the longman anthology of
CONTEMPORARY AMERICAN POETRY

W9-ADW-337

This anthology spans thirty years of unparalleled vigor and achievement in American poetry. Its forty-eight poets, remarkable for their variety in age, geography, temperament, and formal practices, present a composite portrait of current American poetry that is striking in its beauty, energy, and imagination. This is a book whose contents promise to enrich the lives of its readers with delight and reflection for years to come. Included are:

Wallace Stevens
William Carlos
   Williams
John Berryman
Elizabeth Bishop
Robert Francis
Robert Hayden
Randall Jarrell
Robert Lowell
Theodore Roethke
Muriel Rukeyser
William Stafford
John Ashberry
Robert Bly
Robert Creeley
James Dickey
John Haines
Donald Hall
Richard Hugo
Donald Justice
Shirley Kaufman
Galway Kinnell
Denise Levertov
Philip Levine

John Logan
W. S. Merwin
Adrienne Rich
Louis Simpson
Alberta Turner
Richard Wilbur
James Wright
Marvin Bell
Russell Edson
Michael Harper
Sylvia Plath
Stanley Plumly
Dennis Schmitz
Charles Simic
Gary Snyder
Mark Strand
Jean Valentine
Nancy Willard
Charles Wright
Norman Dubie
Laura Jensen
Larry Levis
Thomas Lux
Sandra McPherson

David St. John

The Longman Anthology of Contemporary American

Stuart Friebert *Oberlin College*

David Young *Oberlin College*

Longman
New York & London

POETRY

1950-1980

The Longman Anthology of Contemporary American Poetry 1950–1980

Longman Inc., 1560 Broadway, New York, N.Y. 10036
Associated companies, branches, and representatives
throughout the world.

Developmental Editor: Gordon T.R. Anderson
Editorial and Design Supervisor: Diane Perlmuth
Interior Design: Diana Hrisinko
Manufacturing Supervisor: Marion Hess
Production Supervisor: Ferne Y. Kawahara

Library of Congress Cataloging in Publication Data
Main entry under title:

The Longman anthology of contemporary American
poetry, 1950–1980.

1. American poetry—20th century. I. Friebert,
Stuart, 1931– . II. Young, David P.
PS 613.L6   811'.54'08   81-15630
ISBN 0-582-28267-5 (case)   AACR2
ISBN 0-582-28263-2 (pbk.)

Manufactured in the United States of America

Acknowledgements

"Large Red Man Reading," "This Solitude of Cataracts," "Metaphor as Degeneration," and "Angel Surrounded by Paysans," copyright 1950 by Wallace Stevens; "Final Soliloquy of the Interior Paramour," copyright 1951 by Wallace Stevens; "Puella Parvula," copyright 1949 by Wallace Stevens; "The Irish Cliffs of Moher," "Vacancy in the Park," "Prologues to What is Possible," "The World as Meditation," "A Quiet Normal Life," and "The Poem That Took the Place of a Mountain," copyright 1952 by Wallace Stevens; "Not Ideas About the Thing, but the Thing Itself," copyright 1954 by Wallace Stevens; reprinted from *The Collected Poems of Wallace Stevens,* by permission of Alfred A. Knopf, Inc.

"Pictures from Brueghel," "I Self-Portrait," "II Landscape With the Fall of Icarus," "III The Hunters in the Snow," "Iris," "To a Dog Injured in the Street," "The Artist," "View by Color Photography on a Commercial Calendar," and "The Sparrow" from William Carlos Williams, *Pictures From Brueghel and Other Poems.* Copyright 1953, 1954, 1955, © 1960, 1962 by William Carlos Williams. "The Artist" was first published in *The New Yorker.* All poems reprinted by permission of New Directions.

Dream Song #9, #12, #23, #76, #107, and #366 from *The Dream Songs* by John Berryman. Copyright © 1959, 1962, 1963, 1964, 1965, 1966, 1968, 1969 by John Berryman. "American Lights, Seen from Off Abroad" from *Short Poems* by John Berryman. Copyright © 1958 by John Berryman. "Certainty Before Lunch," "Gislebertus' Eve," and "Washington in Love" from *Delusions, Etc.* by John Berryman. Copyright © 1969, 1971 by John Berryman. Copyright © 1972 by the Estate of John Berryman. Reprinted by permission of Farrar, Straus and Giroux, Inc.

"Over 2000 Illustrations and a Complete Concordance," "The Prodigal," "Sestina," "First Death in Nova Scotia," and "At the Fishhouses" from *The Complete Poems* by Elizabeth Bishop. Copyright © 1947, 1948, 1951, 1956, 1962, 1969 by Elizabeth Bishop. "In the Waiting Room" from *Geography III* by Elizabeth Bishop. Copyright © 1971 by Elizabeth Bishop. Reprinted by permission of Farrar, Straus and Giroux, Inc.

"Cypresses," "Cold," "Bluejay," and "Three Darks Come Down Together," copyright © 1959 by Robert Francis. Reprinted from *The Orb Weaver* by permission of Wesleyan University Press. "Cold" first appeared in *Poetry.*

Love! Love!," copyright 1950 by Theodore Roethke, and "Journey to the Interior," copyright © 1961 by Beatrice Roethke, Administratrix of the Estate of Theodore Roethke, from the book *The Collected Poems of Theodore Roethke*. Reprinted by permission of Doubleday & Company, Inc.

"Children's Elegy" from *Beast in View,* copyright, © Muriel Rukeyser, 1944, 1970. "The Speed of Darkness" from *The Speed of Darkness,* copyright, © Muriel Rukeyser, 1968. "Children, The Sandbar, That Summer" from *Body of Awaking,* copyright, © Muriel Rukeyser, 1958. "Then," "Double Ode," "Resurrection of the Right Side" from *The Gates,* copyright, © Muriel Rukeyser, 1976. All reprinted permission, ICM, 40 W. 57th St., New York, NY 10019.

From *Stories That Could Be True* by William Stafford: "Traveling Through the Dark" copyright © 1960 by William Stafford; "The Rescued Year" copyright © 1964 by William Stafford; "Observation Car and Cigar" copyright © 1965 by William Stafford; "Ceremony" copyright © 1966 by William Stafford; "Any Time" and "Earth Dweller" copyright 1967 by William Stafford; "Bring the North" copyright © 1969 by William Stafford; "In a Museum in the Capital" copyright © 1971 by William Stafford; "Accountability" copyright © 1976 by William Stafford; "At the Playground" copyright © 1977 by William Stafford. "The Epitaph Ending in And" from *The Rescued Year* by William Stafford, copyright © 1965 by William Stafford. All selections reprinted by permission of Harper and Row, Publishers, Inc.

"Notice What This Poem Is Not Doing" from *Things That Happen Where There Aren't Any People* by William Stafford. Copyright © 1980 by William Stafford. Reprinted with the permission of BOA Editions.

"Together Again" from *FIELD* #4, Spring 1971. "School Days" from *FIELD* #18, spring 1978. Reprinted by permission.

"Civilisation and its Discontents," "Glazunoviana," and "Variations, Calypso and Fugue" by John Ashbery are from *Rivers and Mountains* (Holt, Rinehart) © 1962 by John Ashbery; *Some Trees* (Holt) © 1956 by John Ashbery; and *The Double Dream of Spring* (Dutton) © 1970 by John Ashbery. Reprinted by permission of the author.

"Marchenbilder" and "On Autumn Lake" from *Self-Portrait In a Convex Mirror* by John Ashbery. Copyright © 1972, 1973, 1974, 1975 by John Ashbery. "What is Poetry" and "Friends" from *Houseboat Days* by John Ashbery. Copyright © 1975, 1976, 1977 by John Ashbery. "My Erotic Double" from *As We Know* by John Ashbery. Copyright © 1979 by John Ashbery. Reprinted by permission of Viking Penguin Inc.

"Driving Toward the Lac Qui Parle River" from *Silence in the Snowy Fields* © 1962 by Robert Bly. Wesleyan University Press, 1962, reprinted with the permission of Robert Bly.

"Visiting Emily Dickinson's Grave with Robert Francis," "Mourning Pablo Neruda," and "Snowbanks North of the House" from *Man in the Black Coat Turns* © 1981 by Robert Bly. Reprinted by permission of The Dial Press.

From *The Light Around the Body* by Robert Bly: "Three Presidents" copyright

Levine. Reprinted from *Not This Pig* by permission of Wesleyan University Press.

"The Monument and the Shrine," "A Suite of Six Pieces for Siskind," and "Believe It" by John Logan. Printed by permission of the author.

"The Zoo" and "The Pass" from *The Zigzag Walk* by John Logan. Copyright © 1963, 1964, 1965, 1966, 1967, 1968, 1969 by John Logan. Reprinted by permission of the publisher, E.P. Dutton.

"First Prelude. Dream in Ohio: The Father" from *The Bridge of Change: Poems 1974–1980*. Copyright © 1981 by John Logan. Reprinted with the permission of BOA Editions.

"The Last One," "Caesar," "The River of Bees," and "When You Go Away" from W.S. Merwin, *The Lice*. Copyright © 1967 by W.S. Merwin (New York: Atheneum, 1967). "Low Fields and Light" from W.S. Merwin, *Green with Beasts*. Copyright © 1956 by W.S. Merwin in *The First Four Books of Poems*. Copyright © 1975 by W.S. Merwin (New York: Atheneum, 1975). "Departure's Girl-friend" and "Witnesses" from W.S. Merwin, *The Moving Target*. Copyright © 1963 by W.S. Merwin (New York: Atheneum, 1963). "A Door (Do you remember how I beat on the door . . .)" and "The War" from W.S. Merwin, *Writings to an Unfinished Accompaniment*. Copyright © 1973 by W.S. Merwin (New York: Atheneum, 1973). "The Hours of a Bridge" from W.S. Merwin, *The Miner's Pale Children*. Copyright © 1969, 1970 by W.S. Merwin (New York: Atheneum, 1970). "The Broken" from W.S. Merwin, *Houses and Travellers*. Copyright © 1977 by W.S. Merwin (New York: Atheneum, 1977). All poems reprinted with permission of Atheneum Publishers.

"After Dark," "The Burning of Paper Instead of Children," and "Meditations for a Savage Child," reprinted from *Poems, Selected and New, 1950–1974* by Adrienne Rich, with the permission of W.W. Norton & Company, Inc. Copyright © 1974, © 1975, 1973, 1971, 1969, 1966 by W.W. Norton & Company, Inc.

"The Photographer" from *Adventures of the Letter I* by Louis Simpson. Copyright © 1967 by Louis Simpson. Reprinted by permission of Harper & Row, Publishers, Inc.

"Chocolates" and "Why Do You Write about Russia?" from *Caviare at the Funeral* by Louis Simpson. Copyright © 1980 by Louis Simpson. Reprinted by permission of Franklin Watts, Inc.

"Early in the Morning" from *Poets of Today II, Good News of Death and Other Poems* by Louis Simpson. Copyright 1955 Louis Simpson. Reprinted by permission of Charles Scribner's Sons.

"My Father in the Night Commanding No," "On the Lawn at the Villa," and "A Story about Chicken Soup" copyright © 1963 by Louis Simpson. Reprinted from *At the End of the Open Road* by permission of Wesleyan University Press. "My Father in the Night Commanding No" first appeared in *The New Yorker*.

"Learning to Count" and "Choosing a Death" by Alberta T. Turner. Reprinted by permission of the author.

"Water," and "Above Pate Valley" by Gary Snyder. Printed by permission of the author.

"Elegy for My Father," "The Prediction," "Shooting Whales," "Keeping Things Whole," "Where Are the Waters of Childhood?" from *Selected Poems* copyright © 1980 by Mark Strand. Reprinted with the permission of Atheneum Publishers.

"The Second Dream" reprinted by permission of Yale University Press from *The Dream Barker* © 1965 by Jean Valentine.

"Pilgrims" and "Orpheus and Eurydice" from *Pilgrims* by Jean Valentine. Copyright © 1965, 1966, 1967, 1968, 1969 by Jean Valentine. "After Elegies" and "The Knife" from *Ordinary Things* by Jean Valentine. Copyright © 1972, 1973, 1974 by Jean Valentine. "The Messenger," "The Forgiveness Dream: Man from the Warsaw Ghetto," "The Field," "Silences: A Dream of Governments," and "December 21st" from *The Messenger* by Jean Valentine. Copyright © 1974, 1975, 1977, 1978 by Jean Valentine. Reprinted by permission of Farrar, Straus and Giroux, Inc.

"The Insects," "Original Strawberry," "Angels in Winter," "How the Hen Sold Her Eggs to the Stingy Priest," "Questions My Son Asked Me, Answers I Never Gave Him," "Lightness Remembered," "Night Light," "Saint Pumpkin," and "No-Kings and the Calling of Spirits" by Nancy Willard. Reprinted by permission of the author.

"Sitting at Night on the Front Porch," "Snow," "Self-Portrait in 2035," and "Invisible Landscape" copyright © 1977, 1975, 1975, 1976 by Charles Wright. Reprinted from *China Trace* by permission of Wesleyan University Press. "Delta Traveller," and "Virgo Descending" copyright © 1974, 1975 by Charles Wright. Reprinted from *Bloodlines* by permission of Wesleyan University Press. "Dog Creek Mainline" and "Nightdream" copyright © 1972, 1973 by Charles Wright. Reprinted from *Hard Freight* by permission of Wesleyan University Press. "Dog Creek Mainline" and "Nightdream" first appeared in *Poetry.* "Stone Canyon Nocturne" and "Spider Crystal Ascension" copyright © 1976, 1977 by Charles Wright. Reprinted from *China Trace* by permission of Wesleyan University Press. "Stone Canyon Nocturne" first appeared in *The New Yorker.*

"Mount Caribou at Night," "Dog Yoga," "Dog Day Vespers," "Dead Color," and "Hawaii Dantesca" by Charles Wright. Reprinted by the permission of the author.

"February: The Boy Breughel" © 1977 by Norman Dubie. Reprinted by permission of the publisher, George Braziller, Inc.

"The Composer's Winter Dream" and "Coleridge Crossing the Plain of Jars: 1833" first appeared in *FIELD.* Copyright 1980 by Norman Dubie. "The Fox Who Watched for the Midnight Sun" first appeared in *The New Yorker,* copyright © 1978 by The New Yorker Magazine, Inc. These poems are from the book *The Everlastings* by Norman Dubie. Reprinted by permission of Doubleday & Company, Inc. "The Ganges," copyright © 1976 by Norman Dubie and "Elizabeth's War with the Christmas Bear: 1601," copyright © 1977 by Norman Dubie from the book *The City of the Olesha Fruit* by Norman Dubie. These poems first appeared in *The New Yorker.* Reprinted by permission of Doubleday & Company, Inc.

"Household," "Tapwater," and "The Candles Draw Well After All" © 1975, 1976, 1976 by Laura Jensen. Printed by permission of *FIELD.*

"The Red Dog," "The Ajax Samples," "An Age," "The Cloud Parade," "Winter Evening Poem," "House Is an Enigma," and "As the Window Darkens" copyright © 1977 by Laura Jensen, from *Bad Boats,* The Ecco Press. Reprinted by permission.

"Kite" by Laura Jensen, reprinted by permission; © 1977, *The New Yorker Magazine,* Inc.

"Linnets" from *The Afterlife* © 1977 by Larry Levis. Reprinted by permission of the author and the University of Iowa Press.

"The Ownership of the Night" and "For Zbigniew Herbert, Summer, Los Angeles, 1971" from *The Dollmaker's Ghost* by Larry Levis. Copyright © 1981 by Larry Levis. Reprinted by permission of the publisher, E.P. Dutton. ("The Ownership of the Night" first appeared in *The Pushcart Prize IV: Best of the Small Presses* and "For Zbigniew Herbert, Summer, Los Angeles, 1971" first appeared in *FIELD*).

"Man Asleep in the Desert," "Graveyard by the Sea," "Barn Fire," "Farmers," "Solo Native," and "Flying Noises" from *Sunday* by Thomas Lux. Copyright © 1979 by Thomas Lux. Reprinted by permission of Houghton Mifflin Company.

"There Were Some Summers" copyright © 1980 by Thomas Lux. *FIELD,* #22, Spring 1980. Reprinted by permission.

"Butchery," "Collapsars," "Wanting a Mummy," and "Peter Rabbit" reprinted from *Radiation* by Sandra McPherson, The Ecco Press, 1973. Used by permission. "A Coconut for Katerina," and "Gnawing the Breast" reprinted from *The Year of Our Birth* by Sandra McPherson, The Ecco Press, 1979. Used by permission.

"Resigning from a Job in a Defense Industry," "Morning Glory Pool," "Michael," and "Games" by permission of Sandra McPherson.

"The Museum of the Second Creation" appeared originally in *FIELD,* #24, Spring 1981. Used by permission.

"Iris," "Hush," "Slow Dance," and "Dolls" from *Hush* by David St. John. Copyright © 1975, 1976 by David St. John. Reprinted by permission of Houghton Mifflin Company.

"Elegy" was published in *The Ohio Grove,* by David St. John, W.D. Hoffsvant & Sons Press, 1980.

"The Shore" by David St. John. Reprinted by permission; © 1977. *The New Yorker Magazine,* Inc.

Contents

Introduction

This anthology presents the work of forty-eight American poets and covers the thirty-year period from 1950 to 1980. The poets are grouped in five sections, by their birthdates, and each poet is represented by 200 to 300 lines of poetry. We could, of course, have included many more poets; it would be foolish to claim that only forty-eight people produced interesting work in one of the most vigorous creative periods of our national history. But we wanted to present enough work by each poet chosen to enable readers to get well acquainted with that poet's work, and we wanted to leave room for a few long poems that characterized some of the best work done during the years in question. The inclusion of sizable poems like James Dickey's "Falling," Denise Levertov's "Olga Poems," and Larry Levis's "Linnets" is one feature that makes this anthology unusual.

In assembling the poems we aimed for a collection that was neither an exercise in personal taste nor a coldly objective, "historical" account of important writing over the past thirty years. We decided to read every poet who had published two or more books in the period to be covered. We divided the preliminary reading assignment equally. When one of us turned up a number of poems by a candidate that would supply the representation we had in mind, he presented his "nomination" to the other. If the other editor agreed, we then began the process of deciding together on final choices. At that point we always entered into correspondence with the living poets, to consult their preferences and views. We asked them initially for their list of favorites, and we gave them a chance to react to our selection before it became final.

The book as a whole is exciting because it brings together what we consider to be the best poetry of the past three decades. It has both freshness and force. It is fun to read, and should be fun to teach and to argue about. We certainly expect some disagreement from our readers; the anthology does not so much attempt to be definitive about contemporary American poetry—we never see the art of our time with the clarity and sureness of generations to come—as to identify the poets whose work seems to us the most exciting and original.

Two common structures for anthologies are the alphabetical, which makes it easy to find your way around, and the chronological, which attempts to do justice to the fact of literary history. Our book is a hybrid of these possibilities. Within the five groupings, which are basically the decades in which they were born, the poets are presented alphabetically. The groups range in size from two poets to nineteen, and a few words about the character and meaning of each group are in order here.

The first group might have been called "Two Old Masters." It presents two poets from the first generation of great modern writers who were still producing first-quality work after 1950. Wallace Stevens and William Carlos Williams, the two whose poems of the 1950s are of interest here, were also extremely influential to the poets who followed them, and so it is especially germane to have them open our collection. The third "old master" whom we considered including here was W. H. Auden. Auden's presence in this country from 1939 onward had an incalculable effect on contemporary American poetry, but on close inspection we decided that his work is still very much that of a British poet; his presence in this collection would have been misleading. (He also belongs, by virtue of his birthdate, to the second group of poets.) Students who wish to understand American postwar poetry fully, however, will sooner or later want to familiarize themselves with Auden's work.

The second group of poets were all born between 1900 and 1920, with the majority clustered around 1914. Only two poets in this group, Robert Francis, the eldest, and William Stafford, are still alive and writing. They are the exceptions to a somewhat tragic pattern, for in terms of early death, suicide, alcoholism, and mental illness, poets in this group tended to have difficult, unhappy lives. Most of them came of age as poets in the 1940s, and it is interesting to consider the different ways in which they confronted, in their lives and in their art, the looming presence of World War II. Many of the poetic canons in this group are now complete, though truncated in several cases by untimely death. The achievement and variety of this generation, especially as seen in figures like Jarrell, Bishop, and Roethke, is becoming impressively clear.

The next group of poets, born in the 1920s, is by far the largest—nineteen in number—and perhaps for that reason is the most difficult group to generalize about. Nevertheless, certain patterns show up in the lives and work of many of these poets. They tended to begin as formalists, writing poetry based in traditional techniques of rhyme and meter, and using traditional forms like the sonnet, ballad, sestina, and villanelle. Most of them rebelled against this beginning and underwent dramatic stylistic changes. In place of the English tradition they had emulated, they sought foreign influences, such as Spanish and French surrealism, and native precedents for open forms like those of Whitman and Williams. The same rebellion led many of them away from impersonal poems and toward various forms of the subjective, as well as into areas previously off limits to the poet: political activism, feminism, and attempts at personal mythology. These poets are now past fifty, and most are still writing vigorously. The books on their careers are still very much open. In their number and variety, they surely constitute one of the most remarkable generations any national literature has seen.

The next group of poets, who were born in the 1930s, happens to represent our own generation, and we may not be privileged to see them quite as clearly. Nevertheless, looking at these writers as a group, while it confirms a remarkable variety of interests and technical means, suggests that they share in what might be termed a cultural salvage operation. They are much interested in the continuities of the human imagination and its means of helping us survive. And they are less anxious about matters of form and style than the previous generation, less inclined to turn against their own work in search of new definitions of self and new aesthetics. Their tolerance of one another's ways is notable, and their dislike of schools and dogmas concomitantly high. These poets, with the exception of the late Sylvia Plath, are in mid-career; it would be premature to characterize them too fully or predict too confidently the future directions of their work.

The fifth and last group, six poets born in the 1940s, is small because many poets in that age group have yet to produce a substantial amount of strong work. In ten years their numbers will undoubtedly increase and will show their poetic tendencies more fully. If any characteristic emerges from this partial and early sampling, it is an ability to *enter* the lives of others, a tendency that may take the form of dramatic monologue or fictive characterization involving narrative. Interchange with other literary arts and with other forms of knowledge—biography, history, science, psychology—seems a livelier possibility among these poets than with any of their predecessors.

Despite the groupings, our primary emphasis is on the poets as individual artists. For that reason, we have provided each poet's selection with an introduction that explores formal and thematic tendencies in the poet's work. By making our introductions short critical essays, we hope to provoke thought and precipitate discussion. Our comments are not meant to be definitive; if they provide an avenue into the poet's work that will help the reader form opinions, they will have served their purpose.

When it came to the question of annotating the poems selected, we were faced with a dilemma. In a good poem, one could conceivably annotate every line. Safer, perhaps, to offer no annotation. We compromised by providing occasional annotations, meant to suggest how background information can bear on a poem rather than to provide such information in every case. A good reader of poetry must be ready to resort continually to a dictionary and frequently to an encyclopedia and other reference works. Our annotations, in addition to translating foreign words and phrases, are no more than occasional suggestions about how poems use allusion and condense information. We might recount one myth, to show how a poem draws on it; we do not recount all the myths mentioned. A complete annotation of this anthology must be the work of individual readers.

In addition to our introductions and occasional annotations, we have included a selective bibliography at the end of each poet's section. The information in this bibliography includes important titles in the poet's canon and discussions of the poet's work, including interviews, that we have found especially helpful.

The structure and character of this anthology have benefited greatly from the advice and cooperation of the individual poets; many of them were also generous in helping arrange for reasonable permissions fees. We wish to thank them, along with the following: Gordon T.R. Anderson, our Longman editor, a fountain of moral support and useful suggestions; David Walker and Chloe Young, whose reading of the manuscript produced many valuable corrections and clarifications; Andrew Hoover, for timely advice at several stages; and Diane Vreuls, who read every introduction in draft, helped us find a style and tone for the book as a whole, challenged some of our choices among the poems to good effect, and in general provided a steady flow of thoughtful criticism and enthusiastic support.

Stuart Friebert
David Young

The Longman Anthology of Contemporary American Poetry: 1950-1980

Two Poets Born in the Nineteenth Century

PART ONE

Wallace Stevens

(1879–1955)

The starting date of this anthology is 1950; when that year began, Wallace Stevens, an insurance company executive in Hartford, Connecticut, had just turned seventy. He was to live only five more years, but old age and declining health neither forced him into retirement nor affected his artistic vigor. He continued to go to work each day, and to compose his poems while walking to and from the office and on weekends. The later poems are richly inventive, making Stevens's career an interesting counterexample to the familiar story of the poet who dies young or experiences a drying up of talent. On the surface, Stevens's life was remarkably uneventful; but as a poet who went on experimenting and developing into his seventies he is a figure of considerable interest.

Stevens's later poetry has a reputation for being excessively abstract or philosophical, a misconception that the playfulness and imaginative daring of the poems presented here should help dispel. There are, of course, ideas in the air, but not for purposes of solemn demonstration or tedious argument. Stevens is like a juggler who can miraculously add abstract concepts to a swirl of plates, cups, balls, and fruit. All his life he deliberately counterpointed the human desire to propound and generalize with the intrusions of an unruly reality. In his later poems, the magisterial moments of summary, the large perspectives on life and death that exhilarate us (as in "The Poem That Took the Place of a Mountain"), are matched by a skeptical mocking of any pretense to final statements and definitive beliefs. Stevens felt that the world was so shifting and changeable, so illusory and unknowable, that even our best intuitions about it must be momentary and glancing. Poetry, he accordingly thought, might well replace religion as the best way of approaching matters of solace and belief, since dogmas tend to be static and resist change, while metaphor, the mode of the poet, tends to reflect and even celebrate it.

The characters in Stevens's poems are caught between their human need for order and meaning and the shifting, unknowable reality that surrounds them. Their efforts to systematize and fix experience are treated with both tenderness and ridicule. Thus, the man in "This Solitude of Cataracts" cannot enjoy the river he walks beside because he wants "a permanent realization," while the dead who have left the world behind and entered a changeless realm in "Large Red Man Reading" want only to return to this world and "would have wept to step barefoot into reality." Stevens would like us to walk through this world and value it for what it is. "Death is the mother of beauty," as an early poem, "Sunday Morning," baldly puts it: the impermanence of things gives them their meaning and value. What will aid us most on any walk "barefoot into reality" is the imagination. It knows how to relish the forms, colors, and textures of reality without claiming to own or classify them. Better still, it knows that the stories it invents to make sense or order of experience are just that: stories and inventions. The imagination is the true hero of a Stevens poem, and the varied forms it takes in the selection presented here—a large red man, an angel, Penelope, a candle—suggest some of his delight in celebrating it.

Readers encountering Stevens for the first time through this selection will find that it takes awhile to enter the holiday revelry of language and meaning. The simultaneous affirmation and deprecation take time to adjust to, and the nimble shifts of diction and tone may seem to shut us out before they finally invite us in. But to understand one poem thoroughly is to find that the others are suddenly much easier, and before we know it we are hooked. Those whom Stevens's music enchants will want to trace it back through his earlier work to his initial collection, *Harmonium* (1923), and then forward through his middle books, *Ideas of Order* (1935), *The Man with the Blue Guitar* (1937), *Parts of a World* (1942), and *Transport to Summer* (1947). In that context, the poems presented here from *The Auroras of Autumn* (1950) and *The Rock* (the final section of *The Collected Poems* of 1954) will mean even more. There is a large body of commentary on Stevens, not all of it helpful; the critics have been rather solemn and misguided about him. In addition to the poetry, his essays, collected in *The Necessary Angel*, and his letters (*Selected Letters of Wallace Stevens*, edited by his daughter, Holly Stevens) are the best way to extend an acquaintance with him.

What Stevens will finally mean to American poetry is still being determined, but along with William Carlos Williams, he begins to loom as large as Walt Whitman or Emily Dickinson. The stylistic innovations of Stevens, his elegance of manner and consistency of vision, and his confident expansion of the horizons of modern poetry are among the features that have made him attractive to poets who have come after him. His influence on the poets of the last thirty years—on Wilbur, Justice, Ashbery, among others—has been so thorough and so various that it seems especially appropriate to have his work begin this volume.

DY

Large Red Man Reading

There were ghosts that returned to earth to hear his phrases,
As he sat there reading, aloud, the great blue tabulae.
They were those from the wilderness of stars that had expected more.

There were those that returned to hear him read from the poem of life,
Of the pans above the stove, the pots on the table, the tulips among them,
They were those that would have wept to step barefoot into reality,

That would have wept and been happy, have shivered in the frost
And cried out to feel it again, have run fingers over leaves
And against the most coiled thorn, have seized on what was ugly

TWO POETS BORN IN THE NINETEENTH CENTURY

And laughed, as he sat there reading, from out of the purple tabulae,
The outlines of being and its expressing, the syllables of its law:
Poesis, poesis, the literal characters, the vatic lines,

Which in those ears and in those thin, those spended hearts,
Took on color, took on shape and the size of things as they are
And spoke the feeling for them, which was what they had lacked.

This Solitude of Cataracts

He never felt twice the same about the flecked river,
Which kept flowing and never the same way twice, flowing

Through many places, as if it stood still in one,
Fixed like a lake on which the wild ducks fluttered,

Ruffling its common reflections, thought-like Monadnocks.
There seemed to be an apostrophe that was not spoken.

There was so much that was real that was not real at all.
He wanted to feel the same way over and over.

He wanted the river to go on flowing the same way,
To keep on flowing. He wanted to walk beside it,

Under the buttonwoods, beneath a moon nailed fast.
He wanted his heart to stop beating and his mind to rest

In a permanent realization, without any wild ducks
Or mountains that were not mountains, just to know how it would be,

Just to know how it would feel, released from destruction,
To be a bronze man breathing under archaic lapis,

Without the oscillations of planetary pass-pass,
Breathing his bronzen breath at the azury centre of time.

Metaphor as Degeneration

If there is a man white as marble
Sits in a wood, in the greenest part,
Brooding sounds of the images of death,

So there is a man in black space
Sits in nothing that we know,
Brooding sounds of river noises;

WALLACE STEVENS

And these images, these reverberations,
And others, make certain how being
Includes death and the imagination.

The marble man remains himself in space,
The man in the black woods descends unchanged.
It is certain that the river

Is not Swatara. The swarthy water
That flows round the earth and through the skies,
Twisting among the universal spaces,

Is not Swatara. It is being.
That is the flock-flecked river, the water,
The blown sheen—or is it air?

How, then, is metaphor degeneration,
When Swatara becomes this undulant river
And the river becomes the landless, waterless ocean?

Here the black violets grow down to its banks
And the memorial mosses hang their green
Upon it, as it flows ahead.

Puella Parvula

Every thread of summer is at last unwoven.
By one caterpillar is great Africa devoured
And Gibralter is dissolved like spit in the wind.

But over the wind, over the legends of its roaring,
The elephant on the roof and its elephantine blaring,
The bloody lion in the yard at night or ready to spring

From the clouds in the midst of trembling trees
Making a great gnashing, over the water wallows
Of a vacant sea declaiming with wide throat,

Over all these the mighty imagination triumphs
Like a trumpet and says, in this season of memory,
When the leaves fall like things mournful of the past,

Keep quiet in the heart, O wild bitch, O mind
Gone wild, be what he tells you to be: *Puella*.
Write *pax* across the window pane. And then

Be still. The *summarium in excelsis* begins . . .
Flame, sound, fury composed . . . Hear what he says,
The dauntless master, as he starts the human tale.

Angel Surrounded by Paysans

One of the countrymen:
                                                    There is
    A welcome at the door to which no one comes?

The angel:
    I am the angel of reality,
    Seen for the moment standing in the door.

    I have neither ashen wing nor wear of ore
    And live without a tepid aureole,

    Or stars that follow me, not to attend,
    But, of my being and its knowing, part.

    I am one of you and being one of you
    Is being and knowing what I am and know.

    Yet I am the necessary angel of earth,
    Since, in my sight, you see the earth again,

    Cleared of its stiff and stubborn, man-locked set,
    And, in my hearing, you hear its tragic drone

    Rise liquidly in liquid lingerings
    Like watery words awash; like meanings said

    By repetitions of half-meanings. Am I not,
    Myself, only half of a figure of a sort,

    A figure half seen, or seen for a moment, a man
    Of the mind, an apparition apparelled in

    Apparels of such lightest look that a turn
    Of my shoulder and quickly, too quickly, I am gone?

The Irish Cliffs of Moher

Who is my father in this world, in this house,
At the spirit's base?

My father's father, his father's father, his—
Shadows like winds

Go back to a parent before thought, before speech,
At the head of the past.

They go to the cliffs of Moher rising out of the mist,
Above the real,

WALLACE STEVENS

Rising out of present time and place, above
The wet, green grass.

This is not landscape, full of the somnambulations
Of poetry

And the sea. This is my father or, maybe,
It is as he was,

A likeness, one of the race of fathers: earth
And sea and air.

Vacancy in the Park

March . . . Someone has walked across the snow,
Someone looking for he knows not what.

It is like a boat that has pulled away
From a shore at night and disappeared.

It is like a guitar left on a table
By a woman, who has forgotten it.

It is like the feeling of a man
Come back to see a certain house.

The four winds blow through the rustic arbor,
Under its mattresses of vines.

The Poem That Took the Place of a Mountain

There it was, word for word,
The poem that took the place of a mountain.

He breathed its oxygen,
Even when the book lay turned in the dust of his table.

It reminded him how he had needed
A place to go to in his own direction,

How he had recomposed the pines,
Shifted the rocks and picked his way among clouds,

For the outlook that would be right,
Where he would be complete in an unexplained completion:

The exact rock where his inexactnesses
Would discover, at last, the view toward which they had edged,

Where he could lie and, gazing down at the sea,
Recognize his unique and solitary home.

Prologues to What Is Possible

I

There was an ease of mind that was like being alone in a boat at sea,
A boat carried forward by waves resembling the bright backs of rowers,
Gripping their oars, as if they were sure of the way to their destination,
Bending over and pulling themselves erect on the wooden handles,
Wet with water and sparkling in the one-ness of their motion.

The boat was built of stones that had lost their weight and being no longer heavy
Had left in them only a brilliance, of unaccustomed origin,
So that he that stood up in the boat leaning and looking before him
Did not pass like someone voyaging out of and beyond the familiar.

He belonged to the far-foreign departure of his vessel and was part of it,
Part of the speculum of fire on its prow, its symbol, whatever it was,
Part of the glass-like sides on which it glided over the salt-stained water,
As he traveled alone, like a man lured on by a syllable without any meaning,
A syllable of which he felt, with an appointed sureness,
That it contained the meaning into which he wanted to enter,
A meaning which, as he entered it, would shatter the boat and leave the oarsmen
    quiet
As at a point of central arrival, an instant moment, much or little,
Removed from any shore, from any man or woman, and needing none.

II

The metaphor stirred his fear. The object with which he was compared
Was beyond his recognizing. By this he knew that the likeness of him extended
Only a little way, and not beyond, unless between himself
And things beyond resemblance there was this and that intended to be
    recognized,
The this and that in the enclosures of hypotheses
On which men speculated in summer when they were half asleep.

What self, for example, did he contain that had not yet been loosed,
Snarling in him for discovery as his attentions spread,
As if all his hereditary lights were suddenly increased
By an access of color, a new and unobserved, slight dithering,
The smallest lamp, which added its puissant flick, to which he gave
A name and privilege over the ordinary of his commonplace—

WALLACE STEVENS   9

A flick which added to what was real and its vocabulary,
The way some first thing coming into Northern trees
Adds to them the whole vocabulary of the South,
The way the earliest single light in the evening sky, in spring,
Creates a fresh universe out of nothingness by adding itself,
The way a look or a touch reveals its unexpected magnitudes.

The World as Meditation

*J'ai passé trop de temps à travailler mon
violon, à voyager. Mais l'exercise essentiel
du compositeur—la méditation—rien ne l'a
jamais suspendu en moi . . . Je vis un rêve
permanent, qui ne s'arrête ni nuit ni jour.*

GEORGES ENESCO

Is it Ulysses that approaches from the east,
The interminable adventurer? The trees are mended.
That winter is washed away. Someone is moving

On the horizon and lifting himself up above it.
A form of fire approaches the cretonnes of Penelope,
Whose mere savage presence awakens the world in which she dwells.

She has composed, so long, a self with which to welcome him,
Companion to his self for her, which she imagined,
Two in a deep-founded sheltering, friend and dear friend.

The trees had been mended, as an essential exercise
In an inhuman meditation, larger than her own.
No winds like dogs watched over her at night.

She wanted nothing he could not bring her by coming alone.
She wanted no fetchings. His arms would be her necklace
And her belt, the final fortune of their desire.

But was it Ulysses? Or was it only the warmth of the sun
On her pillow? The thought of it kept beating in her like her heart.
The two kept beating together. It was only day.

It was Ulysses and it was not. Yet they had met,
Friend and dear friend and a planet's encouragement.
The barbarous strength within her would never fail.

She would talk a little to herself as she combed her hair,
Repeating his name with its patient syllables,
Never forgetting him that kept coming constantly so near.

A Quiet Normal Life

His place, as he sat and as he thought, was not
In anything that he constructed, so frail,
So barely lit, so shadowed over and naught,

As, for example, a world in which, like snow,
He became an inhabitant, obedient
To gallant notions on the part of cold.

It was here. This was the setting and the time
Of year. Here in his house and in his room,
In his chair, the most tranquil thought grew peaked

And the oldest and the warmest heart was cut
By gallant notions on the part of night—
Both late and alone, above the crickets' chords,

Babbling, each one, the uniqueness of its sound.
There was no fury in transcendent forms.
But his actual candle blazed with artifice.

Final Soliloquy of the Interior Paramour

Light the first light of evening, as in a room
In which we rest and, for small reason, think
The world imagined is the ultimate good.

This is, therefore, the intensest rendezvous.
It is in that thought that we collect ourselves,
Out of all the indifferences, into one thing:

Within a single thing, a single shawl
Wrapped tightly round us, since we are poor, a warmth,
A light, a power, the miraculous influence.

Here, now, we forget each other and ourselves.
We feel the obscurity of an order, a whole,
A knowledge, that which arranged the rendezvous.

Within its vital boundary, in the mind.
We say God and the imagination are one . . .
How high that highest candle lights the dark.

Out of this same light, out of the central mind,
We make a dwelling in the evening air,
In which being there together is enough.

WALLACE STEVENS   11

Not Ideas About the Thing
but the Thing Itself

At the earliest ending of winter,
In March, a scrawny cry from outside
Seemed like a sound in his mind.

He knew that he heard it,
A bird's cry, at daylight or before,
In the early March wind.

The sun was rising at six,
No longer a battered panache above snow . . .
It would have been outside.

It was not from the vast ventriloquism
Of sleep's faded papier-mâché . . .
The sun was coming from outside.

That scrawny cry—it was
A chorister whose c preceded the choir.
It was part of the colossal sun,

Surrounded by its choral rings,
Still far away. It was like
A new knowledge of reality.

Notes

Large Red Man Reading. Stevens sometimes uses color as broadly and emphatically as an Expressionist painter. The hero of this poem is not an American Indian but a figure like someone in a painting by Chagall or Klee.

This Solitude of Cataracts. The pre-Socratic philosopher Heraclitus is said to have characterized time and incessant change by the maxim "You can't step in the same river twice." This poem begins with a deliberate variation on that idea.

Metaphor as Degeneration. Swatara, a mythical river of darkness and nullity, is mentioned in another poem, "The Countryman," and seems to be Stevens's own invention, inspired by the word "swarthy."

Puella Parvula. The title means "poor little girl."

The World as Meditation. The epigraph translates as follows: "I have spent too much time in practicing my violin, in traveling. But the essential exercise of the composer—meditation—has never been interrupted in me. I live in a permanent dream, which does not stop, either by day or by night."

Wallace Stevens

Books

The Necessary Angel (essays), 1951
Collected Poems, 1954
Opus Posthumous, 1957
Letters, ed. Holly Stevens, 1966
The Palm at the End of the Mind: Selected Poems and a Play, ed. Holly Stevens, 1972

Criticism

Frank Kermode, *Wallace Stevens*, 1960; *Wallace Stevens: A Collection of Critical Essays*, ed. Marie Borroff, 1963; Joseph N. Riddel, *The Clairvoyant Eye*, 1965; Helen Vendler, *On Extended Wings*, 1969; Harold Bloom, *Wallace Stevens: The Poems of Our Climate*, 1977

William
Carlos
Williams

(1883–1963)

Williiam Carlos Williams managed to combine a lifelong dedication to poetry with a medical practice in New Jersey. He did this by writing emphatically about the life around him—the ordinary, and even drab, people, events, and landscapes that made up his routine. His poetry combined vigorous formal experimentation, often in the direction of abandoning traditional forms and mastering the possibilities of free verse, of which he remains the most influential practitioner, with a plainness and directness of manner entirely suited to his native subjects and settings: city streets, vacant lots, workers and their tools, a retarded servant girl, a wheelbarrow, scraps of conversation, a sheet of paper rolling along in the wind. Nature is a vigorous presence in his poems, and it is celebrated without ever being idealized; it is puddles rather than lakes, sparrows rather than nightingales, weeds rather than roses. Everything is presented tautly, with a minimum of comment or judgment, in the simplest language and according to a lifelong preference for the concrete as expressed in the famous motto "No ideas but in things."

The music of Williams's poems seems at first to be a deliberate absence of music, and it takes some time to perceive the finely controlled dance that the hesitations and abruptnesses of the free verse line accomplish; reading aloud should include experimentation with the pauses to be found on the page, listening for the plain, emerging music. Our recognition of this unlikely lyricism involves the same kind of delighted surprise that we experience from the poet's ways of finding beauty in unexpected places; subject and style have the same aims, and an aesthetic of discovery through reduction and directness lies behind everything Williams did. To put it in terms of the visual analogies that very much interested him, his poems combine the freshness and daring of cubist painting with the candor and unmediated confrontation of photography.

Williams's career, like Stevens's, was long and productive. Early in the century he began writing romantic, Keatsian poems; he responded to the innovations of modernism in all the arts during the first two decades of the century, briefly sampled the expatriate life that his friend Ezra Pound had chosen, then settled down in New Jersey to his medical practice and his highly distinctive poems. By 1950 he was in the midst of his major long poem, *Paterson*, and the shorter pieces represented here. He had by then developed a poetic device peculiarly suited both to American speech and to his artistic needs, the "variable foot." This was a unit of varying length—one word or several—which was supposed to have the same weight and duration in the poem. Grouped in threes to make up a triadic line, these variable feet led Williams to some of his finest writing, and his excitement about his "new measure" seems in retrospect to have been justified. In a poem like "The Sparrow," we see how the triadic line combines the staccato and fragmentary nature of American speech with a dreamy fluency that is both haunting and hypnotic.

Like Stevens, Williams was enormously influential to the poets who followed, both the more direct imitators who carried on the free verse style (in this collection, most notably, Robert Creeley, Denise Levertov, and Dennis Schmitz) and those who borrowed parts of his aesthetic without trying to approximate his style: Jarrell, Lowell, and a host of others. His personal generosity and availability made him an important figure to younger writers; in the declining years of the late 1950s and early 1960s after he was crippled by a series of strokes, his home was a place of pilgrimage for many American poets.

No poet since Whitman has been so successful in merging his artistic program with his distinctive sense of what it means to be American. As Williams wrote his later poems, American poetry was entering its most vigorous period, and the fact that he could finally take for his subjects the paintings of a Dutch master or a calendar picture of a Swiss landscape without diluting the distinctively native quality of his poetry is one indication of the way in which his art was thoroughly infused with the language, manners, experience, and attitudes of his own country. For that, for his vision of the world's beauty and energy manifesting themselves in unlikely ways and places, and for his technical finesse with a new verse form, all subsequent poets are greatly in his debt.

DY

Pictures from Brueghel

I SELF-PORTRAIT

In a red winter hat blue
eyes smiling
just the head and shoulders

crowded on the canvas
arms folded one
big ear the right showing

the face slightly tilted
a heavy wool coat
with broad buttons

gathered at the neck reveals
a bulbous nose
but the eyes red-rimmed

from over-use he must have
driven them hard
but the delicate wrists

show him to have been a
man unused to
manual labor unshaved his

blond beard half trimmed
no time for any-
thing but his painting

II LANDSCAPE WITH THE FALL OF ICARUS

According to Brueghel
when Icarus fell
it was spring

a farmer was ploughing
his field
the whole pageantry

of the year was
awake tingling
near

the edge of the sea
concerned
with itself

sweating in the sun
that melted
the wings' wax

unsignificantly
off the coast
there was

a splash quite unnoticed
this was
Icarus drowning

III THE HUNTERS IN THE SNOW

The over-all picture is winter
icy mountains
in the background the return

from the hunt it is toward evening
from the left
sturdy hunters lead in

their pack the inn-sign
hanging from a
broken hinge is a stag a crucifix

between his antlers the cold
inn yard is
deserted but for a huge bonfire

that flares wind-driven tended by
women who cluster
about it to the right beyond

the hill is a pattern of skaters
Brueghel the painter
concerned with it all has chosen

a winter-struck bush for his
foreground to
complete the picture   .   .

Iris

a burst of iris so that
come down for
breakfast

we searched through the
rooms for
that

sweetest odor and at
first could not
find its

source then a blue as
of the sea
struck

startling us from among
those trumpeting
petals

To a Dog Injured in the Street

It is myself,
         not the poor beast lying there
               yelping with pain
that brings me to myself with a start—
         as at the explosion
               of a bomb, a bomb that has laid
all the world waste.
         I can do nothing
               but sing about it
and so I am assuaged
         from my pain.

A drowsy numbness drowns my sense
         as if of hemlock
               I had drunk. I think
of the poetry
         of René Char
               and all he must have seen
and suffered
         that has brought him
               to speak only of
sedgy rivers,
         of daffodils and tulips
               whose roots they water,
even to the free-flowing river
         that laves the rootlets
               of those sweet-scented flowers
that people the
         milky
               way

I remember Norma
         our English setter of my childhood
               her silky ears

and expressive eyes.
         She had a litter
               of pups one night
in our pantry and I kicked
         one of them
               thinking, in my alarm,
that they
         were biting her breasts
         to destroy her.

I remember also
        a dead rabbit
              lying harmlessly
on the outspread palm
        of a hunter's hand.
              As I stood by
watching
        he took a hunting knife
              and with a laugh
thrust it
        up into the animal's private parts.
              I almost fainted.

Why should I think of that now?
        The cries of a dying dog
              are to be blotted out
as best I can.
        René Char
              you are a poet who believes
in the power of beauty
        to right all wrongs.
              I believe it also.
With invention and courage
        we shall surpass
              the pitiful dumb beasts,
let all men believe it,
        as you have taught me also
              to believe it.

The Artist

Mr. T.
        bareheaded
              in a soiled undershirt
his hair standing out
        on all sides
              stood on his toes
heels together
        arms gracefully
              for the moment
curled above his head.

Then he whirled about
                    bounded
into the air
          and with an *entrechat*
                    perfectly achieved
completed the figure.
          My mother
                    taken by surprise
where she sat
          in her invalid's chair
                    was left speechless.
Bravo! she cried at last
          and clapped her hands.
                    The man's wife
came from the kitchen:
          What goes on here? she said.
                    But the show was over.

View by Color Photography on a Commercial Calendar

The church of Vice-Morcate
          in the Canton Ticino
                    with its apple blossoms
is beautiful
          as anything I have ever seen
                    in or out of
Switzerland.
          The beauty of holiness
                    the beauty of a man's anger
reflecting his sex
          or a woman's either,
                    mountainous,
or a little stone church
          from a height
                    or
close to the camera
          the apple tree in blossom
                    or the far lake
below
          in the distance—
                    are equal
as they are unsurpassed.

Peace
                    after the event
comes from their contemplation,
            a great peace.
                    The sky is cut off,
there is no horizon
            just the mountainside
                    bordered by water
on which tiny waves

            without passion
                    unconcerned
cover the invisible fish.
            And who but we are concerned
                    with the beauty of apple blossoms
and a small church
            on a promontory,
                    an ancient church—
by the look of its masonry—
            abandoned
                    by a calm lake
in the mountains
            where the sun shines
                    of a springtime
afternoon. Something
            has come to an end here,
                    it has been accomplished.

The Sparrow

(To My Father)

This sparrow
            who comes to sit at my window
                    is a poetic truth
more than a natural one.
            His voice,
                    his movements,
his habits—
            how he loves to
                    flutter his wings
in the dust—
            all attest it;

                        granted, he does it
to rid himself of lice
                but the relief he feels
                        makes him
cry out lustily—
                which is a trait
                        more related to music
than otherwise.
                Wherever he finds himself
                        in early spring,
on back streets
                or beside palaces,
                        he carries on
unaffectedly
                his amours.
                                It begins in the egg,
his sex genders it:
                What is more pretentiously
                        useless
or about which
                we more pride ourselves?

                        It leads as often as not
to our undoing.
                The cockerel, the crow
                        with their challenging voices
cannot surpass
                the insistence
                        of his cheep!
Once
        at El Paso
                toward evening,
I saw—and heard!—
                ten thousand sparrows
                        who had come in from
the desert
                to roost. They filled the trees
                        of a small park. Men fled
(with ears ringing!)
                from their droppings,
                        leaving the premises
to the alligators
                who inhabit
                        the fountain. His image
is familiar
                as that of the aristocratic
                        unicorn, a pity

there are not more oats eaten
        nowadays
                to make living easier
for him.
        At that,
                his small size,
keen eyes,
        serviceable beak
                and general truculence
assure his survival—
        to say nothing
                of his innumerable

brood.
        Even the Japanese
            know him
and have painted him
        sympathetically,
                with profound insight
into his minor
        characteristics.
                Nothing even remotely
subtle
        about his lovemaking.
                He crouches
before the female,
        drags his wings,
            waltzing,
throws back his head
        and simply—
                yells! The din
is terrific.
        The way he swipes his bill
            across a plank
to clean it,
        is decisive.
                So with everything
he does. His coppery
        eyebrows
            give him the air
of being always
        a winner—and yet
            I saw once,
the female of his species
        clinging determinedly
                to the edge of
a water pipe,

                    catch him
                              by his crown-feathers
to hold him
                    silent,
                              subdued,
hanging above the city streets
                    until
                              she was through with him.
What was the use
          of that?
                              She hung there
herself,
                    puzzled at her success.
                    I laughed heartily.
Practical to the end,
          it is the poem
                    of his existence
that triumphed
          finally;
                    a wisp of feathers
flattened to the pavement,
          wings spread symmetrically
                    as if in flight,
the head gone,
          the black escutcheon of the breast
                    undecipherable,
an effigy of a sparrow,
          a dried wafer only,
                    left to say
and it says it
          without offense,
                    beautifully;
This was I,
          a sparrow.
                    I did my best;
farewell.

Notes

Pictures from Brueghel. Williams's admiration for the naturalism, vigor, and scope of Breughel's art makes them kindred spirits. It is interesting to compare Williams's handling of the Icarus painting with W. H. Auden's very different treatment of the same subject in the poem "Musée de Beaux Arts."

To a Dog Injured in the Street. The fifth triad paraphrases the opening lines of

Keats's "Ode to a Nightingale." René Char is a contemporary French poet who was active in the French Resistance movement during World War II.

William Carlos Williams

Books

Collected Earlier Poems, 1938, 1951
Collected Later Poems, 1944, 1948, 1950, 1963
Paterson, Book I, 1946
Paterson, Book II, 1948
Paterson, Book III, 1949
Paterson, Book IV, 1951
The Autobiography of William Carlos Williams, 1951
The Desert Music, 1954
Selected Essays, 1954
Selected Letters, 1957
Pictures from Brueghel, 1962
Selected Poems, 1963, 1968

Criticism, Interviews

William Carlos Williams: A Collection of Critical Essays, ed. J. Hillis Miller, 1966; Thomas Whitaker, *William Carlos Williams*, 1968; Emily Mitchell Wallace, *A Bibliography of William Carlos Williams*, 1968; James Breslin, *William Carlos Williams, An American Artist*, 1970; Jerome Mazzaro, *William Carlos Williams, The Later Poems*, 1973; Paul Marian, *William Carlos Williams: A New World Naked*, 1982

TWO POETS BORN IN THE NINETEENTH CENTURY

Nine Poets
Born
Between
1900 and 1920

PART TWO

John
Berryman

(1914–1972)

From the beginning, the poetry of John Berryman is characterized by tremendous learning mixed in a cauldron of scathing wit. He brooded his life away trying to come to terms with his father's suicide, insulating himself with his writing and teaching until drink and sickness led him finally to take his own life.

He wanted to be remembered as a man who worked hard, and to the end he was at work on lives of Shakespeare and Christ, and on a novel called *Recovery*. He was one of those who lived, and lived by, his poetry, spending literally years on matters of style and form, paying constant tribute to his literary sources and influences. He remained the scholar-poet, and much of what he wrote was a response to reading around in his favorites, Yeats, Apollinaire, Auden, Pound, Stevens, Rilke, Coleridge, Poe, and Kafka, "a wide cast of characters," as he noted elsewhere about the many figures in *The Dream Songs*.

Many critics have called attention to the complex mix of self-pity, delusions of grandeur, and childlike innocence that form the main strings of his cat's cradle; when the poems fail, it is because he pulls one string at the expense of the others. More important, he was trying, as he noted in a remark on his "three epics" (*Homage to Mistress Bradstreet, The Dream Songs*, and the unfinished *Proemio*), to "include instructions to them [his children] on every subject I feel sufficiently strongly about and either know inside-out or am wholly perplext by."

Robert Lowell called *The Dream Songs*, which stand at the center of Berryman's work, "one of the glories of the age, the most heroic work in English poetry since the war" (cited in Cooper's *The Autobiographical Myth of Robert Lowell*). Dense with learning, aflow with cryptic references and dream meanings, sounding a little like a xylophone played by a master musician, *The Dream Songs* are nonetheless, in their strict forms, "provocative, practically an innovation" (Louis Simpson, *A Revolution in Taste*), coming as they did at a time when free verse had gained the upper hand. Introducing *The Dream Songs* in 1966, Berryman said they were about "a white American who sometimes appears in blackface and who has suffered an irreversible loss." They are more personal than he liked to admit; they are also about all of us, and lest we grow too gloomy at the prospect, Berryman added that he and Saul Bellow almost killed themselves laughing at them. One is reminded of Kafka: his work made others feel awful, but he and his friends would read it out loud and laugh themselves silly. So it is up to the reader to watch for the humor and see the poke in the ribs for what it is: the way to start disentangling guilt and innocence.

The poems presented here underline the great sense of fun Berryman had singing the song of his poems. If we're reminded of "The Bells of St. Clements" while reading "American Lights, Seen from Off Abroad," so much the better; we can sing along, making up two-liners about our hometown lights. Berryman's wit in these ditties is tempered by great affection, and his sense of timing is a fine comic's. In "Washington in

Love" the poem's fragmentary character establishes a paradigmatic way of looking at our history that Berryman sought in all subjects. The critic John Haffernden says he came across sixteen pages of notes for an "Ur-Washington in Love" in Berryman's attic. All has been reduced to seven lines in our version, seven little chapter headlines behind which history crackles and flashes. Berryman the teacher is at work here; the reader has to enter history, flesh out the possible versions. "Gislebertus' Eve" gives Berryman another opportunity to romp through the history of great ideas. As in *The Dream Songs*, he invests the speaker (his father? himself as an old-time director of history, à la John Ford, the filmmaker?) with a dramatic presence that identifies "the passion for secrets the passion worst of all"—the word *passion* fairly bristling to escape. Of all the props Berryman used, the sassy cabaret-style monologue allowed him a measure of religious identity in the face of bitter disillusionment and emptiness. From this no-man's-land, this sweep across the history of foolish propositions, or ideas, he could only be saved by parodying the parody: "I too find it delicious."

Whether rubbing our noses in what we have been up to militarily and politically, or confronting us with our personal limitations, *The Dream Songs* lament terrible things that *have* happened between nation and people, leader and follower, father and son. But they play their little anthems out so engagingly that we are caught up in the music, and the image of our going "out," or off the stage, is realized in taut structures under such pressure as to convey a feeling of animated strength.

SF

American Lights, Seen from Off Abroad

Blue go up & blue go down
to light the lights of Dollartown

Nebuchadnezzar had it so good?
wink the lights of Hollywood

I never think, I have so many things,
flash the lights of Palm Springs

I worry like a madwoman over all the world,
affirm the lights, all night, at State

I have no plans, I mean well,
swear the lights of Georgetown

I have the blind staggers
call the lights of Niagara

We shall die in a palace
shout the black lights of Dallas

I couldn't dare less, my favorite son,
fritter the lights of Washington

(I have a brave old So-and-So,
chuckle the lights of Independence, Mo.)

I cast a shadow, what I mean,
blurt the lights of Abilene

Both his sides are all the same
glows his grin with all but shame

He can do nothing night & day
wonder his lovers. So they say.

"Basketball in outer space"
sneers the White New Hampshire House

I'll have a smaller one, later, Mac,
hope the strange lights of Cal Tech

I love you one & all, hate shock,
bleat the lights of Little Rock

I cannot quite focus
cry the lights of Las Vegas

I am a maid of shots & pills,
swivel the lights of Beverly Hills

Proud & odd, you give me vertigo,
fly the lights of San Francisco

I am all satisfied love & chalk,
mutter the great lights of New York

I have lost your way
say the white lights of Boston

Here comes a scandal to blight you to bed.
Here comes a cropper'. That's what I said.

(Lévanto, 7 October 1957)

JOHN BERRYMAN

Certainty Before Lunch

Ninety percent of the mass of the Universe
(90%!) may be gone in collapsars,
pulseless, lightless, forever, if they exist.
My friends the probability man & I

& his wife the lawyer are taking a country walk
in the flowerless April snow in exactly two hours
and maybe won't be back. Finite & unbounded
the massive spirals absolutely fly

distinctly apart, by math *and* observation,
current math, this morning's telescopes
& inference. My wife is six months gone
so won't be coming. That mass must be somewhere!

or not? just barely possibly *may not*
BE anywhere? My Lord, I'm glad we don't
on x or y depend for Your being there.
I know You are there. The sweat is, I am here.

Washington in Love

I

Rectitude, and the terrible upstanding member

II

The music of our musketry is: *beautiful*

III

Intolerable Sally, loved in vain

IV

Mr Adams of Massachusetts . . . I accept, gentlemen.

V

Aloes. Adders. Roman gratitude.

VI

My porch elevation from the Potomac is 174′, 7½″.

Bring the wounded, Martha! *Bring the wounded, men.*

Gislebertus' Eve

Most men are not wicked . . . They
are sleep-walkers, not evildoers.
KAFKA TO G JANOUCH

Eve & her envy roving slammed me down
prone in discrepancy: I can't get things right:
the passion for secrets the passion worst of all,
the ultimate human, from Leonardo & Darwin

to the austere Viennese with the cigar
and Bohr a-musing: 'The opposite of a true
statement is a false statement. But the opposite
of a profound truth may be another profound truth.'

So now we see where we are, which is all-over
we're nowhere, son, and suffering we know it,
rapt in delusion, where weird particles
frantic & Ditheletic orbit our

revolutionary natures. She snaked out a soft
small willing hand, curved her ivory fingers on
a new taste sensation, in reverie over
something other,
sank her teeth in, and offered him a bite.

I too find it delicious.

from **The Dream Songs**
9

Deprived of his enemy, shrugged to a standstill
horrible Henry, foaming. Fan their way
toward him who will
in the high wood: the officers, their rest,
with p.a. echoing: his girl comes, say,
conned in to test

JOHN BERRYMAN

if he's still human, see: she love him, see,
therefore she get on the Sheriff's mike & howl
'Come down, come down'.
Therefore he un-budge, furious. He'd flee
but only Heaven hangs over him foul.
At the crossways, downtown,

he dreams the folks are buying parsnips & suds
and paying rent to foes. He slipt & fell.
It's golden here in the snow.
A mild crack: a far rifle. Bogart's duds
truck back to Wardrobe. Fancy the brain from hell
held out so long. Let go.

12

Sabbath

There is an eye, there was a slit.
Nights walk, and confer on him fear.
The strangler tree, the dancing mouse
confound his vision; then they loosen it.
Henry widens. How did Henry House
himself ever come here?

Nights run. Tes yeux bizarres me suivent
when loth at landfall soft I leave.
The soldiers, Coleridge Rilke Poe,
shout commands I never heard.
They march about, dying & absurd.
Toddlers are taking over. O

ver! Sabbath belling. Snoods converge
on a weary-daring man.
What now can be cleared up? from the Yard the visitors urge.
Belle thro' the graves in a blast of sun
to the kirk moves the youngest witch.
Watch.

23

The Lay of Ike

This is the lay of Ike.
Here's to the glory of the Great White—awk—
who has been running—er—er—things in recent—ech—
in the United—If your screen is black,

ladies & gentlemen, we—I like—
at the Point he was already terrific—sick

to a second term, having done no wrong—
no right—no right—having let the Army—bang—
defend itself from Joe, let venom' Strauss
bile Oppenheimer out of use—use Robb,
who'll later fend for Goldfine—Breaking no laws,
he lay in the White House—sob!!—

who never understood his own strategy—whee—
so Monty's memoirs—nor any strategy,
wanting the ball bulled thro' all parts of the line
at once—proving, by his refusal to take Berlin,
he misread even Clauswitz—wide empty grin
that never lost a vote (O Adlai mine).

76

Henry's Confession

Nothin very bad happen to me lately.
How you explain that? —I explain that, Mr Bones,
terms o' your bafflin odd sobriety.
Sober as man can get, no girls, no telephones,
what could happen bad to Mr Bones?
—*If* life is a handkerchief sandwich,

in a modesty of death I join my father
who dared so long agone leave me.
A bullet on a concrete stoop
close by a smothering southern sea
spreadeagled on an island, by my knee.
—You is from hunger, Mr Bones,

I offers you this handkerchief, now set
your left foot by my right foot,
shoulder to shoulder, all that jazz,
arm in arm, by the beautiful sea,
hum a little, Mr Bones.
—I saw nobody coming, so I went instead.

107

Three 'coons come at his garbage. He be cross,
I figuring porcupine & took Sir poker
unbarring Mr door,

JOHN BERRYMAN

& then screen door. Ah, but the little 'coon,
hardly a foot (not counting tail) got in with
two more at the porch-edge

and they swirled, before some two swerve off
this side of crab tree, and my dear friend held
with the torch in his tiny eyes
two feet off, banded, but then he gave &
shot away too. They were all the same size,
maybe they were brothers,

it seems, and is, clear to me we are brothers.
I wish the rabbit & the 'coons could be friends,
I'm sorry about the poker
but I'm too busy now for nipping or quills
I've given up literature & taken down pills,
and that rabbit doesn't trust me

366

Chilled in this Irish pub I wish my loves
well, well to strangers, well to all his friends,
seven or so in number,
I forgive my enemies, especially two,
races his heart, at so much magnanimity,
can it at all be true?

—Mr Bones, you on a trip outside yourself.
Has you seen a medicine man? You sound will-like,
a testament & such.
Is you going?—Oh, I suffer from a strike
& a strike & three balls: I stand up for much,
Wordsworth & that sort of thing.

The pitcher dreamed. He threw a hazy curve,
I took it in my stride & out I struck,
lonesome Henry.
These Songs are not meant to be understood, you understand.
They are only meant to terrify & comfort.
Lilac was found in his hand.

Notes

American Lights, Seen from Off Abroad. "A brave old So-and-So" refers to former
President Harry S. Truman. "Abilene" should conjure up former President
Dwight D. Eisenhower, who was born there.

Gislebertus' Eve. Gislebertus was a twelfth-century French sculptor. His "Eve" is on the stone panels of St. Lazare at Autun. The "austere Viennese with the cigar" is Sigmund Freud. "Bohr" was Niels Bohr, Danish physicist, who developed a theory of atomic structure. "Ditheletic" means believing in the existence of two antagonistic principles, one good and one evil.

Dream Song 9. The film *High Sierra*, directed by John Ford and starring Humphrey Bogart and Ida Lupino, is the subject of the poem.

Dream Song 12. "Tes yeux bizarres me suivent" means "Your bizarre eyes follow me" which may (if not made up!) be a line from Apollinaire, according to a French scholar consulted.

Dream Song 23: The Lay of Ike. "Ike" is former President Dwight D. Eisenhower. The "Point" is West Point. "Joe" is Senator Joseph McCarthy, who "went after" communists in the military and government. "Strauss" is a commissioner of the Atomic Energy Commission during the Eisenhower administration. "Robb" refers again to Strauss, whose first name was Robert. "Goldfine" is Bernard Goldfine, a businessman involved in shady deals during the Eisenhower administration. "Oppenheimer" is J. Robert Oppenheimer, U.S. nuclear physicist who worked on atomic bombs and was suspected of communist connections. "Monty": Sir Bernard Law Montgomery, British field marshal who became famous during World War II. "Clausewitz" (*sic.*) refers to Karl von Clausewitz (1780–1831), German military officer and author of books on military strategy. "Adlai": Adlai E. Stevenson, former governor of Illinois and twice an unsuccessful candidate against Eisenhower for the presidency.

Dream Song 76. "Mr Bones" is a kind of alter ego for Henry, who, Berryman once said, could be thought of as "Death" come to fetch Henry at the end.

John Berryman

Books

Poems, 1942
The Dispossessed, 1948
Homage to Mistress Bradstreet, 1956
His Thoughts Made Pockets & The Plane Buckt, 1958
Stephen Crane (biography), 1962
77 Dream Songs, 1964
Short Poems, 1967
His Toy, His Dream, His Rest, 1968
The Dream Songs, 1969
Love & Fame, 1972
Delusions, Etc., 1972
Henry's Fate & Other Poems, 1967, 1972
Recovery (novel), 1973
The Freedom of the Poet (essays and stories), 1976

Criticism

William J. Martz, *John Berryman*, 1969; Ernest C. Stefanik, Jr., *John Berryman: A Descriptive Bibliography*, 1972; J. M. Linebarger, *John Berryman*, 1974

Elizabeth
Bishop

(1911–1978)

A pungent sense of wonder inhabits everything that Elizabeth
Bishop wrote, and her powerful capacity for pursuing and cap-
turing the marvelous and the mysterious in her dense, meticu-
lous poems is her leading attribute as an artist. Her poems can be
solemn and rather childlike in their approach to the world, and they can

glitter with wit and sophistication, but these varieties of tone share a purposeful, even relentless, air of pursuit, a boring in on a subject so as to make it reveal, through penetrating observation, its hidden and magical characteristics. In this she goes farther than her friend and mentor, Marianne Moore. Take, for example, the imaginative intensity with which Bishop invades and inhabits the experience of the Prodigal Son in "The Prodigal." At first she seems to be searching out the negative qualities of his exile, but gradually the delight starts to mix in with the miseries to form a truer portrait of the runaway's ambivalence. When the deliberately flat ending (off-rhymed after a series of full rhymes) tells us that "it took him a long time / finally to make his mind up to go home," it doesn't surprise us, given the disquieting beauty of the barn and barnyard, a curious analogue to the Nativity setting that closes "Over 2000 Illustrations and a Complete Concordance."

To speak of a sense of wonder is not to dismiss emotions like dismay and terror. The world's richness is a strangeness too, about which the poet is both candid and precise: "In Mexico the dead man lay / in a blue arcade; the dead volcanoes / glistened like Easter lilies." Two kinds of death, one disquieting and the other comforting, framed by an odd beauty and a strange comparison that allow comfort and disquiet to mix together. What frightens the speaker of this poem ("Over 2000 Illustrations") most turns out to be a "holy grave" that seems empty and meaningless, suggesting that the search for natural wonders and exotic beauty is really a search for divinity and the meaning it would give the world. The speaker must finally imagine the epiphany—in this case the "old Nativity"—that would justify the appetite behind the travels and catalogues of this poem. The poet John Ashbery has called the last line of this poem among the most memorable and mysterious in contemporary poetry. Its sense of glory also suggests a simultaneous innocence and a yielding to extinction.

A private income, a love of travel, and a taste for the exotic allowed Elizabeth Bishop to explore and live in unusual settings. The geographical extremes of her first book, *North and South* (1946), seemed to be New England and Key West, but in her later poems these stretch out to Nova Scotia on the one hand and Brazil on the other. While her years of residence in Brazil produced many fine poems, we found ourselves preferring her "northern" poems, and the present selection reflects that preference. The relative strength of poems like "At the Fishhouses" and "First Death in Nova Scotia," as well as examples not included here, like the fine later poem "The Moose" and the unforgettable story "In the Village" (which was included in her collection of poems, *Questions of Travel*), may have to do with their roots in her childhood. She was born in Worcester, Massachusetts, but because her father died when she was an infant and her mother was committed to a mental institution when she was four, she was raised by her maternal grandparents in Nova Scotia. Poems like "Sestina" and "In the Waiting Room" seem to have a strong autobiographical basis.

It is not surprising that such a poet would be drawn to the formal and obsessive qualities of the sestina, and Elizabeth Bishop has left us two of the best examples in the language, "A Miracle for Breakfast" and the less well known but possibly superior example represented here. It is also not surprising that Bishop is a superb portrayer of childhood. Children are variously presented in this selection, most notably perhaps in "Sestina," "First Death in Nova Scotia," and "In the Waiting Room." This last poem, from her late collection *Geography III* (1976), shows the simplified style of precisely monitored, crisp reportage that especially characterizes her later work. Elizabeth Bishop's poetic canon is one of the smallest among the poets of her generation, but its importance and integrity continue to impress new readers, who discover in her poems a balanced exactness and unsentimental sense of the sublime that are far too rare in poetry.

DY

Over 2000 Illustrations and a Complete Concordance

Thus should have been our travels:
serious, engravable.
The Seven Wonders of the World are tired
and a touch familiar, but the other scenes,
innumerable, though equally sad and still,
are foreign. Often the squatting Arab,
or group of Arabs, plotting, probably,
against our Christian Empire,
while one apart, with outstretched arm and hand
points to the Tomb, the Pit, the Sepulcher.
The branches of the date-palms look like files.
The cobbled courtyard, where the Well is dry,
is like a diagram, the brickwork conduits
are vast and obvious, the human figure
far gone in history or theology,
gone with its camel or its faithful horse.

Always the silence, the gesture, the specks of birds
suspended on invisible threads above the Site,
or the smoke rising solemnly, pulled by threads.
Granted a page alone or a page made up
of several scenes arranged in cattycornered rectangles
or circles set on stippled gray,
granted a grim lunette,
caught in the toils of an initial letter,
when dwelt upon, they all resolve themselves.
The eye drops, weighted, through the lines
the burin made, the lines that move apart
like ripples above sand,
dispersing storms, God's spreading fingerprint,
and painfully, finally, that ignite
in watery prismatic white-and-blue.
Entering the Narrows at St. Johns
the touching bleat of goats reached to the ship.
We glimpsed them, reddish, leaping up the cliffs
among the fog-soaked weeds and butter-and-eggs.
And at St. Peter's the wind blew and the sun shone madly.
Rapidly, purposefully, the Collegians marched in lines,
crisscrossing the great square with black, like ants.
In Mexico the dead man lay
in a blue arcade; the dead volcanoes
glistened like Easter lilies.
The jukebox went on playing "Ay, Jalisco!"
And at Volubilis there were beautiful poppies
splitting the mosaics; the fat old guide made eyes.
In Dingle harbor a golden length of evening
the rotting hulks held up their dripping plush.
The Englishwoman poured tea, informing us
that the Duchess was going to have a baby.
And in the brothels of Marrakesh
the little pockmarked prostitutes
balanced their tea-trays on their heads
and did their belly-dances; flung themselves
naked and giggling against our knees,
asking for cigarettes. It was somewhere near there
I saw what frightened me most of all:
A holy grave, not looking particularly holy,
one of a group under a keyhole-arched stone baldaquin
open to every wind from the pink desert.
An open, gritty, marble trough, carved solid
with exhortation, yellowed
as scattered cattle-teeth;
half-filled with dust, not even the dust
of the poor prophet paynim who once lay there.

ELIZABETH BISHOP

In a smart burnoose Khadour looked on amused.

Everything only connected by "and" and "and."
Open the book. (The gilt rubs off the edges
of the pages and pollinates the fingertips.)
Open the heavy book. Why couldn't we have seen
this old Nativity while we were at it?
—the dark ajar, the rocks breaking with light,
an undisturbed, unbreathing flame,
colorless, sparkless, freely fed on straw,
and, lulled within, a family with pets,
—and looked and looked our infant sight away.

At the Fishhouses

Although it is a cold evening,
down by one of the fishhouses
an old man sits netting,
his net, in the gloaming almost invisible
a dark purple-brown,
and his shuttle worn and polished.
The air smells so strong of codfish
it makes one's nose run and one's eyes water.
The five fishhouses have steeply peaked roofs
and narrow, cleated gangplanks slant up
to storerooms in the gables
for the wheelbarrows to be pushed up and down on.
All is silver: the heavy surface of the sea,
swelling slowly as if considering spilling over,
is opaque, but the silver of the benches,
the lobster pots, and masts, scattered
among the wild jagged rocks,
is of an apparent translucence
like the small old buildings with an emerald moss
growing on their shoreward walls.
The big fish tubs are completely lined
with layers of beautiful herring scales
and the wheelbarrows are similarly plastered
with creamy iridescent coats of mail,
with small iridescent flies crawling on them.
Up on the little slope behind the houses,
set in the sparse bright sprinkle of grass,
is an ancient wooden capstan,
cracked, with two long bleached handles
and some melancholy stains, like dried blood,
where the ironwork has rusted.

The old man accepts a Lucky Strike.
He was a friend of my grandfather.
We talk of the decline in the population
and of codfish and herring
while he waits for a herring boat to come in.
There are sequins on his vest and on his thumb.
He has scraped the scales, the principal beauty,
from unnumbered fish with that black old knife,
the blade of which is almost worn away.

Down at the water's edge, at the place
where they haul up the boats, up the long ramp
descending into the water, thin silver
tree trunks are laid horizontally
across the gray stones, down and down
at intervals of four or five feet.

Cold dark deep and absolutely clear,
element bearable to no mortal,
to fish and to seals . . . One seal particularly
I have seen here evening after evening.
He was curious about me. He was interested in music;
like me a believer in total immersion,
so I used to sing him Baptist hymns.
I also sang "A Mighty Fortress Is Our God."
He stood up in the water and regarded me
steadily, moving his head a little.
Then he would disappear, then suddenly emerge
almost in the same spot, with a sort of shrug
as if it were against his better judgment.
Cold dark deep and absolutely clear,
the clear gray icy water . . . Back, behind us,
the dignified tall firs begin.
Bluish, associating with their shadows,
a million Christmas trees stand
waiting for Christmas. The water seems suspended
above the rounded gray and blue-gray stones.
I have seen it over and over, the same sea, the same,
slightly, indifferently swinging above the stones,
icily free above the stones,
above the stones and then the world.
If you should dip your hand in,
your wrist would ache immediately,
your bones would begin to ache and your hand would burn
as if the water were a transmutation of fire
that feeds on stones and burns with a dark gray flame.
If you tasted it, it would first taste bitter,
then briny, then surely burn your tongue.

It is like what we imagine knowledge to be:
dark, salt, clear, moving, utterly free,
drawn from the cold hard mouth
of the world, derived from the rocky breasts
forever, flowing and drawn, and since
our knowledge is historical, flowing, and flown.

The Prodigal

The brown enormous odor he lived by
was too close, with its breathing and thick hair,
for him to judge. The floor was rotten; the sty
was plastered halfway up with glass-smooth dung.
Light-lashed, self-righteous, above moving snouts,
the pigs' eyes followed him, a cheerful stare—
even to the sow that always ate her young—
till, sickening, he leaned to scratch her head.
But sometimes mornings after drinking bouts
(he hid the pints behind a two-by-four),
the sunrise glazed the barnyard mud with red;
the burning puddles seemed to reassure.
And then he thought he almost might endure
his exile yet another year or more.

But evenings the first star came to warn.
The farmer whom he worked for came at dark
to shut the cows and horses in the barn
beneath their overhanging clouds of hay,
with pitchforks, faint forked lightnings, catching light,
safe and companionable as in the Ark.
The pigs stuck out their little feet and snored.
The lantern—like the sun, going away—
laid on the mud a pacing aureole.
Carrying a bucket along a slimy board,
he felt the bats' uncertain staggering flight,
his shuddering insights, beyond his control,
touching him. But it took him a long time
finally to make his mind up to go home.

Sestina

September rain falls on the house.
In the failing light, the old grandmother
sits in the kitchen with the child
beside the Little Marvel Stove,

reading the jokes from the almanac,
laughing and talking to hide her tears.

She thinks that her equinoctial tears
and the rain that beats on the roof of the house
were both foretold by the almanac,
but only known to a grandmother.
The iron kettle sings on the stove.
She cuts some bread and says to the child,

It's time for tea now; but the child
is watching the teakettle's small hard tears
dance like mad on the hot black stove,
the way the rain must dance on the house.
Tidying up, the old grandmother
hangs up the clever almanac

on its string. Birdlike, the almanac
hovers half open above the child,
hovers above the old grandmother
and her teacup full of dark brown tears.
She shivers and says she thinks the house
feels chilly, and puts more wood in the stove.

It was to be, says the Marvel Stove.
I know what I know, says the almanac.
With crayons the child draws a rigid house
and a winding pathway. Then the child
puts in a man with buttons like tears
and shows it proudly to the grandmother.

But secretly, while the grandmother
busies herself about the stove,
the little moons fall down like tears
from between the pages of the almanac
into the flower bed the child
has carefully placed in the front of the house.

Time to plant tears, says the almanac.
The grandmother sings to the marvellous stove
and the child draws another inscrutable house.

First Death in Nova Scotia

In the cold, cold parlor
my mother laid out Arthur
beneath the chromographs:
Edward, Prince of Wales,

with Princess Alexandra,
and King George with Queen Mary.
Below them on the table
stood a stuffed loon
shot and stuffed by Uncle
Arthur, Arthur's father.

Since Uncle Arthur fired
a bullet into him,
he hadn't said a word.
He kept his own counsel
on his white, frozen lake,
the marble-topped table.
His breast was deep and white,
cold and caressable;
his eyes were red glass,
much to be desired.

"Come," said my mother,
"Come and say good-bye
to your little cousin Arthur."
I was lifted up and given
one lily of the valley
to put in Arthur's hand.
Arthur's coffin was
a little frosted cake,
and the red-eyed loon eyed it
from his white, frozen lake.

Arthur was very small.
He was all white, like a doll
that hadn't been painted yet.
Jack Frost had started to paint him
the way he always painted
the Maple Leaf (Forever).
He had just begun on his hair,
a few red strokes, and then
Jack Frost had dropped the brush
and left him white, forever.

The gracious royal couples
were warm in red and ermine;
their feet were well wrapped up
in the ladies' ermine trains.
They invited Arthur to be
the smallest page at court.
But how could Arthur go,
clutching his tiny lily,

with his eyes shut up so tight
and the roads deep in snow?

In the Waiting Room

In Worcester, Massachusetts,
I went with Aunt Consuelo
to keep her dentist's appointment
and sat and waited for her
in the dentist's waiting room.
It was winter. It got dark
early. The waiting room
was full of grown-up people,
arctics and overcoats,
lamps and magazines.
My aunt was inside
what seemed like a long time
and while I waited I read
the *National Geographic*
(I could read) and carefully
studied the photographs:
the inside of a volcano,
black, and full of ashes;
then it was spilling over
in rivulets of fire.
Osa and Martin Johnson
dressed in riding breeches,
laced boots, and pith helmets.
A dead man slung on a pole
—"Long Pig," the caption said.
Babies with pointed heads
wound round and round with string;
black, naked women with necks
wound round and round with wire
like the necks of light bulbs.
Their breasts were horrifying.
I read it right straight through.
I was too shy to stop.
And then I looked at the cover:
the yellow margins, the date.

Suddenly, from inside,
came an *oh!* of pain
—Aunt Consuelo's voice—
not very loud or long.

I wasn't at all surprised;
even then I knew she was
a foolish, timid woman.
I might have been embarrassed,
but wasn't. What took me
completely by surprise
was that it was *me:*
my voice, in my mouth.
Without thinking at all
I was my foolish aunt,
I—we—were falling, falling,
our eyes glued to the cover
of the *National Geographic,*
February, 1918.

I said to myself: three days
and you'll be seven years old.
I was saying it to stop
the sensation of falling off
the round, turning world
into cold, blue-black space.
But I felt: you are an *I,*
you are an *Elizabeth,*
you are one of *them.*
Why should you be one, too?
I scarcely dared to look
to see what it was I was.
I gave a sidelong glance
—I couldn't look any higher—
at shadowy gray knees,
trousers and skirts and boots
and different pairs of hands
lying under the lamps.
I knew that nothing stranger
had ever happened, that nothing
stranger could ever happen.
Why should I be my aunt,
or me, or anyone?
What similarities—
boots, hands, the family voice
I felt in my throat, or even
the *National Geographic*
and those awful hanging breasts—
held us all together
or made us all just one?
How—I didn't know any
word for it—how "unlikely" . . .

How had I come to be here,
like them, and overhear
a cry of pain that could have
got loud and worse but hadn't?

The waiting room was bright
and too hot. It was sliding
beneath a big black wave,
another, and another.

Then I was back in it.
The War was on. Outside,
in Worcester, Massachusetts,
were night and slush and cold,
and it was still the fifth
of February, 1918.

Notes

Over 2000 Illustrations and a Complete Concordance. Experience of the world presented first in terms of the encyclopedia illustrations the child pores over, then as real travel. A "burin" (line 27) is the tool used by the engraver to etch the plate.

Elizabeth Bishop

Books

North & South, 1946
Poems: North & South—A Cold Spring, 1955
The Diary of Helena Morley (translator), 1957
Questions of Travel, 1965
The Complete Poems, 1969
Anthology of Contemporary Brazilian Poetry (editor, translator), 1972
Geography III, 1976

Criticism, Interviews

Ann Stevenson, *Elizabeth Bishop*, 1966; "An Interview with Elizabeth Bishop," *Shenandoah* 17 (Winter 1966): 3–19; David Kalstone, *Five Temperaments*, 1977; *World Literature Today*, special Elizabeth Bishop issue (Winter 1977); "The Work! A Conversation with Elizabeth Bishop," *Ploughshares* 3 (1977)

Robert Francis

(b. 1901)

I t is a troublesome fact that Robert Francis, one of our best poets, is still so little known. His modest and retiring life near Amherst, Massachusetts, may partly explain his obscurity, along with a relatively slow development—his best poems were written after he turned fifty— and a number of years spent in the shadow of his friend and mentor,

Robert Frost. Then, too, it must be noted that Francis's poems are modest in scale and scope, and that in a time when it has been fashionable for poets to stress angst and anguish, their own and that of others, Francis has made a serious exploration of pleasure and delight. He is, as he says in his autobiography, *The Trouble with Francis* (1971), a deeply pessimistic man; but his poems, while they occasionally reflect that outlook, mostly search out the properties of the natural world and of language that can act to offset or qualify the pessimism.

The short, precise, exquisitely balanced poems that Francis writes find the same properties to celebrate in nature and language: effects of doubling, rhyming, compounding, punning and echoing. The flow of experience reveals curious and chancy links between objects and among words, and the poet catches them on the wing. Francis does not so much create metaphors and forge likenesses as he does find them, discover them, in natural things—toads, cypresses, waxwings, weather—and in words that rhyme, pun, wed in compounds, or reveal sudden family resemblances based on etymology, consonance, or similarity of meaning. For years cypresses have been "teaching birds / In little schools, by little skills, / How to be shadows." The shading of "schools" into "skills" is partly an effect of rhyming and punning, partly an observation of the world. Similarly, the two riders in "Boy Riding Forward Backward" are like 'Swallows that weave and wave and sweep / And skim and swoop and skitter until / The last trees take them." This is a celebration both of the way swallows behave and of the language's capacity for verbs. When good likenesses appear between the words themselves and the things they name or imitate, a special pleasure is created from simultaneous matching in nature and language, the two realities of world and word. "Bluejay" provides a fine example when the bird and the beloved father's unlikely affection for it allow the off-rhyme of "feather" and "father" to bring the poem to its perfect close. Other poems may revel directly in the delights of language—"Hogwash" and "Yes, What?"—or in the felicities of the natural world—"Cold" and "Blue Winter"—but the combination of language as pleasure and nature as beauty, and their delicate interaction, is usually at the heart of a Francis poem. "Silent Poem," a daring series of compound nouns, is a distillation of these interests, a one-of-a-kind poem that only a poet as devoted to language and nature as Francis could possibly have written.

The twin subjects of language and nature both have their human dimension, of course, and Francis can marvel at human virtuosity, as in "Boy Riding Forward Backward" and "Apple Peeler," and delineate human folly, as he does quite variously in "Like Ghosts of Eagles," "December," and "'Paper Men to Air Hopes and Fears.'" Nevertheless, his strongest affirmations of human skill are those implicit in the craft and economy of his poems. Whether their order is of a traditional sort, an apparently effortless use of rhyme and meter, or innovative, Francis's poems are always distinguished by formal excellence, an unusual grace and shapeliness. One senses that they are the products of a great patience and perfectionism, a willingness to work and wait until things come just right. The result is a poem that holds its interest longer than most.

Robert Francis's life, as described in the disarming autobiography cited above, has reflected the patience and economy of the poems. He has lived in near-solitude most of his life, on a minuscule income, learning how to make do with little and live off the land, transferring the lessons of simplicity and independence into the adroit, tough-minded lyric poems he writes and into his lucid prose (besides *The Trouble with Francis*, there is a book of prose "potshots," *The Satirical Rogue on Poetry*, and a memoir, *Frost: A Time to Talk*). The grace and uncanny precision of his poems suggests comparisons with other poets—Herrick, Hardy, Emily Dickinson—but what is finally most notable about Robert Francis is his uniqueness, the distinctive mind and temper that inform each poem. As this book appears, he will have passed his eightieth birthday, still far from sufficiently recognized.

DY

Sheep

From where I stand the sheep stand still
As stones against the stony hill.

The stones are gray
And so are they.

And both are weatherworn and round,
Leading the eye back to the ground.

Two mingled flocks—
The sheep, the rocks.

And still no sheep stirs from its place
Or lifts its Babylonian face.

Blue Winter

Winter uses all the blues there are.
One shade of blue for water, one for ice,
Another blue for shadows over snow.
The clear or cloudy sky uses blue twice—
Both different blues. And hills row after row
Are colored blue according to how far.
You know the bluejay's double-blue device
Shows best when there are no green leaves to show.
And Sirius is a winterbluegreen star.

Boy Riding Forward Backward

Presto, pronto! Two boys, two horses.
But the boy on backward riding forward
Is the boy to watch.

He rides the forward horse and laughs
In the face of the forward boy on the backward
Horse, and *he* laughs

Back and the horses laugh. They gallop.
The trick is the cool barefaced pretense
There is no trick.

They might be flying, face to face,
On a fast train. They might be whitecaps
Hot-cool-headed,

One curling backward, one curving forward,
Racing a rivalry of waves.
They might, they might—

Across a blue of lake, through trees,
And half a mile away I caught them:
Two boys, two horses.

Through trees and through binoculars
Sweeping for birds. Oh, they were birds
All right, all right,

Swallows that weave and wave and sweep
And skim and swoop and skitter until
The last trees take them.

Waxwings

Four Tao philosophers as cedar waxwings
chat on a February berrybush
in sun, and I am one.

Such merriment and such sobriety—
the small wild fruit on the tall stalk—
was this not always my true style?

Above an elegance of snow, beneath
a silk-blue sky a brotherhood of four
birds. Can you mistake us?

To sun, to feast, and to converse
and all together—for this I have abandoned
all my other lives.

Apple Peeler

Why the unbroken spiral, Virtuoso,
Like a trick sonnet in one long, versatile sentence?

Is it a pastime merely, this perfection,
For an old man, sharp knife, long night, long winter?

Or do your careful fingers move at the stir
Of unadmitted immemorial magic?

Solitaire. The ticking clock. The apple
Turning, turning as the round earth turns.

Bluejay

So bandit-eyed, so undovelike a bird
to be my pastoral father's favorite—
skulker and blusterer
whose every arrival is a raid.

Love made the bird no gentler
nor him who loved less gentle.
Still, still the wild blue feather
brings my mild father.

Cold

Cold and the colors of cold: mineral, shell,
And burning blue. The sky is on fire with blue
And wind keeps ringing, ringing the fire bell.

I am caught up into a chill as high
As creaking glaciers and powder-plumed peaks
And the absolutes of interstellar sky.

Abstract, impersonal, metaphysical, pure,
This dazzling art derides me. How should warm breath
Dare to exist—exist, exult, endure?

Hums in my ear the old Ur-father of freeze
And burn, that pre-post-Christian Fellow before
And after all myths and demonologies.

Under the glaring and sardonic sun,
Behind the icicles and double glass
I huddle, hoard, hold out, hold on, hold on.

Cypresses

At noon they talk of evening and at evening
Of night, but what they say at night
Is a dark secret.

Somebody long ago called them the Trees
Of Death and they have never forgotten.
The name enchants them.

Always an attitude of solitude
To point the paradox of standing
Alone together.

How many years they have been teaching birds
In little schools, by little skills,
How to be shadows.

Three Darks Come Down Together

Three darks come down together,
Three darks close in around me:
Day dark, year dark, dark weather.

They whisper and conspire,
They search me and they sound me
Hugging my private fire.

Day done, year done, storm blowing,
Three darknesses impound me
With dark of white snow snowing.

Three darks gang up to end me,
To browbeat and dumbfound me.
Three future lights defend me.

Hogwash

The tongue that mothered such a metaphor
Only the purest purist could despair of.

Nobody ever called swill sweet but isn't
Hogwash a daisy in a field of daisies?

What beside sports and flowers could you find
To praise better than the American language?

Bruised by American foreign policy
What shall I soothe me, what defend me with

But a handful of clean unmistakable words—
Daisies, daisies, in a field of daisies?

"Paper Men to Air Hopes and Fears"

The first speaker said
Fear fire. Fear furnaces
Incinerators, the city dump
The faint scratch of match.

The second speaker said
Fear water. Fear drenching rain
Drizzle, oceans, puddles, a damp
Day and the flush toilet.

The third speaker said
Fear wind. And it needn't be
A hurricane. Drafts, open
Windows, electric fans.

The fourth speaker said
Fear knives. Fear any sharp
Thing, machine, shears
Scissors, lawnmowers.

The fifth speaker said
Hope. Hope for the best
A smooth folder in a steel file.

Like Ghosts of Eagles

The Indians have mostly gone
but not before they named the rivers
the rivers flow on
and the names of the rivers flow with them
    Susquehanna   Shenandoah

The rivers are now polluted plundered
but not the names of the rivers
cool and inviolate as ever
pure as on the morning of creation
    Tennessee   Tombigbee

If the rivers themselves should ever perish
I think the names will somehow somewhere hover
like ghosts of eagles
those mighty whisperers
    Missouri   Mississippi.

Silent Poem

backroad   leafmold   stonewall   chipmunk
underbrush   grapevine   woodchuck   shadblow

woodsmoke   cowbarn   honeysuckle   woodpile
sawhorse   bucksaw   outhouse   wellsweep

backdoor   flagstone   bulkhead   buttermilk
candlestick   ragrug   firedog   brownbread

hilltop   outcrop   cowbell   buttercup
whetstone   thunderstorm   pitchfork   steeplebush

gristmill   millstone   cornmeal   waterwheel
watercress   buckwheat   firefly   jewelweed

ROBERT FRANCIS

gravestone groundpine windbreak bedrock
weathercock snowfall starlight cockcrow

December

Dim afternoon December afternoon
Just before dark, their caps
A Christmas or un-Christmas red
The hunters.

Oh, I tell myself that death
In the woods is far far better
Than doom in the slaughterhouse.
Still, the hunters haunt me.

Does a deer die now or does a hunter
Dim afternoon December afternoon
By cold intent or accident but always
My death?

History

I

History to the historian
Is always his story.

He puts the pieces
Of the past together

To make his picture
To make his peace—

Pieces of past wars
Pieces of past peaces.

But don't ask him
To put the pieces

Of the past together
To make your picture

To make your peace.

II

The Holy See is not by any means
the whole sea and the whole sea
so far as one can see is far from holy.

The Holy See is old but how much older
the sea that is not holy, how vastly
older the sea itself, the whole sea.

The Holy See may last a long time longer
yet how much longer, how vastly longer
the whole sea, the sea itself, the unholy sea

Scrubbing earth's unecclesiastical shores
as if they never never would be clean
like a row of Irish washerwomen

Washing, washing, washing away
far into the unforeseeable future
long after the Holy See no more is seen.

III

Henry Thoreau Henry James and Henry Adams
would never have called history bunk
not Henry James not Henry Adams.

Nor would Henry Adams or Henry James
ever have tried to get the boys
out of the trenches by Christmas.

Only Henry Thoreau might have tried
to get the boys out of the bunk out
of the Christmas out of the trenches.

For Henry Thoreau was anti-bunk Henry James
pro-bunk and what shall we say of Henry Adams
except that all four Henrys are now history?

IV

The great Eliot has come the great Eliot
has gone and where precisely are we now?

He moved from the Mississippi to the Thames
and we moved with him a few miles or inches.

He taught us what to read what not to read
and when he changed his mind he let us know.

ROBERT FRANCIS   61

He coughed discreetly and we likewise coughed;
we waited and we heard him clear his throat.

How to be perfect prisoners of the past
this was the thing but now he too is past.

Shall we go sit beside the Mississippi
and watch the riffraft driftwood floating by?

Yes, What?

What would earth do without her blessed boobs
her blooming bumpkins garden variety
her oafs   her louts   her yodeling yokels
and all her Breughel characters
under the fat-faced moon?

Her nitwits   numskulls   universal
nincompoops   jawohl   jawohl   with all
their yawps   burps   beers   guffaws
her goofs   her goons   her big galoots
under the red-face moon?

Notes

History. The fourth "Henry" in section III, who is famous for having proposed a scheme to end World War I "to get the boys out of the trenches by Christmas" and for having said "History is bunk," is Henry Ford. Section IV takes note of the fact that T. S. Eliot was born in St. Louis.

Robert Francis

Books

Stand With Me Here, 1936
Valhalla and Other Poems, 1938
The Sound I Listened For, 1944
We Fly Away (novel), 1948
The Face Against the Glass, 1950
The Orb Weaver, 1960
Come Out Into the Sun, 1965
The Satirical Rogue on Poetry (criticism), 1968

The Trouble With Francis (autobiography), 1971
Frost: A Time to Talk (memoir), 1972
Like Ghosts of Eagles, 1974
Collected Poems, 1936–1976, 1976
Pot Shots at Poetry (prose), 1980

Criticism

John Holmes, "Constants Carried Forward," *Massachusetts Review* (Summer 1961); David Young, "Out of the Shadow," *New Republic* (7 August 1971); Donald Hall, "Two Poets Named Robert," *Ohio Review* (Fall 1977); Symposium in Honor of Robert Francis's 80th Birthday, *FIELD*, No. 25 (Fall 1981).

Robert
Hayden

(1913–1980)

U ntil 1966, when the *Selected Poems* appeared, Robert Hayden was little known. That seems surprising as we look back at his life's work, which started taking shape in the 1930s. Even the earliest full collection, *Heart-Shape in the Dust* (1940), is much more than an imitation of Auden, or apprenticeship poetry, as some have called it. In the long period that followed until his second volume was published in 1955, Hayden kept working away quietly while teaching at Fisk, until the critics and the public began to pay some attention to him. He has suffered the usual put-down of being considered merely a spokesman for black issues and causes, with a condescending glance at his artistic merits: "the surest poetic talent of any Negro poet in America," as one magazine put it. While there has been little criticism to date that takes the poetry seriously as poetry, he is no longer emerging, and it is clear that his reputation will continue to grow.

Hayden's poems deal with many compelling historical struggles—the Baha'i faith, slavery, Malcolm X, Kennedy, and King—and seem to be seeking a *Dauer im Wechsel*, or permanence in change, as Goethe put it. Many readers will be attracted to the "romantic realist" spirit that Hayden himself felt infused the poems. Ultimately, however, Hayden's stature and power as a poet flow mainly from his uncanny ways of telling stories, both real and imagined. He is as accomplished a modern balladeer of our cities and streets as Philip Levine, with whom Hayden shares Detroit as home ground. It is this fascination with stories, which Hayden tells with rough-cut abandon, chiseling them into brilliant figures at the right moments, that dazzles us. And how his characters talk! We don't mind if people don't really talk like that; we want them to from now on. Aunt Jemima—one of his great women characters—leaps off the pancake box (or better, in Hayden's vision, out of the freak show *he* finds her in) and onto the sand beside us, suggesting, cajoling, whispering a smarter way to live. In "Stars," the "ancestress / childless mother" walking barefoot toward us out of slavery under the beautifully named stars does not speak, but her *mind* is a star. That is the reason she can follow the stars. Hayden's mystery people, like the stars "abstract as future yesterdays," emerge in their true landscapes where we meet them and are startled out of our clichés.

Michael Harper tells of Hayden calling him up again and again, genuinely worried about just the right word or phrasing, still fiddling with poems that had long since been published and honored. Such demonic revising impulses let us sense the tremendous pressure the poems have been put under, as he "molded and resolved with confidence and precision," in Gwendolyn Brooks's words (*Negro Digest*). Another important aspect of the care and skill he brought to each word, rethinking many poems till the day he died, is the exhaustive research he invested in his subjects. "Night, Death, Mississippi," "Runagate Runagate," and the gutsy tribute to Bessie Smith, "Homage to the Empress of the Blues," are not only contemporary ballads that range the imagination and the memory as they track the human experience of slavery and subjugation;

they are historical documents as well, laying bare the facts of those survival stories. It is no wonder that Hayden won the prestigious World Festival of the Arts Prize and the Russell Loines Award and was *twice* named consultant to the Library of Congress. He was a *recording* artist of the facts and fantasies he felt we must not lose sight of, and drove himself to keep us fixed on our rights as well as our responsibilities. But what we find especially moving as we look back at the poems we have chosen is how he could restrain all the learning, all the political and religious fervor he unleashed on most subjects, to preserve the most delicate touch for the hardest of stories to tell: "Those Winter Sundays" takes us to the heart of the love struggle with our parents, and ultimately ourselves. The first stanza is paid out carefully, as if counting out bills on a counter, the alliterative rhythms that would otherwise jump out discordantly smacking into place. The second stanza, reaching back in a nineteenth-century reverie for the memory of the sleeping child waking to see his father up early even on Sunday, making a fire, tightens in the last line on the unexpected adjective: "fearing the chronic angers of that house." Then the marvelous move in the final stanza to an exalted, almost self-consciously poetic turn that casts the real spell: the child-adult lolling at first, "What did I know, what did I know," as if dreaming of guilt and innocence, before seeing ahead to "love's austere and lonely offices." "Offices," with its brace of adjectives, carries us sadly away.

SF

" 'Mystery Boy' Looks for Kin in Nashville"

Puzzle faces in the dying elms
promise him treats if he will stay.
Sometimes they hiss and spit at him
like varmints caught
in a thicket of butterflies.

A black doll,
one disremembered time,
came floating down to him
through mimosa's fancywork leaves and blooms
to be his hidden bride.

From the road beyond the creepered walls
they call to him now and then,
and he'll take off in spite of the angry trees,
hearing like the loudening of his heart
the name he never can he never can repeat.

And when he gets to where the voices were—
Don't cry, his dollbaby wife implores;
I know where they are, don't cry.
We'll go and find them, we'll go
and ask them for your name again.

Aunt Jemima of the Ocean Waves

I

Enacting someone's notion of themselves
(and me), The One And Only Aunt Jemima
and Kokimo The Dixie Dancing Fool
do a bally for the freak show.

I watch a moment, then move on,
pondering the logic that makes of them
(and me) confederates
of The Spider Girl, The Snake-skinned Man . . .

Poor devils have to live somehow.

I cross the boardwalk to the beach,
lie in the sand and gaze beyond
the clutter at the sea.

II

Trouble you for a light?
I turn as Aunt Jemima settles down
beside me, her blue-rinsed hair
without the red bandanna now.

I hold the lighter to her cigarette.
Much obliged. Unmindful (perhaps)
of my embarrassment, she looks
at me and smiles. You sure

do favor a friend I used to have.
Guess that's why I bothered you
for a light. So much like him that I—
She pauses, watching white horses rush

to the shore. Way them big old waves
come slamming whopping in,
sometimes it's like they mean to smash
this no-good world to hell.

ROBERT HAYDEN

Well, it could happen. A book I read—
Crossed that very ocean years ago.
London, Paris, Rome,
Constantinople too—I've seen them all.

Back when they billed me everywhere
as the Sepia High Stepper.
Crowned heads applauded me.
Years before your time. Years and years.

I wore me plenty diamonds then,
and counts or dukes or whatever they were
would fill my dressing room
with the costliest flowers. But of course

there was this one you resemble so.
Get me? The sweetest gentleman.
Dead before his time. Killed in the war
to save the world for another war.

High-stepping days for me
were over after that. Still I'm not one
to let grief idle me for long.
I went out with a mental act—

mind-reading—Mysteria From
The Mystic East—veils and beads
and telling suckers how to get
stolen rings and sweethearts back.

One night he was standing by my bed,
seen him plain as I see you,
and warned me without a single word:
Baby, quit playing with spiritual stuff.

So here I am, so here I am,
fake mammy to God's mistakes.
And that's the beauty part,
I mean, ain't that the beauty part.

She laughs, but I do not, knowing what
her laughter shields. And mocks.
I light another cigarette for her.
She smokes, not saying any more.

Scream of children in the surf,
adagios of sun and flashing foam,
the sexual glitter, oppressive fun. . . .
An antique etching comes to mind:

"The Sable Venus" naked on
a baroque Cellini shell—voluptuous
imago floating in the wake
of slave-ships on fantastic seas.

Jemima sighs, Reckon I'd best
be getting back. I help her up.
Don't you take no wooden nickels, hear?
Tin dimes neither. So long, pal.

Stars

I

Stood there then among
spears and kindled shields,
praising Orion.

II

Betelgeuse Aldebaran
Abstract as future yesterdays
the starlight
crosses eons of meta-space
to us.

Algol Arcturus Almaak

How shall the mind keep warm
save at spectral
fires—how thrive but by the light
of paradox?

Altair Vega Polaris Maia

III

(*Sojourner Truth*)
Comes walking barefoot
out of slavery

ancestress
childless mother

following the stars
her mind a star

Night, Death, Mississippi

I

A quavering cry. Screech-owl?
Or one of them?
The old man in his reek
and gauntness laughs—

One of them, I bet—
and turns out the kitchen lamp,
limping to the porch to listen
in the windowless night.

Be there with Boy and the rest
if I was well again.
Time was. Time was.
White robes like moonlight

In the sweetgum dark.
Unbucked that one then
and him squealing bloody Jesus
as we cut it off.

Time was. A cry?
A cry all right.
He hawks and spits,
fevered as by groinfire.

Have us a bottle,
Boy and me—
he's earned him a bottle—
when he gets home.

II

Then we beat them, he said,
beat them till our arms was tired
and the big old chains
messy and red.

O Jesus burning on the lily cross

Christ, it was better
than hunting bear
which don't know why
you want him dead.

O night, rawhead and bloodybones night

You kids fetch Paw
some water now so's he
can wash that blood
off him, she said.

O night betrayed by darkness not its own

A Road in Kentucky

And when that ballad lady went
    to ease the lover whose life she broke,
oh surely this is the road she took,
    road all hackled through barberry fire,
through cedar and alder and sumac and thorn.

Red clay stained her flounces
    and stones cut her shoes
and the road twisted on to his loveless house
    and his cornfield dying
in the scarecrow's arms.

And when she had left her lover lying
    so stark and so stark, with the Star-of-Hope
drawn over his eyes, oh this is the road
    that lady walked in the cawing light,
so dark and so dark in the briary light.

Homage to the Empress of the Blues

Because there was a man somewhere in a candystripe silk shirt,
gracile and dangerous as a jaguar and because a woman moaned
for him in sixty-watt gloom and mourned him Faithless Love
Twotiming Love Oh Love Oh Careless Aggravating Love.

    She came out on the stage in yards of pearls, emerging like
    a favorite scenic view, flashed her golden smile and sang.

Because grey laths began somewhere to show from underneath
torn hurdygurdy lithographs of dollfaced heaven;
and because there were those who feared alarming fists of snow
on the door and those who feared the riot-squad of statistics,

    She came out on the stage in ostrich feathers, beaded satin,
    and shone that smile on us and sang.

ROBERT HAYDEN   71

Those Winter Sundays

Sundays too my father got up early
and put his clothes on in the blueblack cold,
then with cracked hands that ached
from labor in the weekday weather made
banked fires blaze. No one ever thanked him.

I'd wake and hear the cold splintering, breaking.
When the rooms were warm, he'd call,
and slowly I would rise and dress,
fearing the chronic angers of that house,

Speaking indifferently to him,
who had driven out the cold
and polished my good shoes as well.
What did I know, what did I know
of love's austere and lonely offices?

Runagate Runagate

I

Runs falls rises stumbles on from darkness into darkness
and the darkness thicketed with shapes of terror
and the hunters pursuing and the hounds pursuing
and the night cold and the night long and the river
to cross and the jack-muh-lanterns beckoning beckoning
and blackness ahead and when shall I reach that somewhere
morning and keep on going and never turn back and keep on going

        Runagate
              Runagate
                    Runagate

Many thousands rise and go
many thousands crossing over

                        O mythic North
                 O star-shaped yonder Bible city

Some go weeping and some rejoicing
some in coffins and some in carriages
some in silks and some in shackles

        Rise and go or fare you well

No more auction block for me
no more driver's lash for me

If you see my Pompey, 30 yrs of age,
new breeches, plain stockings, negro shoes;
if you see my Anna, likely young mulatto
branded E on the right cheek, R on the left,
catch them if you can and notify subscriber.
Catch them if you can, but it won't be easy.
They'll dart underground when you try to catch them,
plunge into quicksand, whirlpools, mazes,
turn into scorpions when you try to catch them.

And before I'll be a slave
I'll be buried in my grave

      North star and bonanza gold
      I'm bound for the freedom, freedom-bound
      and oh Susyanna don't you cry for me

             Runagate

               Runagate

II

Rises from their anguish and their power,
          Harriet Tubman,

               woman of earth, whipscarred,
               a summoning, a shining

             Mean to be free

And this was the way of it, brethren brethren,
way we journeyed from Can't to Can.
Moon so bright and no place to hide,
the cry up and the patterollers riding,
hound dogs belling in bladed air.
And fear starts a-murbling, Never make it,
we'll never make it. *Hush that now,*
and she's turned upon us, levelled pistol
glinting in the moonlight:
Dead folks can't jaybird-talk, she says;
you keep on going now or die, she says.

Wanted   Harriet Tubman   alias The General
alias Moses   Stealer of Slaves

In league with Garrison   Alcott   Emerson
Garrett   Douglass   Thoreau   John Brown

ROBERT HAYDEN   73

Armed and known to be Dangerous

Wanted   Reward   Dead or Alive

> Tell me, Ezekiel, oh tell me do you see
> mailed Jehovah coming to deliver me?

Hoot-owl calling in the ghosted air,
five times calling to the hants in the air.
Shadow of a face in the scary leaves,
shadow of a voice in the talking leaves:

> Come ride-a my train

> *Oh that train, ghost-story train*
> *through swamp and savanna movering movering,*
> *over trestles of dew, through caves of the wish,*
> *Midnight Special on a sabre track movering movering,*
> *first stop Mercy and the last Hallelujah.*

> Come ride-a my train

> Mean mean mean to be free.

Notes

"Mystery Boy" Looks for Kin in Nashville. It's said that the poem is based on an account Hayden came across in a newspaper of a young girl (!) who escaped from a sanitarium.

Aunt Jemima of the Ocean Waves. Aunt Jemima is the person who appears on the packages of the Aunt Jemima pancake products.

Stars. Betelgeuse, Aldebaran, Algol, Arcturus, Almaak, Altair, Vega, Polaris, Maia are all stars of various magnitudes that occur in the constellations. Sojourner Truth was a freed slave.

Homage to the Empress of the Blues. This poem celebrates the great blues singer, Bessie Smith.

Runagate Runagate. A runagate is an archaic word for a fugitive or runaway (slave). Harriet Tubman, herself an escaped slave, returned from freedom to help many blacks escape. Garrison was a leader of the abolition movement. Alcott was a U.S. transcendentalist philosopher and reformer. Douglass was the U.S. black leader and orator who fought against slavery.

Robert Hayden

Books

Heart-Shape in the Dust, 1940
Figure of Time, 1955

Selected Poems, 1966
Words in the Mourning Time, 1970
Angle of Ascent, 1975
American Journal, 1982

Interviews, Criticism

How I Write / 1, 1972; *Interviews with Black Writers*, ed. J. O'Brien, 1973; *Conversations with Black Writers, 1*, ed. R. Layman, 1977; Robert Stepto, "After Modernism, After Hibernation," in *Chant of Saints*, 1979

Randall
Jarrell
(1914–1963)

Ted Russell

R andall Jarrell, a poet of great force and originality, stands apart
in many ways from the rest of his generation. Technical bril-
liance and allusive density did not tempt him as they did others.
From poets who had explored the power of plainness and directness—
Whitman, Frost, Rilke, Williams—he drew the inspiration for his own rel-

atively unadorned style, a powerful instrument that speaks candidly to issues at the center of everyday lives. How ordinary people live and how they cope with their terror, need, and ignorance are things Jarrell writes about in a way that few poets have equaled.

A southerner by birth (Nashville, Tennessee), Jarrell spent some childhood years in Hollywood (as lovingly recorded in the "Lost World" poems of his last book), majored in psychology at Vanderbilt, taught briefly at Kenyon (where John Crowe Ransom was a senior teacher and Robert Lowell an undergraduate), served in the Air Force during World War II, and taught for many years at a small women's college (Greensboro) in North Carolina. He was, by all reports, a gifted teacher.

As a writer, Jarrell was something of a double personality. The reviewer and critic was notorious for wit, sophistication, and self-confidence. The poet, in contrast, could seem self-effacing, almost clumsy. In fact, the way in which Jarrell banished his brilliant and urbane side from his poems protected him from clever modishness, allowing him to explore the world with a sense of freshness and wonder. His willingness to be childlike, even to center his poetry on the experiences of childhood, gives him interesting links with Elizabeth Bishop and Theodore Roethke and helps explain his additional success as a writer of children's books.

Hindsight shows us that Jarrell was the poet of his generation who came most fully to terms with the Second World War. Most of the poetry that war produced is no longer read or studied, but Jarrell's war poems continue to exert their power. One secret of their success may lie in the poet's willingness to let the speechless war dead—the soldiers and the concentration camp victims—speak through him. This creates a rhetorical advantage, since it keeps the poems understated and does not put the poet in the position of claiming that he understands the war or can comment on it from a position of easy self-righteousness. The power of poems like "Losses," "The Death of the Ball Turret Gunner" and "Protocols" seems to stem partly from that fact and partly from the poet's uncanny ability—what Keats, in praising Shakespeare, called "negative capability"—to put himself into the lives and imaginations of others, an ability Jarrell also reveals in such later masterpieces as "Seele im Raum."

After the war, almost as though his negative capability had made him want to know the enemy that others would hate and dismiss, Jarrell developed a passionate interest in German culture and civilization; the world of his poems is peopled with culture heroes like Freud, the brothers Grimm, Rilke, Dürer, Richard Strauss, and Goethe. This interest, which contributed so much to his best poetry, is centered on the rich, imaginative world of the German fairy tales. As metaphors for the human condition, as vehicles of psychological insight—both Freud and Jung are immensely relevant here—these tales became the foundation for a number of Jarrell's most searching and mysterious poems, as exemplified in the present selection by "Cinderella," "A Hunt in the Black Forest," and "The House in the Wood."

Not long after the publication of his finest volume (*The Lost World*, 1965), Randall Jarrell was struck by a car while walking at night. Some have called the death a suicide, others an accident. In any case, it was an untimely loss of a poet who had accomplished much and was still growing.

Jarrell's *Complete Poems* is available in paperback. Also of note are his novel, *Pictures from an Institution* (1954), and his three books of essays: *Poetry and the Age* (1954, reprinted 1980), *A Sad Heart at the Supermarket* (1962), and *The Third Book of Criticism* (1969). His children's books include *The Bat Poet* and *The Animal Family*. Jarrell can be doctrinaire in his Freudianism and repetitive in his deliberate plainness, but his best poems are challenging in their range and unforgettable in their compassionate humanity, and his honesty and imaginative depth continue to win him new readers.

DY

Losses

It was not dying: everybody died.
It was not dying: we had died before
In the routine crashes—and our fields
Called up the papers, wrote home to our folks,
And the rates rose, all because of us.
We died on the wrong page of the almanac,
Scattered on mountains fifty miles away;
Diving on haystacks, fighting with a friend,
We blazed up on the lines we never saw.
We died like aunts or pets or foreigners.
(When we left high school nothing else had died
For us to figure we had died like.)

In our new planes, with our new crews, we bombed
The ranges by the desert or the shore,
Fired at towed targets, waited for our scores—
And turned into replacements and woke up
One morning, over England, operational.

It wasn't different: but if we died
It was not an accident but a mistake
(But an easy one for anyone to make).
We read our mail and counted up our missions—
In bombers named for girls, we burned
The cities we had learned about in school—
Till our lives wore out; our bodies lay among
The people we had killed and never seen.
When we lasted long enough they gave us medals;
When we died they said, "Our casualties were low."

They said, "Here are the maps"; we burned the cities.

It was not dying—no, not ever dying;
But the night I died I dreamed that I was dead,
And the cities said to me: "Why are you dying?
We are satisfied, if you are; but why did I die?"

The Death of the Ball Turret Gunner

From my mother's sleep I fell into the State,
And I hunched in its belly till my wet fur froze.
Six miles from earth, loosed from its dream of life,
I woke to black flak and the nightmare fighters.
When I died they washed me out of the turret with a hose.

Protocols

(Birkenau, Odessa; the children speak alternately.)

We went there on the train. *They had big barges that they towed,*
We stood up, there were so many I was squashed.
There was a smoke-stack, then they made me wash.
It was a factory, I think. *My mother held me up*
And I could see the ship that made the smoke.

When I was tired my mother carried me.
She said, "Don't be afraid." But I was only tired.
Where we went there is no more Odessa.
They had water in a pipe—like rain, but hot;
The water there is deeper than the world

And I was tired and fell in in my sleep
And the water drank me. That is what I think.
And I said to my mother, "Now I'm washed and dried,"
My mother hugged me, and it smelled like hay
And that is how you die. And that is how you die.

Seele im Raum

It sat between my husband and my children.
A place was set for it—a plate of greens.
It had been there: I had seen it
But not somehow—but this was like a dream—
Not seen it so that I knew I saw it.
It was as if I could not know I saw it
Because I had never once in all my life
Not seen it. It was an eland.
An eland! *That* is why the children
Would ask my husband, for a joke, at Christmas:
"Father, is it Donner?" He would say, "No, Blitzen."
It had been there always. Now we put silver
At its place at meals, fed it the same food
We ourselves ate, and said nothing. Many times
When it breathed heavily (when it had tried
A long useless time to speak) and reached to me
So that I touched it—of a different size
And order of being, like the live hard side
Of a horse's neck when you pat the horse—
And looked with its great melting tearless eyes
Fringed with a few coarse wire-like lashes
Into my eyes, and whispered to me
So that my eyes turned backward in their sockets
And they said nothing—
                               many times
I have known, when they said nothing,
That it did not exist. If they had heard
They *could* not have been silent. And yet they heard;
Heard many times what I have spoken
When it could no longer speak, but only breathe—
When I could no longer speak, but only breathe.

NINE POETS BORN BETWEEN 1900 AND 1920

And, after some years, the others came
And took it from me—it was ill, they told me—
And cured it, they wrote me: my whole city
Sent me cards like lilac-branches, mourning
As I had mourned—
                          and I was standing
By a grave in flowers, by dyed rolls of turf,
And a canvas marquee the last brown of earth.

It is over.
It is over so long that I begin to think
That it did not exist, that I have never—
And my son says, one morning, from the paper:
"An eland. Look, an eland!"
                          —It was so.

Today, in a German dictionary, I saw *elend*
And the heart in my breast turned over, it was—

It was a word one translates *wretched*.

It is as if someone remembered saying:
"This is an antimacassar that I grew from seed,"
And this were true.
                          And, truly,
One could not wish for anything more strange—
For anything more. And yet it wasn't *interesting* . . .
—It was worse than impossible, it was a joke.

And yet when it was, I *was*—
Even to think that I once thought
That I could see it is to feel the sweat
Like needles at my hair-roots, I am blind

—It was not even a joke, not even a joke.

Yet how can I believe it? Or believe that I
Owned it, a husband, children? Is my voice the voice
Of that skin of being—of what owns, is owned
In honor or dishonor, that is borne and bears—
Or of that raw thing, the being inside it
That has neither a wife, a husband, nor a child
But goes at last as naked from this world
As it was born into it—

And the eland comes and grazes on its grave.

RANDALL JARRELL   81

This is senseless?
Shall I make sense or shall I tell the truth?
Choose either—I cannot do both.

I tell myself that. And yet it is not so,
And what I say afterwards will not be so:
To be at all is to be wrong.
                              Being is being old
And saying, almost comfortably, across a table
From—
          from what I don't know—
                                        in a voice
Rich with a kind of longing satisfaction:
"To own an eland! That's what I call life!"

Cinderella

Her imaginary playmate was a grown-up
In sea-coal satin. The flame-blue glances,
The wings gauzy as the membrane that the ashes
Draw over an old ember—as the mother
In a jug of cider—were a comfort to her.
They sat by the fire and told each other stories.

"What men want. . . ." said the godmother softly—
How she went on it is hard for a man to say.
Their eyes, on their Father, were monumental marble.
Then they smiled like two old women, bussed each other,
Said, "Gossip, gossip"; and, lapped in each other's looks,
Mirror for mirror, drank a cup of tea.

Of cambric tea. But there is a reality
Under the good silk of the good sisters'
Good ball gowns. *She* knew. . . . Hard-breasted, naked-eyed,
She pushed her silk feet into glass, and rose within
A gown of imaginary gauze. The shy prince drank
A toast to her in champagne from her slipper

And breathed, "Bewitching!" Breathed, "I am bewitched!"
—She said to her godmother, "Men!"
And, later, looking down to see her flesh
Look back up from under lace, the ashy gauze
And pulsing marble of a bridal veil,
She wished it all a widow's coal-black weeds.

A sullen wife and a reluctant mother,
She sat all day in silence by the fire.
Better, later, to stare past her sons' sons,
Her daughters' daughters, and tell stories to the fire.
But best, dead, damned, to rock forever
Beside Hell's fireside—to see within the flames

The Heaven to whose gold-gauzed door there comes
A little dark old woman, the God's Mother,
And cries, "Come in, come in! My son's out now,
Out now, will be back soon, may be back never,
Who knows, eh? *We* know what they are—men, men!
But come, come in till then! Come in till then!"

The Elementary Scene

Looking back in my mind I can see
The white sun like a tin plate
Over the wooden turning of the weeds;
The street jerking—a wet swing—
To end by the wall the children sang.

The thin grass by the girls' door,
Trodden on, straggling, yellow and rotten,
And the gaunt field with its one tied cow—
The dead land waking sadly to my life—
Stir, and curl deeper in the eyes of time.

The rotting pumpkin under the stairs
Bundled with switches and the cold ashes
Still holds for me, in its unwavering eyes,
The stinking shapes of cranes and witches,
Their path slanting down the pumpkin's sky.

Its stars beckon through the frost like cottages
(Homes of the Bear, the Hunter—of that absent star,
The dark where the flushed child struggles into sleep)
Till, leaning a lifetime to the comforter,
I float above the small limbs like their dream:

I, I, the future that mends everything.

A Hunt in the Black Forest

After the door shuts and the footsteps die,
He calls out: "Mother?"
The wind roars in the leaves: his cold hands, curled
Within his curled, cold body, his blurred head
Are warmed and tremble; and the red leaves flow
Like cells across the spectral, veined,
Whorled darkness of his vision.
                  The red dwarf
Whispers, "The leaves are turning"; and he reads
The dull, whorled notes, that tremble like a wish
Over the branched staves of the wood.

The stag is grazing in the wood.

A horn calls, over and over, its three notes.
The flat, gasped answer sounds and dies—
The geese call from a hidden sky.
The rain's sound grows into the roar
Of the flood below the falls; the rider calls
To the shape within the shades, a dwarf
Runs back into the brush. But smoke
Drifts to the gelding's nostrils, and he neighs.
From the wet starlight of the glade
A hut sends out its chink of fire.

The rider laughs out: in the branches, birds
Are troubled, stir.

He opens the door. A man looks up
And then slowly, with a kind of smile,
Acts out his own astonishment.
He points to his open mouth: the tongue
Is cut out. Bares his shoulder, points
To the crown branded there, and smiles. The hunter frowns.
The pot bubbles from the embers in the laugh
The mute laughs. With harsh habitual
Impatience, the hunter questions him.
The man nods vacantly—
Shaken, he makes his gobbling sound
Over and over. The hunter ladles from the pot
Into a wooden bowl, the shining stew.
He eats silently. The mute
Counts spoonfuls on his fingers. Come to ten,
The last finger, he laughs out in joy
And scuttles like a mouse across the floor
To the door and the door's darkness. The king breathes hard,

Rises—and something catches at his heart,
Some patient senseless thing
Begins to squeeze his heart out in its hands.
His jerking body, bent into a bow,
Falls out of the hands onto the table,
Bends, bends further, till at last it breaks.
But, broken, it still breathes—a few whistling breaths
That slow, are intermittent, cease.

Now only the fire thinks, like a heart
Cut from its breast. Light leaps, the shadows fall
In the old alternation of the world . . .

Two sparks, at the dark horn of the window,
Look, as stars look, into the shadowy hut,
Turn slowly, searching:
Then a bubbled, gobbling sound begins,
The sound of the pot laughing on the fire.
—The pot, overturned among the ashes,
Is cold as death.

Something is scratching, panting. A little voice
Says, "Let *me*! Let *me*!" The mute
Puts his arms around the dwarf and raises him.

The pane is clouded with their soft slow breaths,
The mute's arms tire; but they gaze on and on,
Like children watching something wrong.
Their blurred faces, caught up in one wish,
Are blurred into one face: a child's set face.

The House in the Wood

At the back of the houses there is the wood.
While there is a leaf of summer left, the wood

Makes sounds I can put somewhere in my song,
Has paths I can walk, when I wake, to good

Or evil: to the cage, to the oven, to the House
In the Wood. It is a part of life, or of the story

We make of life. But after the last leaf,
The last light—for each year is leafless,

Each day lightless, at the last—the wood begins
Its serious existence: it has no path,

No house, no story; it resists comparison . . .
One clear, repeated, lapping gurgle, like a spoon

Or a glass breathing, is the brook,
The wood's fouled midnight water. If I walk into the wood

As far as I can walk, I come to my own door,
The door of the House in the Wood. It opens silently:

On the bed is something covered, something humped
Asleep there, awake there—but what? I do not know.

I look, I lie there, and yet I do not know.
How far out my great echoing clumsy limbs

Stretch, surrounded only by space! For time has struck,
All the clocks are stuck now, for how many lives,

On the same second. Numbed, wooden, motionless,
We are far under the surface of the night.

Nothing comes down so deep but sound: a car, freight cars,
A high soft droning, drawn out like a wire

Forever and ever—is this the sound that Bunyan heard
So that he thought his bowels would burst within him?—

Drift on, on, into nothing. Then someone screams
A scream like an old knife sharpened into nothing.

It is only a nightmare. No one wakes up, nothing happens,
Except there is gooseflesh over my whole body—

And that too, after a little while, is gone.
I lie here like a cut-off limb, the stump the limb has left . . .

Here at the bottom of the world, what was before the world
And will be after, holds me to its black

Breasts and rocks me: the oven is cold, the cage is empty,
In the House in the Wood, the witch and her child sleep.

Field and Forest

When you look down from the airplane you see lines,
Roads, ruts, braided into a net or web—
Where people go, what people do: the ways of life.

Heaven says to the farmer: "What's your field?"
And he answers: "Farming," with a field,
Or: "Dairy-farming," with a herd of cows.
They seem a boy's toy cows, seen from this high.

Seen from this high,
The fields have a terrible monotony.

But between the lighter patches there are dark ones.
A farmer is separated from a farmer
By what farmers have in common: forests,
Those dark things—what the fields were to begin with.
At night a fox comes out of the forest, eats his chickens.
At night the deer come out of the forest, eat his crops.

If he could he'd make farm out of the forest,
But it isn't worth it: some of it's marsh, some rocks,
There are things there you couldn't get rid of
With a bulldozer, even—not with dynamite.
Besides, he likes it. He had a cave there, as a boy;
He hunts there now. It's a waste of land,
But it would be a waste of time, a waste of money,
To make it into anything but what it is.

At night, from the airplane, all you see is lights,
A few lights, the lights of houses, headlights,
And darkness. Somewhere below, beside a light,
The farmer, naked, takes out his false teeth:
He doesn't eat now. Takes off his spectacles:
He doesn't see now. Shuts his eyes.
If he were able to he'd shut his ears,
And as it is, he doesn't hear with them.
Plainly, he's taken out his tongue: he doesn't talk.
His arms and legs: at least, he doesn't move them.
They are knotted together, curled up, like a child's.
And after he has taken off the thoughts
It has taken him his life to learn,
He takes off, last of all, the world.

When you take off everything what's left? A wish,
A blind wish; and yet the wish isn't blind,
What the wish wants to see, it sees.

There in the middle of the forest is the cave
And there, curled up inside it, is the fox.

He stands looking at it.
Around him the fields are sleeping: the fields dream.
At night there are no more farmers, no more farms.
At night the fields dream, the fields *are* the forest.
The boy stands looking at the fox
As if, if he looked long enough—
                              he looks at it.
Or is it the fox that's looking at the boy?
The trees can't tell the two of them apart.

Notes

Losses. Spoken collectively by dead young bomber crews who bombed Germany in World War II. The first stanza deals with their deaths during the training period, the second with their deaths in combat over "The cities we had learned about in school."

The Death of the Ball Turret Gunner. Jarrell's note: "A ball turret was a plexiglass sphere set into the belly of a B-17 or B-24, and inhabited by two .50 caliber machine guns and one man, a short small man. When this gunner tracked with his machine-guns a fighter attacking his bomber from below, he revolved with the turret; hunched upside-down in his little sphere, he looked like the foetus in the womb. The fighters which attacked him were armed with cannon firing explosive shells. The hose was a steam hose."

Protocols. Two experiences of mass extermination, told in tandem by victims who did not understand what was happening to them. The gas used in the "showers" into which the victims were herded is said to have smelled like clover or hay.

Seele im Raum. Jarrell: "'Seele im Raum' is the title of one of Rilke's poems; 'Soul in Space' sounded so glib that I couldn't use it instead. An eland is the largest sort of African antelope—the males are as big as a horse, and you often see people gazing at them, at the zoo, in uneasy wonder." One way to read this poem is to consider it as spoken by a housewife who has been cured of schizophrenia; she remembers her illness with wonder, uneasiness, and a kind of nostalgia. She may have been a mental patient; she was also a visionary.

Cinderella. The poem makes us reconsider the fairy tale's relation to wish fulfillment. Cinderella's wish seems not to have been for her prince after all.

A Hunt in the Black Forest. A child goes to sleep (compare Rilke's Third Duino Elegy) and dreams a dream that is both a German fairy tale and an Oedipal wish fulfillment.

Field and Forest. A more playful version, in an American setting, of the dream journeys enacted in the preceding poems.

Randall Jarrell

Books

Five Young American Poets (with others), 1940
Blood for a Stranger, 1942
Little Friend, Little Friend, 1945
Losses, 1948
The Seven-League Crutches, 1951
Poetry and the Age (criticism), 1953
Pictures from an Institution (novel), 1954
Selected Poems, 1955
The Woman at the Washington Zoo, 1960
A Sad Heart at the Supermarket (essays), 1962

Selected Poems, 1964
The Lost World, 1965
The Third Book of Criticism (essays), 1969
The Complete Poems, 1969
Goethe's Faust: Part One (translation), 1974

Criticism

Charles M. Adams, *Randall Jarrell: A Bibliography*, 1958; Robert Lowell, Peter Taylor, Robert Penn Warren, eds., *Randall Jarrell 1914–1965*, 1967; Suzanne Ferguson, *The Poetry of Randall Jarrell*, 1971

Robert Lowell

(1917–1978)

© Rollie McKenna, 1968

In the best poems of Robert Lowell historical issues are mixed with dilemmas of the self in an explosive tension that illuminates both. Lowell was deeply critical of Americans for their neglect and dislike of their own history, and he associates individual isolation and anguish (which he knew firsthand from periodic mental illness) with America's inability to connect past and present in the form of viable traditions. No doubt this attitude was partly formed by his early apprenticeship to two southern poets, Allen Tate and John Crowe Ransom, who practiced variations on T. S. Eliot's religious conservatism and cultural nostalgia (Lowell was at this time a Roman Catholic convert) in specifically American settings. It can also be traced to his membership in an illustrious New England family whose past was a good deal more distinguished than its present.

Lowell's precocity and technical brilliance caused him to be singled out early as a major poet, a burden that probably made an uneven career more problematic. Certainly there are elements of self-regard in almost everything he wrote, and a writer less convinced of the magnitude of his talent would probably have been more cautious about what he chose to consider publishable work. Lowell continues to be obscured by an inflated reputation that may have to be discredited before we can discover the true nature of his contribution to American letters.

Throughout the 1950s Lowell was a traditional poet—heroic couplets, pastoral elegies, and the like—of formidable dimensions. His dramatic change of manner at the end of the decade was much remarked upon and very influential. Under the influence of a new mentor, William Carlos Williams, he put aside the dense, allusive, ornate manner of the poems he had written in *Lord Weary's Castle* (1946) and *The Mills of the Kavanaughs* (1951) and turned to more open forms and a more personal subject matter that eventually gave rise to the term "confessional poetry." The early style is represented in this selection only by "Noli Me Tangere"; aside from its increasingly dubious value, this first phase of Lowell's career mostly predates our starting point of 1950. The volume that marked Lowell's change, *Life Studies* (1959), is represented here by "Skunk Hour" and "For the Union Dead," which appears as the last poem in some editions under the title "Colonel Shaw and the Massachusetts 54th." The latter poem migrated to his next volume as the title poem, and that collection is also represented here by "July in Washington," "Those Before Us," "Water," and "The Lesson." Between them, *Life Studies* and *For the Union Dead* (1964) represent Lowell at his best, in mid-career when the personal-historical tension was most finely balanced in his work. As the historical had been too dominant in his earlier work, so the personal took over in subsequent volumes. From his later books we have included only one poem, "Turtle," from his last collection, *Day by Day* (1977). There is also an interesting volume of plays, *The Old Glory*, in which his preoccupation with American history leads to some effective adaptations of short stories by Hawthorne and Melville. *Imitations*, a volume of translations/adaptations in which a number of poets are "Lowellized," made to sound like their translator, would seem to be misnamed: it is not that Lowell imitates Baudelaire, Montale, and others but that he makes them imitate him. This volume does contain some dazzling passages, reflections more of Lowell's considerable skills than of his sources.

If Lowell's poetic manner changed drastically with *Life Studies*, certain features of his style remained constant throughout his work. He was fond of strong verbs as a means of charging—and sometimes overcharging—a poem with energy. He used slang effectively, and he could sometimes manage to pile up three adjectives around a noun, a trick few poets can duplicate. When the poems have little substance or vision, this coarse-grained and energized style rings hollow, but when it connects firmly with Lowell's fierce and anguished vision of the demented self in an impoverished landscape, it has an authenticity and weight that are unforgettable.

DY

Noli Me Tangere

We park and stare. A full sky of the stars
Wheels from the pumpkin setting of the moon
And sparks the windows of the yellow farm
Where the red-flanneled madmen look through bars
At windmills thrashing snowflakes by an arm
Of the Atlantic. Soon
The undertaker who collects antiques
Will let his motor idle at the door
And set his pine-box on the parlor floor.
Our homicidal sheriff howled for weeks;

We kiss. The State had reasons: on the whole,
It acted out of kindness when it locked
Its servant in this place and had him watched
Until an ordered darkness left his soul
A *tabula rasa*; when the Angel knocked
The sheriff laid his notched
Revolver on the table for the guest.
Night draws us closer in its bearskin wrap
And our loved sightless smother feels the tap
Of the blind stars descending to the west
To lay the Devil in the pit our hands
Are draining like a windmill. Who'll atone

For the unsearchable quicksilver heart
Where spiders stare their eyes out at their own
Spitting and knotted likeness? We must start:
Our aunt, his mother, stands
Singing *O Rock of Ages*, as the light
Wanderers show a man with a white cane
Who comes to take the coffin in his wain,
The thirsty Dipper on the arc of night.

Skunk Hour

(*For Elizabeth Bishop*)

Nautilus Island's hermit
heiress still lives through winter in her Spartan cottage;
her sheep still graze above the sea.
Her son's a bishop. Her farmer
is first selectman in our village;
she's in her dotage.

Thirsting for
the hierarchic privacy
of Queen Victoria's century,
she buys up all
the eyesores facing her shore,
and lets them fall.

The season's ill—
we've lost our summer millionaire,
who seemed to leap from an L. L. Bean
catalogue. His nine-knot yawl
was auctioned off to lobstermen.
A red fox stain covers Blue Hill.

And now our fairy
decorator brightens his shop for fall;
his fishnet's filled with orange cork,
orange, his cobbler's bench and awl;
there is no money in his work,
he'd rather marry.

One dark night,
my Tudor Ford climbed the hill's skull;
I watched for love-cars. Lights turned down,
they lay together, hull to hull,
where the graveyard shelves on the town. . . .
My mind's not right.

ROBERT LOWELL   93

A car radio bleats,
"Love, O careless Love. . . ." I hear
my ill-spirit sob in each blood cell,
as if my hand were at its throat. . . .
I myself am hell;
nobody's here—

only skunks, that search
in the moonlight for a bite to eat.
They march on their soles up Main Street:
white stripes, moonstruck eyes' red fire
under the chalk-dry and spar spire
of the Trinitarian Church.

I stand on top
of our back steps and breathe the rich air—
a mother skunk with her column of kittens swills the garbage pail.
She jabs her wedge-head in a cup
of sour cream, drops her ostrich tail,
and will not scare.

For the Union Dead

"Relinquunt Omnia Servare Rem Publicam."

The old South Boston Aquarium stands
in a Sahara of snow now. Its broken windows are boarded.
The bronze weathervane cod has lost half its scales.
The airy tanks are dry.

Once my nose crawled like a snail on the glass;
my hand tingled
to burst the bubbles
drifting from the noses of the cowed, compliant fish.

My hand draws back. I often sigh still
for the dark downward and vegetating kingdom
of the fish and reptile. One morning last March,
I pressed against the new barbed and galvanized

fence on the Boston Common. Behind their cage,
yellow dinosaur steamshovels were grunting
as they cropped up tons of mush and grass
to gouge their underworld garage.

NINE POETS BORN BETWEEN 1900 AND 1920

Parking spaces luxuriate like civic
sandpiles in the heart of Boston.
A girdle of orange, Puritan-pumpkin colored girders
braces the tingling Statehouse,

shaking over the excavations, as it faces Colonel Shaw
and his bell-cheeked Negro infantry
on St. Gaudens' shaking Civil War relief,
propped by a plank splint against the garage's earthquake.

Two months after marching through Boston,
half the regiment was dead;
at the dedication,
William James could almost hear the bronze Negroes breathe.

Their monument sticks like a fishbone
in the city's throat.
Its Colonel is as lean
as a compass-needle.

He has an angry wrenlike vigilance,
a greyhound's gentle tautness;
he seems to wince at pleasure,
and suffocate for privacy.

He is out of bounds now. He rejoices in man's lovely,
peculiar power to choose life and die—
when he leads his black soldiers to death,
he cannot bend his back.

On a thousand small town New England greens,
the old white churches hold their air
of sparse, sincere rebellion; frayed flags
quilt the graveyards of the Grand Army of the Republic.

The stone statues of the abstract Union Soldier
grow slimmer and younger each year—
wasp-wasted, they doze over muskets
and muse through their sideburns . . .

Shaw's father wanted no monument
except the ditch,
where his son's body was thrown
and lost with his "niggers."

The ditch is nearer.
There are no statues for the last war here;
on Boylston Street, a commercial photograph
shows Hiroshima boiling

ROBERT LOWELL   95

over a Mosler Safe, the "Rock of Ages"
that survived the blast. Space is nearer.
When I crouch to my television set,
the drained faces of Negro school-children rise like balloons.

Colonel Shaw
is riding on his bubble,
he waits
for the blessèd break.

The Aquarium is gone. Everywhere,
giant finned cars nose forward like fish;
a savage servility
slides by on grease.

Water

It was a Maine lobster town—
each morning boatloads of hands
pushed off for granite
quarries on the islands,

and left dozens of bleak
white frame houses stuck
like oyster shells
on a hill of rock,

and below us, the sea lapped
the raw little match-stick
mazes of a weir,
where the fish for bait were trapped.

Remember? We sat on a slab of rock.
From this distance in time,
it seems the color
of iris, rotting and turning purpler,

but it was only
the usual gray rock
turning the usual green
when drenched by the sea.

The sea drenched the rock
at our feet all day,
and kept tearing away
flake after flake.

One night you dreamed
you were a mermaid clinging to a wharf-pile,
and trying to pull
off the barnacles with your hands.

We wished our two souls
might return like gulls
to the rock. In the end,
the water was too cold for us.

The Lesson

No longer to lie reading *Tess of the d'Urbervilles*,
while the high, mysterious squirrels
rain small green branches on our sleep!

All that landscape, one likes to think it died
or slept with us, that we ourselves died
or slept then in the age and second of our habitation.

The green leaf cushions the same dry footprint,
or the child's boat luffs in the same dry chop,
and we are where we were. We were!

Perhaps the trees stopped growing in summer amnesia;
their day that gave them veins is rooted down—
and the nights? They are for sleeping now as then.

Ah the light lights the window of my young night,
and you never turn off the light,
while the books lie in the library, and go on reading.

The barberry berry sticks on the small hedge,
cold slits the same crease in the finger,
the same thorn hurts. The leaf repeats the lesson.

Those Before Us

They are all outline, uniformly gray,
unregenerate arrowheads sloughed up by the path here,
or in the corners of the eye, they play
their thankless, fill-in roles. They never were.

ROBERT LOWELL   97

Wormwood on the veranda! Plodding needles
still prod the coarse pink yarn into a dress.
The muskrat that took a slice of your thumb still huddles,
a mop of hair and a heart-beat on the porch—

there's the tin wastebasket where it learned to wait
for us playing dead, the slats it mashed in terror,
its spoor of cornflakes, and the packing crate
it furiously slashed to matchwood to escape.

Their chairs were *ex cathedra*, yet if you draw back the blinds,
(as full of windows as a fishnet now)
you will hear them conspiring, slapping hands
across the bent card-table, still leaf-green.

Vacations, stagnant growth. But in the silence,
some one lets out his belt to breathe, some one
roams in negligee. Bless the confidence
of their sitting unguarded there in stocking feet.

Sands drop from the hour-glass waist and swallow tail.
We follow their gunshy shadows down the trail—
those before us! Pardon them for existing.
We have stopped watching them. They have stopped watching.

July in Washington

The stiff spokes of this wheel
touch the sore spots of the earth.

On the Potomac, swan-white
power launches keep breasting the sulphurous wave.

Otters slide and dive and slick back their hair,
raccoons clean their meat in the creek.

On the circles, green statues ride like South American
liberators above the breeding vegetation—

prongs and spearheads of some equatorial
backland that will inherit the globe.

The elect, the elected ... they come here bright as dimes,
and die dishevelled and soft.

We cannot name their names, or number their dates—
circle on circle, like rings on a tree—

NINE POETS BORN BETWEEN 1900 AND 1920

but we wish the river had another shore,
some further range of delectable mountains,

distant hills powdered blue as a girl's eyelid.
It seems the least little shove would land us there,

that only the slightest repugnance of our bodies
we no longer control could drag us back.

Turtle

I pray for memory—
an old turtle,
absentminded, inelastic,
kept afloat by losing touch . . .
no longer able to hiss or lift
a useless shield against the killer.

Turtles age, but wade out amorously,
half-frozen fossils, yet knight-errant
in a foolsdream of armor.
The smaller ones climb rocks to broil in comfort.

Snapping turtles only submerge.
They have survived . . . not by man's philanthropy.

I hunted them in school vacations.
I trampled an acre of driftstraw
floating off the muskrats' loose nests.
Here and there, a solitary turtle
craned its brown Franciscan cowl
from one of twenty waterholes.
In that brew, I stepped
on a turtle's smooth, invisible back.
It was like escaping quicksand.
I drew it in my arms by what I thought was tail—
a tail? I held a foreleg.
I could have lost a finger.

This morning when
the double-brightness of the winter sun
wakes me from the film of dreaming,
my bedroom is unfamiliar. I see

three snapping turtles squatted on my drifting clothes—
two rough black logs ... the third is a nuzzler
dressed in see-through yellow tortoiseshell,
a puppy squeaking and tweaking
my empty shirt for milk.

They are stale and panting;
what is dead in me wakes their appetite.
When they breathe, they seem to crack apart,
crouched motionless on tiptoe
with crooked smiles
and high-school nicknames on their tongues,
as if they wished to relive
the rawness that let us meet as animals.
Nothing has passed between us but time.

"You've wondered where we were these years?
Here are we."

They lie like luggage—
my old friend the turtle ... Too many pictures
have screamed from the reel ... in the rerun,
the snapper holds on till sunset—
in the awful instantness of retrospect,
its beak
works me underwater drowning by my neck,
as it claws away pieces of my flesh
to make me small enough to swallow.

Notes

Noli Me Tangere. "Touch me not." This is part 1 of a two-part poem, "The Death of the Sheriff." A *tabula rasa* (line 15) is a blank tablet and, by traditional inference, a mind or memory with nothing in it. "Wain" is an old word for wagon; one of the names for the Big Dipper is "Charles's Wain."

Skunk Hour. The setting is Maine. L. L. Bean is a Maine mail-order store famous for clothing and other gear for campers, sportsmen, and fishermen. A Tudor Ford is simply "two-door," as typically shortened in want-ads.

For the Union Dead. The monument by the sculptor St. Gaudens to the Civil War regiment of black soldiers led by Colonel Shaw stands on the north side of Boston Common, facing the Statehouse. The epigraph translates as "They left everything behind to serve their country."

Those Before Us. "*Ex cathedra*," literally "from the chair," refers to pronouncements made by virtue of an important office (e.g., a bishop or pope).

July in Washington. The city of Washington, D.C., is laid out in the shape of a wheel.

NINE POETS BORN BETWEEN 1900 AND 1920

Robert Lowell

Books

Land of Unlikeness, 1944
Lord Weary's Castle, 1946
The Mills of the Kavanaughs, 1951
Life Studies, 1959
Imitations (translations), 1961
For the Union Dead, 1964
The Old Glory (plays), 1965
Near the Ocean, 1967
The Voyage & Other Versions of Poems by Baudelaire (translations), 1968
Aeschylus, *Prometheus Bound* (translation), 1969
Notebook, 1967–68, 1969, rev. 1970
The Dolphin, 1973
For Lizzie and Harriet, 1973
History, 1973
Selected Poems, 1976
Day by Day, 1977
Aeschylus, *The Oresteia* (translation), 1979

Criticism, Interviews

Jerome Mazzaro, *The Achievement of Robert Lowell, 1939–1959*, 1960; Interview, *Paris Review*, 25 (Spring 1961); Jerome Mazzaro, *The Poetic Themes of Robert Lowell*, 1965; Thomas Parkinson, ed., *Robert Lowell: A Collection of Critical Essays*, 1968; Philip Cooper, *The Autobiographical Myth of Robert Lowell*, 1970; Richard Fein, *Robert Lowell*, 1970; Michael Lond and Robert Boyers, eds., *Robert Lowell: A Portrait of the Artist in His Time*; Marjorie Perloff, *The Poetic Art of Robert Lowell*, 1973; Alan Williamson, *Pity the Monsters: The Political Vision of Robert Lowell*, 1974; Stephen Yenser, *Circle to Circle: The Poetry of Robert Lowell*, 1975; Stephen Gould Axelrod, *Robert Lowell: Life and Art*, 1978

Theodore Roethke

(1908–1963)

Frank Murphy

T heodore Roethke grew up in Saginaw, Michigan, where his father ran a nursery and floral business. As his poetry matured, he ventured back to his childhood for subject matter, to the greenhouse and its associations with nurture and growth. The first poems in this selection, "Cuttings," "Cuttings (later)," "Child on Top of a Greenhouse," and "My Papa's Waltz," from the 1948 volume *The Lost Son and Other Poems*, represent his initial engagement with these materials and strike the note of his artistic authenticity: an eye for minute natural detail coupled with a gift for distinctive verbal music. They were followed, in *Praise to the End*! (1951), by poems violently experimental as to form and sensibility, represented here by "The Shape of the Fire" and "I Cry, Love! Love!" These poems re-create the child's world not from the safe perspective of the adult but by reenacting its terrors, wonders, mysteries, and confusions. Their deliberate childishness has confused readers and critics, but Roethke's fellow poets tended to recognize and respond immediately to the originality of these poems, and it was probably his example (along with Robert Lowell's in *Life Studies* a few years later) that led to the new era of formal experiment in American poetry.

Roethke was fundamentally a nature poet. His poetry is a study of the self in the natural world, a history of its quest for an ecstatic union with nature, a transcendence. This preoccupation links Roethke not only with Romantic poets but with American Transcendentalists and indeed with all mystics who strike a pantheistic note. The affinity with these traditions is clear in the extended and confident pair of poems that close this selection: the first section of "Meditations of an Old Woman" and "Journey to the Interior," the latter from the "North American Sequence" of his last collection, *The Far Field*. But the presence of this quest throughout Roethke's work should help readers who are aware of it to find their way through the difficult middle sequences (here represented by "The Shape of the Fire" and "I Cry, Love! Love!"), in which coherence comes and goes and the sense of purpose is often precarious. It helps to see these poems as resembling the action paintings of the abstract expressionists with which they were contemporaneous. They use language for its own sake, as a medium of spontaneous and studious play rather than an instrument of steady communication. Roethke argued that "we must permit poetry to extend consciousness as far, as deeply, as particularly as it can," and spoke of writing poems "which try in their rhythms to catch the very movement of the mind itself." To this end he imitated nursery rhymes, proverbs and sayings, the infant babble that takes pleasure in speech as pure sound, rhythm, and iteration, as well as the ramblings of hysteria and mental illness. The collage of possibilities that results is often bewildering. But the poems have an aim, to "trace the spiritual history of a protagonist," and their lyrical closing sections reveal how much they were an effort to bring the self through confusion and need to an equilibrium in which oneness with nature is the source of a mystical contentment.

The nervous, blustery man who wrote these romantic lyrics was a fine teacher of poetry and creative writing, but an unhappy individual, suffering periodically from mental breakdowns and never fully at home in the world he loved so deeply. His work can be derivative—of Yeats, Eliot, and Dylan Thomas especially—and is no doubt uneven, but his best poems seem destined to last. A *Collected Poems* is available in paperback, and the letters and notebooks have been collected, edited, and published. There is also a sympathetic biography, *The Glass House*, by Allan Seager.

DY

Cuttings

Sticks-in-a-drowse droop over sugary loam,
Their intricate stem-fur dries;
But still the delicate slips keep coaxing up water;
The small cells bulge;

One nub of growth
Nudges a sand-crumb loose,
Pokes through a musty sheath
Its pale tendrilous horn.

Cuttings

(*later*)

This urge, wrestle, resurrection of dry sticks,
Cut stems struggling to put down feet,
What saint strained so much,
Rose on such lopped limbs to a new life?

I can hear, underground, that sucking and sobbing,
In my veins, in my bones I feel it,—
The small waters seeping upward,
The tight grains parting at last.
When sprouts break out,
Slippery as fish,
I quail, lean to beginnings, sheath-wet.

Child on Top of a Greenhouse

The wind billowing out the seat of my britches,
My feet crackling splinters of glass and dried putty,
The half-grown chrysanthemums staring up like accusers,
Up through the streaked glass, flashing with sunlight,
A few white clouds all rushing eastward,
A line of elms plunging and tossing like horses,
And everyone, everyone pointing up and shouting!

My Papa's Waltz

The whiskey on your breath
Could make a small boy dizzy;
But I hung on like death:
Such waltzing was not easy.

We romped until the pans
Slid from the kitchen shelf;
My mother's countenance
Could not unfrown itself.

The hand that held my wrist
Was battered on one knuckle;
At every step you missed
My right ear scraped a buckle.

You beat time on my head
With a palm caked hard by dirt,
Then waltzed me off to bed
Still clinging to your shirt.

The Shape of the Fire

1

What's this? A dish for fat lips.
Who says? A nameless stranger.
Is he a bird or a tree? Not everyone can tell.

Water recedes to the crying of spiders.
An old scow bumps over black rocks.
A cracked pod calls.

THEODORE ROETHKE

Mother me out of here. What more will the bones allow?
Will the sea give the wind suck? A toad folds into a stone.
These flowers are all fangs. Comfort me, fury.
Wake me, witch, we'll do the dance of rotten sticks.

Shale loosens. Marl reaches into the field. Small birds pass over water.
Spirit, come near. This is only the edge of whiteness.
I can't laugh at a procession of dogs.

In the hour of ripeness the tree is barren.
The she-bear mopes under the hill.
Mother, mother, stir from your cave of sorrow.

A low mouth laps water. Weeds, weeds, how I love you.
The arbor is cooler. Farewell, farewell, fond worm.
The warm comes without sound.

2

Where's the eye?
The eye's in the sty.
The ear's not here
Beneath the hair.
When I took off my clothes
To find a nose,
There was only one shoe
For the waltz of To,
The pinch of Where.

Time for the flat-headed man. I recognize that listener,
Him with the platitudes and rubber doughnuts,
Melting at the knees, a varicose horror.
Hello, hello. My nerves knew you, dear boy.
Have you come to unhinge my shadow?
Last night I slept in the pits of a tongue.
The silver fish ran in and out of my special bindings;
I grew tired of the ritual of names and the assistant keeper of the mollusks:
Up over a viaduct I came, to the snakes and sticks of another winter,
A two-legged dog hunting a new horizon of howls.
The wind sharpened itself on a rock;
A voice sang:

Pleasure on ground
Has no sound,
Easily maddens
The uneasy man.

Who, careless, slips
In coiling ooze
Is trapped to the lips,
Leaves more than shoes;

Must pull off clothes
To jerk like a frog
On belly and nose
From the sucking bog.

My meat eats me. Who waits at the gate?
Mother of quartz, your words writhe into my ear.
Renew the light, lewd whisper.

3

The wasp waits.
        The edge cannot eat the center.
The grape glistens.
        The path tells little to the serpent.
An eye comes out of the wave.
        The journey from flesh is longest.
A rose sways least.
        The redeemer comes a dark way.

4

Morning-fair, follow me further back
Into that minnowy world of weeds and ditches,
When the herons floated high over the white houses,
And the little crabs slipped into silvery craters.
When the sun for me glinted the sides of a sand grain,
And my intent stretched over the buds at their first trembling.

That air and shine: and the flicker's loud summer call:
The bearded boards in the stream and the all of apples;
The glad hen on the hill; and the trellis humming.
Death was not. I lived in a simple drowse:
Hands and hair moved through a dream of wakening blossoms.
Rain sweetened the cave and the dove still called;
The flowers leaned on themselves, the flowers in hollows;
And love, love sang toward.

I Cry, Love! Love!

1

Went weeping, little bones. But where?
Wasps come when I ask for pigeons.
The sister sands, they slipper soft away.
What else can befall?

    Delight me otherly, white spirit,—
    Some errand, obscure as the wind's circuit,
    A secret to jerk from the lips of a fish.
    Is circularity such a shame?
    A cat goes wider.

What's a thick? Two-by-two's a shape.
This toad could waltz on a drum;
I hear a most lovely huzza:
I'm king of the boops!

2

Reason? That dreary shed, that hutch for grubby schoolboys!
The hedgewren's song says something else.
I care for a cat's cry and the hugs, live as water.
I've traced these words in sand with a vestigial tail;
Now the gills are beginning to cry.
Such a sweet noise: I can't sleep for it.
Bless me and the maze I'm in!
Hello, thingy spirit.

    Mouse, mouse, come out of the ferns,
    And small mouths, stay your aimless cheeping:
    A lapful of apples sleeps in this grass.
    That anguish of concreteness!—
    The sun playing on loam,
    And the first dust of spring listing over backlots,—
    I proclaim once more a condition of joy.
    Walk into the wind, willie!

In a sodden place, all raps and knocks approve.
A dry cry comes from my own desert;
The bones are lonely.
Beginnings start without shade,
Thinner than minnows.
The live grass whirls with the sun,
Feet run over the simple stones,
There's time enough.
Behold, in the lout's eye,
Love.

        NINE POETS BORN BETWEEN 1900 AND 1920

I hear the owls, the soft callers, coming down from the hemlocks.
The bats weave in and out of the willows,
Wing-crooked and sure,
Downward and upward,
Dipping and veering close to the motionless water.

A fish jumps, shaking out flakes of moonlight.
A single wave starts lightly and easily shoreward,
Wrinkling between reeds in shallower water,
Lifting a few twigs and floating leaves,
Then washing up over small stones.

The shine on the face of the lake
Tilts, backward and forward.
The water recedes slowly,
Gently rocking.

Who untied the tree? I remember now.
We met in a nest. Before I lived.
The dark hair sighed.
We never enter
Alone.

From **Meditations of an Old Woman**

First Meditation

1

On love's worst ugly day,
The weeds hiss at the edge of the field,
The small winds make their chilly indictments.
Elsewhere, in houses, even pails can be sad;
While stones loosen on the obscure hillside,
And a tree tilts from its roots,
Toppling down an embankment.

The spirit moves, but not always upward,
While animals eat to the north,
And the shale slides an inch in the talus,
The bleak wind eats at the weak plateau,
And the sun brings joy to some.
But the rind, often, hates the life within.

THEODORE ROETHKE

How can I rest in the days of my slowness?
I've become a strange piece of flesh,
Nervous and cold, bird-furtive, whiskery,
With a cheek soft as a hound's ear.
What's left is light as a seed;
I need an old crone's knowing.

2

Often I think of myself as riding—
Alone, on a bus through western country.
I sit above the back wheels, where the jolts are hardest,
And we bounce and sway along toward the midnight,
The lights tilting up, skyward, as we come over a little rise,
Then down, as we roll like a boat from a wave-crest.

All journeys, I think, are the same:
The movement is forward, after a few wavers,
And for a while we are all alone,
Busy, obvious with ourselves,
The drunken soldier, the old lady with her peppermints;
And we ride, we ride, taking the curves
Somewhat closer, the trucks coming
Down from behind the last ranges,
Their black shapes breaking past;
And the air claps between us,
Blasting the frosted windows,
And I seem to go backward,
Backward in time:

> Two song sparrows, one within a greenhouse,
> Shuttling its throat while perched on a wind-vent,
> And another, outside, in the bright day,
> With a wind from the west and the trees all in motion.
> One sang, then the other,
> The songs tumbling over and under the glass,
> And the men beneath them wheeling in dirt to the cement benches,
> The laden wheelbarrows creaking and swaying,
> And the up-spring of the plank when a foot left the runway.

Journey within a journey:
The ticket mislaid or lost, the gate
Inaccessible, the boat always pulling out
From the rickety wooden dock,
The children waving;
Or two horses plunging in snow, their lines tangled,
A great wooden sleigh careening behind them,
Swerving up a steep embankment.

For a moment they stand above me,
Their black skins shuddering:
Then they lurch forward,
Lunging down a hillside.

3

As when silt drifts down through muddy pond-water,
Settling in small beads around weeds and sunken branches,
And one crab, tentative, hunches himself before moving along the bottom,
Grotesque, awkward, his extended eyes looking at nothing in particular,
Only a few bubbles loosening from the ill-matched tentacles,
The tail and smaller legs slipping and sliding slowly backward—
So the spirit tries for another life,
Another way and place in which to continue;
Or a salmon, tired, moving up a shallow stream,
Nudges into a back-eddy, a sandy inlet,
Bumping against sticks and bottom-stones, then swinging
Around, back into the tiny maincurrent, the rush of brownish-white water,
Still swimming forward—
So, I suppose, the spirit journeys.

4

I have gone into the waste lonely places
Behind the eye; the lost acres at the edge of smoky cities.
What's beyond never crumbles like an embankment,
Explodes like a rose, or thrusts wings over the Caribbean.
There are no pursuing forms, faces on walls:
Only the motes of dust in the immaculate hallways,
The darkness of falling hair, the warnings from lint and spiders,
The vines graying to a fine powder.
There is no riven tree, or lamb dropped by an eagle.

There are still times, morning and evening:
The cerulean, high in the elm,
Thin and insistent as a cicada,
And the far phoebe, singing,
The long plaintive notes floating down,
Drifting through leaves, oak and maple,
Or the whippoorwill, along the smoky ridges,
A single bird calling and calling;
A fume reminds me, drifting across wet gravel;
A cold wind comes over stones;
A flame, intense, visible,
Plays over the dry pods,
Runs fitfully along the stubble,
Moves over the field,

Without burning.
      In such times, lacking a god,
      I am still happy.

Journey to the Interior

1

In the long journey out of the self,
There are many detours, washed-out interrupted raw places
Where the shale slides dangerously
And the back wheels hang almost over the edge
At the sudden veering, the moment of turning.
Better to hug close, wary of rubble and falling stones.
The arroyo cracking the road, the wind-bitten buttes, the canyons,
Creeks swollen in midsummer from the flash-flood roaring into the narrow
      valley.
Reeds beaten flat by wind and rain,
Grey from the long winter, burnt at the base in late summer.
—Or the path narrowing,
Winding upward toward the stream with its sharp stones,
The upland of alder and birchtrees,
Through the swamp alive with quicksand,
The way blocked at last by a fallen fir-tree,
The thickets darkening,
The ravines ugly.

2

I remember how it was to drive in gravel,
Watching for dangerous down-hill places, where the wheels whined beyond
      eighty—
When you hit the deep pit at the bottom of the swale,
The trick was to throw the car sideways and charge over the hill, full of the
      throttle.
Grinding up and over the narrow road, spitting and roaring.
A chance? Perhaps. But the road was part of me, and its ditches,
And the dust lay thick on my eyelids,—Who ever wore goggles?—
Always a sharp turn to the left past a barn close to the roadside,
To a scurry of small dogs and a shriek of children,
The highway ribboning out in a straight thrust to the North,
To the sand dunes and fish flies, hanging, thicker than moths,

Dying brightly under the street lights sunk in coarse concrete,
The towns with their high pitted road-crowns and deep gutters,
Their wooden stores of silvery pine and weather-beaten red court-houses,
An old bridge below with a buckled iron railing, broken by some idiot plunger;
Underneath, the sluggish water running between weeds, broken wheels, tires,
     stones.
And all flows past—
The cemetery with two scrubby trees in the middle of the prairie,
The dead snakes and muskrats, the turtles gasping in the rubble,
The spikey purple bushes in the winding dry creek bed—
The floating hawks, the jackrabbits, the grazing cattle—
I am not moving but they are,
And the sun comes out of a blue cloud over the Tetons,
While, farther away, the heat-lightning flashes.
I rise and fall in the slow sea of a grassy plain,
The wind veering the car slightly to the right,
Whipping the line of white laundry, bending the cottonwoods apart,
The scraggly wind-break of a dusty ranch-house.
I rise and fall, and time folds
Into a long moment;
And I hear the lichen speak,
And the ivy advance with its white lizard feet—
On the shimmering road,
On the dusty detour.

3

I see the flower of all water, above and below me, the never receding,
Moving, unmoving in a parched land, white in the moonlight:
The soul at a still-stand,
At ease after rocking the flesh to sleep,
Petals and reflections of petals mixed on the surface of a glassy pool,
And the waves flattening out when the fishermen drag their nets over the stones.

In the moment of time when the small drop forms, but does not fall,
I have known the heart of the sun,—
In the dark and light of a dry place,
In a flicker of fire brisked by a dusty wind.
I have heard, in a drip of leaves,
A slight song,
After the midnight cries.

I rehearse myself for this:
The stand at the stretch in the face of death,
Delighting in surface change, the glitter of light on waves,
And I roam elsewhere, my body thinking,
Turning toward the other side of light,
In a tower of wind, a tree idling in air,

THEODORE ROETHKE   113

Beyond my own echo,
Neither forward nor backward,
Unperplexed, in a place leading nowhere.

As a blind man, lifting a curtain, knows it is morning,
I know this change:
On one side of silence there is no smile;
But when I breathe with the birds,
The spirit of wrath becomes the spirit of blessing,
And the dead begin from their dark to sing in my sleep.

Notes

The Shape of the Fire and *I Cry, Love! Love!* These poems do not so much require
annotation as an approach that is relaxed as to exact meanings and firm
connections. They use questions, interjections, commands, aphorisms, and other
magical or superstitious forms of language to re-create a sense of spiritual crisis
and emotional need that moves toward a musical, rather than narrative,
resolution in their closing sections. They repay meditation and close attention,
but more for their ability to create a verbal world that imitates "the very
movement of the mind itself" than for their status as logical or coherent
discourse.

Theodore Roethke

Books

Open House, 1941
The Lost Son and Other Poems, 1948
Praise to the End, 1951
The Waking, Poems: 1933–1953, 1953
Words for the Wind, 1958
The Far Field, 1964
On the Poet and His Craft (essays), 1965
The Collected Poems of Theodore Roethke, 1966
Selected Letters of Theodore Roethke, ed. Mills, 1968
Straw for the Fire. From the Notebooks of Theodore Roethke,
    1943–63, ed. Wagoner, 1972

Criticism, Interviews

Ralph Mills, *Theodore Roethke*, 1963; Arnold Stein, ed., *Theodore Roethke: Essays on
the Poetry*, 1965; Karl Malkoff, *Theodore Roethke: an Introduction to the Poetry*, 1966;
Allan Seager, *The Glass House: The Life of Theodore Roethke*, 1968; Gary Lane, ed.,

A Concordance to the Poems of Theodore Roethke, 1972; Richard Allen Blessing, *Theodore Roethke's Dynamic Vision*, 1974; Rosemary Sullivan, *Theodore Roethke, The Garden Master*, 1975; Jenijoy La Belle, *The Echoing Wood of Theodore Roethke*, 1976; Keith R. Moul, *Theodore Roethke's Career: An Annotated Bibliography*, 1977; Jay Parrini, *Theodore Roethke: An American Romantic*, 1979

Muriel
Rukeyser

(1913–1980)

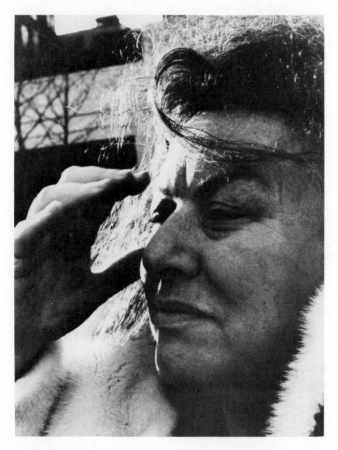

A s more and more contributions by women to all fields are being uncovered and studied, it is becoming clear that those of Muriel Rukeyser to the twin arts of poetry and translation are major and substantial. She herself could remark, in the preface to her collected poems, "It never occurred to me that my poems would be collected until after my lifetime." We are not surprised that they were. After early work that Jarrell reviewed harshly for its slide into rhetoric on a grand scale—allowing only that "she is sometimes so original . . ." (*Poetry & the Age*)—she continued to develop as a poet, richly exploring dream world, nightmare, and sexual fantasy in imagery and rhythms that even Jarrell sensed would come to speak for "the Common Woman of the century." She was born early enough to experience World War I and participate in the political and social developments of the 1920s and '30s, thoughtfully intense and excited at the prospects for social change—see especially her early poems on flying and mining—and she died in 1980, having marched for causes she believed in and having continued to write poems that followed the times. She reached for two things, as she put it: "the evidence itself," as well as "the unverifiable fact, as in sex, dream, the parts of life in which we dive deep" (*The Life of Poetry*). She was especially pleased that her last publisher printed vast amounts of scientific work. "I care very much about that meeting-place, of science and poetry," she wrote.

In her work in general, and the poems presented here in particular, the speaking voice attempts to guide the reader in ways she admired in her favorite writers, Whitman, Dante, and Baudelaire: by making much of the music of speech, as well as its negative shape, or counterpoint, of silence; and by focusing on human experience, which for her meant watching people caught up in landscapes they would never leave—man/woman, husband/wife, and especially, parents/children, as protagonists and antagonists alike. "Bringing them back to life," she said she wanted mainly to animate them, to have them "speak these days." She stresses everyone's need to learn language and use it richly, "not leaving it to the unborn poets." Especially the children must confront their own predicament and not rely on adults' perceptions—"and nothing was what they said . . ." is the child's lament in one of the poems.

"Do I move toward form, do I use all my fears?" she asked. Mature writer that she was, she realized our fears must not only be faced but must be *used* as well, and these poems approach this ideal: Past the phrases, past the pieces, they move toward their songs, singing of us in unexpected lines and structures, the prevailing voice that of an ancient sleepwalker:

> A whisper attempts me, I whisper without stammer
> I walk the long hall to the time of a metronome
> set by a child's gun-target   left-right
> the power of eyesight is very slowly arriving
>   in this late impossible daybreak
>   all the blue flowers open.

MURIEL RUKEYSER   117

One can compare this passage, and many others in the later poems, to her contemporary, Roethke, as well as to subsequent work by poets like Jean Valentine.

Elsewhere, in an essay, Rukeyser recalls Lucretius "moving the sleeping images toward the light." Reading the poems of the last books, *The Speed of Darkness, Breaking Open,* and *The Gates,* we look across with her "at the real / vulnerable   involved   naked / devoted to the present" of all we care for, set down in extraordinary, natural places—the long hall, for instance—in which nothing is safe. No wonder she worries at the end of *The Gates,* "How shall we speak to the infant beginning to run? / All those beginning to run?"

SF

From **Eighth Elegy**

Children's Elegy

. . . That is what they say, who were broken off from love:
However long we were loved, it was not long enough.

We were afraid of the broad big policeman,
of lions and tigers, the dark hall and the moon.

After our father went, nothing was ever the same,
when mother did not come back, we made up a war-game.

My cat was sitting in the doorway when the planes
went over, and my cat saw mother cry;
furry tears, fire fell, wall went down;
did my cat see mother die?

Mother is gone away, my cat sits here coughing.
I cough and sit. I am nobody's nothing.

However long they loved us, it was not long enough.
For we have to be strong, to know what they did, and then
our people are saved in time, our houses built again.

You will not know, you have a sister and brother;
My doll is not my child, my doll is my mother.

However strong we are, it is not strong enough.
I want to grow up. To come back to love. . . .

Children, the Sandbar, that Summer

Sunlight the tall women may never have seen.
Men, perhaps, going headfirst into the breakers,
But certainly the children at the sandbar.
Shallow glints in the wave suspended
We knew at the breaker line, running that shore
At low tide, when it was safe. The grasses whipped
And nothing was what they said: not safety, nor the sea.
And the sand was not what they said, but various,
Lion-grained, beard-grey. And blue. And green.
And each grain casting its shadow down before
Childhood in tide-pools where all things are food.
Behind us the shores emerged and fed on tide.
We fed on summer, the round flowers in our hands
From the snowball bush entered us, and prisoner wings,
And shells in spirals, all food.
                                    All keys to unlock
Some world, glinting as strong as noon on the sandbar,
Where men and women give each other children.

The Speed of Darkness

I

Whoever despises the clitoris despises the penis
Whoever despises the penis despises the cunt
Whoever despises the cunt despises the life of the child.

Resurrection music,   silence,   and surf.

II

No longer speaking
Listening with the whole body
And with every drop of blood
Overtaken by silence

But this same silence is become speech
With the speed of darkness.

III

Stillness during war, the lake.
The unmoving spruces.

Glints over the water.
Faces, voices.   You are far away.
A tree that trembles.

I am the tree that trembles and trembles.

IV

After the lifting of the mist
after the lift of the heavy rains
the sky stands clear
and the cries of the city risen in day
I remember the buildings are space
walled, to let space be used for living
I mind this room is space
this drinking glass is space
whose boundary of glass
lets me give you drink and space to drink
your hand, my hand being space
containing skies and constellations
your face
carries the reaches of air
I know I am space
my words are air.

V

Between   between
the man : act   exact
woman : in curve   senses in their maze
frail orbits, green tries,   games of stars
shape of the body speaking its evidence

VI

I look across at the real
vulnerable   involved   naked
devoted to the present of all I care for
the world of its history leading to this moment.

VII

Life the announcer.
I assure you
there are many ways to have a child.
I bastard mother
promise you
there are many ways to be born.

They all come forth
in their own grace.

VIII

Ends of the earth join tonight
with blazing stars upon their meeting.

These sons,   these sons
fall burning into Asia.

IX

Time comes into it.
Say it.   Say it.

The universe is made of stories,
not of atoms.

X

Lying
blazing beside me
you rear beautifully and up—
your thinking face—
erotic body reaching
in all its colors and lights—
your erotic face
colored and lit—
not colored body-and-face
but now entire,
colors   lights   the world thinking and reaching.

XI

The river flows past the city.

Water goes down to tomorrow
making its children   I hear their unborn voices
I am working out the vocabulary of my silence.

XII

Big-boned man young and of my dream
Struggles to get the live bird out of his throat.
I am he am I?   Dreaming?
I am the bird am I?   I am the throat?

A bird with a curved beak.
It could slit anything, the throat-bird.

Drawn up slowly.   The curved blades, not large.
Bird emerges   wet   being born
Begins to sing.

XIII

My night awake
staring at the broad rough jewel
the copper roof across the way
thinking of the poet
yet unborn in this dark
who will be the throat of these hours.
No.   Of those hours.
Who will speak these days,
if not I,
if not you?

Then

When I am dead, even then,
I will still love you, I will wait in these poems,
When I am dead, even then
I am still listening to you.
I will still be making poems for you
out of silence;
silence will be falling into that silence,
it is building music.

Double Ode

for Bill and Alison

I

Wine and oil gleaming within their heads,
I poured it into the hollow of their bodies
but they did not speak. The light glittered.
Lit from underneath they were. Water
pouring over her face, it
made the lips move and the eyes move, she
spoke:
Break open.

He did not speak.
A still lake shining in his head,
until I knew that the sun and the moon
stood in me with one light.

II

They began to breathe and glitter. Morning
overflowed, gifts poured from their sex
upon my throat and my breast.
They knew. They laughed. In their tremendous games
night revolved and shook my bed. I
woke in a cold morning.
Your presences
allow me to begin to make myself
carried on your shoulders, swayed in your arms.
Something is flashing among the colors. I
move without being allowed. I
move with the blessing of the sky and the sea.

III

Tonight I will try again for the music of truth
since this one and that one of mine are met with death.
It is a blind lottery, a cheap military trumpet
with all these great roots black under the earth
while a muscle-legged man
stamps in his red and gold
rough wine, creatures in nets, swords through their spines
and all their cantillation in our thought.

Glitter and pedestal under my female powers
a woman singing horses, blind cities of concrete, moon
comes to moonrise as a dark daughter.
I am the poet of the night of women
and my two parents are the sun and the moon,
a strong father of that black double likeness,
a bell kicking out of the bell-tower,
and a mother who shines and shines his light.

Who is the double ghost whose head is smoke?
Her thighs hold the wild infant, a trampled country
and I will fly in, in all my fears.
Those two have terrified me, but I live,
their silvery line of music gave me girlhood
and fierce male prowess and a woman's grave
eternal double music male and female,
inevitable blue, repeated evening
of the two.   Of the two.

MURIEL RUKEYSER

IV

But these two figures are not the statues east and west
at my long window on the river they are mother and father
but not my actual parents only their memory.
Not memory but something builded in my cells

Father with your feet cut off
mother cut down to death
cut down my sister in the selfsame way
and my abandoned husband a madman of the sun
and you dark outlaw the other one when do we speak
The song flies out of all of you the song
starts in my body, the song
it is in my mouth, the song
it is on my teeth, the song
it is pouring the song
wine and lightning
the rivers coming to confluence
in me entire.

V

But that was years ago. My child is grown.
His wife and he in exile, that is, home,
longing for home, and I home, that is exile, the much-loved country
like the country called parents, much-loved that was, and exile.
His wife and he turning toward the thought
of their own child, conceive we say, a child.
Now rise in me the old dealings: father, mother,
not years ago, but in my last-night dream,
waking this morning, the two Mexican figures
black stone with their stone hollows I fill with water,
fill with wine, with oil, poems and lightning.
Black in morning dark, the sky going blue,
the river going blue.

Moving toward new form I am—
carry again
all the old gifts and wars.

VI

Black parental mysteries
groan and mingle in the night.
Something will be born of this.

Pay attention to what they tell you to forget
pay attention to what they tell you to forget
pay attention to what they tell you to forget

Farewell the madness of the guardians
the river, the window, they are the guardians,
there is no guardian, it is all built into me.

Do I move toward form, do I use all my fears?

Resurrection of the Right Side

When the half-body dies its frightful death
forked pain, infection of snakes, lightning, pull down the voice. Waking
and I begin to climb the mountain on my mouth,
word by stammer, walk stammered, the lurching deck of earth.
Left-right with none of my own rhythms
the long-established sex and poetry.
                      I go running in sleep,
but waking stumble down corridors of self, all rhythms gone.

The broken movement of love   sex out of rhythm
one halted name   in a shattered language
ruin of French-blue lights behind the eyes
slowly the left hand extends a hundred feet
and the right hand follows follows
but still the power of sight is very weak
but I go rolling this ball of life, it rolls
and I follow it whole up the slowly-brightening slope

A whisper attempts me, I whisper without stammer
I walk the long hall to the time of a metronome
set by a child's gun-target   left-right
the power of eyesight is very slowly arriving
        in this late impossible daybreak
        all the blue flowers open

Muriel Rukeyser

Books

Theory of Flight, 1935
A Turning Wind, 1939
Beast in View, 1944
The Green Wave, 1948
The Life of Poetry (essays), 1949
Selected Poems, 1951
Body of Waking, 1958

Waterlily Fire: Poems 1935–1962, 1962
The Speed of Darkness, 1968
Breaking Open, 1973
The Gates, 1976
Collected Poems, 1978

Criticism

Rachel Blau DuPlessis, "The Critique of Consciousness and Myth in Levertov, Rich, and Rukeyser," in *Shakespeare's Sisters: Feminist Essays on Women Poets*, ed. Gilbert and Gubar, 1979. Louise Kertesz, *The Poetic Vision of Muriel Rukeyser*, 1979

William Stafford

(b. 1914)

A t first glance, the poems of William Stafford seem simple and direct. Their plain and relaxed manner may remind us of Robert Frost. Like Frost, however, Stafford proves on closer examination to be a very elusive poet with a distinctive private vision that slips through our grasp when we try to identify, summarize, or paraphrase it. His world is regional—he writes of the lives and landscapes of the American Midwest and West—but it is also universal, seen *sub specie aeternitatis*, in a god's-eye view that subsumes all petty issues. His speakers and narrators tend to report moments when they are taken beyond the bounds of ordinary experience, and instead of showing the terror or exhilaration most of us would feel, they tend to react with a combination of equanimity and heightened awareness. The speaker of "Ceremony" has had his hand mangled by a muskrat, but he listens entranced to the calling of an owl and experiences a vision of expanded space and time that transcends the immediacy of his pain and the disconcerting nature of his encounter. The narrator of "Traveling Through the Dark" has an unpleasant, difficult task to face—the disposal of a dead deer and her unborn but still living fawn—but his ability to enlarge his consciousness ("around our group I could hear the wilderness listen") seems to make his personal emotions of distress or guilt disappear into his sense of awe. The voice of "Accountability" matches the ultimates of cold and space against the trucks, taverns, schools, military posters, and "fragmentary explorations" of wise thinkers, to show how these large, indifferent forces surround and chasten our fragile human world.

Stafford is tender about our foolishness; his tone is neither the satirist's nor the prophet's. But his sense of the precariousness of our giving and taking of meaning from nature, all our brave certainties and frightened temporizings, can be quietly, if good-humoredly, inexorable. Poems like "At the Playground" and "The Epitaph Ending in And" are not the products of a sensibility that cultivates easy answers or comforting evasions.

What are the origins of this modest gaze and voice that turn out to have such ineffable ways of seeing and saying the world, this soft-spoken sidling into the visionary? One answer may be found in the poem "The Rescued Year," almost certainly an account of Stafford's Kansas boyhood, in which the lessons he learned from his father are shown to have stood him in good stead as a man and as a writer ever since. His father is contrasted with the preacher, whose voice booms like "empty silos" while his father's "mean attention" and "wonderfully level gaze" go far beyond the knowledge of the man in the pulpit. The father's creed is a realistic seeing of the world as it is—"to glance around and understand"— that takes the patient witness toward unsought knowledge and truth. It makes the "dull town" an Aladdin's lamp and puts the Stafford family into the company of the old man "who spent his life knowing, / unable to tell how he knew." Indeed, the memory of that year and those lessons rescues them from time itself so that the past informs the present as a long-gone train that is able to ripple miraculously backward into the station.

Stafford's religious beliefs—United Brethren—made him a conscientious objector during the Second World War. He worked in labor camps, an experience recorded in a small prose memoir, *Down in My Heart*. After the war he studied in the Writing Program at the University of Iowa, and in 1948 moved to Oregon, where he taught at Lewis and Clark College in Portland until his recent retirement. Stafford came to notice later than many of his contemporaries, but his first sizable collection, *Traveling Through the Dark* (1962), won a National Book Award. He has been a remarkably prolific poet, generous in sending work to little magazines, and much of his poetry still remains uncollected. He has described his unusual writing methods: getting up early every day and writing in an undirected, random fashion, without worrying much about purpose at that early stage, a meditative ritual of sorts. His writer's sensibility seems to wander through the world in the same way that his gaze does, curious and tolerant, taking things as they come and regarding the manifestations of the extraordinary, whether comforting, as in "Earth Dweller," or frightening, as in "In a Museum in the Capital," with calm good humor. The writing method that leaves the subjects and outcomes of poems such an open question has produced, inevitably, an uneven canon, and it has also tended to give us poems that are open to interpretation. "Notice What This Poem Is Not Doing" is merely the most obvious example in this selection of a poem that leaves large areas of interpretation and creation to the reader. Two very different accounts of what the poem is "not doing" would be unlikely to dismay or upset Stafford; he seems ready to live with a latitude of response in the same way that he lives with the vagaries and mysteries of the natural world, sustained by an odd and private faith in the large forces that exist beyond and around our lives.

William Stafford still lives in Portland, though he travels and reads his work widely, one of the most admired presences on the current poetry scene: handy, shrewd, generous, with a whiff of the metaphysical about him, a man like the one in "The Rescued Year" for whom the truth, once it was ready, "didn't care how it came."

DY

Ceremony

On the third finger of my left hand
under the bank of the Ninnescah
a muskrat whirled and bit to the bone.
The mangled hand made the water red.

That was something the ocean would remember:
I saw me in the current flowing through the land,
rolling, touching roots, the world incarnadined,
and the river richer by a kind of marriage.

While in the woods an owl started quavering
with drops like tears I raised my arm.
Under the bank a muskrat was trembling
with meaning my hand would wear forever.

In that river my blood flowed on.

Traveling Through the Dark

Traveling through the dark I found a deer
dead on the edge of the Wilson River road.
It is usually best to roll them into the canyon:
that road is narrow; to swerve might make more dead.

By glow of the tail-light I stumbled back of the car
and stood by the heap, a doe, a recent killing;
she had stiffened already, almost cold.
I dragged her off; she was large in the belly.

My fingers touching her side brought me the reason—
her side was warm; her fawn lay there waiting,
alive, still, never to be born.
Beside that mountain road I hesitated.

The car aimed ahead its lowered parking lights;
under the hood purred the steady engine.
I stood in the glare of the warm exhaust turning red;
around our group I could hear the wilderness listen.

I thought hard for us all—my only swerving—,
then pushed her over the edge into the river.

The Rescued Year

Take a model of the world so big
it is the world again, pass your hand,
press back that area in the west where no one lived,
the place only your mind explores. On your thumb
that smudge becomes my ignorance, a badge
the size of Colorado: toward that state by train
we crossed our state like birds and lodged—
the year my sister gracefully
grew up—against the western boundary
where my father had a job.

Time should go the way it went
that year: we weren't at war; we had
each day a treasured unimportance;
the sky existed, so did our town;
the library had books we hadn't read;
every day at school we learned and sang,
or at least hummed and walked in the hall.

In church I heard the preacher; he said
"Honor!" with a sound like empty silos
repeating the lesson. For a minute I held
Kansas Christian all along the Santa Fe.
My father's mean attention, though, was busy—this
I knew—and going home his wonderfully level gaze
would hold the state I liked, where little happened
and much was understood. I watched my father's finger
mark off huge eye-scans of what happened in the creed.

Like him, I tried. I still try,
send my sight like a million pickpockets
up rich people's drives; it is time
when I pass for every place I go to be alive.
Around any corner my sight is a river,
and I let it arrive: rich by those brooks
his thought poured for hours
into my hand. His creed: the greatest ownership
of all is to glance around and understand.

That Christmas Mother made paper
presents; we colored them with crayons
and hung up a tumbleweed for a tree.
A man from Hugoton brought my sister
a present (his farm was tilted near oil
wells; his car ignored the little
bumps along our drive: nothing
came of all this—it was just part of the year).

I walked out where a girl I knew would be;
we crossed the plank over the ditch
to her house. There was popcorn on the stove,
and her mother recalled the old days, inviting me back.
When I walked home in the cold evening,
snow that blessed the wheat had roved
along the highway seeking furrows,
and all the houses had their lights—
oh, that year did not escape me: I rubbed
the wonderful old lamp of our dull town.

That spring we crossed the state again,
my father soothing us with stories:
the river lost in Utah, underground—
"They've explored only the ones they've found!"—
and that old man who spent his life knowing,
unable to tell how he knew—
"I've been sure by smoke, persuaded
by mist, or a cloud, or a name:
once the truth was ready"—my father smiled
at this—"it didn't care how it came."

In all his ways I hold that rescued year—
comes that smoke like love into the broken
coal, that forms to chunks again and lies
in the earth again in its dim folds, and comes a sound,
then shapes to make a whistle fade,
and in the quiet I hold no need, no hurry:
any day the dust will move, maybe settle;
the train that left will roll back into our station,
the name carved on the platform unfill with rain,
and the sound that followed the couplings back
will ripple forward and hold the train.

Observation Car and Cigar

Tranquility as his breath, his eye a camera
that believes, he follows rails that only last
one trip, then vanish. (Suppose America
tried and then was the West once more, but this time
no one found it? He has felt that much
alone.) Remembering with smoke, he uses
the haze as authentic (the authentic loves not kept
for display fade authentically and become
priceless, never to be exchanged). A silver

evening light follows the train silently
over a great bridge. Like a camera that
believes, he follows an arch into faded
authentic scenes that bring something presented again
and yet all new: traveling, our loves are brought
before us and followed securely into a new evening.

The Epitaph Ending in And

In the last storm, when hawks
blast upward and a dove is
driven into the grass, its broken wings
a delicate design, the air between
wracked thin where it stretched before,
a clear spring bent close too often
(that Earth should ever have such wings
burnt on in blind color!), this will be
good as an epitaph:

Doves did not know where to fly, and

Any Time

Vacation? Well, our children took our love apart:
"Why do you hold Daddy's hand?" "Susy's mother
doesn't have gray in her hair." And scenes crushed
our wonder—Sun Valley, Sawtooths, those reaches
of the Inland Passage, while the children took our
simple love apart.

(Children, how many colors does the light have?
Remember the wide shafts of sunlight, roads
through the trees, how light examines the road hour
by hour? It is all various, no simple on-off colors.
And love does not come riding west through the
trees to find you.)

"Daddy, tell me your best secret." (I have woven
a parachute out of everything broken; my scars
are my shield; and I jump, daylight or dark,
into any country, where as I descend I turn
native and stumble into terribly human speech
and wince recognition.)

"When you get old, how do you know what to do?"
(Waves will quiet, wind lull; and in that
instant I will have all the time in the world;
something deeper than birthdays will tell me all I need.)
"But will you do right?" (Children, children,
oh see that waterfall.)

Earth Dweller

It was all the clods at once become
precious; it was the barn, and the shed,
and the windmill, my hands, the crack
Arlie made in the axe handle: oh, let me stay
here humbly, forgotten, to rejoice in it all;
let the sun casually rise and set.
If I have not found the right place,
teach me; for, somewhere inside, the clods are
vaulted mansions, lines through the barn sing
for the saints forever, the shed and windmill
rear so glorious the sun shudders like a gong.

Now I know why people worship, carry around
magic emblems, wake up talking dreams
they teach to their children: the world speaks.
The world speaks everything to us.
It is our only friend.

Bring the North

Mushroom, Soft Ear, Old Memory,
Root come to tell the air:
bring the Forest Floor along
the valley; bring all that comes
blue into passes, long shores
around a lake, talk, talk, talk,
miles, then deep. Bring that story.

Unfold a pack by someone's door—
wrapped in leather, brought in brown,
what the miles collect.
Leave sound in an empty
house in its own room there,
a little cube hung like a birdcage
in the attic, with a swinging door.
Search out a den: try natural,
no one's, your own, a dirt
floor. Accept them all.

One way to find your place is like
the rain, a million requests
for lodging, one that wins, finds
your cheek: you find your home,
a storm that walks the waves.
You hear that cloak whip, those
chilly hands take night apart.
In split Heaven you see one sudden
eye on yours, and yours in it,
scared, falling, fallen.

Mushroom, Soft Ear, Memory
attend what is.
Bring the North.

In a Museum in the Capital

Think of the shark's tiny brain
trapped in that senseless lust,
ripped through the tide, dismayed.

Think of The Great, helpless,
their very purposes caught
like ice that cannot be else.

And even The Wise are framed—
plans bound like a vise on the face,
and vanity roaring its claims.

The clock ticks on, every second
wandering down like a snowflake,
while an avalanche whispers our names.

WILLIAM STAFFORD   135

Together Again

When I drive, every bridge is
a gift, and the power that swoops
the wires is ready to let go.
The little car radio drinks and drinks
whatever comes true out of the sky.

Were our lost ones ever to come
home, and be hale, all four of my
own would come, the center a place
again and the hiss of the river past
a bit of grass the only sound, our whole lives—

And drama enough, this time.

At the Playground

Away down deep and away up high,
a swing drops you into the sky.
Back, it draws you away down deep,
forth, it flings you in a sweep
all the way to the stars and back
—Goodby, Jill; Goodby, Jack:
shuddering climb wild and steep,
away up high, away down deep.

Accountability

Cold nights outside the taverns in Wyoming
pickups and big semi's lounge idling, letting their
haunches twitch now and then in gusts of powder snow,
their owners inside for hours, forgetting as well
as they can the miles, the circling plains, the still town
that connects to nothing but cold and space and a few
stray ribbons of pavement, icy guides to nothing
but bigger towns and other taverns that glitter and wait:
Denver, Cheyenne.

Hibernating in the library of the school on the hill
a few pieces by Thomas Aquinas or Saint Teresa
and the fragmentary explorations of people like Alfred
North Whitehead crouch and wait amid research folders
on energy and military recruitment posters glimpsed
by the hard stars. The school bus by the door, a yellow
mound, clangs open and shut as the wind finds a loose
door and worries it all night, letting the hollow
students count off and break up and blow away
over the frozen ground.

Notice What This Poem is Not Doing

The light along the hills in the morning
comes down slowly, naming the trees
white, then coasting the ground for stones to nominate.

Notice what this poem is not doing.

A house, a house, a barn, the old
quarry, where the river shrugs—
how much of this place is yours?

Notice what this poem is not doing.

Every person gone has taken a stone
to hold, and catch the sun. The carving
says, "Not here, but called away."

Notice what this poem is not doing.

The sun, the earth, the sky, all wait.
The crows and redbirds talk. The light
along the hills has come, has found you.

Notice what this poem has not done.

WILLIAM STAFFORD   137

School Days

1

After the test they sent an expert
questioner to our school: "Who is this
kid Bohr?" When Bohr came in
he asked the expert, "Who are you?"
and for a long time they looked at each other,
and Bohr said, "Thanks, I thought so." Then
they talked about why the test was given.
Afterwards they shook hands, and Bohr walked
slowly away. He turned and called out, "You passed."

2

Enough sleet had pasted over the window
by three o'clock so we couldn't tell if it was dark—
and our pony would be out there in the little shed
waiting to take us home. Teacher banked the stove
with an extra log. That was the storm
of 1934. For two days we waited,
singing and praying, and I guess it worked,
even though the snow drifted over the roof.
But the pony was dead when they dug us out.

3

At a tiny desk inside my desk, a doll
bends over a book. In the book is a feather
found at the beach, from a dead gull.
While Miss Leonard reads "The Highwayman,"
I bend over my book and cry,
and fly all alone through the night
toward being the person I am.

Notes

Bring the North.—Why the capitalizations in the first stanza? The poet seems to
be creating a muse or god of the forest, a presence of the kind the Indians
believed in, from whom special knowledge can be invoked or requested.

School Days. "Bohr" is Niels Bohr, the Danish physicist who made significant
contributions to modern atomic theory. "The Highwayman," a melodramatic
poem by Alfred Noyes, was at one time a standard item in high school textbooks.

William Stafford

Books

Down in My Heart (prose), 1947
West of Your City: Poems, 1960
Traveling Through the Dark, 1962
The Rescued Year, 1966
Allegiances, 1970
Someday, Maybe, 1973
Stories That Could Be True: New and Collected Poems, 1977
Writing the Australian Crawl: Views on the Writer's Vocation (essays), 1978
Things That Happen Where There Aren't Any People, 1980

Criticism, Interviews

Three articles on Stafford in *Modern Poetry Studies* 6 (Spring 1975); Alberta Turner, "William Stafford and the Surprise Cliché," *South Carolina Review* 7 (April 1975); Jonathan Holden, *The Mark to Turn: A Reading of William Stafford's Poetry*, 1976; George Lensing and Ronald Moran, *Four Poets of the Emotive Imagination: Robert Bly, James Wright, Louis Simpson and William Stafford*, 1976

Nineteen Poets Born Between 1920 and 1930

PART THREE

John Ashbery

(b. 1927)

Readers unfamiliar with this century's experimental traditions in the arts (Dada and Surrealist poetry, abstract painting, serial music, etc.) are apt to be bewildered by John Ashbery's poetry. They may begin by taking it too seriously. Then, when they have discovered its playful, parodic, and deliberately arbitrary elements, they may wrongly conclude that there is no serious intent behind it, no substance under its brilliantly manipulated surfaces. Most of all, they will be frustrated if they bring an expectation of constancy to an art obsessed with shifting and changing possibilities. You must enjoy unpredictability—of tone, subject, and style—if you are to like John Ashbery. While most poets operate at a "middle distance" of consistent attitude and set relation of work to reader, Ashbery is usually either closer or farther away than we expect, veering from an unusually candid and forthright manner at one moment to perfectly specious and impenetrable statements and combinations at the next. We must be ready for anything in reading Ashbery because this eclectic, dazzling, inventive creator of travesties and treatises is most of all ready to include anything, go anywhere, say what is least expected, in the service of an aesthetic dedicated to liberating poetry from predictable conventions and tired traditions.

The flight from tradition becomes a tradition of its own, of course, and the attack on conventions creates new ones. Thus it is that we have learned how to "read" abstract paintings, for example, recognizing that they can "express" emotional states without representing a known visual world, and acknowledging that their emphasis on their own medium— line, color, shape, texture—is a way of making us aware of them as objects that do not so much comment on the world as join it, as separate things in their own right. It is much more difficult to achieve this effect with works of art made of language, however, since language is insistently communicative and referential. But poems by early modern masters like Wallace Stevens, insofar as they seem to be about the nature of language and the enterprise of making poetry from it, anticipate the giddy exhilaration with which Ashbery makes language into "language," skating along the borders of sense and nonsense, meaning and gibberish, rational and irrational; he is the foremost current practitioner in English of an avant-garde "tradition of the new," centered in French culture and beginning with Cubism, Dada, and Apollinaire, that has touched all writers and artists since. As one poet put it recently, whether or not we consciously subscribe to this tradition, it is now part of the very air we breathe, so that John Ashbery, different as he may seem from most working poets, represents the extreme of a tendency to which all poets respond to some degree.

All this is not to claim that Ashbery's poems are best viewed as if they were Jackson Pollock canvases or Andy Warhol soup cans. This poet's gifts are in fact stylistic and musical. His strengths are the strengths of a good writer: an inventive imagination, a sharp eye for the rich possibilities of juxtaposition, an ear that makes him a superb mimic, and an appetite for the artistic transformations to which banality can be subjected. His weaknesses are a writer's too: a certain preciousness, an apparent absence of self-criticism that makes his work uneven, a tendency to lengthiness that can induce boredom. But because so few working poets share Ashbery's full allegiance to the modern experimental tradition described above, and so many painters and not a few composers do, the value of analogies to the other arts in his case remains a useful way of helping readers approach his poems.

Our relation to any given Ashbery poem ought to be highly speculative. If we happen to know where the details were appropriated—for example, recognizing the derivation of "Glazunoviana" from a famous geometry problem—we may feel quite at home with the way in which they are assembled playfully with an eye toward a semiserious culminating statement. If we do not, we need to proceed with more caution. How much does "Civilisation and its Discontents," for example, have to do with Freud's book by that title? Who is the speaker? Whom is he addressing? How much should the narrative elements be seen as part of some genuine story and how much as pseudo-narrative fragments in a large collage? To rush into single-minded answers to such questions would be not only to misread the poem by limiting its possibilities but to deprive ourselves of the enjoyable uncertainties Ashbery has prepared for us. As we read the poem's touching but perfectly silly closing stanza ("I had already swallowed the poison / And could only gaze into the distance . . ."), the mixture of possibilities, from Freud to romantic novels and operas, is what should most engage us. That the poem is primarily a love poem seems clear enough, but that it may be addressed to the reader by the writer is one of many possibilities we cannot afford to overlook.

At times the fun of Ashbery's poems is more overt, as in the hilarious "Variations, Calypso and Fugue on a Theme of Ella Wheeler Wilcox," where the badness of the lady's original quatrain becomes the inspiration for an exuberant tour of the terrible rhyming of calypso lyrics and a host of other garrulous, awful styles of fantasy and platitude. Read aloud, preferably with a steel band accompaniment in the background, this poem should move listeners toward bursts of helpless laughter. It is good to be reminded that the language of Chaucer, Donne, Swift, and Byron still has rich comic possibilities for poetry.

Laced into Ashbery's fun, both overt and sly, is a plangent, romantic melancholy that is perfectly serious and often quite moving, and we must be ready to respond to that as well. He writes of the limits of language and art with great feeling, as well as the traditional poetic subjects of love and loss, old age and death, isolation and community, belief and skepticism. The present selection does not stress all these facets of Ashbery's work, nor can it adequately represent his effective work in longer poems (e.g., "The Skaters" and "Self-Portrait in a Convex Mirror"). This controversial and gifted poet has been so copious and restless that readers who wish a full portrait of his poetic achievement, good and bad, will need to read him more widely. All his collections, from the brilliant first book, *Some Trees*, to the most recent as of this writing, *Shadow Train*, are currently in print.

DY

Glazunoviana

The man with the red hat
And the polar bear, is he here too?
The window giving on shade,
Is that here too?
And all the little helps,
My initials in the sky,
The hay of an arctic summer night?

The bear
Drops dead in sight of the window.
Lovely tribes have just moved to the north.
In the flickering evening the martins grow denser.
Rivers of wings surround us and vast tribulation.

Civilisation and its Discontents

A people chained to aurora
I alone disarming you

Millions of facts of distributed light

Helping myself with some big boxes
Up the steps, then turning to no neighbourhood;
The child's psalm, slightly sung
In the hall rushing into the small room.
Such fire! leading away from destruction.
Somewhere in outer ether I glimpsed you
Coming at me, the solo barrier did it this time.
Guessing us staying true to be at the blue mark
Of the threshold. Tired of planning it again and again,
The cool boy distant, and the soaked-up
Afterthought, like so much rain, or roof.

The miracle took you in beside him.
Leaves rushed the window, there was clear water and the sound of a lock.
Now I never see you much any more.
The summers are much colder than they used to be
In that other time, when you and I were young.
I miss the human truth of your smile,
The halfhearted gaze of your palms,
And all things together, but there is no comic reign
Only the facts you put to me. You must not, then,
Be very surprised if I am alone: it is all for you,
The night, and the stars, and the way we used to be.

There is no longer any use in harping on
The incredible principle of daylong silence, the dark sunlight
As only the grass is beginning to know it.

The wreath of the north pole,
Festoons for the late return, the shy pensioners
Agasp on the lamplit air. What is agreeable
Is to hold your hand. The gravel
Underfoot. The time is for coming close. Useless
Verbs shooting the other words far away.

I had already swallowed the poison
And could only gaze into the distance at my life
Like a saint's with each day distinct.
No heaviness in the upland pastures. Nothing
In the forest. Only life under the huge trees
Like a coat that has grown too big, moving far away,
Cutting swamps for men like lapdogs, holding its own,
Performing once again, for you and for me.

Variations, Calypso and Fugue on a Theme of Ella Wheeler Wilcox

"For the pleasures of the many
May be ofttimes traced to one
As the hand that plants an acorn
Shelters armies from the sun."
And in places where the annual rainfall is 0071 inches
What a pleasure to lie under the tree, to sit, stand, and get up under the tree!
Im wunderschönen Monat Mai
The feeling is of never wanting to leave the tree,
Of predominantly peace and relaxation.

Do you step out from under the shade a moment,
It is only to return with renewed expectation, of expectation fulfilled.
Insecurity be damned! There is something to all this, that will not elude us:
Growing up under the shade of friendly trees, with our brothers all around.
And truly, young adulthood was never like this:
Such delight, such consideration, such affirmation in the way the day goes 'round
    together.
Yes, the world goes 'round a good deal faster
When there are highlights on the lips, unspoken and true words in the heart,
And the hand keeps brushing away a strand of chestnut hair, only to have it fall
    back into place again.
But all good things must come to an end, and so one must move forward
Into the space left by one's conclusions. Is this growing old?

Well, it is a good experience, to divest oneself of some tested ideals, some old
    standbys,
And even finding nothing to put in their place is a good experience,
Preparing one, as it does, for the consternation that is to come.
But—and this is the gist of it—what if I dreamed it all,
The branches, the late afternoon sun,
The trusting camaraderie, the love that watered all,
Disappearing promptly down into the roots as it should?
For later in the vast gloom of cities, only there you learn
How the ideas were good only because they had to die,
Leaving you alone and skinless, a drawing by Vesalius.
This is what was meant, and toward which everything directs:
That the tree should shrivel in 120-degree heat, the acorns
Lie around on the worn earth like eyeballs, and the lead soldiers shrug and slink
    off.

So my youth was spent, underneath the trees
I always moved around with perfect ease

I voyaged to Paris at the age of ten
And met many prominent literary men

Gazing at the Alps was quite a sight
I felt the tears flow forth with all their might

A climb to the Acropolis meant a lot to me
I had read the Greek philosophers you see

In the Colosseum I thought my heart would burst
Thinking of all the victims who had been there first

On Mount Ararat's side I began to grow
Remembering the Flood there, so long ago

On the banks of the Ganges I stood in mud
And watched the water light up like blood

JOHN ASHBERY   147

The Great Wall of China is really a thrill
It cleaves through the air like a silver pill

It was built by the hand of man for good or ill
Showing what he can do when he decides not to kill

But of all the sights that were seen by me
In the East or West, on land or sea,
The best was the place that is spelled H-O-M-E.

Now that once again I have achieved home
I shall forbear all further urge to roam

There is a hole of truth in the green earth's rug
Once you find it you are as snug as a bug

Maybe some do not like it quite as much as you
That isn't all you're going to do.

You must remember that it is yours
Which is why nobody is sending you flowers

This age-old truth I to thee impart
Act according to the dictates of your art

Because if you don't no one else is going to
And that person isn't likely to be you.

It is the wind that comes from afar
It is the truth of the farthest star

In all likelihood you will not need these
So take it easy and learn your ABC's

And trust in the dream that will never come true
'Cause that is the scheme that is best for you
And the gleam that is the most suitable too.

"MAKE MY DREAM COME TRUE." This message, set in 84-point Hobo type, startled in the morning editions of the paper: the old, half-won security troubles the new pause. And with the approach of the holidays, the present is clearly here to stay: the big brass band of its particular moment's consciousness invades the plazas and the narrow alleys. Three-fourths of the houses in this city are on narrow stilts, finer than a girl's wrists: it is largely a question of keeping one's feet dry, and of privacy. In the morning you forget what the punishment was. Probably it was something like eating a pretzel or going into the back yard. Still, you can't tell. These things could be a lot clearer without hurting anybody. But it does not follow that such issues will produce the most dynamic capital gains for you.

Friday. We are really missing you.

"The most suitable," however, was not the one specially asked for nor the one hanging around the lobby. It was just the one asked after, day after day—what spilled over, claimed by the spillway. The distinction of a dog, of how a dog walks. The thought of a dog walking. No one ever referred to the incident again. The case was officially closed. Maybe there were choruses of silent gratitude, welling up in the spring night like a column of cloud, reaching to the very rafters of the sky—but this was their own business. The point is no ear ever heard them. Thus, the incident, to call it by one of its names—choice, conduct, absent-minded frown might be others—came to be not only as though it had never happened, but as though it never *could* have happened. Sealed into the wall of all that season's coming on. And thus, for a mere handful of people—roustabouts and degenerates, most of them—it became the only true version. Nothing else mattered. It was bread by morning and night, the dates falling listlessly from the trees—man, woman, child, festering glistering in a single orb. The reply to "hello."

> Pink purple and blue
> The way you used to do

The next two days passed oddly for Peter and Christine, and were among the most absorbing they had ever known. On the one hand, a vast open basin—or sea; on the other a narrow spit of land, terminating in a copse, with a few broken-down outbuildings lying here and there. It made no difference that the bey—b-e-y this time, oriental potentate—had ordained their release, there was this funny feeling that they should always be there, sustained by looks out over the ether, missing Mother and Alan and the others but really quiet, in a kind of activity that offers its own way of life, sunflower chained to the sun. Can it ever be resolved? Or are the forms of a person's thoughts controlled by inexorable laws, as in Dürer's Adam and Eve? So mutually exclusive, and so steep— Himalayas jammed side by side like New York apartment buildings. Oh the blame of it, the de-crescendo. My vice is worry. Forget it. The continual splitting up, the ear-shattering volumes of a polar ice-cap breaking up are just what you wanted. You've got it, so shut up.

> The crystal haze
> For days and days

Lots of sleep is an important factor, and rubbing the eyes. Getting off the subway he suddenly felt hungry. He went into one place, a place he knew, and ordered a hamburger and a cup of coffee. He hadn't been in this neighborhood in a long time—not since he was a kid. He used to play stickball in the vacant lot across the street. Sometimes his bunch would get into a fight with some of the older boys, and he'd go home tired and bleeding. Most days were the same though. He'd say "Hi" to the other kids and they'd say "Hi" to him. Nice bunch of guys. Finally he decided to take a turn past the old grade school he'd attended as a kid. It was a rambling structure of yellow brick, now gone in seediness and shabbiness which the late-afternoon shadows mercifully softened. The gravel playground in front was choked with weeds. Large trees and shrubbery would do no harm flanking the main entrance. Time farted.

> The first shock rattles the cruets in their stand,
> The second rips the door from its hinges.

"My dear friend," he said gently, "you said you were Professor Hertz. You must pardon me if I say that the information startles and mystifies me. When you are stronger I have some questions to ask you, if you will be kind enough to answer them."

No one was prepared for the man's answer to that apparently harmless statement.

Weak as he was, Gustavus Hertz raised himself on his elbow. He stared wildly about him, peering fearfully into the shadowy corners of the room.

"I will tell you nothing! Nothing, do you hear?" he shrieked. "Go away! Go away!"

Märchenbilder

Es war einmal . . . No, it's too heavy
To be said. Besides, you aren't paying attention any more.
How shall I put it?
"The rain thundered on the uneven red flagstones.

The steadfast tin soldier gazed beyond the drops
Remembering the hat-shaped paper boat, that soon . . ."
That's not it either.
Think about the long summer evenings of the past, the queen anne's lace.

Sometimes a musical phrase would perfectly sum up
The mood of a moment. One of those lovelorn sonatas
For wind instruments was riding past on a solemn white horse.
Everybody wondered who the new arrival was.

Pomp of flowers, decorations
Junked next day. Now look out of the window.
The sky is clear and bland. The wrong kind of day
For business or games, or betting on a sure thing.

The trees weep drops
Into the water at night. Slowly couples gather.
She looks into his eyes. "It would not be good
To be left alone." He: "I'll stay

As long as the night allows." This was one of those night rainbows
In negative color. As we advance, it retreats; we see
We are now far into a cave, must be. Yet there seem to be
Trees all around, and a wind lifts their leaves, slightly.

I want to go back, out of the bad stories.
But there's always the possibility that the next one . . .
No, it's another almond tree, or a ring-swallowing frog . . .
Yet they are beautiful as we people them

With ourselves. They are empty as cupboards.
To spend whole days drenched in them, waiting for the next whisper,
For the word in the next room. This is how the princes must have behaved,
Lying down in the frugality of sleep.

On Autumn Lake

Leading liot act to foriage is activity
Of Chinese philosopher here on Autumn Lake thoughtfully inserted in
Plovince of Quebec—stop it! I will not. The edge hugs
The lake with ever-more-paternalistic insistence, whose effect
Is in the blue way up ahead. The distance

By air from other places to here isn't much, but
It doesn't count, at least not the way the
Shore distance—leaf, tree, stone; optional (fern, frog, skunk);
And then stone, tree, leaf; then another optional—counts.
It's like the "machines" of the 19th-century Academy.
Turns out you didn't need all that training
To do art—that it was even better not to have it. Look at
The Impressionists—some of 'em had it, too, but preferred to forget it
In vast composed canvases by turns riotous
And indigent in color, from which only the notion of space is lacking.

I do not think that this
Will be my last trip to Autumn Lake
Have some friends among many severe heads
We all scholars sitting under tree
Waiting for nut to fall. Some of us studying
Persian and Aramaic, others the art of distilling
Weird fragrances out of nothing, from the ground up.
In each the potential is realized, the two wires
Are crossing.

Friends

> I like to speak in rhymes,
> because I am a rhyme myself.
> NIJINSKY

I saw a cottage in the sky.
I saw a balloon made of lead.
I cannot restrain my tears, and they fall
On my left hand and on my silken tie,
But I cannot and do not want to hold them back.

JOHN ASHBERY

One day the neighbors complain about an unpleasant odor
Coming from his room. *I went for a walk*
But met no friends. Another time I go outside
Into the world. It rocks on and on.
It was rocking before I saw it
And is presumably doing so still.

The banker lays his hand on mine.
His face is as clean as a white handkerchief.
We talk nonsense as usual.
I trace little circles on the light that comes in
Through the window on saw-horse legs.
Afterwards I see that we are three.
Someone had entered the room while I was discussing my money problems.
I wish God would put a stop to this. I
Turn and see the new moon through glass. I am yanked away
So fast I lose my breath, a not unpleasant feeling.

I feel as though I had been carrying the message for years
On my shoulders like Atlas, never feeling it
Because of never having known anything else. In another way
I am involved with the message. I want to put it down
(In two senses of "put it down") so that you
May understand the agreeable destiny that awaits us.
You sigh. Your sighs will admit of no impatience,
Only a vast crater lake, vast as the sea.
In which the sky, smaller than that, is reflected.

I reach for my hat
And am bound to repeat with tact
The formal greeting I am charged with.
No one makes mistakes. No one runs away
Any more. I bite my lip and
Turn to you. Maybe now you understand.

The feeling is a jewel like a pearl.

What is Poetry

The medieval town, with frieze
Of boy scouts from Nagoya? The snow

That came when we wanted it to snow?
Beautiful images? Trying to avoid

Ideas, as in this poem? But we
Go back to them as to a wife, leaving

The mistress we desire? Now they
Will have to believe it

As we believe it. In school
All the thought got combed out:

What was left was like a field.
Shut your eyes, and you can feel it for miles around.

Now open them on a thin vertical path.
It might give us—what?—some flowers soon?

My Erotic Double

He says he doesn't feel like working today.
It's just as well. Here in the shade
Behind the house, protected from street noises,
One can go over all kinds of old feeling,
Throw some away, keep others.
                       The wordplay
Between us gets very intense when there are
Fewer feelings around to confuse things.
Another go-round? No, but the last things
You always find to say are charming, and rescue me
Before the night does. We are afloat
On our dreams as on a barge made of ice,
Shot through with questions and fissures of starlight
That keep us awake, thinking about the dreams
As they are happening. Some occurrence. You said it.

I said it but I can hide it. But I choose not to.
Thank you. You are a very pleasant person.
Thank you. You are too.

Notes

Glazunoviana. Alesandr Glazunov (1865–1936) was a Russian composer. The window, the bear, and the man in the red hat come from a riddle about the North Pole.

Civilisation and its Discontents. The title is after a famous work by Freud (1930).

Variations. . . . Ella Wheeler Wilcox (1855–1919) was an American poet and journalist whose bad poems (e.g., *Poems of Passion*, 1883, and *Poems of Pleasure*, 1888) enjoyed great popularity.

Märchenbilder. The title means "fairy-tale images." The opening words, *"Es war einmal,"* are the traditional "once upon a time" beginning.

Friends. Nijinsky (1890–1950) was a famous Russian ballet dancer whose career was cut short by insanity. His journal, which is quoted in the epigraph, is a moving record of his illness and isolation.

John Ashbery

Books

Some Trees, 1956
The Tennis Court Oath, 1962
Rivers and Mountains, 1966
A Nest of Ninnies (novel, with James Schuyler), 1969
The Double Dream of Spring, 1970
Three Poems, 1972
Self-Portrait in a Convex Mirror, 1975
Houseboat Days, 1977
3 Plays, 1978
As We Know, 1979
Shadow Train, 1981

Criticism, Interviews

David Kermani, *John Ashbery: A Comprehensive Bibliography,* 1976; David Shapiro, *John Ashbery: An Introduction to the Poetry,* 1979; David Kalstone, *Five Temperaments,* 1977; Jonathan Holden, *The Rhetoric of the Contemporary Lyric,* 1980

Robert
Bly

(b. 1926)

William Stafford

R obert Bly is rightly considered one of the dominant forces in contemporary American poetry. As a translator (he has introduced many overlooked and even unknown, European, South American, and Asian writers to American readers in vigorous translations), as an editor and publisher (of *The Fifties* and *The Sixties*), and as a poet, he has played a major role in shaping what we read, how we read, and what we know about the role of the artist in our society.

Bly's friendship with other poets of his generation has meant that his ideas about literary values and concerns have been as influential in practice as in theory. James Wright provides the most notable example of this. The two poets worked closely together during the crucial years that produced Bly's *Silence in the Snowy Fields* and Wright's *The Branch Will Not Break*, and the results of their mutual influence are everywhere evident in these two books. Discussing "Fishing on a Lake at Night," a poem Bly had worked on for many years, he wrote, "The 'we' in the last line are all intellectuals, I guess, but in the poem Jim and me." This clue helps us reconsider the early work Bly and Wright were producing side by side. Desperate to shake off all formal aspects that run counter to artistic intentions, they exhorted each other to write *American* poems in plain language. Bly's friendships with other poets, especially Donald Hall, Louis Simpson, and Galway Kinnell, and, more briefly, James Dickey and John Haines, have also left their mark (one thinks of the young Ezra Pound in searching for an analogy). From the reading and writing Bly urged on them, two key principles emerge: poetry must arrive at a visionary sense of the world through the least rhetorical means, and must be a kind of surrealist Puritan transcendentalism in the process; or, as he put it elsewhere, poems should "try to achieve 'two presences' by adopting the line with simple syntax." To accomplish this, poems need images that burn what is seen into place.

The "line with simple syntax" is the lifeblood of Bly's poems, adopted partly for didactic reasons, the chief argument against falsely abstract language that comes from too much appreciation of earlier periods and styles; and partly because Bly needs simple syntax to carry his strong opinions on national and private matters—lying and deceit, anger and fear—to a large public. In spite of the many exclamation points that ring out the assertions of the poems, the voice speaking them can and often does drop down to be quiet, to "talk low," as one poem says of two people out in a boat. In "Listening to Bach," the fifth section of "Six Winter Privacy Poems," the ecstatic shouting is tuned down for our inner ear: "There is someone inside this music / who is not well described by the names / of Jesus, or Jehovah, or the Lord of Hosts!" Indeed, and there is someone inside the poems as well who is better described as a meditator, albeit an exhorting one—"I want to be..., I want to be..." is the way many poems seem to speak. Tomas Tranströmer, the Swedish poet Bly has translated, says of his own poems that they are "active meditations, they want to wake us up"; it is a view that applies to Bly's work as well.

Given this focus on bare-bones structure and simple diction and syntax, it is no accident that Bly has turned more and more to the prose poem. "August Rain" and "Visiting Emily Dickinson's Grave with Robert Francis" are among his finest examples in the genre. These poems look lovingly, closely, in a childlike way, at things that are part of the natural world; but as they do they make astonishing comparisons. In "August Rain," starting with a "simple" scene—it is raining—we are quickly caught up in a biblical flood of spiritual as well as physical proportions. As "The . . . earth turns blacker, it absorbs the rain needles without a sound"; it is as if the poem itself absorbed its words without a sound. In "Visiting Emily Dickinson's Grave" the comparison of the distance between her house and grave to the immense distance through which "Satan and his helpers rose and fell, oh vast areas, the distances between stars, between the first time love is felt in the sleeves of a dress, and the death of the person who was in that room . . ." is extremely moving for the way the poet sees eternal forces manifested in simple details, simple objects. Bly has an exciting sense of scale.

Bly was one of the organizers of "Poets Reading Against the Vietnam War"; he has always assumed the role of citizen-poet, who believes poetry is the conscience of the age. While our selections have taken little account of his pointedly political poems (with the exception of "Turning Away from Lies" and "Three Presidents"), a recent poem like "Mourning Pablo Neruda" stirs our moral senses as much as famous poems (like "The Teeth Mother Naked at Last") that moved audiences during the war. The strangely skinny shape of "Mourning Pablo Neruda" is like a vase for its elemental language. The monologue of the driver, his eye on the jar of water beside him in the car like some animal he is about to release, resists abstraction and rhetoric as it accounts for Neruda's death: "For the dead remain inside / us, as water / remains / inside granite— / hardly at all—" We'd perhaps been expecting the word "forever," the exclaiming word most poets cannot seem to avoid, where we read "hardly at all." But this is a poem of releasing, of letting go, and saying the right good-bye. Of not pretending to understand what cannot be understood. In a famous Bashō poem that Bly has translated, the morning glory, though we must learn to regard it, is one more thing that cannot be our friend. Bly's poetry is about establishing the limits of what we can see, hear and sense, of looking at "the other," as Rilke insisted we must, without confusing worlds.

SF

Driving Toward the Lac Qui Parle River

I

I am driving; it is dusk; Minnesota.
The stubble field catches the last growth of sun.
The soybeans are breathing on all sides.
Old men are sitting before their houses on carseats
In the small towns. I am happy,
The moon rising above the turkey sheds.

II

The small world of the car
Plunges through the deep fields of the night,
On the road from Willmar to Milan.
This solitude covered with iron
Moves through the fields of night
Penetrated by the noise of crickets.

III

Nearly to Milan, suddenly a small bridge,
And water kneeling in the moonlight.
In small towns the houses are built right on the ground;
The lamplight falls on all fours in the grass.
When I reach the river, the full moon covers it;
A few people are talking low in a boat.

Three Presidents

Andrew Jackson

I want to be a white horse!
I want to be a white horse on the green mountains!
A horse that runs over wooden bridges, and sleeps
In abandoned barns . . .

Theodore Roosevelt

When I was President, I crushed snails with my bare teeth.
I slept in my underwear in the White House.
I ate the Cubans with a straw, and Lenin dreamt of *me* every night.
I wore down a forest of willow trees. I ground the snow,
And sold it.

The mountains of Texas shall heal our cornfields,
Overrun by the yellow race.
As for me, I want to be a stone. Yes!
I want to be a stone laid down thousands of years ago,
A stone with almost invisible cracks!
I want to be a stone that holds up the edge of the lake house,
A stone that suddenly gets up and runs around at night,
And lets the marriage bed fall; a stone that leaps into the water,
Carrying the robber down with him.

John F. Kennedy

I want to be a stream of water falling—
Water falling from high in the mountains, water
That dissolves everything,   .
And is never drunk, falling from ledge to ledge, from glass to glass.
I want the air around me to be invisible, resilient,
Able to flow past rocks.
I will carry the boulders with me to the valley.
Then ascending I will fall through space again:
Glittering in the sun, like the crystal in sideboards,
Goblets of the old life, before it was ruined by the Church.
And when I ascend the third time, I will fall forever,
Missing the earth entirely.

Turning Away from Lies

1

If we are truly free, and live in a free country,
When shall I be without this heaviness of mind?
When shall I have peace? Peace this way and peace that way?
I have already looked beneath the street
And there I saw the bitter waters going down,
The ancient worms eating up the sky.

2

Christ did not come to redeem our sins
The Christ Child was not obedient to his parents
The Kingdom of Heaven does not mean the next life
No one in business can be a Christian
The two worlds are both in this world

The saints rejoice out loud upon their beds!
Their song moves through the troubled sea
The way the holy tortoise moves
From dark blue into troubled green,
Or ghost crabs move above the dolomite.
The thieves are crying in the wild asparagus.

Fishing on a Lake at Night

Someone has left a light on at the boathouse
to guide the fishermen back after dark.
The light makes no sound as it comes.
It flies over the waves like a bird with one wing.
Its path is a boatful of the dead, trying to return to life
over the broken waters.
                And the light
simply comes, bearing no gifts,
as if the camels had arrived without the Wise Men.
It is steady, holding us to our old mountain home.
Now as we watch the moon rises over the popple forest.
It too arrives without fuss,
it goes between the boards around the pulp-cutter's house—
the same fence we pass through by opening the gate.

A Long Walk Before the Snows Began

1

Nearly winter. All day the sky gray. Earth heavy.
The cornfields dead. I walk over the soaked
cornstalks knocked flat in rows,
a few grains of white sleet on the leaves.

2

White sleet also in the black plowing.
I turn and go west—tracks, pushed deep!
I am walking with an immense deer.
He passed three days ago.

I reach the creek at last, nearly dusk.
New snow on the river ice, under willow branches,
open places like the plains of North China,
where the mice have been, just a half hour ago.

Six Winter Privacy Poems

1

About four, a few flakes.
I empty the teapot out in the snow,
      feeling shoots of joy in the new cold.
By nightfall, wind,
the curtains on the south sway softly.

2

My shack has two rooms; I use one.
The light falls on my table,
and I fly into one of my own poems—
I can't tell you where—
as if I appeared where I am now,
in a wet field, snow falling.

3

More of the fathers are dying each day.
It is time for the sons.
Bits of darkness are gathering around them.
The bits appear as flakes of light.

4

SITTING ALONE

There is a solitude like black mud!
Sitting in the darkness singing
I can't tell if this joy
is from the body, or the soul, or a third place!

5

LISTENING TO BACH

There is someone inside this music
who is not well described by the names
of Jesus, or Jehovah, or the Lord of Hosts!

ROBERT BLY   161

When I woke, new snow had fallen.
I am alone, yet someone else is with me,
drinking coffee, looking out at the snow.

August Rain

After a month and a half without rain, at last, in late August, darkness comes at three in the afternoon, a cheerful thunder begins, and at last the rain. I set a glass out on a table to measure the rain, and suddenly buoyant and affectionate go indoors to find my children. They are upstairs, playing quietly alone in their doll-filled rooms, hanging pictures, thoughtfully moving "the small things that make them happy" from one side of the room to another. I feel triumphant, without need of money, far from the grave. I walk over the grass, watching the soaked chairs, and the cooled towels, and sit down on my stoop, dragging a chair out with me. The rain deepens. It rolls off the porch roof, making a great puddle near me. The bubbles slide toward the puddle edge, are crowded, and disappear. The black earth turns blacker, it absorbs the rain needles without a sound. The sky is low, everything silent, as when parents are angry. . . . What has failed and been forgiven—the leaves from last year unable to go on, lying near the foundation, dry under the porch, retreat farther into the shadow, they give off a faint hum, as of birds' eggs, or the tail of a dog.

The older we get the more we fail, but the more we fail the more we feel a part of the dead straw of the universe, the corners of barns with cowdung twenty years old, the chairs fallen back on their heads in deserted houses, the belts left hanging over the chairback after the bachelor has died in the ambulance on the way to the city, these objects also belong to us, they ride us as the child holding on to the dog's fur, these appear in our dreams, they are more and more near us, coming in slowly from the wainscoting, they make our trunks heavy, accumulating between trips, they lie against the ship's side, and will nudge the hole open that lets the water in at last.

Snowbanks North of the House

Those great sweeps of snow that stop suddenly six feet from the house . . .
Thoughts that go so far.
The boy gets out of high school and reads no more books;
the son stops calling home.
The mother puts down her rolling pin and makes no more bread.
And the wife looks at her husband one night at a party, and loves him no more.

162

The energy leaves the wine, and the minister falls leaving the church.
It will not come closer—
the one inside moves back, and the hands touch nothing, and are safe.

The father grieves for his son, and will not leave the room where the coffin
    stands.
He turns away from his wife, and she sleeps alone.

And the sea lifts and falls all night, the moon goes on through the unattached
    heavens alone.
The toe of the shoe pivots
in the dust . . .
And the man in the black coat turns, and goes back down the hill.
No one knows why he came, or why he turned away, and did not climb the hill.

Visiting Emily Dickinson's Grave
with Robert Francis

A black iron fence closes the graves in, its ovals delicate as wine stems. They
resemble those chapel windows on the main Aran island, made narrow in the 4th
century so that not too much rain would drive in . . . It is April, clear and dry.
Curls of grass rise around the nearby gravestones.

The Dickinson house is not far off. She arrived here one day, at 56, Robert
says, carried over the lots between by six Irish laboring men, when her brother
refused to trust her body to a carriage. The coffin was darkened with violets and
pine boughs, as she covered the immense distance between the solid Dickinson
house and this plot.

The distance is immense, the distances through which Satan and his helpers
rose and fell, oh vast areas, the distances between stars, between the first time
love is felt in the sleeves of the dress, and the death of the person who was in that
room . . . the distance between the feet and head as you lie down, the distance be-
tween the mother and father, through which we pass reluctantly.

My family "address an Eclipse every morning, which they call their
'Father.' " Each of us crosses that distance at night, arriving out of sleep on
hands and knees, astonished we see a hump in the ground where we thought a
chapel would be . . . it is a grassy knoll. And we clamber out of sleep, holding on
to it with our hands . . .

Mourning Pablo Neruda

Water is practical
especially in
August.

Faucet water
that drops
into the buckets
I carry
to the young
willow trees
whose leaves have been eaten
off by grasshoppers.
Or this jar of water
that lies next
to me
on the carseat
as I drive to my shack.
When I look down,
the seat all
around the jar
is dark,
for water doesn't intend
to give, it gives
anyway,
and the jar of water
lies there
quivering
as I drive
through a countryside
of granite quarries,
stones
soon to be shaped
into blocks for the dead,
the only
thing they have
left that is theirs.

For the dead remain inside
us, as water
remains
inside granite—
hardly at all—
for their job is to go
away,
and not come back,
even when we ask them, but
water comes to us—
it doesn't care
about us, it goes
around us, on the way
to the Minnesota River,

to the Mississippi River,
to the Gulf,
always closer
to where
it has to be,
No one lays flowers
on the grave
of water,
for it is not
here,
it is
gone.

Robert Bly

Books

Twenty Poems of Georg Trakl (translations, with James Wright), 1961
Silence in the Snowy Fields, 1962
The Light Around the Body, 1967
Knut Hamsen, *Hunger* (translation), 1967
Tomas Tranströmer: Twenty Poems (translations), 1970
The Teeth Mother Naked at Last, 1970
Neruda and Vallejo: Selected Poems (translations, with John Knoepfle and James Wright), 1971
Sleepers Joining Hands, 1973
Lorca and Jiménez: Selected Poems (translations), 1973
Leaping Poetry (essays and translations), 1975
The Morning Glory, 1975
Friends, You Drank Some Darkness: Three Swedish Poets (translations), 1976
This Body is Made of Camphor and Gopherwood, 1977
The Kabir Book: Forty-Four of the Ecstatic Poems of Kabir (translations), 1977
Vicente Aleixandre: Twenty Poems (translations, with Lewis Hyde), 1977
This Tree Will Be Here for a Thousand Years, 1979
Rainer Maria Rilke: Selected Poems (translations), 1981
The Man in the Black Coat Turns, 1981

Interviews, Criticism

Talking All Morning: Collected Interviews and Conversations, 1979; George Lensing and Ronald Moran, *Four Poets of the Emotive Imagination: Robert Bly, James Wright, Louis Simpson and William Stafford*, 1976

Robert Creeley

(b. 1926)

William Stafford

A New Englander by birth, and in his way a poetic descendent of Emily Dickinson, Robert Creeley was perhaps most formed as an artist by his experiences at Black Mountain College in North Carolina where, like Denise Levertov, he came under the influence of Charles Olson, edited the *Black Mountain Review*—one of several lively little magazines founded right after World War II that tried to change the nature and direction of American poetry—and mixed with other emerging American artists. Creeley has also lived on Mallorca, where he founded the Divers Press; in Mexico; and in Buffalo, New York, where he has taught for many years at the University of Buffalo.

Much has been made of Charles Olson's influential essay "Projective Verse," with its discussion of the "possibilities of the breath" as well as its focus on our "listenings," and it no doubt helped Creeley to his vision of the poem: a tightly orchestrated voice-print of intimate exchanges between speaker and listener; "things made of words," he likes to say. Having grown up on a farm, with a sense of all speech as saying what needs saying and no more, Creeley was ready to investigate the borders between speech and silence, an issue that has obsessed other contemporary poets, most notably the great European poet Paul Celan.

Looking for a minimal structure to explore language, as the painter Mark Rothko had explored the nature of color in his striped shapes, Creeley came to plow the same furrow again and again, planting within its narrow borders the most complicated exchanges on friendship, family, love, and death. Mixing sophisticated classical subjects (in "Damon & Pythias," for example) with nursery rhymes and rhythms, he achieves an effect at once tender and frightening: Heads seem to roll at the ends of phrases, and courses are set we hadn't counted on. In the midst of these tales, their little structures squared off in a grid of sharp breaths, a peculiar, mad-singing voice keeps breaking the myth. "They are all dead now," the child who has had to grow up too fast announces in a frightening, matter-of-fact way. We hear strains of "boom, boom, all fall down," a kind of baby talk by way of Gertrude Stein and e.e. cummings with its strange but familiar syncopations and repetitions.

In "A Gift of Great Value," gift-horse (Trojan horse?), Freud, and Maurice Sendak all come together for the windy ride from birth to death. In "The Turn," a sleight-of-hand, now-you-see-it, now-you-don't strategy is behind the oddly holidaylike visit the voiceless, faceless humans pay to a land of harsh and illusory scenery and perform a mimetic dance armed with a stalk of celery as their only prop. Both "The City" and "The Statue" function in similar ways, almost as if Creeley had wound them up and set them off, creating moving tableaux vivants. In "Time," Creeley sets his poetic dictum clearly before us, in verse: "Each moment is / of such paradoxical / definition—a / waterfall that would /

flow backward / if it could." This view of time has its own limits, can only be played back and forth: As soon as we dig down to our ancestors (with that iron shovel, in "And"), we discover them dead and must turn around ("The Turn"), come back up, start all over again. Creeley's poems are not mere make-believe; they are a form of knowledge and, within their own propositions, true: "I propose to you / a body bleached, a body / which would be dead / were it not alive" ("The Statue").

SF

Damon & Pythias

When he got into bed,
he was dead.

Oh god, god, god, he said.
She watched him take off his shoes

and kneel there
to look for the change which had fallen

out of his pocket.
Old Mr. Jones

whom nobody loves
went to market for it,

and almost found it
under a table,

but by that time was unable.
And the other day two men,

who had been known as friends,
were said to be living together again.

After Lorca

(*for M. Marti*)

The church is a business, and the rich
are the business men.
                When they pull on the bells, the
poor come piling in and when a poor man dies, he has a wooden
cross, and they rush through the ceremony.

But when a rich man dies, they
drag out the Sacrament
and a golden Cross, and go *doucement, doucement*
to the cemetery.

And the poor love it
and think it's crazy.

A Gift of Great Value

Oh that horse I see so high
when the world shrinks into its
relationships, my mother
sees as well as I.

She was born, but I bore with her.
This horse was a mighty occasion!
The intensity of its feet! The height
of its immense body!

Now then in wonder at evening, at
the last small entrance of the night,
my mother calls it, and I
call it *my father.*

With angry face, with no
rights, with impetuosity and
sterile vision—and a great
wind we ride.

And

A pretty party for people
to become engaged in, she was

twentythree, he
was a hundred and twentyseven times

all the times, over and over
and under and under she went

down stairs, thru doorways,
glass, alabaster, an iron shovel

stood waiting and
she lifted it to dig

back
and back to mother,

father and brother,
grandfather and grandmother—

They are all dead now.

The Turn

Each way the turn
twists, to be apprehended:
now she is
there, now she

is not, goes, but
did she, having gone,
went before
the eye saw

nothing. The tree
cannot walk, all its
going must
be violence. They listen

to the saw cut, the
roots scream. And in eating
even a stalk of celery
there will be pathetic screaming.

But what we want
is not what we get.
What we saw, we think
we will see again?

We will not. Moving,
we will
move, and then
stop.

The City

Not from that
could you get it,
nor can things
comprise a form

just to be made.
Again, let
each be this or
that, they, together,

are many whereas,
one by one,
each is a wooden
or metal or even

water, or vegetable,
flower, a crazy orange
sun, a windy
dirt, and here is

a place to sit
shaded by tall buildings
and a bed that
grows leaves on

all its branches
which are
boards I know
soon enough.

The Statue

I propose to you
a body bleached, a body
which would be dead
were it not alive.

We will stand it up
in the garden, which
we have taken such pains
to water. All the flowers

will grow at its feet,
and evenings it will
soften there as the darkness
comes down from such space.

Perhaps small sounds
will come from it, perhaps
the wind only, but its
mouth, could one see it,

will flutter. There will be
a day it walks just before
we come to look at it, but by then
it will have returned to its place.

Time

Moment to
moment the
body seems

to me to
be there: a
catch of

air, pattern
of space—Let's
walk today

all the way
to the beach,
let's think

of where we'll be
in two years'
time, of where

we *were*. Let
the days go.
Each moment is

of such paradoxical
definition—a
waterfall that would

flow backward
if it could. It
can? My time,

one thinks,
is drawing to
some close. This

feeling comes
and goes. No
measure ever serves

enough, enough—
so "finish it"
gets done, alone.

NINETEEN POETS BORN BETWEEN 1920 AND 1930

Notes

Damon & Pythias. According to Roman legend, Damon was a Syracusan who barely escaped suffering the death penalty as a voluntary hostage for his friend Pythias.

After Lorca. Federico Garcia Lorca (1898–1936) was a Spanish poet and playwright; *doucement* means "softly" or "sweetly."

Robert Creeley

Books

The Kind of Act of, 1953
A Form of Women, 1959
For Love: Poems 1950–1960, 1962
The Island (novel), 1963
The Gold Diggers and Other Stories, 1965
Words, 1967
Pieces, 1968
A Quick Graph: Collected Notes and Essays, 1970
A Day Book, 1972
Selected Poems, 1976
Hello: A Journal, February 29–May 3, 1976, 1978
Later, 1979

Criticism, Interviews

Martin Duberman, *Black Mountain: An Exploration in Community,* 1972; Mary Novik, *Robert Creeley: An Inventory, 1945–1970,* 1973; Donald Allen, *Contexts of Poetry: Interviews 1961–1971,* 1973

James Dickey

(b. 1923)

William Stafford

The southerner's talent for storytelling and exaggeration that is familiar to us through the fiction of writers like William Faulkner, Eudora Welty, and Flannery O' Connor has been manifested less frequently in the work of poets. James Dickey surely exemplifies one way in which the southern imagination can be turned to the possibilities of poetry. In Dickey's poems, yarns, tall tales, and grotesque characters aspire to the universal condition of myth. The effort to bring them to that pitch and status can produce poems that seem labored and pretentious; but when the combination works, the result is exciting and fresh, not least for the way in which the ordinary and extraordinary interact. In "Bread," for example, the meal that celebrates the rescue of some World War II aviators whose bomber crashed in a swamp is both a miraculous feast shot through with associations of biblical miracle (manna, pentecostal fire, loaves and fishes, the Last Supper) and at the same time a very modest affair in a mess tent, consisting of standard armed forces fare: powdered eggs, canned fruit cocktail, and Spam. Similarly, in "Hedge Life," the tiny creatures (voles, shrews, wrens, snakes) that live in the hedge remain real and ordinary to us at the same time that their home gradually expands in meaning to become a mythical kingdom.

The selection of James Dickey's work presented here totals no more than four poems because we wanted to demonstrate, through one long poem, the way in which his storytelling abilities, vivid imagination, drive to create myth, and propensity for length can combine to produce a poem as potent and distinctive as 'Falling." Dickey was a fighter pilot in World War II and Korea, and his imagination often responds best to stories that involve flight in some way. "Bread" illustrates this on a small scale, "Falling" on a large one. Starting from a news item about a stewardess who was accidentally sucked out through the emergency door of an airliner in flight, Dickey imagines himself into the experience in a way that re-creates it powerfully for his readers and achieves a memorable, expressive effect we can call mythic. As her terrible fall becomes an exhilarated skydive and striptease, a freeing of the self from ordinary restraints and the desperate allegiance to life, a Rilkean embrace of death and a fallen—or falling!—condition, the stewardess changes from an ordinary person to a kind of fertility goddess and scapegoat, a transformation made plausible and exciting by the poem's narrative drive and imaginative intensity. Especially when read aloud, this poem is both sure-fire entertainment and a distinctive literary achievement.

James Dickey's narrative talents are also evident in his novel, *Deliverance* (1970), which was a popular though not a critical success. After his military service, Dickey was for many years an advertising executive in Atlanta, Georgia, before turning full-time to writing. His role at Jimmy Carter's inaugural, and the popular appeal of his poems, especially through their narrative strength and relative accessibility, have made him one of our better-known poets. He lives in Columbia, South Carolina, where he teaches at the university. *Poems 1957–1967* brings together most of his strongest work, though there have been subsequent volumes (e.g., *The Strength of Fields* and *Puella*).

DY

Bread

Old boys, the cracked boards spread before
You, bread and spam   fruit cocktail   powder
Of eggs. I who had not risen, but just come down
From the night sky   knew always this was nothing
Like home   for under the table I was cut deep
    In the shoes

To make them like sandals no stateside store
Ever sold   and my shirtsleeves were ragged as
Though chopped off by propellers in the dark.
It was all our squadron, old boys: it was thus
I sat with you on your first morning
    On the earth,

Old boys newly risen from a B-25 sinking slowly
Into the swamps of Ceram. Patrick said
We got out   we got out on the wings
And lived there   we spread our weight
Thin as we could   arms and legs spread, we lay
    Down night and day,

We lived on the wings. When one of us got to one
Knee to spear a frog   to catch a snake
To eat, we lost another inch. O that water,
He said. O that water. Old boys, when you first
Rose, I sat with you in the mess-tent
    On solid ground,

At the unsinkable feast, and looked at the bread
Given to lizard-eaters. They set it down
And it glowed from under   your tongues
Fluttered   you reached   the scales fell
From your eyes   all of us weightless from living
    On wings so long

No one could escape   no one could sink or swim
Or fly. I looked at your yellow eyeballs
Come up   evolved   drawn out of the world's slime

Amphibious eyes   and Patrick said Bread
Is good   I sat with you in my own last war
    Poem   I closed my eyes

I ate the food I ne'er had eat.

Hedge Life

At morning we all look out
As our dwelling lightens; we have been somewhere.
With dew our porous home
Is dense, wound up like a spring,

Which is solid as motherlode
At night. Those who live in these apartments
Exist for the feeling of growth
As thick as it can get, but filled with

Concealment. When lightning
Strikes us, we are safe; there is nothing to strike, no bole
For all-fire's shattered right arm.
We are small creatures, surviving

On the one breath that grows
In our lungs in the complex green, reassured in the dawn-
silver heavy as wool. We wait
With crowded excitement

For our house to spring
Slowly out of night-wet to the sun; beneath us,
The moon hacked to pieces on the ground.
None but we are curled

Here, rising another inch,
Knowing that what held us solid in the moon is still
With us, where the outside flowers flash
In bits, creatures travel

Beyond us like rain,
The great sun floats in a fringed bag, all stones quiver
With the wind that moves us.
We trade laughters silently

Back and forth, and feel,
As we dreamed we did last night, our noses safe in our fur,
That what is happening to us in our dwelling
Is true: That on either side

As we sleep, as we wake, as we rise
Like springs, the house is winding away across the fields,
Stopped only momentarily by roads,
King-walking hill after hill.

The Flash

Something far off   buried deep and free
In the country   can always strike you dead
Center of the brain. There is never anything

It could be   but you go dazzled
Dazzled   and all the air in that
Direction swarms   waits

For that day-lightning,
For hoe blade   buckle   bifocal
To reach you. Whatever it does

Again is worth waiting for
Worth stopping the car   worth standing alone
For   and arranging the body

For light to score off you
In its own way, and send
Across the wheat   the broad silent

Blue valley, your long-awaited,
Blinding, blood-brotherly
Beyond-speech answer.

Falling

*A 29-year-old stewardess fell . . . to her
death tonight when she was swept
through an emergency door that sud-
denly sprang open . . . The body . . .
was found . . . three hours after the
accident.*

NEW YORK TIMES

The states when they black out and lie there rolling   when they turn
To something transcontinental   move by   drawing moonlight out of the great
One-sided stone hung off the starboard wingtip   some sleeper next to
An engine is groaning for coffee   and there is faintly coming in
Somewhere the vast beast-whistle of space. In the galley with its racks
Of trays   she rummages for a blanket   and moves in her slim tailored
Uniform to pin it over the cry at the top of the door. As though she blew

The door down with a silent blast from her lungs   frozen   she is black
Out finding herself   with the plane nowhere and her body taking by the throat
The undying cry of the void   falling   living   beginning to be something
That no one has ever been and lived through   screaming without enough air

Still neat   lipsticked   stockinged   girdled by regulation   her hat
Still on   her arms and legs in no world   and yet spaced also strangely
With utter placid rightness on thin air   taking her time   she holds it
In many places   and now, still thousands of feet from her death she seems
To slow   she develops interest   she turns in her maneuverable body

To watch it. She is hung high up in the overwhelming middle of things in her
Self   in low body-whistling wrapped intensely   in all her dark dance-weight
Coming down from a marvellous leap   with the delaying, dumbfounding ease
Of a dream of being drawn   like endless moonlight to the harvest soil
Of a central state of one's country   with a great gradual warmth coming
Over her   floating   finding more and more breath in what she has been using
For breath   as the levels become more human   seeing clouds placed honestly
Below her left and right   riding slowly toward them   she clasps it all
To her and can hang her hands and feet in it in peculiar ways   and
Her eyes opened wide by wind, can open her mouth as wide   wider   and suck
All the heat from the cornfields   can go down on her back with a feeling
Of stupendous pillows stacked under her   and can turn   turn as to someone
In bed   smile, understood in darkness   can go away   slant   slide
Off tumbling   into the emblem of a bird with its wings half-spread
Or whirl madly on herself   in endless gymnastics in the growing warmth
Of wheatfields rising toward the harvest moon.   There is time to live
In superhuman health   seeing mortal unreachable lights far down seeing
An ultimate highway with one late priceless car probing it   arriving
In a square town   and off her starboard arm the glitter of water catches
The moon by its one shaken side   scaled, roaming silver   My God it is good
And evil   lying in one after another of all the positions for love
Making   dancing   sleeping   and now cloud wisps at her no
Raincoat   no matter   all small towns brokenly brighter from inside
Cloud   she walks over them like rain   bursts out to behold a   Greyhound
Bus shooting light through its sides   it is the signal to go straight
Down like a glorious diver   then feet first   her skirt stripped beautifully
Up   her face in fear-scented cloths   her legs deliriously bare   then
Arms out   she slow-rolls over   steadies out   waits for something great
To take control of her   trembles near feathers   planes head-down
The quick movements of bird-necks turning her head   gold eyes the insight-
eyesight of owls blazing into the hencoops   a taste for chicken overwhelming
Her   the long-range vision of hawks enlarging all human lights of cars
Freight trains   looped bridges   enlarging the moon racing slowly
Through all the curves of a river   all the darks of the midwest blazing
From above. A rabbit in a bush turns white   the smothering chickens
Huddle   for over them there is still time for something to live
With the steaming half-idea of a long stoop   a hurtling   a fall
That is controlled   that plummets as it wills   turns gravity
Into a new condition, showing its other side like a moon   shining
New Powers   there is still time to live on a breath made of nothing
But the whole night   time for her to remember to arrange her skirt
Like a diagram of a bat   tightly it guides her   she has this flying-skin

JAMES DICKEY   179

Made of garments   and there are also those sky-divers on TV   sailing
In sunlight   smiling under their goggles   swapping batons back and forth
And He who jumped without a chute and was handed one by a diving
Buddy. She looks for her grinning companion   white teeth   nowhere
She is screaming   singing hymns   her thin human wings spread out
From her neat shoulders   the air beast-crooning to her   warbling
And she can no longer behold the huge partial form of the world   now
She is watching her country lose its evoked master shape   watching it lose
And gain   get back its houses and peoples   watching it bring up
Its local lights   single homes   lamps on barn roofs   if she fell
Into water she might live   like a diver   cleaving   perfect   plunge

Into another   heavy silver   unbreathable   slowing   saving
Element: there is water   there is time to perfect all the fine
Points of diving   feet together   toes pointed   hands shaped right
To insert her into water like a needle   to come out healthily dripping
And be handed a Coca-Cola   there they are   there are the waters
Of life   the moon packed and coiled in a reservoir   so let me begin
To plane across the night air of Kansas   opening my eyes   superhumanly
Bright   to the dammed moon   opening the natural wings of my jacket
By Don Loper   moving like a hunting owl toward the glitter of water
One cannot just fall   just tumble screaming all that time   one must use
It   she is now through with all   through all   clouds   damp   hair
Straightened   the last wisp of fog pulled apart on her face like wool revealing
New darks   new progressions of headlights along dirt roads   from chaos

And night   a gradual warming   a new-made, inevitable world of one's own
Country   a great stone of light in its waiting waters   hold   hold out
For water: who knows when what correct young woman must take up her body
And fly   and head for the moon-crazed inner eye of midwest imprisoned
Water   stored up for her years   the arms of her jacket slipping
Air up her sleeves to go   all over her? What final things can be said
Of one who starts out sheerly in her body in the high middle of night
Air   to track down water like a rabbit where it lies like life itself
Off to the right in Kansas? She goes toward   the blazing-bare lake
Her skirts neat   her hands and face warmed more and more by the air
Rising from pastures of beans   and under her   under chenille bedspreads
The farm girls are feeling the goddess in them struggle and rise brooding
On the scratch-shining posts of the bed   dreaming of female signs
Of the moon   male blood like iron   of what is really said by the moan
Of airliners passing over them at dead of midwest midnight   passing
Over brush fires   burning out in silence on little hills   and will wake
To see the woman they should be   struggling on the rooftree to become
Stars: for her the ground is closer   water is nearer   she passes
It   then banks   turns   her sleeves fluttering differently as she rolls
Out to face the east, where the sun shall come up from wheatfields   she must
Do something with water   fly to it   fall in it   drink it   rise

From it   but there is none left upon earth   the clouds have drunk it back
The plants have sucked it down   there are standing toward her only
The common fields of death   she comes back from flying to falling
Returns to a powerful cry   the silent scream with which she blew down
The coupled door of the airliner   nearly   nearly losing hold
Of what she has done   remembers   remembers the shape at the heart
Of cloud   fashionably swirling   remembers she still has time to die
Beyond explanation. Let her now take off her hat in summer air the contour
Of cornfields   and have enough time to kick off her one remaining
Shoe with the toes   of the other foot   to unhook her stockings
With calm fingers, noting how fatally easy it is to undress in midair
Near death   when the body will assume without effort any position
Except the one that will sustain it   enable it to rise   live
Not die   nine farms hover close   widen   eight of them separate, leaving
One in the middle   then the fields of that farm do the same   there is no
Way to back off   from her chosen ground   but she sheds the jacket
With its silver sad impotent wings   sheds the bat's guiding tailpiece
Of her skirt   the lightning-charged clinging of her blouse   the intimate
Inner flying-garment of her slip in which she rides like the holy ghost
Of a virgin   sheds the long windsocks of her stockings   absurd
Brassiere   then feels the girdle required by regulations squirming
Off her: no longer monobuttocked   she feels the girdle flutter   shake
In her hand   and float   upward   her clothes rising off her   ascending
Into cloud   and fights away from her head the last sharp dangerous shoe
Like a dumb bird   and now will drop in   SOON   now will drop

In like this   the greatest thing that ever came to Kansas   down   from all
Heights   all levels of American breath   layered in the lungs from the frail
Chill of space to the loam where extinction slumbers in corn tassels thickly
And breathes like rich farmers counting: will come among them after
Her last superhuman act   the last slow careful passing of her hands
All over her unharmed body   desired by every sleeper in his dream:
Boys finding for the first time their loins filled with heart's blood
Widowed farmers whose hands float under light covers to find themselves
Arisen at sunrise   the splendid position of blood unearthly drawn
Toward clouds   all feel something   pass over them as she passes
Her palms over *her* long legs   *her* small breasts   and deeply between
Her thighs   her hair shot loose from all pins   streaming in the wind
Of her body   let her come openly   trying at the last second to land
On her back   This is it   THIS
                              All those who find her impressed
In the soft loam   gone down   driven well into the image of her body
The furrows for miles flowing in upon her where she lies very deep
In her mortal outline   in the earth as it is in cloud   can tell nothing
But that she is there   inexplicable   unquestionable   and remember
That something broke in them as well   and began to live and die more
When they walked for no reason into their fields to where the whole earth

Caught her   interrupted her maiden flight   told her how to lie   she cannot
Turn   go away   cannot move   cannot slide off it and assume another
Position   no sky-diver with any grin could save her   hold her in his arms
Plummet with her   unfold above her his wedding silks   she can no longer
Mark the rain with whirling women that take the place of a dead wife
Or the goddess in Norwegian farm girls   or all the back-breaking whores
Of Wichita. All the known air above her is not giving up quite one
Breath   it is all gone   and yet not dead   not anywhere else
Quite   lying still in the field on her back   sensing the smells
Of incessant growth try to lift her   a little sight left in the corner
Of one eye   fading   seeing something wave   lies believing
That she could have made it   at the best part of her brief goddess
State   to water   gone in headfirst   come out smiling   invulnerable
Girl in a bathing-suit ad   but she is lying like a sunbather at the last
Of moonlight   half-buried in her impact on the earth   not far
From a railroad trestle   a water tank   she could see if she could
Raise her head from her modest hole   with her clothes beginning
To come down all over Kansas   into bushes   on the dewy sixth green
Of a gold course   one shoe   her girdle coming down fantastically
On a clothesline, where it belongs   her blouse on a lightning rod:

Lies in the fields   in *this* field   on her broken back as though on
A cloud she cannot drop through   while farmers sleepwalk without
Their women from houses   a walk like falling toward the far waters
Of life   in moonlight   toward the dreamed eternal meaning of their farms
Toward the flowering of the harvest in their hands   that tragic cost

Feels herself go   go toward   go outward   breathes at last fully
Not   and tries   less   once   tries   tries   AH, GOD—

James Dickey

Books

Into the Stone (in *Poets of Today*, VII), 1960
Drowning with Others, 1962
Helmets, 1964
The Suspect in Poetry (criticism), 1964
Buckdancer's Choice, 1965
Poems, 1957–1967
Babel to Byzantium (criticism), 1968
Deliverance (novel), 1970
The Eye-Beaters, Blood, Victory, Madness, Buckhead and Mercy, 1970
The Zodiac, 1976
The Strength of Fields, 1979
Puella, 1981

Criticism, Interviews

Richard Howard, *Alone With America: Essays on the Art of Poetry in the United States Since 1950*, 1969, rev. 1980; *Self-Interviews*, 1970; John Graham, interview with Dickey in *The Writer's Voice: Conversations with Contemporary Writers*, ed. George Garrett, 1973; Norman Silverstein, "James Dickey's Muscular Eschatology," in *Contemporary Poetry in America*, ed. Robert Boyers, 1974

John
Haines

(b. 1924)

William Stafford

T he son of a navy man, John Haines also served in the navy during World War II, and so it is not surprising that water imagery plays a dominant role in his work. He also spent a lot of time "on the road," exploring the Pacific Northwest, and his poems are attempts to wake us up to the calls of the natural world. When he writes of the artistic world of others, which he has been doing more and more (see especially his poems on Klee, Ryder, and David Smith; there are others), he walks the paintings and sculptures he's describing as if they were landscapes he must physically survive. In "Wolves," he puts it like this: "Their voices rang through the frozen / water of my human sleep." And in "Paul Klee" : "There are also disasters at sea, / compasses gone wrong— // only because of a gentle / submarine laughter, / no one is drowning." He is a modest traveler, reverent about what he sees on his journeys, and patiently attentive to the natural habitat of creatures and things. He spent the years 1954 to 1969 homesteading in Alaska, and in his essay "The Writer as Alaskan: Beginnings and Reflections," we meet a veritable mountain man, who stops by lost roads to watch mountain sheep for hours, or comes across a grave marker in a remote place ("history is no more than sunlight / on a weathered cross"), events that are enough to set off his imagination. In short, he is a poet who writes about one of our last frontiers, and who stands comparison with Thoreau and Frost. Like theirs, Haines's landscapes are not romanticized or glorified, though he goes his own ways with imagery and subject matter.

Haines's primary concern is with the meaning of wildness and wilderness, their relation to civilization, and by extension, how they work as a feature of art, a source of its archetypal power. A poem like "Lake in the Sky" is like a great Luminist (post–Hudson River) canvas, and marks Haines's place in the American tradition of celebrating the wilderness in literature and painting. Haines's way with these powerful themes is to speak in matter-of-fact tones that convey exact information about his subjects. Using repetitions of sounds, rhymes, and near-rhymes carefully, he pays, as he has said, "at times exasperating attention to details of experience, small clues of feeling that often seem about to disappear entirely."

Haines has always fashioned his poems with a rigor and honesty that give the reader a feeling of fresh discovery, of hearing "news"—the title of an early book is *Winter News* (1966)—but he has begun to move away from poems that speak merely of isolation and rugged individualism to poems (especially the ones about other artists and their landscapes) that release us from familiar experiences and everyday bonds and jolt us into a double consciousness: He sees real landscapes as if looking at art, and artistic landscapes as if they were real. When he invokes the industrial world, as in "Homage to David Smith," there's a savagery and terror that comes at us in the finished surfaces of mechanized materials, and we risk being "bent in a terrible heat, // five fixed and glowing figures / who are not men." These poems take us into places where we are not in control, and the message is, "Beware the images you allow to represent you, they may do so only too well...." Though Haines calls many of his poems "dreams," there is a stark simplicity about them that has shed the weight of associations and focusses sharply on the bleak landscapes in view. In "The End of the Street," the bleakness is set against the calm in knowing that "your evening is here," but there is a double meaning to this that is chilling.

There is no easy anthropomorphizing, no condescension to the savage world in these poems. For us who are "always on the point of falling asleep," it's "too late now to storm the silence / on God's forbidden mountain"; we "have to go on as the century darkens" ("The Middle Ages"), like Dürer's knight, with his double vision of the Devil and Death. But the poem is a place to meditate in.

SF

If the Owl Calls Again

at dusk
from the island in the river,
and it's not too cold,

I'll wait for the moon
to rise,
then take wing and glide
to meet him.

We will not speak,
but hooded against the frost
soar above
the alder flats, searching
with tawny eyes.

And then we'll sit
in the shadowy spruce and
pick the bones
of careless mice,

while the long moon drifts
toward Asia
and the river mutters
in its icy bed.

And when morning climbs
the limbs
we'll part without a sound,

fulfilled, floating
homeward as
the cold world awakens.

Wolves

Last night I heard wolves howling,
their voices coming from afar
over the wind-polished ice—so much
brave solitude in that sound.

They are death's snowbound sailors:
they know only a continual
drifting between moonlit islands,
their tongues licking the stars.

But they sing as good seamen should,
and tomorrow the sun will find them,
yawning and blinking
the snow from their eyelashes.

Their voices rang through the frozen
water of my human sleep,
blown by the night wind
with the moon for an icy sail.

To Vera Thompson

(*Buried in the Old Military Cemetery at Eagle, Alaska*)

Woman whose face
is a blurred map of roots,
I might be buried here
and you dreaming in the warmth
of this late northern summer.

Say I was the last
soldier on the Yukon,
my war fought out
with leaves and thorns.

Here is the field;
it lies thick with horsetail,
fireweed, and stubborn rose.

JOHN HAINES

The wagons and stables
followed the troopers
deep into soil and smoke.
When a summer visitor
steps over the rotting sill
the barracks floor
thumps with a hollow sound.

Life and death grow quieter
and lonelier here by the river.
Summer and winter
the town sleeps and settles,
history is no more than sunlight
on a weathered cross.

The picket fence sinks
to a row of mossy shadows,
the gate locks with a rusty pin.
Stand there now
and say that you loved me,
that I will not be forgotten
when a ghostwind
drifts through the canyon
and our years grow deep
in a snow of roses and stones.

The End of the Street

It would be at the end
of a bad winter,
the salty snow turning black,
a few sparrows cheeping
in the ruins of
a dynamited water tower.

The car is out of gas;
someone has gone to look.

Your evening is here.

The Middle Ages

Always on the point of falling asleep,
the figures of men and beasts.

Faces, deeply grained with dirt,
a soiled finger pointing inward.

Like Dürer's Knight, always haunted
by two companions:

the Devil, with a face like a matted hog,
disheveled and split;

and Death, half dog, half monkey,
a withered bishop with an hourglass.

There's a cold lizard underfoot,
the lancehead glitters in its furry collar;

but it's too late now to storm the silence
on God's forbidden mountain.

You have to go on as the century darkens,
the reins still taut in that armored fist.

Ryder

The moonlight has touched them all . . .

The dream hulk with its hollows
driven black,
the ancient helmsman, his handbones
glinting with salt and memory.

Under the sail of sleep, torn and flapping,
night's crowded whale broaches,
heaving another Jonah
to the shoal of a broken world.

Jehovah's arm outstretched
like a locust cloud at sea,

and the moon itself,
a pale horse of torment flying . . .

Paul Klee

The hot mice feeding in red,
the angry child
clutching a blue watermelon—
these are the sun and moon.

JOHN HAINES   189

The Tunisian patch,
where beneath some crooked
black sticks
a woman's face is burning.

There are also disasters at sea,
compasses gone wrong—

only because of a gentle
submarine laughter,
no one is drowning.

Men Against the Sky

Across the Oregon plateau
I saw strange man-figures
made up from rivets and girders,
harnessed with cables;

tall, electric, burning
in the strong evening light,
they marched into the sunset.

Their outstretched arms were bearing
away the life of that country . . .

A scorched silence fell over
the shadowy red buttes,
and sank forever
in a town with one long street.

They left behind the smell
of sagebrush mixed with ashes,
black bands of cattle
quietly drifting;

a dry lake filling with moonlight,
and one old windmill,
its broken arms
clattering in the darkness.

The Lake in the Sky

Once more evening on the earth
lies awash at our feet,
the light of many wrecked suns.

Look down in this furnace of water
clearing of smoke:
our people are there,
black reeds erect or bending
upon the night,
each one afloat on his shadow;
now the fisherman
burns on his rock alone.

A figure flaming in oak leaves
stands here beside us;
he tells of ripening acorns,
and dust glittering at summer's end;
of someone lost on a mountain
plunging green in the west,
that far-off splashing.

Two beaver in the lighted depths,
sleek and afire,
bound for the shore of a cloud.
Swallows like flares,
soaring alive in the dark . . .
All that is left of the sun
is a red dog lapping the shallows.

Evening games, voices of men
and women parting in the dusk,
singing out of sunken campgrounds;
the firewheel turns, the light
from the ring on your finger darkens . . .

Certain Dead

With your assistance, departed citizens,
the future became a road
lined with bonfires, coffins,
and empty houses.

JOHN HAINES

Whenever we looked at you
we saw you wrapped in old uniforms,
hauling on flags, handing out
paper poppies and boyscout medals.

Cunning and boastful,
you led our children into a field
to let the straw out of dummies,
to drill interminably
with brooms on their shoulders,
their foreheads forever
marked with your cross of ashes.

I have seen a photograph of that time,
a soldier sprawled against an embankment,
with his shirt blown open,
his young face a rotting flower.
At his feet this weathering caption:

Es war ein Traum.

It was time your dead faces let go
and went back to nature.
Like matted leaves, sour and damp,
they lie there now,
feeding your country's dwindling soil.

Homage to David Smith

We are made of angle-iron and crossbrace,
we live and we die
in the sunlight of polished steel,
in the night of painted iron.

All that surrounds us and by which
we will be judged—
these incompleted circles,
perforated diaphragms,
gnawed shields, unfinished arrows—
will be taken as signs

pointing inward to an iron self,
or else toward the scrapyard
to which we seem to be rolling—

great studded wheels grinding
over the pavement,
leaving behind us crushed glass,
pieces of flattened tin.

And riding the space-drawn carriage,
as if they were weighted
and bent in a terrible heat,

five fixed and glowing figures
who are not men.

Notes

The Middle Ages. Albrecht Dürer, German painter and engraver (1471–1528); see especially the engraving "The Knight, Death, and the Devil."
Ryder. Albert Pinkham Ryder, American painter (1847–1917).
Paul Klee. Swiss artist (1879–1940).
Homage to David Smith. David Smith, American sculptor (1906–1965).

John Haines

Books

Winter News, 1966
The Stone Harp, 1971
Cicada, 1977
Selected Poems, 1982

Essays

"At White River," in *Fifty Contemporary Poets: The Creative Process*, ed. A. Turner, 1977; *From the Beginning*, 1981

Donald
Hall

(b. 1928)

Mark Olenicki

The poems of Donald Hall show a remarkable variety of subjects
and forms, but one of the constants that links them is a concern
with the nature of time. Like many poets, past and present,
Hall is fascinated by process and change, and his poems seek out those
moments when time is transcended or understood. They might be de-

scribed as a quest for such transcendence, a quest that turns up in metaphors of travel, like the river journey in "The Long River" or the last flight in "The Old Pilot." The sense of mystery involved in our confrontations with time is expressed in images as various as the accordion in "Wedding Party," the abandoned airfield in "An Airstrip in Essex, 1960," and the strange group of associations that come together in "Swan." Whether we call it change or mortality, the question of how we can reconcile our lives with this force remains an open one, but the sculptures of Henry Moore, as characterized in "Reclining Figure," with their representation of movement in a permanent form ("Then the knee of the wave / turned to stone"), suggest art's power to engineer such truces. Moore may also interest Hall by the fact of his productive old age; Hall has always been fascinated by longevity in artists, and has interviewed and written about many elderly poets: Frost, Pound, Eliot, MacLeish. Father figures? Perhaps. But certainly successful creators over long spans, reflecting a harmonious existence in and with the temporal process.

Nature is another source of such harmony. In the poem "New Hampshire" the natural world, which includes the ruins of abandoned homesteads where "A bear sleeps in a cellar hole," exists as an accommodation of changelessness and change, and can absorb even the anomalous wrecked aircraft, an image from other Hall poems where the combat aircraft of both world wars seem to stand for death and change. The natural energy that brings raspberries—"a quarrel of vines"—and bees from the "spilled body" of the wreck seems to argue for the restorative powers of nature. The poem is prophetic of Hall's own recent move to New Hampshire, where he has settled on the farm of his grandparents and begun to write poems that investigate the timescapes in the rhythms and details of farm life. Hence the "ten thousand years" of man-sheep association witnessed in "The Black Faced Sheep," and the "generation on generation" in "Names of Horses."

Donald Hall was born and raised in Connecticut and educated at Harvard, Oxford, and Stanford. He taught for many years at the University of Michigan. His first book, *Exiles and Marriages* (1956), cultivated wit and formal elegance, primary values of the period that produced it, but in the 1960s his work began to change, reflecting the influence of American poetry's new preoccupation with surrealism and "deep image" poetry. Poems in this "middle" period sometimes experiment with the less noticed formal possibilities of syllabics, as in "The Long River," which uses a stanza with a set number of syllables to each line in the pattern 4-4-5-4-4, and "Apples," with its intricate stanza of 3-11-5-9 (or 7)-3-11. While poems like "Swan" and "An Airstrip in Essex, 1960" show Hall as a very successful practitioner of the laconic, mysterious "deep image" manner, a more expansive and discursive side of his nature, represented by "The Old Pilot" among the earlier poems included here, has characterized his recent work. From the volume *Kicking the Leaves* (1978), we have drawn three examples: "Ox Cart Man," "The Black Faced Sheep," and "Names of Horses." If these latest poems seem to lack some of the tension and concentration of earlier pieces, they rise to powerful and deeply felt statements and portraits by the intensity with which they fix themselves to their subjects and manage to be celebratory and elegiac at the same time.

Donald Hall has also been active as an anthologist, editor, critic, and writer of prose memoirs. *Remembering Poets* (1978) and *String Too Short to Be Saved* (reissued, 1979) are expertly written volumes of reflection and reminiscence.

DY

Wedding Party

The pock-marked player of the accordion
Empties and fills his squeeze box in the corner,
Kin to the tiny man who pours champagne,
Kin to the caterer. These solemn men,
Amid the sounds of silk and popping corks,
Stand like pillars. And the white bride
Moves through the crowd as a chaired relic moves.

Now all at once the pock-marked player grows
Immense and terrible beside the bride
Whose marriage withers to a rind of years
And curling photographs in a dry box;
And in the storm that hurls upon the room
Above the crowd he holds his breathing box
That only empties, fills, empties, fills.

The Long River

The musk-ox smells
in his long head
my boat coming. When
I feel him there,
intent, heavy,

the oars make wings
in the white night,
and deep woods are close
on either side
where trees darken.

I rowed past towns
in their black sleep
to come here. I rowed
by northern grass
and cold mountains.

The musk-ox moves
when the boat stops,
in hard thickets. Now
the wood is dark
with old pleasures.

An Airstrip in Essex, 1960

It is a lost road into the air.
It is a desert
among sugar beets.
The tiny wings
of the Spitfires of nineteen-forty-one
flake in the mud of the Channel.

Near the road a brick pillbox
totters under a load of grass,
where Home Guards waited
in the white fogs of the invasion winter.

Goodnight, old ruined war.

In Poland the wind rides on a jagged wall.
Smoke rises from the stones; no, it is mist.

The Old Pilot

in memory of Philip Thompson

He discovers himself on an old airfield.
He thinks he was there before,
but rain has washed out the lettering of a sign.

DONALD HALL   197

A single biplane, all struts and wires,
stands in the long grass and wildflowers.
He pulls himself into the narrow cockpit
although his muscles are stiff
and sits like an egg in a nest of canvas.
He sees that the machine gun has rusted.
The glass over the instruments
has broken, and the red arrows are gone
from his gas gauge and his altimeter.
When he looks up, his propeller is turning,
although no one was there to snap it.
He lets out the throttle. The engine catches
and the propeller spins into the wind.
He bumps over holes in the grass,
and he remembers to pull back on the stick.
He rises from the land in a high bounce
which gets higher, and suddenly he is flying again.
He feels the old fear, and rising over the fields
the old gratitude. In the distance, circling
in a beam of late sun like birds migrating,
there are the wings of a thousand biplanes.

New Hampshire

A bear sleeps in a cellar hole; pine needles
heap over a granite doorstep; a well brims
with acorns and the broken leaves of an oak
which grew where an anvil rusted in a forge.

Inside an anvil, inside a bear, inside a leaf,
a bark of rust grows on the tree of a gas pump;
EAT signs gather like leaves in the shallow
cellars of diners; a wildcat waits for deer

on the roof of a car. Blacktop buckled by frost
starts goldenrod from the highway. Fat honey bees
meander among raspberries, where a quarrel
of vines crawls into the spilled body of a plane.

Swan

December, nightfall at three-thirty.
I climb Mill Hill
past hawthorn and wild cherry,
mist in the hedgerows.
Smoke blows
from the orange edges of fire
working the wheat
stubble. "Putting
the goodness back.
into the soil."

Driving; the fog
matted around the headlights;
suddenly, a thudding
white shape in the whiteness,
running huge and frightened, lost
from its slow stream . . .

The mill drew up to power
the dark underneath it
through tunnels like the roots of a beech
that spread to the poles
and down to the center of the earth.

Fire breaks out in the fields.
The wheel of the mill does not turn.

Fog stacked in the hedges.

The windmill
flies, clattering its huge wings, to the swamp.
I make out cliffs of the Church,
houses drifting like glaciers.

I envy the man hedging and ditching,
trimming the hawthorn, burning branches
while wasps circle in the smoke of their nest,
clearing a mile of lane, patches of soot
like closed holes to a cave of fire,

DONALD HALL   199

the man in his cottage
who smokes his pipe in the winter, in summer
digging his garden in ten o'clock light,
the man grafted entirely to rain and air,
stained dark
by years of hedging and ditching.

5

The close-packed surface of the roots
of a root-bound plant
when I break the pot away,
the edges white
and sleek as a swan . . .

Apples

They have gone
into the green hill, by doors without hinges,
or lifting city
manhole covers to tunnels
lined with grass,
their skin soft as grapes, their faces like apples.

The peacock
feather, its round eye, sees dancers underground.
The curved spot on this
apple is a fat camel, is a
fly's shadow,
is the cry of a marigold. Looking hard,

I enter:
I am caught in the web of a gray apple,
I struggle inside
an immense apple of blowing sand,
I blossom
quietly from a window-box of apples.

For one man
there are seven beautiful ladies with buns
and happy faces
in yellow dresses with green sashes
to bring him
whiskey. The rungs of a ladder tell stories

to his friend.
Their voices like apples brighten in the wind.

Now they are dancing
with fiddles and ladies and trumpets
in the round
hill of the peacock, in the resounding hill.

"Reclining Figure"

from Henry Moore's sculpture

Then the knee of the wave
turned to stone.

By the cliff of her flank
I anchored,

in the darkness of harbors
laid-by.

Ox Cart Man

In October of the year,
he counts potatoes dug from the brown field,
counting the seed, counting
the cellar's portion out,
and bags the rest on the cart's floor.

He packs wool sheared in April, honey
in combs, linen, leather
tanned from deerhide,
and vinegar in a barrel
hooped by hand at the forge's fire.

He walks by ox's head, ten days
to Portsmouth Market, and sells potatoes,
and the bag that carried potatoes,
flaxseed, birch brooms, maple sugar, goose
feathers, yarn.

When the cart is empty he sells the cart.
When the cart is sold he sells the ox,
harness and yoke, and walks
home, his pockets heavy
with the year's coin for salt and taxes,

DONALD HALL

and at home by fire's light in November cold
stitches new harness
for next year's ox in the barn,
and carves the yoke, and saws planks
building the cart again.

The Black Faced Sheep

Ruminant pillows! Gregarious soft boulders!

If one of you found a gap in a stone wall,
the rest of you—rams, ewes, bucks, wethers, lambs;
mothers and daughters, old grandfather-father,
cousins and aunts, small bleating sons—
followed onward, stupid
as sheep, wherever
your leader's sheep-brain wandered to.

My grandfather spent all day searching the valley
and edges of Ragged Mountain,
calling "Ke-*day!*" as if he brought you salt,
"Ke-*day!* Ke-*day!*"

✳   ✳   ✳

When a bobcat gutted a lamb at the Keneston place
in the spring of eighteen-thirteen
a hundred and fifty frightened black faced sheep
lay in a stupor and died.

✳   ✳   ✳

When the shirt wore out, and darns in the woolen
shirt needed darning,
a woman in a white collar
cut the shirt into strips and braided it,
as she braided her hair every morning.

In a hundred years
the knees of her great-granddaughter
crawled on a rug made from the wool of sheep
whose bones were mud,
like the bones of the woman, who stares
from an oval in the parlor.

NINETEEN POETS BORN BETWEEN 1920 AND 1930

*　*　*

I forked the brambly hay down to you
in nineteen-fifty. I delved my hands deep
in the winter grass of your hair.

When the shearer cut to your nakedness in April
and you dropped black eyes in shame,
hiding in barnyard corners, unable to hide,
I brought grain to raise your spirits,
and ten thousand years
wound us through pasture and hayfield together,
threads of us woven
together, three hundred generations
from Africa's hills to New Hampshire's.

*　*　*

You were not shrewd like the pig.
You were not strong like the horse.
You were not brave like the rooster.

Yet none of the others looked like a lump of granite
that grew hair,
and none of the others
carried white fleece as soft as dandelion seed
around a black face,
and none of them sang such a flat and sociable song.

*　*　*

In November a bearded man, wearing a lambskin apron,
slaughtered an old sheep for mutton
and hung the carcass in north shade
and cut from the frozen sides all winter, to stew in a pot
on the fire that never went out.

*　*　*

Now the black faced sheep have wandered and will not return,
though I search the valleys
and call "Ke-*day*" as if I brought them salt.

Now the railroad draws
a line of rust through the valley. Birch, pine, and maple
lean from cellarholes
and cover the dead pastures of Ragged Mountain
except where machines make snow
and cables pull money up hill, to slide back down.

DONALD HALL

∗   ∗   ∗

At South Danbury Church twelve of us sit—
cousins and aunts, sons—

where the great-grandfathers of the forty-acre farms
filled every pew.
I look out the window at summer places,
at Boston lawyers' houses
with swimming pools cunningly added to cowsheds,
and we read an old poem aloud, about Israel's sheep
—and I remember faces and wandering hearts,
dear lumps of wool—and we read

that the rich farmer, though he names his farm for himself,
takes nothing into his grave;
that even if people praise us, because we are successful,
we will go under the ground
to meet our ancestors collected there in the darkness;
that we are all of us sheep, and death is our shepherd,
and we die as the animals die.

Names of Horses

All winter your brute shoulders strained against collars, padding
and steerhide over the ash hames, to haul
sledges of cordwood for drying through spring and summer,
for the Glenwood stove next winter, and for the simmering range.

In April you pulled cartloads of manure to spread on the fields,
dark manure of Holsteins, and knobs of your own clustered with oats.
All summer you mowed the grass in meadow and hayfield, the mowing machine
clacketing beside you, while the sun walked high in the morning;
and after noon's heat, you pulled a clawed rake through the same acres,
gathering stacks, and dragged the wagon from stack to stack,
and the built hayrack back, uphill to the chaffy barn,
three loads of hay a day from standing grass in the morning.

Sundays you trotted the two miles to church with the light load
of a leather quartertop buggy, and grazed in the sound of hymns.
Generation on generation, your neck rubbed the windowsill
of the stall, smoothing the wood as the sea smooths glass.

When you were old and lame, when your shoulders hurt bending to graze
one October the man, who fed you and kept you, and harnessed you every
    morning,
led you through corn stubble to sandy ground above Eagle Pond,
and dug a hole beside you where you stood shuddering in your skin,

and lay the shotgun's muzzle in the boneless hollow behind your ear,
and fired the slug into your brain, and felled you into your grave,
shoveling sand to cover you, setting goldenrod upright above you,
where by next summer a dent in the ground made your monument.

For a hundred and fifty years, in the pasture of dead horses,
roots of pine trees pushed through the pale curves of your ribs,
yellow blossoms flourished above you in autumn, and in winter
frost heaved your bones in the ground—old toilers, soil makers:

O Roger, Mackerel, Riley, Ned, Nellie, Chester, Lady Ghost.

Donald Hall

Books

Exiles & Marriages, 1955
The Dark Houses, 1958
String Too Short to Be Saved: Childhood Reminiscences (prose), 1961, 1979
A Roof of Tiger Lilies, 1964
Henry Moore (biography), 1966
The Alligator Bride: Poems New and Selected, 1969
The Yellow Room, 1971
Writing Well (textbook), 1973
The Town of Hill, 1975
Dock Ellis in the Country of Baseball (with Dock Ellis; biography), 1976
Goatfoot Milktongue Twinbird: Interviews, Essays, and Notes on Poetry, 1970–1976, 1978
Remembering Poets: Reminiscences and Opinions (essays), 1978
Kicking the Leaves, 1978
Oxford Book of American Literary Anecdotes, 1981

Criticism, Interviews

Robert Bly, "Some Notes on Donald Hall," *FIELD*, 2 (Spring 1970); Scott
Chisholm, "An Interview with Donald Hall," *Tennessee Poetry Journal* 2 (Winter
1971); Ralph J. Mills, Jr., "Donald Hall's Poetry," *Iowa Review* 2 (Winter 1971)

Richard
Hugo

(b. 1923)

William Stafford

R ichard Hugo grew up in Seattle and was educated at the University of Washington. He served as a bombardier during World War II and worked for Boeing for nearly thirteen years. Like Jarrell and Dickey, he draws heavily on his wartime experiences, but he writes more with the fractured vision of Vonnegut, say, in *Slaugh-*

terhouse Five. Hugo is an inveterate traveler, who must keep going back to places that are important, or discover new ones as if they'd been his real home all along. Part of his appeal lies in his ability to take us, physically and spiritually, to locations our heritage forces us to seek (a book published in 1975, *What Thou Lovest Well, Remains American*, points especially in this direction). Most of his poems explore the twin "rights" of freedom of self and freedom to travel that Americans prize so highly, concerns that link Hugo to other poets in this collection, most notably Stevens, Dickey, Stafford, and Kaufman.

Since 1964, Hugo has been teaching at the University of Montana, and, more recently, serving as editor of the Yale Series of Younger Poets. His teaching and editing (particularly his interest in discovering new poets and fostering their careers) go hand in hand with his writing, and he has been one of our most eloquent, incisive essayists on the problems of writing and teaching writing. Since he has a deep sense of what he himself is up to, we do well to begin by looking at some statements he has made in lectures and essays published under the title *The Triggering Town* (1979): "I came from a town with a bad reputation, too," he says. At the heart of the issues he raises in these essays is this parabolic view:

> The poem is always in your hometown, but you have a better chance of finding it in another.... At home, not only do you know that ... the grocer is a newcomer who took over after the former grocer committed suicide, you have complicated emotional responses that defy sorting out. With the strange town, you can assume all knowns are stable, and you owe the details nothing emotionally.... However, not just any town will do. Though you've never seen it before, it must be a town you've lived in all your life.

In his typically tough-minded but soft-spoken way, Hugo goes on to isolate the fine distinction that he takes to be the central issue for contemporary poetry:

> With the private poet, and most good poets of the last century or so have been private poets, the words, at least certain key words, mean something to the poet they don't mean to the reader. A sensitive reader perceives this relation of poet to word and in a way that relation—the strange way the poet emotionally possesses his vocabulary—is one of the mysteries and preservative forces of the art.

Hugo's towns, or places, range the whole world, from Montana taverns to cemeteries on the Isle of Skye, off Scotland. They are stops on his private underground railway, where he pokes around in abandoned houses, quarries, and churches, or walks down old roads till they jump back to life and his "adequate self" emerges. Trying his hand at fiction for a spell, he said, "I settled back into poems for good...seemed to use poems to create some adequate self...I could be tough in a poem...." If Hugo seems slightly obsessed by the quality of "toughness" (the word occurs often in his essays), it is not Hemingway we should think of. Hugo is talking about striking a balance between selves—which all good poems must manage—of finding the "right" relationship between things, as the title of a recent collection suggests: *The Right Madness on Skye* (1980).

As he himself has warned, achieving this balance is difficult business; poems must "move and not contain more information than is necessary." At times, his poems try to cover too much ground; he crowds things together, and seems to seek the most difficult ways for saying things, with a raspy energy that leaves the reader gasping. Haunted by his material, he plunges straight on, from fact to association to next fact to more associations to pure discourse and back to fact. Which is not to suggest that he loses control of his material; indeed, though he is celebrated for his informal ways with words, he is in fact a master at iambic pentameter and syllabics, as a reading aloud of the poems in this selection will amply demonstrate. He also has full command of more formal structures, as witness his use of the demanding form of the villanelle to treat a difficult and heartbreaking subject, "The Freaks at Spurgin Road Field." But even here, as in the denser poems, he works in modes curiously close to the way the mind works when we are tired, at once exhilarated and exhausted. A second major theme running through the poems is a fascination with the phenomenon of consciousness. Hugo comments on this process in a poem not included here, "Limited Access": "A novel fakes a start in every bar, / gives way to gin and talk. The talk gives way / to memories of elk, and elk were never here". Having stumbled onto those elk, the poet has a new responsibility to learn from the slip: "That day haunted me, came back unexpected," Hugo writes of how an experience he was tracking in Italy "came back unwelcome to remind me how we learn little from our positive experiences, how we slip back too easily into this ungenerous world of denial and possession."

We have tried to represent almost all the major books Hugo has published over the past twenty years, since *A Run of Jacks* (1961) appeared. However different his structures and moods seem from collection to collection, moving as he does from simple forms in the early poems to what would become a whole book of *31 Dreams and 13 Letters*, his approach is always of a man leaning your way, saying just for the two of you, as in "Open Country": "And you come back here / where land has ways of going on / and the shadow of a cloud / crawls like a freighter, no port in mind, / no captain, and the charts dead wrong." To test such stories by historical or personal experience would seem to be as mistaken as to try to prove the existence of "The Lady in Kicking Horse Reservoir" by dragging the water. There are no maps, no charts, save for what the mind's eye, the imagination, can see and tell of.

SF

1614 Boren

Room on room, we poke debris for fun,
chips of dolls, the union picnic flag,
a valentine with a plump girl in a swing
who never could grow body hair or old
in all that lace (her flesh the color
of a salmon egg), a black-edged scroll
regretting death: "whereas—Great Architect—
has seen it fit—the lesser aerie here—
great aerie in the sky—deep sympathy."
Someone could have hated this so much . . .
he owns a million acres in Peru.

What does the picture mean, hung where it is
in the best room? Peace, perhaps. The calm road
leading to the house half hid by poplars,
willows and the corny vines bad sketches used
around that time, the white canal in front
with two innocuous boats en route,
the sea suggested just beyond the bar,
the world of harm behind the dormant hill.

Why could room 5 cook and 7 not?
These dirty rooms were dirty even then,
the toilets ancient when installed,
and light was always weak and flat
like now, or stark from a bare bulb.
And the boarders when they spoke of this
used "place" and "house," the one with photos
of Alaska on his wall said "edifice."
This home could be a joke on the horizon—
bad proportions and the color of disease.

But the picture, where? The Netherlands
perhaps. There are Netherland canals.
But are they bleached by sky, or scorched
pale gray by an invader's guns?
It can't exist. It's just a sketcher's whim.
The world has poison and the world has sperm
and water looks like water, not like milk
or a cotton highway. There's a chance
a man who sweated years in a stale room,
probably one upstairs, left the picture here
on purpose, and when he moved believed
that was the place he was really moving from.

The Church on Comiaken Hill

The lines are keen against today's bad sky
about to rain. We're white and understand
why Indians sold butter for the funds
to build this church. Four hens and a rooster
huddle on the porch. We are dark
and know why no one climbed to pray. The priest
who did his best to imitate a bell
watched the river, full of spirits, coil
below the hill, relentless for the bay.

A church abandoned to the wind is portent.
In high wind, ruins make harsh music.
The priest is tending bar. His dreams have paid
outrageous fees for stone and mortar.
His eyes are empty as a chapel
roofless in a storm. Greek temples seem
the same as forty centuries ago.
If we used one corner for a urinal,
he wouldn't swear we hadn't worshipped here.

The chickens cringe. Rain sprays chaos where
the altar and the stained glass would have gone
had Indians not eaten tribal cows
one hungry fall. Despite the chant,
salmon hadn't come. The first mass
and a phone line cursed the river.
If rain had rhythm, it would not be Latin.

Children do not wave as we drive out.
Like these graves ours may go unmarked.
Can we be satisfied when dead
with daffodils for stones? These Indians—
whatever they once loved or used for God—
the hill—the river—the bay burned by the moon—
they knew that when you die you lose your name.

Napoli Again

Long before I hear it, Naples bright
with buildings trumpets from the hill.
A tugboat toots "*paisan*" and I am back.
That dock I sailed from eighteen years ago.
This bay had a fleet of half-sunk ships.
Where those dapper men are drinking wine,
a soldier beat an urchin with a belt.
Fountains didn't work. I remember stink.
Streets and buildings all seemed brown.

Romans hate such recent ruins,
bombed-out houses you do not repair.
Better pillars one must work to date.
Forget the innocent cut down,
cats gone crazy from the bombs
waiting down those alleys for delicious eyes.
Here, the glass replaced in *galleria* roofs,
cappuccino too high priced, it's hard
to go back years and feed the whores for free.

I'll never think of virgin angels here.
Did I walk this street before,
protesting: I am kind. You switch the menu,
gyp me on the bill. Remember me? My wings?
The silver target and the silver bomb?
Take the extra coin. I only came
to see you living and the fountains run.

The Lady in Kicking Horse Reservoir

Not my hands but green across you now.
Green tons hold you down, and ten bass curve
teasing in your hair. Summer slime
will pile deep on your breast. Four months of ice
will keep you firm. I hope each spring
to find you tangled in those pads
pulled not quite loose by the spillway pour,
stars in dead reflection off your teeth.

Lie there lily still. The spillway's closed.
Two feet down most lakes are common gray.
This lake is dark from the black blue Mission range
climbing sky like music dying Indians once wailed.
On ocean beaches, mystery fish
are offered to the moon. Your jaws go blue.
Your hands start waving every wind.
Wave to the ocean where we crushed a mile of foam.

We still love there in thundering foam
and love. Whales fall in love with gulls
and tide reclaims the Dolly skeletons
gone with a blast of aching horns to China.
Landlocked in Montana here·
the end is limited by light, the final note
will trail off at the farthest point we see,
already faded, lover, where you bloat.

All girls should be nicer. Arrows rain
above us in the Indian wind. My future
should be full of windy gems, my past
will stop this roaring in my dreams.
Sorry. Sorry. Sorry. But the arrows sing:
no way to float her up. The dead sink
from dead weight. The Mission range
turns this water black late afternoons.

One boy slapped the other. Hard.
The slapped boy talked until his dignity
dissolved, screamed a single 'stop'
and went down sobbing in the company pond.
I swam for him all night. My only suit
got wet and factory hands went home.
No one cared the coward disappeared.
Morning then: cold music I had never heard.

NINETEEN POETS BORN BETWEEN 1920 AND 1930

Loners like work best on second shift.
No one liked our product and the factory closed.
Off south, the bison multiply so fast
a slaughter's mandatory every spring
and every spring the creeks get fat
and Kicking Horse fills up. My hope is vague.
The far blur of your bones in May
may be nourished by the snow.

The spillway's open and you spill out
into weather, lover down the bright canal
and mother, irrigating crops
dead Indians forgot to plant.
I'm sailing west with arrows to dissolving foam
where waves strand naked Dollys.
Their eyes are white as oriental mountains
and their tongues are teasing oil from whales.

A Map of Montana in Italy

On this map white. A state thick as a fist
or blunt instrument. Long roads weave and cross
red veins full of rage. Big Canada, map maker's
pink, squats on our backs, planning bad winters
for years, and Glacier Park's green with my envy
of Grizzly Bears. On the right, antelope sail
between strands of barbed wire and never
get hurt, west, I think, of Plevna, say near
Sumatra, or more west, say Shawmut,
anyway, on the right, east on the plains.
The two biggest towns are dull deposits
of men getting along, making money, driving
to church every Sunday, censoring movies and books.
The two most interesting towns, Helena, Butte,
have the good sense to fail. There's too much
schoolboy in bars—I'm tougher than you—
and too much talk about money.
Jails and police are how you dream Poland—
odd charges, bad food and forms you must fill
stating your religion. In Poland say none.
With so few Negroes and Jews we've been reduced
to hating each other, dumping our crud
in our rivers, mistreating the Indians.

Each year, 4000 move, most to the west
where ocean currents keep winter in check.
This map is white, meaning winter, ice
where you are, helping children who may be
already frozen. It's white here too
but back of me, up in the mountains where
the most ferocious animals
are obsequious wolves. No one fights
in the bars filled with pastry. There's no
prison for miles. But last night the Italians
cheered the violence in one of our westerns.

Drums in Scotland

Trumpets. A valley opens and beyond
the valley, closed and open sea. This land
is tough north music. Green cannot hide
the rock it hides and if horizon softens
into roll, it is the terrible drums
you dream are rolling. It is a curved sword
carving gray. It is counter roll
to rolling sky. And you were never wanted.

Rain. Small windows muting light until
the living room was dull, a hunger
that would go on hunger for the girl.
No warmth in eyes, arms, anything
but words. No warmth in words. The cat
kept staring and the woman in the kitchen
banged about. What good words were you saying
that the small girl listened? You walked
two miles to visit every Sunday and she
always said come in. No invitation
needed in the country. You just went and lied.

That's a long sky there from Scotland.
Same gray. Same relentless drive
of sky and music. It is your dream,
that terrible rolling drum. You were never
wanted and she always said come in.

The Freaks at Spurgin Road Field

The dim boy claps because the others clap.
The polite word, handicapped, is muttered in the stands.
Isn't it wrong, the way the mind moves back.

One whole day I sit, contrite, dirt, L.A.
Union Station, 46, sweating through last night.
The dim boy claps because the others clap.

Score, 5 to 3. Pitcher fading badly in the heat.
Isn't it wrong to be or not be spastic?
Isn't it wrong, the way the mind moves back.

I'm laughing at a neighbor girl beaten to scream
by a savage father and I'm ashamed to look.
The dim boy claps because the others clap.

The score is always close, the rally always short.
I've left more wreckage than a quake.
Isn't it wrong, the way the mind moves back.

The afflicted never cheer in unison.
Isn't it wrong, the way the mind moves back
to stammering pastures where the picnic should have worked.
The dim boy claps because the others clap.

In Your Bad Dream

Morning at nine, seven ultra-masculine men
explain the bars of your cage are silver
in honor of our emperor. They finger the bars
and hum. Two animals, too far to name,
are fighting. One, you are certain, is destined
to win, the yellow one, the one who from here
seems shaped like a man. Your breakfast
is snake but the guard insists eel. You say hell
I've done nothing. Surely that's not a crime.
You say it and say it. When men leave, their hum
hangs thick in the air as scorn. Your car's
locked in reverse and running. The ignition
is frozen, accelerator stuck, brake shot.
You go faster and faster back. You wait for the crash.
On a bleak beach you find a piano the tide
has stranded. You hit it with a hatchet.

You crack it. You hit it again and music
rolls dissonant over the sand. You hit it
and hit it driving the weird music from it.
A dolphin is romping. He doesn't approve.
On a clean street you join the parade. Women
line the streets and applaud, but only the band.
You ask to borrow a horn and join in.
The bandmaster says we know you can't play.
You are embarrassed. You pound your chest
and yell meat. The women weave into the dark
that is forming, each to her home. You know
they don't hear your sobbing crawling the street
of this medieval town. You promise money
if they'll fire the king. You scream a last promise—
Anything. Anything. Ridicule my arm.

Open Country

It is much like ocean the way it opens
and rolls. Cows dot the slow climb of a field
like salmon trawls dot swells, and here or there
ducks climb on no definite heading.
Like water it is open to suggestion,
electric heron, and every moon
tricky currents of grass.

                    Let me guess;
when you repair the damaged brain
of a beaten child or bring to a patient
news that will never improve, you need
a window not a wall to turn to.
And you come back here
where land has ways of going on
and the shadow of a cloud
crawls like a freighter, no port in mind,
no captain, and the charts dead wrong.

Notes

1614 Boren. The street address of an abandoned roominghouse.
Napoli Again. "Napoli" is Naples, Italy. "Galleria" are arched or covered pas-
sageways, usually with shops on either side. "Cappucino" is a special blend of

Italian coffee, served with whipped cream. "Coin" refers to the coin that one throws into the fountain for good luck.

The Lady in Kicking Horse Reservoir. "Dollys" are small locomotives, especially used in quarries or construction sites.

Richard Hugo

Books

A Run of Jacks, 1961
Death of the Kapowsin Tavern, 1965
Good Luck in Cracked Italian, 1969
The Lady in Kicking Horse Reservoir, 1973
What Thou Lovest Well, Remains American, 1975
31 Letters and 13 Dreams, 1977
Selected Poems, 1979
White Center, 1980
The Right Madness on Skye, 1980
Death and the Good Life (mystery novel), 1981

Essays, Criticism

The Triggering Town (lectures and essays), 1979; F. Garber, "Large Man in the Mountains: The Recent Work of Richard Hugo," *Western American Literature* 10 (November 1975)

Donald Justice

(b. 1925)

Christian Haller

Donald Justice is celebrated as a teacher of poets, and the control and precision of his poetry, as well as its range and experimentation, suggest how much he has had to offer his students. It is important not to neglect the teacher's work in favor of his pupils; this poet has quietly produced a body of work that puts him among the leading figures of his generation. His output has been modest because his standards are high, but the recent publication of a *Selected Poems* (1979), spanning some twenty-five years of writing, has made clear just how effective and original a poet he is.

Justice's poems have great depth as well as great concentration. Much of their power stems from his command of technique, reminding us that a deep interest in the musical and formal possibilities of language is no less likely to result in lasting work than the poems of writers with visionary, psychological, or philosophical preoccupations. A few details, cannily placed, as in the third section of "Dreams of Water," can speak volumes. A truly thoughtful rhyme, like "father" and "lather" in "Men at Forty," can make language and reality meet in a way that is nothing short of magical. Short poems that capture the essence of large subjects (e.g., "On the Death of Friends in Childhood") are unforgettable.

Like many writers of his generation, Justice learned a great deal from W. H. Auden, the English poet whose presence in America from 1939 until his death in 1973 made his great influence inevitable if not always helpful. For many poets in that period, coming of age was a matter of attempting to retain the formal values and stylistic flair acquired through emulating Auden while ridding themselves of derivative mannerisms and developing a personal vision. Among the poems selected here, "Dreams of Water" shows the influence of Auden most clearly (compare Auden's "Three Dreams"), but it is an uncharacteristic side of Auden—more suggestive, less discursive—and Justice has naturalized it splendidly for his own purposes. Indeed, the two-stress line of that poem, also found here in "Bus Stop," has been so effectively exploited by Justice for its dreamy and yet jerky rhythms that it can be said to be more his than Auden's. Auden would have made "Bus Stop" a clever bit of moralizing; Justice invests it with a sense of melancholy beauty that is as haunting as a painting by Edward Hopper.

A poem by Donald Justice may offer us generalized portraiture like "Men at Forty" or fictive biographies like "A Dancer's Life." It may cross musical with painterly possibilities, as in "Sonatina in Yellow," or explore elegant variations on a theme, as in "Elsewheres" and "White Notes." Even when its subject matter is personal, it drives toward an objective treatment of it, as in "Childhood," where the raw material may be Justice's own Florida boyhood, but the aim is an artistic investigation of the "mythical childhood" explored by the earlier writers (Wordsworth, Rimbaud, Hart Crane, Alberti) to whom it is dedicated. Whatever their form and mode, Justice's poems tend to become small, dreamlike worlds in which people face death, the fear of growing old, the unknown, and the mysteries of human isolation. Since these worlds are generally melancholy in their perceptions, we may wonder why they give us so much satisfaction until we realize that they are so truly and perfectly complete as artifacts that they tell us as much about pleasure as about pain.

As a teacher for many years at the Iowa Writer's Workshop, Donald Justice has taught many of the poets included in this volume: Marvin Bell, Mark Strand, Charles Wright, Larry Levis, Laura Jensen, and David St. John. But Justice's career as a poet of craft, consistency, and rigorous attention to detail, a student of human emotions and the human imagination, makes him an example to poets beyond his own classroom.

DY

Landscape with Little Figures

There were some pines, a canal, a piece of sky.
The pines are the houses now of the very poor,
Huddled together, in a blue, ragged wind.
Children go whistling their dogs, down by the mudflats,
Once the canal. There's a red ball lost in the weeds.
It's winter, it's after supper, it's goodbye.
O goodbye to the houses, the children, the little red ball,
And the pieces of sky that will go on falling for days.

On the Death of Friends in Childhood

We shall not ever meet them bearded in heaven,
Nor sunning themselves among the bald of hell;
If anywhere, in the deserted schoolyard at twilight,
Forming a ring, perhaps, or joining hands
In games whose very names we have forgotten.
Come, memory, let us seek them there in the shadows.

Dreams of Water

1

An odd silence
Falls as we enter
The cozy ship's-bar.

The captain, smiling,
Unfolds his spyglass
And offers to show you

The obscene shapes
Of certain islands,
Low in the offing.

I sit by in silence.

2

People in raincoats
Stand looking out from
Ends of piers.

A fog gathers;
And little tugs,
Growing uncertain

Of their position,
Start to complain
With the deep and bearded

Voices of fathers.

3

The season is ending.
White verandas
Curve away.

The hotel seems empty
But once inside,
I hear a great splashing.

Behind doors
Grandfathers loll
In steaming tubs,

Huge, unblushing.

Men at Forty

Men at forty
Learn to close softly
The doors to rooms they will not be
Coming back to.

DONALD JUSTICE   221

At rest on a stair landing,
They feel it moving
Beneath them now like the deck of a ship,
Though the swell is gentle.

And deep in mirrors
They rediscover
The face of the boy as he practices tying
His father's tie there in secret

And the face of that father,
Still warm with the mystery of lather.
They are more fathers than sons themselves now.
Something is filling them, something

That is like the twilight sound
Of the crickets, immense,
Filling the woods at the foot of the slope
Behind their mortgaged houses.

Bus Stop

Lights are burning
In quiet rooms
Where lives go on
Resembling ours.

The quiet lives
That follow us—
These lives we lead
But do not own—

Stand in the rain
So quietly
When we are gone,
So quietly . . .

And the last bus
Comes letting dark
Umbrellas out—
Black flowers, black flowers.

And lives go on.
And lives go on
Like sudden lights
At street corners

Or like the lights
In quiet rooms
Left on for hours,
Burning, burning.

Elsewheres
South

The long green shutters are drawn.
Against what parades?

Closing our eyes against the sun,
We try to imagine

The darkness of an interior
Where something might still happen:

The razor lying open
On the cool marble washstand,

The drip of something—is it water?—
Upon stone floors.

North

Already it is midsummer
In the Sweden of our lives.

The peasants have joined hands,
They are circling the haystacks.

We watch from the veranda.
We sit, mufflered,

Humming the tune in snatches
Under our breath.

We tremble sometimes,
Not with emotion.

Waiting Room

Reading the signs,
We learn what to expect—

The trains late,
The machines out of order.

We learn what it is
To stare out into space.

Great farms surround us,
Squares of a checkerboard.

Taking our places, we wait,
We wait to be moved.

A Dancer's Life

The lights in the theater fail. The long racks
Of costumes abandoned by the other dancers
Trouble Celeste. The conductor asks
If she is sad because autumn is coming on,

But when autumn comes she is merely pregnant and bored.
On her way back from the holidays, a man
Who appears to have no face rattles the door
To her compartment. *How disgusting*, she thinks;

How disgusting it always must be to grow old.
Dusk falls, and a few drops of rain.
On the train window trembles the blurred
Reflection of her own transparent beauty,

And through this, beautiful ruined cities passing,
Dark forests, and people everywhere
Pacing on lighted platforms, some
Beating their children, some apparently dancing.

The costumes of the dancers sway in the chill darkness.
Now sinking into sleep is like sinking again
Into the lake of her youth. Her parents
Lean from the rail of a ferryboat waving, waving.

As the boat glides farther out across the waves.
No one, it seems, is meeting her at the station.
The city is frozen. She warms herself
In the pink and and scented twilight of a bar.

The waiter who serves her is young. She nods assent.
The conversation dies in bed. Later,
She hurries off to rehearsal. In the lobby,
Dizzy still with the weight of her own body,

She waits, surrounded by huge stills of herself
And bright posters announcing events to come.

NINETEEN POETS BORN BETWEEN 1920 AND 1930

Her life—she feels it closing about her now
Like a small theater, empty, without lights.

White Notes

1

Suddenly there was a dress,
Inhabited, in motion.

It contained a forest,
Small birds, rivers.

It contained the ivory
Of piano keys,
White notes.

Across the back of a chair
Skins of animals
Dried in the moon.

2

It happened.
Your body went out of your body.

It rose
To let the air in,
The night.

From the sheets it rose,
From the bare floor.
Floating.

Over roofs,
Smaller and smaller,
Lost.

Entangled now
In the cold arms
Of distant street lamps.

3

The city forgets where you live.
It wanders through many streets,
And the streets turn, confused,
Upon one another.

DONALD JUSTICE

Parks have deserted themselves.
All night, awnings are whipped
And cannot remember.

O forgotten umbrella . . .
Darkness saw you, air
Displaced you, words
Erased you.

4

And afterwards.
After the quenching of the street lamps,
Long after the ivory could have been brought back to life by any touch.

Afterwards, when I might have told you
The address of your future.
Long after the future.

When the umbrella had been closed forever.
Then, when not even the moon
Would have the power to bruise you any more.

Then, in another time.

Sonatina in Yellow

Du schnell vergehendes Daguerrotyp
In meinen langsamer vergehenden Händen.
RILKE

The pages of the album,
As they are turned, turn yellow; a word,
Once spoken, obsolete,
No longer what was meant. Say it.
The meanings come, or come back later,
Unobtrusive, taking their places.

Think of the past. Think of forgetting the past.
It was an exercise requiring further practice;
A difficult exercise, played through by someone else.
Overheard from another room, now,
It seems full of mistakes.
                          So the voice of your father,
Rising as from the next room still
With all the remote but true affection of the dead,
Repeats itself, insists,

Insisting you must listen, rises
In the familiar pattern of reproof
For some childish error, a nap disturbed,
Or vase, broken or overturned;
Rises and subsides. And you do listen.
Listen and forget. Practice forgetting.

Forgotten sunlight still
Blinds the eyes of faces in the album.
The faces fade, and there is only
A sort of meaning that comes back,
Or for the first time comes, but comes too late
To take the places of the faces.

                          Remember
The dead air of summer. Remember
The trees drawn up to their full height like fathers,
The underworld of shade you entered at their feet.
Enter the next room. Enter it quietly now,
Not to disturb your father sleeping there. *He stirs.*
Notice his clothes, how scrupulously clean,
Unwrinkled from the nap; his face, freckled with work,
Smoothed by a passing dream. The vase
Is not yet broken, the still young roses
Drink there from perpetual waters. *He rises, speaks* . . .

Repeat it now, no one was listening.
So your hand moves, moving across the keys.
And slowly the keys grow darker to the touch.

Childhood

J'ai heurté, savez-vous, d'incroyables Florides . . .
          RIMBAUD

TIME: the thirties
PLACE: Miami, Florida

Once more beneath my thumb the globe turns—
And doomed republics pass in a blur of colors . . .

            Winter mornings now, my grandfather,
Head bared to the mild sunshine, likes to spread
The Katzenjammers out around a white lawn chair
To catch the stray curls of citrus from his knife.

Chameleons quiver in ambush; wings
Of monarchs beat above bronze turds, feasting . . .
                              And there are pilgrim ants
Eternally bearing incommensurate crumbs
Past slippered feet.—There,
In the lily pond, my own face wrinkles
With the slow teasings of a stick.
                         The long days pass, days
Streaked with the colors of the first embarrassments . . .
And Sundays, among kin, happily ignored,
I sit nodding, somnolent with horizons:
                         Myriad tiny suns
Drown in the deep mahogany polish of the chair-arms;
Bunched cushions prickle through starched cotton . . .
                              Already
I know the pleasure of certain solitudes.
I can look up at a ceiling so theatrical
Its stars seem more aloof than the real stars;
And pre-depression putti blush in the soft glow
Of exit signs. Often I blink, re-entering
The world—or catch, surprised, in a shop window,
My ghostly image skimming across nude mannequins.
Drawbridges, careless of traffic, lean there
Against the low clouds—early evening . . .
                              All day
There is a smell of ocean longing landward.
And, high on his frail ladder, my father
Stands hammering great storm shutters down
Across the windows of the tall hotels,
Swaying. Around downed wires, across broken fronds,
Our Essex steers, bargelike and slow . . .
                         Westward now,
The smoky rose of oblivion blooms, hangs;
And on my knee a small red sun-glow, setting.
For a long time I feel, coming and going in waves,
The stupid wish to cry. I dream . . .
                              And there are
Colognes that mingle on the barber's hands
Swathing me in his striped cloth Saturdays, downtown.
Billy, the midget haberdasher, stands grinning
Under the winking neon goat, his sign—
And Flagler's sidewalks fill. Slowly
The wooden escalator rattles upward
Towards the twin fountains of a mezzanine
Where boys, secretly brave, prepare to taste
The otherness trickling there, forbidden . . .
And then the warm cashews in cool arcades!

O counters of spectacles!—where the bored child first
Scans new perspectives squinting through strange lenses;
And the mirrors, tilting, offer back toy sails
Stiffening breezeless towards green shores of baize . . .

How thin the grass looks of the new yards—
And everywhere
The fine sand burning into the bare heels
With which I learn to crush, going home,
The giant sandspurs of the vacant lots.
Iridescences of mosquito hawks
Glimmer above brief puddles filled with skies,
Tropical and changeless. And sometimes,
Where the city halts, the cracked sidewalks
Lead to a coral archway still spanning
The entrance to some wilderness of palmetto—

Forlorn suburbs, but with golden names!

—Dedicated to the poets of a mythical childhood—
Wordsworth, Rimbaud, Hart Crane, and Alberti

Notes

A Dancer's Life. Justice notes, "Most of the details . . . were remembered, perhaps wrongly, from early Bergman movies, scripts, and criticism."

Sonatina in Yellow. The epigraph, from Rilke's poem on a youthful portrait of his father as a cadet, translates, "You quickly fading daguerreotype / In my more slowly fading hands."

Donald Justice

Books

The Summer Anniversaries, 1960
Contemporary French Poetry (edited, with Alexander Aspel), 1965
Night Light, 1967
Departures, 1973
Selected Poems, 1979

Criticism

Richard Howard, *Alone With America: Essays on the Art of Poetry in the United States Since 1950*, 1969, rev. 1980; Greg Simon, "On Donald Justice," *American Poetry Review* 2 (1976)

Shirley
Kaufman

(b. 1923)

© Karen Benzian

F*rom One Life to Another*, the latest collection by Shirley Kaufman, tracks the break-up of a long marriage and the new life she has made for herself in Jerusalem. The daughter of Eastern European immigrants, she grew up in Seattle and lived most of her life in San

Francisco before settling in Israel in 1973. She has always possessed, she says, a "west coast sensibility," and like Jeffers, Snyder, and Duncan, she seeks strong visual experiences as beginnings for poems; eschews the narrative stance in favor of what she calls "related fragments"; is partial to open, less organized structures that "let incoherence spill over . . . so I can feel my way through a poem as it occurs, instead of adding it up afterward." This resolve has led her to be patient, to work for weeks at a time only to put poems aside for a fresh look still later, and results finally in long, sustained landscapes that are about "different ways of looking at the same central theme." So it is particularly apt that our selection focuses on "Looking at Henry Moore's Elephant Skull Etchings in Jerusalem During the War," a poem that demonstrates her talent for making the long poem work. She lived through the October war, with daily shopping trips through markets that might be bombed ("Well, the man I always bought oranges from is dead"); and learned to control the difficult, sometimes excruciating subject matter by having learned from Olson and Williams about the rhythmic principles implicit in her own speech, her own breath. The result is utterances that pull the material apart into clear little shapes, *haiku*-like in their precision, true to the many irrational and unconnected feelings riding her:

> Simpson calls it impulse. The pulse inside. It's something physical. And yet. And yet. Who stops to think how he breathes? Or where the next breath's coming from? After the first gasp, entering the light, we go on breathing. And yet. There's more to life than breathing.
>
> (from an essay on "The Line")

Breathing marks the moment of birth. Many of Kaufman's poems center on the stirring of life from the skin of death: "It's my face / staring out of her picture / wrinkled and old / as a newborn infant // pushed there / ahead of myself" ("Nechama," a poem about her grandmother's death). And again, "if the thin membranes and the thick / weep in the naked bone // then the whole elephant can rise up / out of its flesh" ("Looking at Henry Moore's Elephant Skull Etchings")—and the startling metamorphosis that follows, the woman giving birth to the elephant so that the loss may be redeemed, and turning into what she gives birth to: "There's an elephant inside me / crowding me out / . . . I taste the coarse hairs / crowding the back of my mouth" In an essay on the use of place in contemporary poetry, Kaufman says, "Our bodies, or more precisely, our inner spaces, are the center of our experience. . . . Women are busy giving birth to themselves." The way Lowell, or Hugo, or James Wright return to places to repossess them, Kaufman returns to *birth* places: "There is a way to enter / if you remember / where you came from"—the soft internal off-rhyme ("enter/remember") serving to rock us back to beginnings.

For Kaufman, though she often returns to the United States, beginnings have to do with questions like "What does it mean to be Jewish, to return to the Jewish homeland, to be an Israeli?" To deepen her ties to art in general, and the Israeli experience in particular, she has been learning Hebrew and translating Israeli poets like Kovner and Gilboa, learning with them to return to the Bible more steadfastly than she had before for stories about roots, exile, place and displacement: "So I sit at my desk in Jerusalem, looking back at Seattle and San Francisco, looking back at the women in the Bible who keep getting into my poems, looking down through excavated layers...at the ruins..., the violent history of this country where I now live."

SF

His wife

But it was right that she
looked back. Not to be
curious, some lumpy
reaching of the mind
that turns all shapes to pillars.
But to be only who she was
apart from them, the place
exploding, and herself
defined. Seeing them melt
to slag heaps and the flames
slide into their mouths.
Testing her own lips then,
the coolness, till
she could taste the salt.

Nechama

They changed her name
to Nellie. All the girls.
To be American.
And cut her hair.

She couldn't give up
what she thought she lost.

Streets like ceiling cracks
she looked up watching
where the same boy bicycled always
to the gate of her Russian house.
She saw him tremble
in the steam over her tea
after the samovar was gone.
She was Anna Karenina
married to somebody else.

✳ ✳ ✳

Oh she was beautiful. She could turn
into an egret with copper hair.
She could turn into a fig tree.
She could turn into a Siberian wolfhound.
She could turn into an opal
turning green. She could drown us
in the lake of her soft skin.

Rhythm of chopping garlic
motion as language in her wrists
warming her hands
rubbing it
over the leg of lamb.

✳ ✳ ✳

Leaving the kitchen she would cry
over pictures telling us
nothing new

till the small light by her bed
kept getting lost under the blanket
where she crawled looking
for something she forgot
or money in her old house
under the hankies looking
for spare parts.

She swallowed what we brought
because we said to.

✳ ✳ ✳

The rabbi knows
the 23rd psalm backwards
and he pretends he came for a wedding.

SHIRLEY KAUFMAN   233

Do me a favor she still pleads
under the roses
begging for proof of faithfulness
or love. If I say yes
she might ask anything like
stay with me
or take me home.

＊　＊　＊

It's my face staring
out of her picture
wrinkled and old
as a newborn infant

pushed there
ahead of myself

or memorizing lines
over and over in a soundproof room
until the smile is stuck there
and the lips stay frozen
like a hole in the ice
where a child fell in.

Looking at Henry Moore's Elephant Skull Etchings in Jerusalem During the War

It wants to be somewhere else
remembering anything somewhere
private where it can lie down

floating in the warm belly
of the Dead Sea

so that the skull keeps
growing in the room

and the loose skin

until the whole head sees
its feet

from a great distance.

234

* * *

Heavy as earth is heavy
under its own weight

it's the same skin
wrinkled on the back of hills

grey in the early morning
on the Jericho Road.

* * *

The brain scooped out of it
lets in the light
we knew at the beginning

when our eyes were dazzled

pushed
without wanting to be pushed

out of the dark.

* * *

The mind of the elephant
has nothing to lose

* * *

I was begging you
not to go
when you closed the door

and left me
watching the skull's
round openings

the eyelids gone.

* * *

There are caverns
under our feet
with rivers running deep in them.

They hide
in the sides of cliffs
at Rosh Hanikra
where the sea breaks in.

SHIRLEY KAUFMAN

There is a way to enter
if you remember
where you came from

how to breathe under water
make love in a trap.

* * *

Step over the small bones
lightly when you feel them
tripping your feet.

* * *

Fear hangs over your shoulder
like a gun it digs in my arm

but the live head knows
that the eyes get used to darkness

fingers learn how to read
the signs they touch.

* * *

Ditches where bones stand up
and shake their fists at us

sons in the shadows
and the shadows flattened
like grass rolled over

one-eyed Cyclops
slit of a concrete bunker
we prowl through
looking for flowers.

* * *

We are going down a long slide
into the secret chamber
we bought our tickets for the ride

the passage is narrow
and we can't find ourselves
in the trick mirrors

we lie down in the fetal position
back to back
each of us in his own eye socket

NINETEEN POETS BORN BETWEEN 1920 AND 1930

marvelous holes
the mind looked out of
filling with dust.

* * *

My lips on the small
rise of forehead above your eyes

mouths of the women in Ramallah
who spit when the soldiers go by

huge head of an infant
shoved out of the birth canal

faces stretched over us like tents
wet bandages over burns

and the white skull balder
than rock under the smile.

* * *

If the smooth joining of the bone
makes arches from here to there

if the intricate structure yields
arms resting desert landscapes mother and child

if the thin membranes and the thick
weep in the naked bone

then the whole elephant can rise up
out of its flesh

as in the torso of Apollo

something is pulsing
in the vacant skull

making us change.

* * *

I don't want to stand
on our balcony with the lights out
black buildings
street lamps
and headlights turned off

and nothing
against the sky

SHIRLEY KAUFMAN

the stars get closer
but it's not the same
as what you plug in.

* * *

There's an elephant inside me
crowding me out
he sees Jerusalem
through my eyes my skin
is stretched tight
over the elephant's skin his wrinkles
begin to break through
I taste the coarse hairs
crowding the back of my mouth
I fall down gagging over my four feet
my nose turns into a tongue with nostrils

it starts to grow.

* * *

I see bodies in the morning kneel
over graves and bodies under them
the skin burned off
their bones laid out in all the cold
tunnels under the world.

There is a photograph in the next room
of a dead child
withered against its mother
between the dry beans of her breasts

there is no blood
under the shrunk skin

their skulls are already visible.

* * *

The elephants come after us
in herds now

they will roll over us
like tanks

we are too sad to move

our skulls
much smaller than theirs
begin to shine.

Déjà Vu

Whatever they wanted for their sons
will be wanted forever, success,
the right wife, they should be
good to their mothers.

One day they meet at the rock
where Isaac was cut free
at the last minute. Sarah stands
with her shoes off under the dome
showing the tourists with their Minoltas
around their necks the place
where Mohammed flew up to heaven.
Hagar is on her knees
in the women's section praying.

They bump into each other at the door,
the dark still heavy on their backs
like the future always coming after them.
Sarah wants to find out what happened
to Ishmael but is afraid to ask.
Hagar's lips make a crooked seam
over her accusations.

They know that the world is flat,
and if they move to the edge
they're sure to fall over. They know
they can only follow their own feet
the way they came.
Jet planes fly over their heads
as they walk out of each other's lives
like the last time, silent, not mentioning
the angels of god and the bright
miracles of birth and water. Not telling
that the boys are gone.

The air ticks slowly. It's August
and the heat is sick of itself
waiting all summer for rain.

Sarah is in her cool villa.
She keeps her eyes on the pot
so it won't boil over.
She brings the food to the table
where he's already seated
reading the afternoon paper.
He's always reading the paper
or listening to the news,

SHIRLEY KAUFMAN   239

the common corruptions they don't
even speak about now.
Guess who I met she says talking
across the dessert.

Hagar shops in the market.
There's a run on chickens, the grapes
are finished and the plums are soft.
She fills her bag with warm bread
fresh from the oven thinking
there's nothing to forgive,
I got what I wanted
from the old man.
The flight in the wilderness
is a morning stroll.
She buys a kilo of ripe figs. She
climbs the dusty path home.

Notes

His Wife. The reference is to Lot's wife, who was changed to a pillar of salt for
looking back during the flight from Sodom (Gen. 13: 1–12, 19).

Shirley Kaufman

Books

The Floor Keeps Turning, 1969
Gold Country, 1973
Abba Kovner, *A Canopy in the Desert* (translations), 1973
Amir Gilboa, *The Light of Lost Suns* (translations), 1979
From One Life to Another, 1979

Essays

"Here and There: The Use of Place in Contemporary Poetry," *FIELD 23* (Fall
1980).

Galway Kinnell

(b. 1927)

William Stafford

I n a poem called "Spindrift" (not included here), Galway Kinnell sits
on a beach, looking back the way he has come, noting that "My
footprints / Slogging for the absolute / Already begin vanishing."
The moment is typical in many ways. The poet presents himself as the

protagonist of his poem, moving through a natural setting but preoccupied with metaphysical questions and concerned, not to say obsessed, with his own ephemerality. The edge of wry self-deprecation in the ironic distance between his romantic quest for the absolute and his very temporary impact on the world, as well as in the characterization implied by "slogging," is typical too. Kinnell is a visionary who is also perfectly capable of laughing at himself, though the humor does not so much undermine the seriousness as make it modern and palatable: Any poet who can introduce an experience of mystical knowledge with the phrase "Just now I had a funny sensation" ("Ruins Under the Stars") is someone we are apt to feel we can trust.

The poet-protagonist who walks beaches, climbs mountains, encounters animals, meditates in ruins, and stares at the night sky, "the old stars rustling and whispering," is looking for comforts in a harsh and violent universe; and they are few and far between. Civilization, for example a "SAC bomber . . . crawling across heaven," seems confused and purposeless much of the time. Wilderness, wildness, violence, the upsurge of primitive energies in the self and in nature: These are more real but they are also frightening, awesome. Art's role is to provide a little music, something to go with the crickets' shrilling, the elegies of birds, the crunch and crackle of porcupines, to cheer us up even as we are consumed by the fires and energies of life, as we face the death that is a part of us ("the pre-trembling of a house that falls") as soon as we are born. Were it not for Kinnell's ability to create unlikely but convincing music, like the boys in "Freedom, New Hampshire" improvising on their tissue-covered combs, his world and his poems would be gloomy indeed.

The present selection, five poems, emphasizes Kinnell's musical talents. These lie partly in his ability to manipulate rich patterns of sound; reading the first section of "Ruins Under the Stars" aloud is a good place to start tasting and savoring his distinctive verbal music. But his musical gifts are organizational as well, and one can trace in these poems his development as a poet through experimentation with poems of musical structure, "suites" in which short lyrical sections accumulate around a major theme. The form is a descendant of the Romantic ode, and its great modern practitioner is Yeats. Spiritually, Kinnell may be closer to some of his declared favorites—Villon, Rilke, Frost—but formally he is a successor to Yeats, and the progress he has made with a poem organized like a musical composition is evident in the present selection. "Freedom, New Hampshire," his memorable elegy for his brother from his first volume, *What a Kingdom It Was* (1960), gives us three sections in which we watch the two boys encountering birth, death, and the generative energies of nature in the country setting where they grew up. In the fourth section, these experiences are recapitulated as the poem moves on to the experience of human loss and grief; the bitter, beautiful conclusion is the stronger for our having been prepared by the sections preceding it, each with its own scenery, music, and movement.

In "Ruins Under the Stars," from Kinnell's next collection, the suite structure has reached a more clearly musical and less temporal formulation. No implied narrative exists, and the temporal notations—"All day," "Every night," "Sometimes," "This morning," "Just now"—act to discount linear progression as important to the poem's variations on the theme of living in time and sensing the presence of the timeless. This same investigation of the interaction of physical and spiritual, visible and invisible, is the main enterprise of the even more dazzling set of variations, "Flower Herding on Mount Monadnock,' the title poem of the second collection (1964). By having as many as ten sections, by using the archetypal structure of the quest as a climb toward knowledge, with the poet as a kind of daft shepherd of the wildflowers, and by teasing us with narrative features, this poem invites our delight in its inventive play with contradictions and paradoxes. There is certainly no "slogging" here, and the climb is more like an elated rise, an acceptance as well as a conquering of gravity and decay, accomplished by a strong musical sense and musical order, a dance up the mountainside.

The interest in longer poems that accumulate from shorter sections led Kinnell finally to the writing of a book-length poem in ten parts, modeled loosely on Rilke's *Duino Elegies*, each part a musical suite or sequence in seven sections, of the kind that earlier poems had developed so successfully. From that major effort, *The Book of Nightmares* (1971), we have included one sequence, the seventh of ten, "Little Sleep's-Head Sprouting Hair in the Moonlight." Any excerpting from *The Book of Nightmares* does it an injustice, since common lines of imagery and recurrent themes run through the entire poem, developing a cumulative meaning and force. Readers who wish to experience the full effect of "Little Sleep's-Head" are urged to read the whole poem from which it is taken. They will find it a fascinating and risky enterprise. In it the poet, thinking about his children and the fact of their mortality, seems less able to come to terms with death and change than he did in, say, "Freedom, New Hampshire," so that the book's appeal will be greatest to those readers most able to share its obsession with impermanence. At the same time, Kinnell pushes his characteristic humor and self-mockery into gothic and macabre regions where the excess is apt either to overwhelm the reader with admiration or produce a strong negative reaction. Still controversial, and still being digested and assessed ten years after its appearance, *The Book of Nightmares* is probably the most interesting poem of its kind since Hart Crane's *The Bridge* or Williams's *Paterson*. Since publishing it, Kinnell has produced one new collection, *Mortal Acts, Mor-*

tal Words (1980), from which we have chosen one short poem, "Day-break."

Besides his influential and widely admired poetry, Galway Kinnell has published significant translations—of Villon, Yvan Goll, Yves Bonnefoy—as well as a novel, *Black Light* (1966). He has taught at a number of universities as writer-in-residence, and currently lives part of the year in Sheffield, Vermont, and part in New York, where he is heading a new writing program at NYU.

DY

Freedom, New Hampshire

1

We came to visit the cow
Dying of fever,
Towle said it was already
Shovelled under, in a secret
Burial-place in the woods.
We prowled through the woods
Weeks, we never

Found where. Other
Kids other summers
Must have found the place
And asked, Why is it
Green here? The rich
Guess a grave, maybe,
The poor think a pit

For dung, like the one
We shovelled in in the fall
That came up green
The next year, that may as well
Have been the grave
Of a cow or something
For all that shows. A kid guesses
By whether his house has a bathroom.

We found a cowskull once; we thought it was
From one of the asses in the Bible, for the sun
Shone into the holes through which it had seen
Earth as an endless belt carrying gravel, had heard
Its truculence cursed, had learned how sweat
Stinks, and had brayed—shone into the holes
With solemn and majestic light, as if some
Skull somewhere could be Baalbek or the Parthenon.

That night passing Towle's Barn
We saw lights. Towle had lassoed a calf
By its hind legs, and he tugged against the grip
Of the darkness. The cow stood by chewing millet.
Derry and I took hold, too, and hauled.
It was sopping with darkness when it came free.
It was a bullcalf. The cow mopped it awhile,
And we walked around it with a lantern.

And it was sunburned, somehow, and beautiful.
It took a dug as the first business
And sneezed and drank at the milk of light.

When we got it balanced on its legs, it went wobbling
Towards the night. Walking home in darkness
We saw the July moon looking on Freedom New Hampshire,
We smelled the fall in the air, it was the summer,
We thought, Oh this is but the summer!

Once I saw the moon
Drift into the sky like a bright
Pregnancy pared
From a goddess who thought
To be beautiful she must keep slender—
Cut loose, and drifting up there
To happen by itself—
And waning, in lost labor;

As we lost our labor
Too—afternoons
When we sat on the gate
By the pasture, under the Ledge,
Buzzing and skirling on toilet-
papered combs tunes
To the rumble-seated cars
Taking the Ossipee Road

On Sundays; for
Though dusk would come upon us
Where we sat, and though we had
Skirled out our hearts in the music,
Yet the dandruffed
Harps we skirled it on
Had done not much better than
Flies, which buzzled, when quick

We trapped them in our hands,
Which went silent when we
Crushed them, which we bore
Downhill to the meadowlark's
Nest full of throats
Which Derry charmed and combed
With an Arabian air, while I
Chucked crushed flies into

Innards I could not see,
For the night had fallen
And the crickets shrilled on all sides
In waves, as if the grassleaves
Shrieked by hillsides
As they grew, and the stars
Made small flashes in the sky,
Like mica flashing in rocks

On the chokecherried Ledge
Where bees I stepped on once
Hit us from behind like a shotgun,
And where we could see
Windowpanes in Freedom flash
And Loon Lake and Winnipesaukee
Flash in the sun
And the blue world flashing.

4

The fingerprints of our eyeballs would zigzag
On the sky; the clouds that came drifting up
Our fingernails would drift into the thin air;
In bed at night there was music if you listened,
Of an old surf breaking far away in the blood.

Kids who come by chance on grass green for a man
Can guess cow, dung, man, anything they want.
To them it is the same. To us who knew him as he was
After the beginning and before the end, it is green
For a name called out of the confusions of the earth—

Winnipesaukee coined like a moon, a bullcalf
Dragged from the darkness where it breaks up again,
Larks which long since have crashed for good in the grass
To which we fed the flies, buzzing ourselves like flies,
While the crickets shrilled beyond us, in July . . .

The mind may sort it out and give it names—
When a man dies he dies trying to say without slurring
The abruptly decaying sounds. It is true
That only flesh dies, and spirit flowers without stop
For men, cows, dung, for all dead things; and it is good, yes—

But an incarnation is in particular flesh
And the dust that is swirled into a shape
And crumbles and is swirled again had but one shape
That was this man. When he is dead the grass
Heals what he suffered, but he remains dead,
And the few who loved him know this until they die.

For my brother, 1925–1957

Ruins Under the Stars

1

All day under acrobat
Swallows I have sat, beside ruins
Of a plank house sunk to its windows
In burdock and raspberry canes,
The roof dropped, the foundation broken in,
Nothing left perfect but axe-marks on the beams.

A paper in a cupboard talks about "Mugwumps,"
In a V-letter a farmboy in the Marines has "tasted battle . . ."
The apples are pure acid on the tangle of boughs,
The pasture has gone to popple and bush.
Here on this perch of ruins
I listen for the crunch of the porcupines.

2

Overhead the skull-hill rises
Crossed on top by the stunted apple,
Infinitely beyond it, older than love or guilt,
Lie the stars ready to jump and sprinkle out of space.

Every night under the millions of stars
An owl dies or a snake sloughs his skin,
But what if a man feels the dark
Homesickness for the inconceivable realm?

3

Sometimes I see them,
The south-going Canada geese,
At evening, coming down
In pink light, over the pond, in great,
Loose, always dissolving V's—
I go out into the field,
Amazed and moved, and listen
To the cold, lonely yelping
Of those tranced bodies in the sky,
Until I feel on the point
Of breaking to a sacred, bloodier speech.

4

This morning I watched
Milton Norway's sky-blue Ford
Dragging its ass down the dirt road
On the other side of the valley.

Later, off in the woods I heard
A chainsaw agonizing across the top of some stump.
A while ago the tracks of a little, snowy,
SAC bomber went crawling across heaven.

What of that little hairstreak
That was flopping and batting about
Deep in the goldenrod—
Did she not know, either, where she was going?

5

Just now I had a funny sensation,
As if some angel, or winged star,
Had been perched nearby watching, maybe speaking.
I turned, in the chokecherry bush
There was a twig just ceasing to tremble . . .

The bats come spelling the swallows.
In the smoking heap of old antiques
The porcupine-crackle starts up again,
The bone-saw, the pure music of this sphere,
And up there the old stars rustling and whispering.

Flower Herding on Mount Monadnock

I can support it no longer.
Laughing ruefully at myself
For all I claim to have suffered
I get up. Damned nightmarer!

It is New Hampshire out there,
It is nearly the dawn.
The song of the whippoorwill stops
And the dimension of depth seizes everything.

2

The song of a peabody bird goes overhead
Like a needle pushed five times through the air,
It enters the leaves, and comes out little changed.

The air is so still
That as they go off through the trees
The love songs of birds do not get any fainter.

3

The last memory I have
Is of a flower which cannot be touched,

Through the bloom of which, all day,
Fly crazed, missing bees.

4

As I climb sweat gets up my nostrils,
For an instant I think I am at the sea,

One summer off Cap Ferrat we watched a black seagull
Straining for the dawn, we stood in the surf,

Grasshoppers splash up where I step,
The mountain laurel crashes at my thighs.

5

There is something joyous in the elegies
Of birds. They seem
Caught up in a formal delight,
Though the mourning dove whistles of despair.

GALWAY KINNELL

But at last in the thousand elegies
The dead rise in our hearts,
On the brink of our happiness we stop
Like someone on a drunk starting to weep.

6

I kneel at a pool,
I look through my face
At the bacteria I think
I see crawling through the moss.

My face sees me,
The water stirs, the face,
Looking preoccupied,
Gets knocked from its bones.

7

I weighed eleven pounds
At birth, having stayed on
Two extra weeks in the womb.
Tempted by room and fresh air
I came out big as a policeman
Blue-faced, with narrow red eyes.
It was eight days before the doctor
Would scare my mother with me.

Turning and craning in the vines
I can make out through the leaves
The old, shimmering nothingness, the sky.

8

Green, scaly moosewoods ascend,
Tenants of the shaken paradise,

At every wind last night's rain
Comes splattering from the leaves,

It drops in flurries and lies there,
The footsteps of some running start.

9

From a rock
A waterfall
A single trickle like a strand of wire
Breaks into beads halfway down.

I know
The birds fly off
But the hug of the earth wraps
With moss their graves and the giant boulders.

10

In the forest I discover a flower.

The invisible life of the thing
Goes up in flames that are invisible
Like cellophane burning in the sunlight.

It burns up. Its drift is to be nothing.

In its covertness it has a way
Of uttering itself in place of itself,
Its blossoms claim to float in the Empyrean,

A wrathful presence on the blur of the ground.

The appeal to heaven breaks off.
The petals begin to fall, in self-forgiveness.
It is a flower. On this mountainside it is dying.

Little Sleep's-Head Sprouting Hair
in the Moonlight

1

You scream, waking from a nightmare.

When I sleepwalk
into your room, and pick you up,
and hold you up in the moonlight, you cling to me
hard,
as if clinging could save us. I think
you think
I will never die, I think I exude
to you the permanence of smoke or stars,
even as
my broken arms heal themselves around you.

GALWAY KINNELL   251

I have heard you tell
the sun, *don't go down*, I have stood by
as you told the flower, *don't grow old*,
don't die. Little Maud,

I would blow the flame out of your silver cup,
I would suck the rot from your fingernail,
I would brush your sprouting hair of the dying light,
I would scrape the rust off your ivory bones,
I would help death escape through the little ribs of your body,
I would alchemize the ashes of your cradle back into wood,
I would let nothing of you go, ever,

until washerwomen
feel the clothes fall asleep in their hands,
and hens scratch their spell across hatchet blades,
and rats walk away from the cultures of the plague,
and iron twists weapons toward the true north,
and grease refuses to slide in the machinery of progress,
and men feel as free on earth as fleas on the bodies of men,
and lovers no longer whisper to the presence beside them in the dark, *O*
     corpse-to-be . . .

And yet perhaps this is the reason you cry,
this the nightmare you wake screaming from:
being forever
in the pre-trembling of a house that falls.

3

In a restaurant once, everyone
quietly eating, you clambered up
on my lap: to all
the mouthfuls rising toward
all the mouths, at the top of your voice
you cried
your one word, *caca! caca! caca!*
and each spoonful
stopped, a moment, in midair, in its withering
steam.

Yes,
you cling because
I, like you, only sooner
than you, will go down
the path of vanished alphabets,
the roadlessness
to the other side of the darkness,

your arms
like the shoes left behind,
like the adjectives in the halting speech
of old men,
which once could call up the lost nouns.

4

And you yourself,
some impossible Tuesday
in the year Two Thousand and Nine, will walk out
among the black stones
of the field, in the rain.

and the stones saying
over their one word. *ci-git. ci-git. ci-git.*

and the raindrops
hitting you on the fontanel
over and over, and you standing there
unable to let them in.

5

If one day it happens
you find yourself with someone you love
in a café at one end
of the Pont Mirabeau, at the zinc bar
where white wine stands in upward opening glasses,

and if you commit then, as we did, the error
of thinking,
one day all this will only be memory,

learn,
as you stand
at this end of the bridge which arcs,

from love, you think, into enduring love,
learn to reach deeper
into the sorrows
to come—to touch
the almost imaginary bones
under the face, to hear under the laughter
the wind crying across the black stones. Kiss
the mouth
which tells you, *here,*
here is the world. This mouth. This laughter. These temple bones.

The still undanced cadence of vanishing.

GALWAY KINNELL

In the light the moon
sends back, I can see in your eyes

the hand that waved once
in my father's eyes, a tiny kite
wobbling far up in the twilight of his last look:

and the angel
of all mortal things lets go the string.

Back you go, into your crib.

The last blackbird lights up his gold wings: *farewell*.
Your eyes close inside your head,
in sleep. Already
in your dreams the hours begin to sing.
Little sleep's-head sprouting hair in the moonlight,
when I come back
we will go out together,

we will walk out together among
the ten thousand things,
each scratched too late with such knowledge, *the wages*
of dying is love.

Daybreak

On the tidal mud, just before sunset,
dozens of starfishes
were creeping. It was
as though the mud were a sky
and enormous, imperfect stars
moved across it as slowly
as the actual stars cross heaven.
All at once they stopped,
and as if they had simply
increased their receptivity
to gravity they sank down
into the mud; they faded down
into it and lay still; and by the time
pink of sunset broke across them
they were as invisible
as the true stars at daybreak.

Galway Kinnell

Books

What a Kingdom It Was, 1960
Flower Herding on Mount Monadnock, 1964
Black Light (novel), 1965
The Poems of François Villon (translations), 1965, rev. 1977
Yves Bonnefoy, *On the Motion and Immobility of Douve* (translation), 1968
Body Rags, 1968
Yvan Goll, *Lackawanna Elegy* (translations), 1970
The Book of Nightmares, 1971
The Avenue Bearing the Initial of Christ into the New World: Poems 1946–64, 1974
Mortal Acts, Mortal Words, 1980

Criticism, Interviews

Conrad Hilberry, "The Structure of Galway Kinnell's *The Book of Nightmares*," *FIELD*, 12 (Spring 1975); Ralph Mills, *Cry of the Human*, 1975; *Walking Down the Stairs: Selections from Interviews*, 1978

Denise Levertov

(b. 1923)

Judith McDowell

F ew poets could lay claim to a more exotic heritage than Denise
Levertov. Her father was a Russian Jew, descended from the
founder of Habad Hasidism, who became an Anglican minister in
England. Her mother, Beatrice Spooner-Jones, was a descendant of the

Welsh tailor and mystic Angel Jones of Mold. She was educated at home and trained in classical ballet, and her first book, *The Double Image*, was published in England right after the war (1946). In 1947 she met and married the American writer Mitchell Goodman, and in 1948 moved with him to the United States. Once settled here, she rapidly trained herself in the free verse tradition of William Carlos Williams, forming friendships with Robert Creeley, Charles Olson, and Robert Duncan, members of the Black Mountain "school." The notion of a school is confining for any good poet, however, and Denise Levertov's sense of kinship with writers of other persuasions, like Galway Kinnell, suggests that her values and allegiances are appropriately complex.

Levertov's mastery of free verse is clearly based on her ability to make it sing. Her Welsh-Russian-Jewish heritage informs her work with a sense of vision and celebration that takes the fullest advantage of the musical possibilities inherent in the English language in general and the movements of American speech in particular. "Six Variations," from her 1961 volume, *The Jacob's Ladder*, is both a declaration and a demonstration of her aesthetic. It finds beauty in unlikely places and activities, after the manner of Dr. Williams, but it also celebrates the transformation of such discovery into verbal form, the "intelligent music" of the dog's drinking "in irregular measure." The wedding of image and sound, as in "the fluted / cylinder of a new ashcan a dazzling silver," is her special gift and delight, and her early books are impressive demonstrations both of her growing technical virtuosity and her powers of close observation and shrewd insight.

If "Six Variations" declares an aesthetic, the "Olga Poems" constitutes one of its finest validations, and we have left out many other fine Levertov poems to make room for this masterpiece. This poem's tremendous effort of re-creation—of the past, of the bond between the estranged sisters, of Olga herself in a composite and moving portrait—is also a musical accomplishment of the most impressive kind, a suite of water music cascading and tumbling through its own images and emotions like the "falls and rapids of the music" of Olga's playing of Beethoven and the brown-gold brooks that recall her eyes.

As the poem suggests, Olga was a political radical and activist, and that seems to have been one source of difference between the two sisters. The writing of her elegy for her sister, as it happens, came just at the time (1964) when Denise Levertov was herself beginning to be deeply involved in the antiwar movement protesting America's role in Vietnam. In the years that followed, it was almost as though Olga's candle burned in her all over again, and her poetry changed appreciably. Given her passionate belief that poetry and life must interact constantly and directly, it was perhaps inevitable that a life absorbed by political issues would result in an "engaged" and more overtly didactic and polemical poetry, but this was a dilemma in which she was by no means alone among American poets in the late 1960s.

There has always been something of the teacher in the work of Denise Levertov. Her books have had titles like *O Taste and See*, and her early poems urge readers to make the most of the physical world and the senses. When that strain predominates, it can limit her effectiveness, but the two recent poems that conclude our selection, "Earliest Spring" and "Continuum," reaffirm the continuity and strength that have made her one of our finest and most interesting poets. They stress her ability to go out into the nature of things; to observe them with a clarity that renews their meaning for us; and to turn her observation into precise, resonant language, a poetry as natural and authentic as we could hope to have.

DY

Six Variations

i

We have been shown
how Basket drank—
and old man Volpe the cobbler
made up what words he didn't know
so that his own son, even,
laughed at him: but with respect.

ii

Two flutes! How close
to each other they move
in mazing figures,
never touching, never
breaking the measure,
as gnats dance in
summer haze all afternoon, over
shallow water sprinkled
with mottled blades of willow—
two flutes!

Shlup, shlup, the dog
as it laps up
water
makes intelligent
music, resting
now and then to
take breath in irregular
measure.

iv

When I can't
strike one spark from you,
when you don't
look me in the eye,
when your answers
come
        slowly, dragging
their feet, and furrows
change your face,
when the sky is a cellar
with dirty windows,
when furniture
obstructs the body, and bodies
are heavy furniture coated
with dust—time
for a lagging leaden pace,
a short sullen line,
measure
of heavy heart and
cold eye.

v

The quick of the sun that gilds
broken pebbles in sidewalk cement
and the iridescent
spit, that defiles and adorns!
Gold light in blind love does not distinguish
one surface from another, the savor
is the same to its tongue, the fluted
cylinder of a new ashcan a dazzling silver,
the smooth flesh of screaming children a quietness, it is all
a jubilance, the light catches up
the disordered street in its apron,
broken fruitrinds shine in the gutter.

Lap up the vowels
of sorrow,
       transparent, cold
water-darkness welling
up from the white sand.
Hone the blade
of a scythe to cut swathes
of light sound in the mind.
Through the hollow globe, a ring
of frayed rusty scrapiron,
is it the sea that shines?
Is it a road at the world's edge?

Olga Poems

(*Olga Levertoff, 1914–1964*)

i

By the gas-fire, kneeling
to undress,
scorching luxuriously, raking
her nails over olive sides, the red
waistband ring—

(And the little sister
beady-eyed in the bed—
or drowsy, was I? My head
a camera—)

Sixteen. Her breasts
round, round, and
dark-nippled—

who now these two months long
is bones and tatters of flesh in earth.

ii

The high pitch of
nagging insistence, lines
creased into raised brows—

Ridden, ridden—
the skin around the nails
nibbled sore—

You wanted
to shout the world to its senses,
did you?—to browbeat

the poor into joy's
socialist republic—
What rage

and human shame swept you
when you were nine and saw
the Ley Street houses,

grasping their meaning as *slum*.
Where I, reaching that age,
teased you, admiring

architectural probity, circa
eighteen-fifty, and noted
pride in the whitened doorsteps.

Black one, black one,
there was a white
candle in your heart.

iii

i

Everything flows
              she muttered into my childhood,
pacing the trampled grass where human puppets
rehearsed fates that summer,
stung into alien semblances by the lash of her will—

everything flows—
I looked up from my Littlest Bear's cane armchair
and knew the words came from a book
and felt them alien to me

but linked to words we loved
                          from the hymnbook—*Time
like an ever-rolling stream / bears all its sons away*—

ii

Now as if smoke or sweetness were blown my way
I inhale a sense of her livingness in that instant,
feeling, dreaming, hoping, knowing boredom and zest like anyone
                                                      else—
a young girl in the garden, the same alchemical square

I grew in, we thought sometimes
too small for our grand destinies—
                              But dread
was in her, a bloodbeat, it was against the rolling dark
oncoming river she raised bulwarks, setting herself
to sift cinders after early Mass all of one winter,

labelling her desk's normal disorder, basing
her verses on Keble's *Christian Year*, picking
those endless arguments, pressing on

to manipulate lives to disaster . . . To change,
to change the course of the river! What rage for order
disordered her pilgrimage—so that for years at a time

she would hide among strangers, waiting
to rearrange all mysteries in a new light.

iii

Black one, incubus—
        she appeared
riding anguish as Tartars ride mares

over the stubble of bad years.

In one of the years
    when I didn't know if she were dead or alive
I saw her in a dream

haggard and rouged
        lit by the flare
from an eel-or cockle-stand on a slum street—

was it a dream? I had lost

all sense, almost, of
    who she was, what—inside of her skin,
under her black hair
                dyed blonde—

it might feel like to be, in the wax and wane of the moon,
in the life I feel as unfolding, not flowing, the pilgrim years—

iv

On your hospital bed you lay
in love, the hatreds
that had followed you, a
comet's tail, burned out

as your disasters bred of love
burned out,
while pain and drugs
quarreled like sisters in you—

lay afloat on a sea
of love and pain—how you always
loved that cadence, 'Underneath
are the everlasting arms'—

all history
burned out, down
to the sick bone, save for

that kind candle.

v

i

In a garden grene whenas I lay—

you set the words to a tune so plaintive
it plucks its way through my life as through a wood.

As through a wood, shadow and light between birches,
gliding a moment in open glades, hidden by thickets of holly

your life winds in me.   In Valentines
a root protrudes from the greensward several yards from its tree

we might raise like a trapdoor's handle, you said,
and descend long steps to another country

where we would live without father or mother
and without longing for the upper world. *The birds
sang sweet, O song, in the midst of the daye,*

and we entered silent mid-Essex churches on hot afternoons
and communed with the effigies of knights and their ladies

and their slender dogs asleep at their feet,
the stone so cold—   *In youth*

is pleasure, in youth is pleasure.

ii

Under autumn clouds, under white
wideness of winter skies you went walking
the year you were most alone

returning to the old roads, seeing again
the signposts pointing to Theydon Garnon
or Stapleford Abbots or Greensted,

crossing the ploughlands (whose color I named *murple*,
a shade between brown and mauve that we loved
when I was a child and you

not much more than a child) finding new lanes
near White Roding or Abbess Roding; or lost in Romford's
new streets where there were footpaths then—

frowning as you ground out your thoughts, breathing deep
of the damp still air, taking
the frost into your mind unflinching.

How cold it was in your thin coat, your down-at-heel shoes—
tearless Niobe, your children were lost to you
and the stage lights had gone out, even the empty theater

was locked to you, cavern of transformation where all
had almost been possible.
                    How many books
you read in your silent lodgings that winter,
how the plovers transpierced your solitude out of doors with their
                                        strange cries
I had flung open my arms in longing, once, by your side
stumbling over the furrows—

Oh, in your torn stockings, with unwaved hair,
you were trudging after your anguish
over the bare fields, soberly, soberly.

                    vi

Your eyes were the brown gold of pebbles under water.
I never crossed the bridge over the Roding, dividing
the open field of the present from the mysteries,
the wraiths and shifts of time-sense Wanstead Park held suspended,
without remembering your eyes. Even when we were estranged
and my own eyes smarted in pain and anger at the thought of you.
And by other streams in other countries; anywhere where the light
reaches down through shallows to gold gravel. Olga's
brown eyes. One rainy summer, down in the New Forest,
when we could hardly breathe for ennui and the low sky,
you turned savagely to the piano and sightread
straight through all the Beethoven sonatas, day after day—
weeks, it seemed to me. I would turn the pages some of the time,

go out to ride my bike, return—you were enduring in the
falls and rapids of the music, the arpeggios rang out, the rectory
trembled, our parents seemed effaced.
I think of your eyes in that photo, six years before I was born,
the fear in them. What did you do with your fear,
later? Through the years of humiliation,
of paranoia and blackmail and near-starvation, losing
the love of those you loved, one after another,
parents, lovers, children, idolized friends, what kept
compassion's candle alight in you, that lit you
clear into another chapter (but the same book) 'a clearing
in the selva oscura,
a house whose door
swings open, a hand beckons
in welcome'?
        I cross
so many brooks in the world, there is so much light
dancing on so many stones, so many questions my eyes
smart to ask of your eyes, gold brown eyes,
the lashes short but the lids
arched as if carved out of olivewood, eyes with some vision
of festive goodness in back of their hard, or veiled, or shining,
unknowable gaze . . .

May–August, 1964

Earliest Spring

Iron scallops border the path, barely
above the earth; a purplish starling lustre.

Earth a different dark, scumbled, bare
between clumps of wintered-over stems.

Slowly, from French windows opened
to first, mild, pale, after-winter morning,

we inch forward, looking: pausing, examining
each plant. It's boring. The dry stalks
are tall as I, up to her thigh. But then—
'Ah! Look! A snowdrop!' she cries,
satisfied, and I see

thin sharp green darning-needles
stitch through the sticky gleam of dirt,

belled with white!
'And another!
And here, look, and here.'
A white carillon.
Then she stoops to show me precise
bright green check-marks

vivid on inner petals,
each outer petal
filing down to a point.
And more:
'Crocuses—yes, here they are . . .'

and these point upward, closed
tight as eyelids waiting a surprise,

egg-yoke gold or mauve;
and she brings my gaze

to filigree veins of violet
traced upon white, that make

the mauve seem. This is the earliest
spring of my life. Last year

I was a baby, and what I saw then
is forgotten. Now I'm a child. Now I'm not bored

at moving step by step,
slow, down the path. Each pause

brings us to bells or flames.

Continuum

Some beetle trilling
its midnight utterance.

Voice of the scarabee,
dungroller,
working survivor . . .

I recall how each year
returning from voyages, flights
over sundown snowpeaks,
cities crouched over darkening lakes,
hamlets of wood and smoke,
I find
> the same blind face upturned to the light
> and singing
> the one song,

> the same weed managing
> its brood of minute stars
> in the cracked flagstone.

Notes

Six Variations. "Basket" was Gertrude Stein's dog.

Olga Poems. "*Everything flows*," the view of Heraclitus, the pre-Socratic philosopher. Final section—"The quoted lines—'a clearing / in the selva oscura . . .'—are an adaptation of some lines in 'Selva Oscura' by the late Louis MacNeice, a poem much loved by my sister, Olga" (Levertov's note). *Selva oscura* means "dark wood," the place where Dante finds himself at the outset of *The Divine Comedy*.

Denise Levertov

Books

The Double Image, 1946
Here and Now, 1956
Overland to the Islands, 1958
With Eyes at the Back of Our Heads, 1960
The Jacob's Ladder, 1961
O Taste and See, 1964
The Sorrow Dance, 1967
Eugene Guillevic, Selected Poems (translations), 1969
Relearning the Alphabet, 1970
To Stay Alive, 1971
Footprints, 1972
The Poet in the World (essays), 1975
The Freeing of the Dust, 1975

Life in the Forest, 1978
Collected Earlier Poems: 1940–1960, 1979
Light Up the Cave (essays), 1982
Writing in the Dark, 1982

Criticism, Interviews

Linda Wagner, *Denise Levertov*, 1967; Robert Wilson, *A Bibliography of Denise Levertov*, 1972; Linda Wagner, ed. *Denise Levertov: In Her Own Province*, 1979; Rachel Blau DuPlessis, "The Critique of Consciousness and Myth in Levertov, Rich, and Rukeyser," in *Shakespeare's Sisters: Feminist Essays on Women Poets*, ed. Gilbert and Gubar, 1979

Philip Levine

(b. 1928)

The poems of Philip Levine are absorbed with the past. They write down every detail, and do not flinch from the syntax and structure of prose if that is what it takes to sweep things up for a hard, close look: "Something has fallen wordlessly / and holds still on the black driveway... / You pick it up... / When you raise your sunglasses / to see exactly what you have / you see it is only a shadow // that has darkened your fingers" ("Something Has Fallen"). On reading the poems, it's as if we have waked from a heavy sleep; the remains of things seen, smelled, and touched continue to haunt us, and there are no hymns to pity or forgiveness in sight. In a much-quoted interview, Levine has said, "In a curious way, I'm not much interested in language. In my ideal poem, no words are noticed. You look through them into a vision of people, see the place . . . ." Any writer who gets in the way of the vision, who uses language to call attention to itself, is on the wrong track, Levine goes on to imply.

Interviewed on numerous occasions, Levine has stressed again and again his identification with "men and women I met as an industrial worker and bum in America." A favorite among his own books is *The Names of the Lost* (1976), whose poems make it clear that he is not willing to forget his "heroes," the blacks and whites who have left their home towns for exhausting work in hostile cities, where their ways and language won't do. The title poem of his most praised collection, and one of the most celebrated poems of our time, "They Feed They Lion," not only pays homage to speech patterns Levine overheard on his jobs but invokes by its ritualizing structure and diction, with the biblical power of psalms, images of what oppressors have always done to oppressed. Pouncing on the phrase "they feed they lion," Levine rediscovers in its sprung rhythms the fresh, stark, serious power that spirituals evoke and achieves a kind of Blakean effect in the poem's orchestration. As in other Levine poems that consider civilization's wholesale slaughter of livestock (e.g., "Not This Pig," "Angel Butcher," and "Animals Are Passing from Our Lives"—poems not included here), he addresses the horrifying fact that we destroy in order to eat. The poem closes on a composite biblical figure, a sort of avenging angel: "From they sack and they belly opened / And all that was hidden burning on the oil-stained earth / They feed they Lion and he comes." We have made an animal of our hunger, we have fed the anti-Christ, who will devour us.

Most Levine poems do not back away from the most brutal experiences that his "loners and losers" endure. As Hayden Carruth has remarked, Levine's poems "are about the kind of courage that people have when courage fails." Levine's gift lies in telling these cruel stories in intimate, elegiac tones that keep obvious themes and standard rhetoric at bay. From early small-press books like *Silent in America; Vivas for Those Who Failed* (1965), to the recent *7 Years from Somewhere* (1979), a title with the ring of a contemporary ballad, Levine has been a poet of the people, in the tradition of Whitman and Sandburg, who follows the fatal scent of his characters through the streets (even the mother in "Late Moon" is perceived as a cast-off). The redeeming feature of these characters is that they have, in Rimbaud's words, "more strengths than saints, more sense than explorers." Levine is privy to stories in the holy way of cellmates (see "Heaven"), and the poems stand as monuments to what humankind has suffered, from the Spanish Civil War on through the Holocaust to the political prisons in many countries today. Levine, whose memory serves him well, writes of ultimate innocence.

Though Levine seems preoccupied with dramatic and narrative voices in many poems, and has said that he likes those poems best in which "the speaker is clearly not me," our selection honors his more mystical and metaphysical poems, his heartaches, in which he can visualize *anything* that affects him. These poems range human emotion in the various modes Levine is master of, from tight structures ("Late Moon," "The Helmet") to the incantatory rhythms of the delicate "Milkweed": Slipping back into a kind of schoolboy reverie, the speaker finally realizes he is now, and only now, smart enough to see what didn't seem at all important before. Here, as in other poems, a major theme is sounded: We reclaim little but love it a lot.

Like other poets whose immigrant parents suffered during the Great Depression, Levine as a young man had to face World War II, industrial pollution, and the waste of land on a huge scale. On a smaller scale perhaps, but just as searing for him, was the personal disharmony he was witness to in the furious neighborhood arguments over socialism, communism, and anarchy. However scarred this all left him, Levine managed to escape these beginnings, graduated from Wayne State University and the Writer's Workshop at the University of Iowa, and has been teaching undergraduates since 1958 at California State University at Fresno—teaching them, one suspects, in such a way as to ensure that they will know their first obligation as artists is to be true to what really happens.

SF

Heaven

If you were twenty-seven
and had done time for beating
your ex-wife and had
no dreams you remembered
in the morning, you might
lie on your bed and listen
to a mad canary sing

and think it all right to be
there every Saturday
ignoring your neighbors, the streets,
the signs that said join,
and the need to be helping.
You might build, as he did,
a network of golden ladders
so that the bird could roam
on all levels of the room;
you might paint the ceiling blue,
the floor green, and shade
the place you called the sun
so that things came softly to order
when the light came on.
He and the bird lived
in the fine weather of heaven;
they never aged, they
never tired or wanted
all through that war,
but when it was over
and the nation had been saved,
he knew they'd be hunted.
He knew, as you would too,
that he'd be laid off
for not being braver,
and it would do no good
to show how he had taken
clothespins and cardboard
and made each step safe.
It would do no good
to have been one of the few
that climbed higher and higher
even in time of war,
for now there would be the poor
asking for their share,
and hurt men in uniforms,
and no one to believe
that heaven was really here.

They Feed They Lion

Out of burlap sacks, out of bearing butter,
Out of black bean and wet slate bread,
Out of the acids of rage, the candor of tar,

Out of creosote, gasoline, drive shafts, wooden dollies,
They Lion grow.
                    Out of the gray hills
Of industrial barns, out of rain, out of bus ride,
West Virginia to Kiss My Ass, out of buried aunties,
Mothers hardening like pounded stumps, out of stumps,
Out of the bones' need to sharpen and the muscles' to stretch,
They Lion grow.
                    Earth is eating trees, fence posts,
Gutted cars, earth is calling in her little ones,
"Come home, Come home!" From pig balls,
From the ferocity of pig driven to holiness,
From the furred ear and the full jowl come
The repose of the hung belly, from the purpose
They Lion grow.
                    From the sweet glues of the trotters
Come the sweet kinks of the fist, from the full flower
Of the hams the thorax of caves,
From "Bow Down" come "Rise Up,"
Come they Lion from the reeds of shovels,
The grained arm that pulls the hands,
They Lion grow.
                    From my five arms and all my hands,
From all my white sins forgiven, they feed,
From my car passing under the stars,
They Lion, from my children inherit,
From the oak turned to a wall, they Lion,
From they sack and they belly opened
And all that was hidden burning on the oil-stained earth
They feed they Lion and he comes.

Late Moon

2 a.m.
December, and still no moon
rising from the river.

My mother
home from the beer garden
stands before the open closet

her hands still burning.
She smooths the fur collar,
the scarf, opens the gloves

crumpled like letters.
Nothing is lost
she says to the darkness, nothing.

The moon finally above the town.
The breathless stacks,
the coal clumps,

the quiet cars
whitened at last
Her small round hand whitens,

the hand a stranger held
and released
while the Polish music wheezed.

I'm drunk, she says,
and knows she's not. In her chair
undoing brassiere and garters

she sighs
and waits for the need
to move.

The moon descends
in a spasm of silver
tearing the screen door,

the eyes of fire
drown in the still river,
and she's herself.

The little jewels
on cheek and chin
darken and go out,

and in darkness
nothing falls
staining her lap.

Clouds

1

Dawn. First light tearing
at the rough tongues of the zinnias,
at the leaves of the just born.

Today it will rain. On the road
black cars are abandoned, but the clouds
ride above, their wisdom intact.

They are predictions. They never matter.
The jet fighters lift above the flat roofs,
black arrowheads trailing their future.

2

When the night comes small fires go out.
Blood runs to the heart and finds it locked.

Morning is exhaustion, tranquilizers, gasoline,
the screaming of frozen bearings,
the failures of will, the TV talking to itself.

The clouds go on eating oil, cigars,
housewives, sighing letters,
the breath of lies. In their great silent pockets
they carry off all our dead.

3

The clouds collect until there's no sky.
A boat slips its moorings and drifts
toward the open sea, turning and turning.

The moon bends to the canal and bathes
her torn lips, and the earth goes on
giving off her angers and sighs

and who knows or cares except these
breathing the first rains,
the last rivers running over iron.

4

You cut an apple in two pieces
and ate them both. In the rain
the door knocked and you dreamed it.
On bad roads the poor walked under cardboard boxes.

The houses are angry because they're watched.
A soldier wants to talk with God
but his mouth fills with lost tags.

The clouds have seen it all, in the dark
they pass over the graves of the forgotten
and they don't cry or whisper.

PHILIP LEVINE

They should be punished every morning,
they should be bitten and boiled like spoons.

The Helmet

All the way
on the road to Gary
he could see
where the sky shone
just out of reach
and smell the rich
smell of work
as strong as money,
but when he got there
the night was over.

People were going
to work and back,
the sidewalks were lakes
no one walked on,
the diners were saying
time to eat
so he stopped
and talked to a woman
who'd been up late
making helmets.

There are white hands
the color of steel,
they have put their lives
into steel,
and if hands could lay down
their lives these hands
would be helmets.
He and the woman
did not lie down

not because
she would praise
the steel helmet
boarding a train
for no war,
not because
he would find
the unjewelled crown
in a surplus store
where hands were sold.

They did not lie down
face to face
because of the waste
of being so close
and they were too tired
of being each other
to try to be lovers
and because they had
to sit up straight
so they could eat.

Milkweed

Remember how unimportant
they seemed, growing loosely
in the open fields we crossed
on the way to school. We
would carve wooden swords
and slash at the luscious trunks
until the white milk started
and then flowed. Then we'd
go on to the long day after
day of the History of History
or the tables of numbers and order
as the clock slowly paid
out the moments. The windows
went dark first with rain
and then snow, and then the days,
then the years ran together and not
one mattered more than
another, and not one mattered.

Two days ago I walked
the empty woods, bent over,
crunching through oak leaves,
asking myself questions
without answers. From somewhere
a froth of seeds drifted by touched
with gold in the last light
of a lost day, going with
the wind as they always did.

Something Has Fallen

Something has fallen wordlessly
and holds still on the black driveway.

You find it, like a jewel,
among the empty bottles and cans

where the dogs toppled the garbage.
You pick it up, not sure

if it is stone or wood
or some new plastic made

to replace them both.
When you raise your sunglasses

to see exactly what you have
you see it is only a shadow

that has darkened your fingers,
a black ink or oil,

and your hand suddenly smells
of classrooms when the rain

pounded the windows and you
shuddered thinking of the cold

and the walk back to an empty house.
You smell all of your childhood,

the damp bed you struggled from
to dress in half-light and go out

into a world that never tired.
Later, your hand thickened and flat,

slid out of a rubber glove,
as you stood, your mask raised

to light a cigarette and rest
while the acid tanks that were

yours to clean went on bathing
the arteries of broken sinks.

Remember, you were afraid
of the great hissing jugs.

There were stories of burnings,
of flesh shredded to lace.

On other nights men spoke
of rats as big as dogs.

Women spoke of men
who trapped them in corners.

Always there was grease that hid
the faces of worn faucets, grease

that had to be eaten one
finger-print at a time,

there was oil, paint, blood,
your own blood sliding across

your nose and running over
your lips with that bright, certain

taste that was neither earth
or air, and there was air,

the darkest element of all,
falling all night

into the bruised river
you slept beside, falling

into the glass of water
you filled two times for breakfast

and the eyes you turned upward
to see what time it was.

Air that stained everything
with its millions of small deaths,

that turned all five fingers
to grease or black ink or ashes.

Notes

They Feed They Lion. It seems appropriate to recall the following quotation, from
New Testament Apocrypha, by E. Hennecke, edited by W. Schneemelcher:
> Jesus has said:
> Blessed is the lion that
> the man will devour, and the lion
> will become man. And loathsome is the
> man that the lion will devour,
> and the lion will become man.

> *Gospel of Thomas*, Logion 7,
> translated by GEORGE OGG

Philip Levine

Books

On the Edge, 1963
Not This Pig, 1968
Red Dust, 1971
Pili's Wall, 1971
They Feed They Lion, 1972
1933, 1974
The Names of the Lost, 1976
Ashes: Poems Old and New, 1979
7 Years from Somewhere, 1979
One for the Rose, 1981

Interviews, Criticism

Don't Ask (interviews), 1981; "And See if the Voice Will Enter You: An Interview with Philip Levine," *Ohio Review* 26 (Winter 1975); Calvin Bedient, "An Interview with Philip Levine," *Parnassus* 6 (1978); Charles Molesworth, "The Burned Essential Oil: The Poetry of Philip Levine," *Hollins Critic* 12 (December 1975)

John Logan

(b. 1923)

The poetry of John Logan combines immense human sympathy with a love of language's expressive possibilities. His ideal for poetry is that it might, as Stevens said, help people live their lives: making them whole, healing emotional wounds, strengthening the sense of human community. Like many other poets of his generation, Logan writes candidly about his own life much of the time, and his work reflects both the strengths and the weaknesses of the "confessional" style. In his best poems subjectivity is tempered by a commitment to the objective power of art. Many of his poems celebrate creativity, sometimes by tracing the lives and translating the poems of favorite poets—Rimbaud, Heine, Cummings, Trakl, Rilke, Keats—and sometimes by taking inspiration from painters like Morris Graves and photographers like Aaron Siskind. Logan's central ideal remains the work of art that can inspire, explain, and heal; his many poems about family and love relationships (typical titles are "Lines to His Son on Reaching Adolescence," "Grandmother Dead in the Aeroplane," and "Poem for My Friend Peter at Pihana") represent direct attempts to realize that goal.

Each of the poems by Logan in this selection can be said to represent a characteristic mode or method. In "The Monument and the Shrine," he takes history and one of its heroes, George Washington, as his subjects, but the drama of the poem is typically realized by reporting the poet's visit to the Washington Monument and Mount Vernon. If we compare this with John Berryman's poem on George Washington ("Washington in Love"), we can see how much Logan's use of himself as protagonist is essential to his enterprise. It leads to the moment of vision in which "the lost / Ghosts of his life" break forth and we glimpse the hero's physical actuality: "The sand glint of his boot, / The flick of his coat on the weeds." The balance of personal involvement and impersonal artistry—the poem's notation is precise and its movement exact—inspires our confidence and trust.

"A Suite of Six Pieces for Siskind" reflects Logan's habit of writing about works of art and artists, and his special preoccupation with Aaron Siskind's photography; poems on Siskind's work appear in several of Logan's collections. This "suite" (compare the Kinnell and Levertov uses of this form) is a fascinating exercise in sound, movement, and close observation. It hums with an implicit tension between the camera's objectivity and the necessary subjectivity of the perceiver, who tends to progress in each section from not recognizing the image to recognizing it to transcending it. And the sections together show that perception alters the perceiver and affects what is perceived next, another way in which human beings differ from cameras.

A similar spirit of observation, with recognitions of perception's give and take, informs "The Zoo." The humor of this poem gives it its special flavor. Both the animals and the human beings are observed with wit and compassion, and the unexpectedly moving ending is the stronger for the context of amusement out of which it grows. Logan as traveler and observer is typified by "The Pass," one of many landscape poems in his canon. Its off-rhyme couplets exemplify the deceptively casual expertise Logan brings to his writing. Finally, "Believe It" and the selection from *Poem in Progress* sample Logan's most recent work. In these long-line poems fantastic images—the freaks in "Believe It," the beautifully imagined dream-ship in the second poem—are the instruments by which the poet engages favorite themes: the human need for love, the quest for wholeness and understanding, the poem as expression of unprecedented emotional honesty.

Born and raised in Red Oak, Iowa, John Logan studied at Coe College, Iowa University, Georgetown, and Notre Dame. Married in 1945 and later divorced, he is the father of nine children. He has taught at many universities and traveled widely, but for many years his home base has been the University of Buffalo. His Roman Catholicism was strongly evident in his first book, *A Cycle for Mother Cabrini* (1955); his subsequent poetry is better characterized by Karl Malkoff's phrase, as that of an "existential humanist," centering its faith and hope in human possibility and human love.

DY

The Monument and the Shrine

I

At focus in the national
Park's ellipse a marker
Draws tight the guys of

Miles, opposite the national
Obelisk with its restless oval
Peoples who shall be

Deeply drawn to its
Austerities: or
For a moment try the mystery

Of the god-like eye, before
Our long climb down past relic
Schoolboy names and states

And one foolish man
Climbs up, his death high
In his elliptic face.

A double highway little
Used in early spring
Goes to the end of the land

Where Washington's chandeliers
Are kept, his beds and chairs,
His roped-off relic kitchen

Spits, his pans; his floors
Are worn underneath the dead
Pilgrims' feet; outside

The not-so-visited tomb,
And over the field and fence
His legendary river:

And so I walk although
The day is cold for this;
I eat a thin slice

Of bread and one remarkable
Egg perfectly shaped.
A perfect oriental por-

Celain sheen of white.
Suddenly the lost
Ghosts of his life

Broke from the trees and from the cold
Mud pools where he played
A boy and set as a man

The sand glint of his boot,
The flick of his coat on the weeds;
His wheels click in the single road.

A Suite of Six Pieces for Siskind

1

A white notch as of bone
for a lost gun,
its prongs as roots
of a mammoth overturned tooth—

or like the odd feet
of some ultimate, melancholy freak—
looks into a profound honeycomb
the texture (odor?) of a morel mushroom.

2

The tip
of a leaf
is the wing of a bird
pinned (stretched) to a board.

3

A smashed piece of terracotta
shaped as the bottom
of a whale's mouth
(edges shorn of teeth)

stands upright
like a little, sacred shrine.
And on the shattered tongue
of this relic is

the impress of a stone chalice.

4

A glowing spi-
ral of white
paint

across a concrete post
or telephone pole
lights up this solemn, chalk tale:

I love mama.

5

Why a film of mud
blisters into the shape of a sun!
its black
rays like a baroque work

of sculpture seem to shiver
when an ancient,
fair cloth
is stripped off.

JOHN LOGAN

6

A luminous, thin
long winged worm

or trout
like an animal of light

swims into the deep humours of my eye
bringing this fish pale day.

The Zoo

1

Like a child the wise porpoise
at the Brookfield Zoo plays
in the continuous, universal game
of fish becoming man.

2

Llamas pray to the gods for snow. They chant
that it shall fall upon their artificial mount.
The llamas do not yearn
for tossed gumdrops or for popped corn.

Look,
even the great brown handsome official Kodiak
bear
has caramel in its hair.
Incomparable as he knows he is
the tough, tall golden lion looks at us
indifferent across
his molded hill, his helpful moat;
and, pregnant with a beast it ate,
the vicious, obvious and obscene
greedy-eyed old python
hauls itself along.

3

Gorillas lope and glare and crash
the glass in the Primate House.
The steaming place is packed
with folks who want to look
as at a wedding or a wake.

We advance. We retreat. We test. We wait.
We hope to see something masturbate.
We want to find a kind of King Kong
(magnificent but wrong)
caught and salted safe as us
behind the bars of flesh.
behind the glass of the face.

Twenty charming little tropical monkey kids
jabber in the phony trees. The gibbon is unkempt.
The yellow baboons bark, and they travel in groups.

There, ugly and alone,
awful and no longer young,
is that ornery thing
an orangutan.
Disconsolate, contrite,
red-haired widow who was once a wife
you pace and turn, and turn and pace
then sit on your repulsive ass
and with a hairy hand
and thumb delicately pinch an egg and
kiss its juice deep into your head.
Oh misery! Misery! You wretched bride.

Why only the silver monkey
glows and rests quietly,
nearly everything well,
a bit back in its tunnel
(which is lit
with its own created light).

This Primate House echoes
with our mixed cries;
it reeks with our ambiguous breath.
Each one caged as an oracle
I feel each upright animal
can tell
how much my life is a human life,
how much an animal death.

South Bend, April 1963

The Pass

Buttercups about the rocks and the sky
colored lupine lies

quiet in the brilliant grass
on the island by Deception Pass.

My young brother, his friends and I carefully
walk we

walk carefully along the edge
of the high flying bridge

and all look down
where gulls fall and rise over The Sound.

The awful height stirs in me
the huge, uneasy

gull
of my own soul.

I will not lean farther
over the bridge's sill with the others

(who can savor such a thrill). I will go back
and read the plaque

upon the rock.
But first I watch

a small, red speedboat hurry
beneath, pulling white, excited water flurries

like a living flag.
It passes a tug,

black and brown
(newly painted green

door) moving sure
as an old shepherd goes, before

a tremendous family of floating logs.
I wait until the tug's

completely underneath the span
(by then

even the wake of the younger boat is gone)
and turn

to walk back
alone toward the rock.

Believe It

There is a two-headed goat, a four-winged chicken
and a sad lamb with seven legs
whose complicated little life was spent in Hopland,
California. I saw the man with doubled eyes
who seemed to watch in me my doubts about my spirit.
Will it snag upon this aging flesh?

There is a strawberry that grew
out of a carrot plant, a blade
of grass that lanced through a thick rock,
a cornstalk nineteen feet two inches tall grown by George
Osborne of Silome, Arkansas.
There is something grotesque growing in me I cannot tell.

It has been waxing, burgeoning, for a long time.
It weighs me down like the chains of the man of Lahore
who began collecting links on his naked body
until he crawled around the town carrying the last
thirteen years of his life six hundred seventy pounds.
Each link or each lump in me is an offense against love.

I want my own lit candle lamp buried in my skull
like the Lighthouse Man of Chung King,
who could lead the travelers home.
Well, I am still a traveler and I don't know where
I live. If my home is here, inside my breast,
light it up! And I will invite you in as my first guest.

From *Poem in Progress*

I

First Prelude. Dream in Ohio: The Father

My ship passes over-slowly through the foreign lands
her lovers all are from. There is not much time. The boat
brushes, feels the banks of these beautiful canals. But
there is no one you will see in the unusual
houses with their strange-shaped, attractive red and white suites
of dining—or brownish, burnished bedroom—furniture.
Their decorators are inventive and avant-garde
though slightly color-blind. Even if they *are* empty,

nothing's ripped up from the floors and we can see that there's
no thievery. Toward the back
of the ship with its frothing, fountaining wake, I walk
underneath elaborate glass pendant chandeliers,
their candle-lit tears turned golden
with the muting dust of the last years above this old
and red San Francisco brocade.
I stand at the ship's stern chain. Sure,
it's dangerous to be here! Drift-
ing all this weird weekend through land-locked midwestern towns.
I think of that possible slip
out of the ship's fastenings
into the long sleep of the wake.
But I wave though. I try to greet,
as the boat moves on quietly through the avenues,
some aging men on corners in this alien place.
But they only talk among themselves. How can they miss
this ship in the streets, these old men—
miss *me* trying to salute them? Father, I suppose
it's you again. Why did you stop
hunting for the vivid pheasants in the fields
or having a beer with your friends
in the old Westerlund Cafe
when I was young in Red Oak, Iowa? Oh, I once
thought we might have talked, might try to have something to say.
Instead I ran my buddy's car ninety miles an hour
down highway 48 outside of town and jacked off
when I got home. Father, I love you still—
still yearn for your advice. Shall I turn back toward the tip
of the ship? There is someone alive close by upstairs
in this many-tiered boat. I can hear them as the ageless, orange moon ri-
ses over the small hill or houses. Well, I will go
up there to the sailors perhaps
or the families or the whores—
whoever *lives* on this ghosted ship that floats through the streets
where absolutely anything goes, and there *are* no shores.

John Logan

Books

A Cycle for Mother Cabrini, 1955
Ghosts of the Heart, 1960
Spring of the Thief, 1963
The Zigzag Walk, 1969
The Anonymous Lover, 1973
Poem in Progress, 1975
Selected Poems: Only the Dreamer Can Change the Dream, 1981
The Bridge of Change, 1981

Criticism, Interviews

Ballet for the Ear, ed. A. Poulin, 1981

W. S.
Merwin

(b. 1927)

Although W. S. Merwin was recognized as a promising poet
during the 1950s, it was during the 1960s and '70s that he
gained a wide audience and grew to be one of our most original
and most widely imitated poets. The first selection here, "Low Fields

and Light," from his fourth collection, *The Drunk in the Furnace* (1960), shows his new style coming into being. The subject—a flat, monochromatic landscape that merges mysteriously with the sea—is disorienting because of the success with which the poem's language and manner seem to match it. The speaker is bemused, the language dazed and repetitive. In earlier poems Merwin had written about ancient myths and legendary places; here he begins to create myth, or a mythic sense of experience. We know that the sea-fields described here may be in Virginia, but we also recognize that their power for the speaker, as for us, derives from the way they seem to point beyond themselves. The poem looks ahead to Merwin's major work, a haunted and haunting poetry in which isolation and nullity are projected with an authority and specificity that remind us of myth.

The voice that has begun to emerge in "Low Fields and Light" is not that of an ordinary person. It is exalted and impersonal, the voice of someone who knows about or speaks from a mythic world. We could call it bardic, noting as we do that it is a voice most of Merwin's contemporaries have eschewed. Merwin can use it to create a character, as in "Departure's Girl-friend," which asks us to take its speaker both as a specific person and an abstraction. We balance between our sense of her dilemma as personal and our knowledge that she is a surreal personification of human loneliness. This dual effect is a challenge, testing the reader's ability to entertain uncertainty.

A very different use of the voice can be seen in "The Last One," where it seems to emanate from a primitive storyteller, a shaman recounting a myth of de-creation and desolation. Here the duality arises from our recognition that the story is at once deliberately timeless, a parable, and at the same time a modern political protest against the technological arrogance that has led to the defoliation of forests in Vietnam and to other forms of environmental misuse. "The Last One," along with the mordant "Caesar," reminds us that Merwin was one of the few poets to produce effective political poetry during the 1960s and '70s. To realize that "Caesar" was written not long after John Kennedy's assassination is to be able to identify the raw historical reality behind it, but its power of survival presumably stems from the fact that it refuses to be tied to one politician's death, to Kennedy or to some Roman ruler, or even to one set of political attitudes. Whatever its occasion, it rises toward the expressive power to sum up large areas of human experience that we say myth possesses.

A mythmaker must be cautious about his use of particulars. Merwin's expert juggling of abstractions and concrete details is surely one secret of his distinctive style. It is almost as if they exchange roles. "Witnesses," for example, uses specific details—mouse, curtain, clock, gloves, knives—but it keeps them at a careful, generalized distance. Imagine them any more specific (e.g., "Windup mouse," "digital clock," "switchblade knives"), and you realize how much their deliberately generalized quality contributes to their characterization of evening as a sinister stranger with sinister accomplices. "The River of Bees" shows us, even in its title, how Merwin drains reality of substance in order to make it magical. A river is physical, bees are physical, but a river of bees is a combination so dreamlike and compelling that it points to another realm, whether metaphysical or of the imagination. The poem that follows can be described as a mingling of memory, dream, and meditation, but even its "messages"—"Men think they are better than grass" or "we were not born to survive / Only to live"—seem mysterious in a context that contains such ineffable details as "the noise of death drawing water." The poem's alternation between clarity and opacity keeps us off balance without completely frustrating us, and it remains one of the most memorable lyrics in *The Lice* (1967), Merwin's most influential collection.

To admit that stylistic and rhetorical formulas are at work in this style is not to dissipate its magic. Sometimes Merwin uses deliberate reversals, as in "We are the echo of the future" or the poem, not included here, titled "On the Anniversary of My Death" and beginning "Every year without knowing it I have passed the day...." Even the notion of the spiders, in "The Broken," as trying to mend the air, can be seen to stem from a program in which norms are systematically turned inside out. But knowing how these effects may have been accomplished leaves us the more impressed by the way they attack our expectations and stir our emotions. The range of forms, from short lyric to dramatic monologue to verse narrative to prose text, is impressive too. From the two collections of Merwin's prose pieces (*The Miner's Pale Children* [1970] and *Houses and Travelers* [1977]), we have drawn two short examples that show how Merwin extends his rhetoric of mythic absence and chilly narrative into small tales and dense prose texts. They can be as accessible as "The Broken" or as difficult as "The Hours of a Bridge," which imagines its way into the sensibility of an object in quite astonishing ways.

One of our most literate writers, Merwin has demonstrated his wide interests and international affiliations by becoming the most active and successful translator of his generation. He has given us persuasive versions of older texts—Perseus, *The Song of Roland*, *The Poem of the Cid*—and of important modern writers like Neruda, Mandelstam, and Jean Follain. While some of these writers, Follain especially, may be thought of as influences, Merwin's style must be recognized as very much his own, a brilliant contribution to the best possibilities of modernism.

Unlike most of his contemporaries, Merwin has never taught regularly to support himself, but has preferred to concentrate on writing and translating. His friendships with other writers are warm and extensive, going back to his undergraduate days at Princeton with Galway Kinnell. At present he lives most of the year in Hawaii.

DY

Low Fields and Light

I think it is in Virginia, that place
That lies across the eye of my mind now
Like a grey blade set to the moon's roundness,
Like a plain of glass touching all there is.

The flat fields run out to the sea there.
There is no sand, no line. It is autumn.
The bare fields, dark between fences, run
Out to the idle gleam of the flat water.

And the fences go on out, sinking slowly,
With a cow-bird half-way, on a stunted post, watching
How the light slides through them easy as weeds
Or wind, slides over them away out near the sky.

Because even a bird can remember
The fields that were there before the slow
Spread and wash of the edging light crawled
There and covered them, a little more each year.

My father never ploughed there, nor my mother
Waited, and never knowingly I stood there
Hearing the seepage slow as growth, nor knew
When the taste of salt took over the ground.

But you would think the fields were something
To me, so long I stare out, looking
For their shapes or shadows through the matted gleam, seeing
Neither what is nor what was, but the flat light rising.

Departure's Girl-friend

Loneliness leapt in the mirrors, but all week
I kept them covered like cages. Then I thought
Of a better thing.

And though it was late night in the city
There I was on my way
To my boat, feeling good to be going, hugging
This big wreath with the words like real
Silver: *Bon Voyage*.

        The night
Was mine but everyone's, like a birthday.
Its fur touched my face in passing. I was going
Down to my boat, my boat,
To see it off, and glad at the thought.
Some leaves of the wreath were holding my hands
And the rest waved good-bye as I walked, as though
They were still alive.

And all went well till I came to the wharf, and no one.

I say no one, but I mean
There was this young man, maybe
Out of the merchant marine,
In some uniform, and I knew who he was; just the same
When he said to me where do you think you're going,
I was happy to tell him.

But he said to me, it isn't your boat,
You don't have one. I said, it's mine, I can prove it:
Look at this wreath, I'm carrying to it,
Bon Voyage. He said, This is the stone wharf, lady,
You don't own anything here.

        And as I
Was turning away, the injustice of it
Lit up the buildings, and there I was
In the other and hated city
Where I was born, where nothing is moored, where
The lights crawl over the stone like flies, spelling now,
Now, and the same fat chances roll
Their many eyes; and I step once more
Through a hoop of tears and walk on, holding this
Buoy of flowers in front of my beauty,
Wishing myself the good voyage.

Witnesses

Evening has brought its
Mouse and let it out on the floor,
On the wall, on the curtain, on
The clock. You with the gloves, in the doorway,
Who asked you to come and watch?

As the bats flower in the crevices
You and your brothers
Raise your knives to see by.
Surely the moon can find her way to the wells
Without you. And the streams
To their altars.

As for us, we enter your country
With our eyes closed.

The Last One

Well they'd made up their minds to be everywhere because why not.
Everywhere was theirs because they thought so.
They with two leaves they whom the birds despise.
In the middle of stones they made up their minds.
They started to cut.

Well they cut everything because why not.
Everything was theirs because they thought so.
It fell into its shadows and they took both away.
Some to have some for burning.

Well cutting everything they came to the water.
They came to the end of the day there was one left standing.
They would cut it tomorrow they went away.
The night gathered in the last branches.
The shadow of the night gathered in the shadow on the water.
The night and the shadow put on the same head.
And it said Now.

Well in the morning they cut the last one.
Like the others the last one fell into its shadow.
It fell into its shadow on the water.
They took it away its shadow stayed on the water.

W.S. MERWIN

297

Well they shrugged they started trying to get the shadow away.
They cut right to the ground the shadow stayed whole.
They laid boards on it the shadow came out on top.
They shone lights on it the shadow got blacker and clearer.
They exploded the water the shadow rocked.
They built a huge fire on the roots.
They sent up black smoke between the shadow and the sun.
The new shadow flowed without changing the old one.
They shrugged they went away to get stones.

They came back the shadow was growing.
They started setting up stones it was growing.
They looked the other way it went on growing.
They decided they would make a stone out of it.
They took stones to the water they poured them into the shadow.
They poured them in they poured them in the stones vanished.
The shadow was not filled it went on growing.
That was one day.

The next day was just the same it went on growing.
They did all the same things it was just the same.
They decided to take its water from under it.
They took away water they took it away the water went down.
The shadow stayed where it was before.
It went on growing it grew onto the land.
They started to scrape the shadow with machines.
When it touched the machines it stayed on them.
They started to beat the shadow with sticks.
Where it touched the sticks it stayed on them.
They started to beat the shadow with hands.
Where it touched the hands it stayed on them.
That was another day.

Well the next day started about the same it went on growing.
They pushed lights into the shadow.
Where the shadow got onto them they went out.
They began to stomp on the edge it got their feet.
And when it got their feet they fell down.
It got into eyes the eyes went blind.

The ones that fell down it grew over and they vanished.
The ones that went blind and walked into it vanished.
The ones that could see and stood still
It swallowed their shadows.
Then it swallowed them too and they vanished.
Well the others ran.

The ones that were left went away to live if it would let them.
They went as far as they could.
The lucky ones with their shadows.

Caesar

My shoes are almost dead
And as I wait at the doors of ice
I hear the cry go up for him Caesar Caesar

But when I look out the window I see only the flatlands
And the slow vanishing of the windmills
The centuries draining the deep fields

Yet this is still my country
The thug on duty says What would you change
He looks at his watch he lifts
Emptiness out of the vases
And holds it up to examine

So it is evening
With the rain starting to fall forever

One by one he calls night out of the teeth
And at last I take up
My duty

Wheeling the president past banks of flowers
Past the feet of empty.stairs
Hoping he's dead

The River of Bees

In a dream I returned to the river of bees
Five orange trees by the bridge and
Beside two mills my house
Into whose courtyard a blind man followed
The goats and stood singing
Of what was older

Soon it will be fifteen years

He was old he will have fallen into his eyes

I took my eyes
A long way to the calendars
Room after room asking how shall I live

One of the ends is made of streets
One man processions carry through it
Empty bottles their
Image of hope
It was offered to me by name

W.S. MERWIN

Once once and once
In the same city I was born
Asking what shall I say

He will have fallen into his mouth
Men think they are better than grass

I return to his voice rising like a forkful of hay

He was old he is not real nothing is real
Nor the noise of death drawing water

We are the echo of the future

On the door it says what to do to survive
But we were not born to survive
Only to live

When You Go Away

When you go away the wind clicks around to the north
The painters work all day but at sundown the paint falls
Showing the black walls
The clock goes back to striking the same hour
That has no place in the years

And at night wrapped in the bed of ashes
In one breath I wake
It is the time when the beards of the dead get their growth
I remember that I am falling
That I am the reason
And that my words are the garment of what I shall never be
Like the tucked sleeve of a one-armed boy

The Hours of a Bridge

When the black.
    When the lamps fill, when the lamps empty.
    When a prayer. With no one praying it. Oh yes there is someone but they
are hanging back, hanging back. All through the darkness. In the daytime they
are nothing but a long gasp. When a prayer they let the prayer go ahead by itself
and they hang back and become deserted.

When a prayer again. No shoes running after it with a limp. Or is that the prayer? No stars. Above or below. And still long long before.

When a rat. When a flag. A long flag.

When the battle will cross. But that will be by its own light. Between the smug statues.

When the sins of the night, in a butcher's cart. The same cart that is used for the plagues. A dog painted on the side. A dog walking under it. Mist walking on each side. The wheels and the cart and the dogs and the mist and the sins all unaware of each other.

When the man with the red hood that looks black. Going home.

When the battle will cross again, coming back. When the statues will all become statues of the death of the air.

When the dawn's cat. Sits right down. By a coat, getting light.

When the coat is disturbed water runs out of it. Old water. Old old water.

But the best thing for us, we believe, is to go on for as long as we can, living upstream, tending our instruments by night. On the one bank.

●

The Broken

The spiders started out to go with the wind on its pilgrimage. At that time they were honored among the invisibles—more sensitive than glass, lighter than water, purer than ice. Even the lightning spoke well of them, and it seemed as though they could go anywhere. But as they were travelling between cold and heat, cracks appeared in them, appeared in their limbs, and they stopped, it seemed they had to stop, had to leave the company of the wind for a while and stay in one place until they got better, moving carefully, hiding, trusting to nothing. It was not long before they gave up trying to become whole again, and instead undertook to mend the air. Neither life nor death, they said, would slip through it any more.

After that they were numbered among the dust—makers of ghosts.

The wind never missed them. There were still the clouds.

A Door

Do you remember how I beat on the door
kicked the door
as though I or the door were a bad thing
later it opened
I went in
nothing
starlight
snowing

an empty throne
snow swirling on the floor
around the feet

and on an instrument
we had been trying
to speak to each other
on which we had been trying to speak
to each other for long
for time
pieces lying apart there
giving off
echoes of words our last words *implor*
 ing
 implor
 ing
by deaf starlight for a moment

and you know we
have danced in such a room
I came in late and you
were far from the door
and I had to dance with
not you after not you before
I could reach you
but this was later than anyone
could have thought

thin
snow falling
in an empty bell
lighting that chair

could I turn at all

now should I kneel

and no door anywhere

The War

There are statues moving into a war
as we move into a dream
we will never remember

they lived before us
but in the dream we may die

and each carrying
one wing as in life
we may go down all the steps of the heart
into swamp water
and draw our hands down after us
out of the names

and we may lose one by one our features
the stone may say good-bye to us
we may say good-bye to the stone
forever
and embark
like a left foot alone in the air
and hear at last voices like small bells
and be drawn ashore

and wake with the war going on

W. S. Merwin

Books

A Mask for Janus, 1952
The Dancing Bears, 1954
Green With Beasts, 1956
The Poem of the Cid (translation), 1959
The Drunk in the Furnace, 1960
The Satires of Perseus (translations), 1961
Spanish Ballads (translations), 1961
The Moving Target, 1963
The Song of Roland, 1963
The Lice, 1967
Selected Translations, 1948–1968, 1968
Transparence of the World: Poems of Jean Follain (translations), 1969
The Carrier of Ladders, 1970
The Miner's Pale Children (prose), 1970
Asian Figures (translations), 1973
Writings to an Unfinished Accompaniment, 1973
Selected Poems of Osip Mandelstam (translations, with Clarence Brown), 1974
The First Four Books of Poems, 1975
The Compass Flower, 1977
Houses and Travelers (prose), 1977
Selected Translations, 1968–1978, 1979

Criticism

Richard Howard, *Alone with America*, 1969; Harvey Gross, "The Writing on the Void: The Poetry of W. S. Merwin," *Iowa Review* 1 (1970); Jan Gordon, "The Dwelling of Disappearance: W. S. Merwin's *The Lice*," *Modern Poetry Studies* 3 (1972); Jarold Ramsey, "The Continuities of W. S. Merwin," *Massachusetts Review* 14 (1973); Laurence Lieberman, "The Church of Ash," in *Contemporary Poetry in America; Essays and Interviews*, ed. Robert Boyers, 1974

NINETEEN POETS BORN BETWEEN 1920 AND 1930

Adrienne Rich

(b. 1929)

From 1954 on, Adrienne Rich began dating her poems. "Writing is tentative and exploratory," she said, "and one needs to allow poems to speak for their moment." Somewhat later, and more tellingly, she added, "The meaning of a poem becomes clear to me only as

305

I see what happens in my life; poems are more like premonitions than conclusions." These statements characterize her formal break with the past. Early books had brought her considerable recognition; impressed by her technical control and mastery of forms, Auden selected *A Change of World* for the 1951 Yale Series of Younger Poets Award, and Jarrell praised her second collection, *The Diamond Cutters*, for similar reasons. She herself says that these first poems were mere exercises for poems she hadn't written; that while she learned her craft from various male poets all the way from Yeats and Thomas to Stevens and Frost, she realized that "formalism was part of the strategy: like asbestos gloves it allowed me to handle materials I couldn't pick up bare-handed."

But her life, and the nation's life, were starting to come apart. The 1950s and the early '60s, with their sit-ins and marches, political assassinations and antiwar movement, were painful and unbalancing. Married and committed to raising her children during those years, she could only read "in fierce snatches, scribble in notebooks, write poetry in fragments . . . but felt that politics was not something 'out there' but something 'in here' and of the essence of my condition." A revolution was also going on in *Sexual Politics*, as Kate Millett's book defined it, and women everywhere were "awakening." In Rich's thoughtful essay "When We Dead Awaken: Writing as Re-Vision" (on her own poem as well as Ibsen's play by the same name, which raises issues about how the male artist uses women in creating culture), she asks passionate, searching questions about men-women relationships and probes into matters she had addressed in her third book of poems. *Snapshots of a Daughter-in-Law* (1963) is an album of candid accounts of how women have been led to treat other women. From this time on, in forms that are beginning to open up, Rich's poems focus on the destructiveness women face in our society; and one of her central means is to mix moral and political issues with her art.

"After Dark" (dated 1964) is a poem about her relationship with her father, who had supported and encouraged her (too much? too soon?). It also reflects her personal and historical struggle to achieve a whole new "psychic geography" (her term), which would be made up of a language and images for the experiences women were only becoming aware of. The poem works through initial angers that many a poet has stopped at (Plath, for example)—where both father and daughter ("Blood is a sacred poison") were in prison—and moves to a tranquil place where both can give each other what they need. Though death finally comes for the father ("the blunt barge // bumps along the shore"), the poem ends on a dream that frees them of their fears. Rich has discovered, she says, that "poems are like dreams, in them you put what you don't know you know."

What Rich was on the way to knowing emerges even more clearly from a spirited exchange she had with Galway Kinnell, whose essay "Poetry, Personality and Death" prompted her to write a response she called "Poetry, Personality and Wholeness." She agreed with Kinnell that certain male poets were on the right track in moving beyond mere personality toward a persona or an abstract "I," but she felt that these were still an evasion. Only an inward look would authenticate the "I," rather than idealize it, she argued. She mentions Emily Dickinson as a model, whose muse was "The Soul," a power unto itself. Rich believes it is the acceptance of the loneliness implicit in this notion that will make for a healthier poetry. She continued to pursue these matters in a remarkable collection of essays, *On Lies, Secrets and Silence* (1979), as well as in a book of poems, *The Dream of a Common Language* (1977), whose title points to her ultimate goal.

The Will to Change (1971), from which "The Burning of Paper Instead of Children" is taken, shows her coming into her own. The woman in the poem is distressed by other things than her neighbor, "a scientist and art-collector." Burning books is one matter, but what if the whole nature of human relationships, in its sexual and political dimensions, has been corrupted by "the oppressor's language," a language that has no means left to talk of wholeness, to talk with "joy instead of dread"? Working with montage techniques common to the films and theater of the period, Rich explores breaks in the double helix of love-talk and love-making: "you enter without knowing / what it is you enter." The implicit danger, which she describes with fierce images, is that all speech will burn up ("my mouth is burning") and disappear for any woman or man: "In America we have only the present tense. I am in danger. You are in danger." The language has taken on the quality of a military manual, and can only sound rote now.

In *Diving into the Wreck* (1973), one of the most famous books of the decade, whose title poem has become a shibboleth for the feminist movement, Rich breaks down the artificial barriers "between private and public, between Vietnam and lover's bed, between the deepest images we carry out of our dreams and the most daylight events 'out in the world.'" We have chosen to represent this later stage of her work by the long poem "Meditations for a Savage Child," at the expense of many strong smaller texts. We do so for two reasons: wherever possible, we want the long poem to be a hallmark of this collection; and to celebrate Rich's artful ways with the complex structure of this "double text." Though she has used collage and montage methods previously—especially when she works with events in the news—"Meditations" is a poem that incorporates her themes and techniques on an impressive scale. The wild child is a perfect choice of subject for her. His needs, his uniqueness, are subverted (as women's have been for so long) by the scientists' needs to teach him their values. These are not out-and-out monsters, however: "There was a profound indifference to the objects of our pleasures and of our fictitious needs...." They are frighteningly aware of what they do, but cannot relinquish the "objects of their caring," which become the center of the child's curriculum. When they speak in a figurative language— "these scars bear witness"—Rich cuts across it for the literal meaning: "There where every wound is registered / as scar tissue // A cave of scars!" She mirrors precisely what we feel when we read the account of what they have done: "When I try to speak / my throat is cut... / Yet always the tissue / grows over, white as silk / hardly a blemish / maybe a hieroglyph for scream." The woman at the lecture who raises her hand has them dead to rights, these scientists who mean so well: "*You have the power / in your hands, you control our lives— / why do you want our pity too?*" Why indeed. In wanting it both ways, these clinicians "*can do things to you.*" Rich has turned lecture hall into courtroom, and those who examine and pronounce in our name are on trial.

Adrienne Rich's life is still changing. In addition to publishing *Of Woman Born: Motherhood as Experience and Institution* (1976), as challenging a book as we have had on the subject, and teaching and lecturing in ways that question the whole university system, she has recently co-founded a lesbian feminist journal, *Sinister Wisdom*, that issues from her home in western Massachusetts.

SF

After Dark

1

You are falling asleep and I sit looking at you
old tree of life
old man whose death I wanted
I can't stir you up now.

Faintly a phonograph needle
whirs round in the last groove
eating my heart to dust.
That terrible record! how it played

down years, wherever I was
in foreign languages even
over and over, *I know you better*
than you know yourself   I know

you better than you know
yourself   I know
you   until, self-maimed,
I limped off, torn at the roots,

stopped singing a whole year,
got a new body, new breath,
got children, croaked for words,
forgot to listen

or read your *mene tekel* fading on the wall,
woke up one morning
and knew myself your daughter.
Blood is a sacred poison.

Now, unasked, you give ground.
We only want to stifle
what's stifling us already.
Alive now, root to crown, I'd give

—oh,—something—not to know
our struggles now are ended.
I seem to hold you, cupped
in my hands, and disappearing.

When your memory fails—
no more to scourge my inconsistencies—
the sashcords of the world fly loose.
A window crashes

suddenly down. I go to the woodbox
and take a stick of kindling
to prop the sash again.
I grow protective toward the world.

2

Now let's away from prison—
Underground seizures!
I used to huddle in the grave
I'd dug for you and bite

my tongue for fear it would babble
—*Darling*—
I thought they'd find me there
someday, sitting upright, shrunken,

my hair like roots and in my lap
a mess of broken pottery—
wasted libation—
and you embalmed beside me.

ADRIENNE RICH

No, let's away. Even now
there's a walk between doomed elms
(whose like we shall not see much longer)
and something—grass and water—

an old dream-photograph.
I'll sit with you there and tease you
for wisdom, if you like,
waiting till the blunt barge

bumps along the shore.
Poppies burn in the twilight
like smudge pots.
I think you hardly see me

but—this is the dream now—
your fears blow out,
off, over the water.
At the last, your hand feels steady.

1964

The Burning of Paper Instead of Children

I was in danger of
verbalizing my moral
impulses out of existence.
DANIEL BERRIGAN,
on trial in Baltimore

1. My neighbor, a scientist and art-collector, telephones me in a state of violent emotion. He tells me that my son and his, aged eleven and twelve, have on the last day of school burned a mathematics textbook in the backyard. He has forbidden my son to come to his house for a week, and has forbidden his own son to leave the house during that time. "The burning of a book," he says, "arouses terrible sensations in me, memories of Hitler; there are few things that upset me so much as the idea of burning a book."

Back there: the library, walled
with green Britannicas
Looking again

in Dürer's *Complete Works*
for MELANCOLIA, the baffled woman

the crocodiles in Herodotus
the Book of the Dead
the *Trial of Jeanne d'Arc*, so blue
I think, It is her color

and they take the book away
because I dream of her too often

love and fear in a house
knowledge of the oppressor
I know it hurts to burn

2. To imagine a time of silence
or few words
a time of chemistry and music

the hollows above your buttocks
traced by my hand
or, *hair is like flesh*, you said

an age of long silence

relief

from this tongue   this slab of limestone
or reinforced concrete
fanatics and traders
dumped on this coast wildgreen clayred
that breathed once
in signals of smoke
sweep of the wind

knowledge of the oppressor
this is the oppressor's language

yet I need it to talk to you

3. *People suffer highly in poverty and it takes dignity and intelligence to overcome this suffer-*
ing. Some of the suffering are: a child did not had dinnner last night: a child steal because he
did not have money to buy it: to hear a mother say she do not have money to buy food for her
children and to see a child without cloth it will make tears in your eyes.

(the fracture of order
the repair of speech
to overcome this suffering)

4. We lie under the sheet
after making love, speaking
of loneliness
relieved in a book
relived in a book
so on that page
the clot and fissure
of it appears
words of a man
in pain
a naked word

entering the clot
a hand grasping
through bars:

deliverance

What happens between us
has happened for centuries
we know it from literature

still it happens

sexual jealousy
outflung hand
beating bed

dryness of mouth
after panting

there are books that describe all this
and they are useless

You walk into the woods behind a house
there in that country
you find a temple
built eighteen hundred years ago
you enter without knowing
what it is you enter

so it is with us

no one knows what may happen
though the books tell everything

burn the texts   said Artaud

5. I am composing on the typewriter late at night, thinking of today. How well
we all spoke. A language is a map or our failures. Frederick Douglass wrote an
English purer than Milton's. People suffer highly in poverty. There are methods
but we do not use them. Joan, who could not read, spoke some peasant form of
French. Some of the suffering are: it is hard to tell the truth; this is America; I
cannot touch you now. In America we have only the present tense. I am in dan-
ger. You are in danger. The burning of a book arouses no sensation in me. I
know it hurts to burn. There are flames of napalm in Catonsville, Maryland. I
know it hurts to burn. The typewriter is overheated, my mouth is burning, I can-
not touch you and this is the oppressor's language.

1968

Meditations for a Savage Child

(*The prose passages are from
J-M Itard's account of* The Wild
Boy of Aveyron, *as translated by
G. and M. Humphrey*)

I

*There was a profound indifference to the objects of our pleasures and of our fictitious needs;
there was still . . . so intense a passion for the freedom of the fields . . . that he would certainly
have escaped into the forest had not the most rigid precautions been taken . . .*

In their own way, by their own lights
they tried to care for you
tried to teach you to care
for objects of their caring:

        glossed oak planks, glass
        whirled in a fire
        to impossible thinness

to teach you names
for things
you did not need

        muslin shirred against the sun
        linen on a sack of feathers
        locks, keys
        boxes with coins inside

they tried to make you feel
the importance of

        a piece of cowhide
        sewn around a bundle
        of leaves impressed with signs

to teach you language:
the thread their lives
were strung on

II

*When considered from a more general and philosophic point of view, these scars bear witness . . .
against the feebleness and insufficiency of man when left entirely to himself, and in favor of
the resources of nature which . . . work openly to repair and conserve that which she tends
secretly to impair and destroy.*

ADRIENNE RICH

I keep thinking about the lesson of the human ear
which stands for music, which stands for balance—
or the cat's ear which I can study better
the whorls and ridges exposed
It seems a hint dropped about the inside of the skull
which I cannot see
lobe, zone, that part of the brain
which is pure survival

The most primitive part
I go back into at night
pushing the leathern curtain
with naked fingers
then
with naked body

There where every wound is registered
as scar tissue

A cave of scars!
ancient, archaic wallpaper
built up, layer on layer
from the earliest, dream-white
to yesterday's, a red-black scrawl
a red mouth slowly closing

Go back so far there is another language
go back far enough the language
is no longer personal

these scars bear witness
but whether to repair
or to destruction
I no longer know

III

*It is true that there is visible on the throat a very extended scar which might throw some doubt
upon the soundness of the underlying parts if one were not reassured by the appearance of the
scar . . .*

When I try to speak
my throat is cut
and, it seems, by his hand

The sounds I make are prehuman, radical
the telephone is always
ripped-out

and he sleeps on
Yet always the tissue
grows over, white as silk

hardly a blemish
maybe a hieroglyph for scream

Child, no wonder you never wholly
trusted your keepers

IV

A hand with the will rather than the habit of crime had wished to make an attempt on the life of this child . . . left for dead in the woods, he will have owed the prompt recovery of his wound to the help of nature alone.

In the 18th century infanticide
reaches epidemic proportions:
old prints attest to it: starving mothers
smothering babies in sleep
abandoning newborns in sleet
on the poorhouse steps
gin-blurred, setting fire to the room

I keep thinking of the flights we used to take
on the grapevine across the gully
littered with beer-bottles where dragonflies flashed
we were 10, 11 years old
wild little girls with boyish bodies
flying over the moist
shadow-mottled earth
till they warned us to stay away from there

Later they pointed out
the venetian blinds
of the abortionist's house
we shivered

Men can do things to you
was all they said

V

And finally, my Lord, looking at this long experiment . . . whether it be considered as the methodical education of a savage or as no more than the physical and moral treatment of one of those creatures ill-favored by nature, rejected by society and abandoned by medicine, the care that has been taken and ought still to be taken of him, the changes that have taken place, and those that can be hoped for, the voice of humanity, the interest inspired by such a desertion and a destiny so strange—all these things recommend this extraordinary young man to the attention of scientists, to the solicitude of administrators, and to the protection of the government.

1.   The doctor in "Uncle Vanya":
    They will call us fools,
    blind, ignorant, they will
    despise us

    devourers of the forest
    leaving teeth of metal in every tree
    so the tree can neither grow
    nor be cut for lumber

    Does the primeval forest
    weep
    for its devourers

    does nature mourn
    our existence

    is the child with arms
    burnt to the flesh of its sides
    weeping eyelessly for man

2.   At the end of the distinguished doctor's
    lecture
    a young woman raises her hand:
    You have the power
    in your hands, you control our lives—
    why do you want our pity too?

    Why are men afraid
    why do you pity yourselves
    why do the administrators
    lack solicitude, the government
    refuse protection,
    why should the wild child
    weep for the scientists
    why

1972

Notes

After Dark. "Mene tekel" is from "mene, mene, tekel, upharsin"—numbered, numbered, weighed and divided: from the Bible, (Daniel 5:25). The writing on the wall, interpreted by Daniel to mean that God had weighed Belshazzar and his kingdom and found them wanting.

Two Shakespearan references weight this poem with glances at other fathers and daughters. "Our struggles now are ended" recalls Prospero's speech beginning "Our revels now are ended," after the interruption of Miranda's wedding masque. In 2, "Now let's away from prison" reverses King Lear's "Come, let's away to prison," after he and Cordelia have been reunited and arrested.

Adrienne Rich

Books

A Change of World, 1951
The Diamond Cutters, 1955
Snapshots of a Daughter-in-Law: Poems, 1954–1962, 1963, 1967
Necessities of Life: Poems 1962–1965, 1966
Leaflets: Poems 1965–1968, 1969
The Will to Change: Poems 1968–1970, 1971
Diving into the Wreck: Poems 1971–1972, 1973
Poems: Selected and New, 1950–1974, 1975
Twenty-One Love Poems, 1976
Of Woman Born: Motherhood as Experience and Institution (prose), 1976
The Dream of a Common Language: Poems 1974–1977, 1978
On Lies, Secrets and Silence: Selected Prose 1966–1978, 1979
A Wild Patience Has Taken Me This Far: Poems 1978–1981, 1981

Essays, Criticism

"Poetry, Personality and Wholeness: A Response to Galway Kinnell" in *A Field Guide to Contemporary Poetry and Poetics*, ed. Friebert and Young, 1980; Barbara C. Gelpi and Albert Gelpi, eds., *Adrienne Rich's Poetry: A Norton Critical Edition* (1975); David Kalstone, *Five Temperaments* (1977); Rachel Blau DuPlessis, "The Critique of Consciousness and Myth in Levertov, Rich, and Rukeyser," in *Shakespeare's Sisters: Feminist Essays on Women Poets*, ed. Gilbert and Gubar, 1979

Louis
Simpson

(b. 1923)

L ouis Simpson grew up in Jamaica, in the British West Indies. His
father was a prominent lawyer of Scottish descent, his mother
from a family of Russian Jews who had immigrated to the United
States early in this century. In 1940 he came to the United States to

study at Columbia University. He joined the army in 1943 and saw action with the 101st Airborne Division during the Allied invasion of Europe. After the war he returned to his studies in New York, working toward a Ph.D. and holding a job with a publishing firm. He documents these and other details of his life in his thoughtful autobiography, *North of Jamaica.*

As a young poet in the 1950s, Simpson wrote poems in rhyme and meter, after the fashion that seems to have been set partly by the presence of W. H. Auden and partly by an intense need for order and tradition created by the war. One of the best of the young formalists, Simpson wrote of his war experiences in quatrains and ballad meters, and produced sweeping poems on historical subjects like the Renaissance and the settling of North America. As "Early in the Morning," our selection from this phase of Simpson's works demonstrates, Simpson's formal lyrics are witty and sinewy, elegant without being overrefined or derivative.

"My Father in the Night Commanding No," first published in 1961, shows Simpson moving away from his early formalism. It uses rhyme and meter, but more subtly. Moreover, something different is happening with the voice, with what we might call the poet's relation to the poem. The distant, controlled manner of "Early in the Morning" is being replaced by a more direct and urgent tone. The reach of this poem is exciting too. It seems to be based in personal memory, but its interest is clearly in the archetypal power of childhood. Looking back to our earliest years (compare Donald Justice's poem "Childhood") is like looking into a myth, and the distance between the speaker and his past is not so much an opportunity for detached and witty comment as an occasion for profound recognition and sorrow.

In the next poem, "On the Lawn at the Villa," we can see how complete Simpson's break with the traditional style finally became. After the opening line, which is the same as the title and very reminiscent of the 1950s manner, the poem suddenly says: "That's the way to start, eh, reader?" From then on, we are on a completely different footing. The safe distance between author, reader, and subject has been abandoned, and the jettisoning of old rules and rhetoric leaves us charged with working out a new relationship to poet and poem. Similarly, in "A Story about Chicken Soup," the poet says of his relatives: "But the Germans killed them. / I know it's in bad taste to say it, / But it's true. The Germans killed them all." This has been Simpson's manner from his 1963 volume, *At the End of the Open Road,* right up to the present. He addresses us directly, he writes straightforwardly and often quite prosaically, and he abandons artifice and tradition in favor of a clipped candor.

Simpson's prosaic style can be deceptive. It may strike readers as arbitrary or antipoetic, but poems like "The Photographer," "Chocolates," and "Why Do You Write About Russia?" prove on closer examination to be superbly controlled and effectively organized. They speak to large contemporary issues in ways that startle us and make us reconsider our attitudes. While they may take up social and political issues directly, to call them polemical would be to oversimplify them, for their tones and attitudes are generally quite complex. "Why Do You Write About Russia?," especially, may appear disjointed, but in its apparent meandering it manages to track the random associations of the mind and imagination and at the same time pursue a purposeful exploration of the deep sources of poetry. Remembering his mother's stories of cold and poverty, told in a setting of tropical comfort and a voice of tender reassurance, the poet concludes: "So it is with poetry: whatever numbing horrors / it may speak of, the voice itself / tells of love and infinite wonder." The rest of the poem elaborates on that paradox, that balance, in an increasingly luminous way.

Louis Simpson, then, continues as he began, writing poems of craft and considerable originality. After some years of teaching in California, at Berkeley, he has been since 1967 a professor at the State University of New York at Stony Brook, Long Island.

DY

Early in the Morning

Early in the morning
The dark Queen said,
"The trumpets are warning
There's trouble ahead."
Spent with carousing,
With wine-soaked wits,
Antony drowsing
Whispered, "It's
Too cold a morning
To get out of bed."

The army's retreating
The fleet has fled,
Caesar is beating
His drums through the dead.
"Antony, horses!
We'll get away,

Gather our forces
For another day . . ."
"It's a cold morning,"
Antony said.

Caesar Augustus
Cleared his phlegm.
"Corpses disgust us.
Cover them."
Caesar Augustus
In his time lay
Dying, and just as
Cold as they,
On the cold morning
Of a cold day.

My Father in the Night Commanding No

My father in the night commanding No
Has work to do. Smoke issues from his lips;
    He reads in silence.
The frogs are croaking and the streetlamps glow.

And then my mother winds the gramophone;
The Bride of Lammermoor begins to shriek—
    Or reads a story
About a prince, a castle, and a dragon.

The moon is glittering above the hill.
I stand before the gateposts of the King—
    So runs the story—
Of Thule, at midnight when the mice are still.

And I have been in Thule! It has come true—
The journey and the danger of the world,
    All that there is
To bear and to enjoy, endure and do.

Landscapes, seascapes . . . where have I been led?
The names of cities—Paris, Venice, Rome—
    Held out their arms.
A feathered god, seductive, went ahead.

Here is my house. Under a red rose tree
A child is swinging; another gravely plays.
    They are not surprised
That I am here; they were expecting me.

LOUIS SIMPSON

And yet my father sits and reads in silence,
My mother sheds a tear, the moon is still,
    And the dark wind
Is murmuring that nothing ever happens.

Beyond his jurisdiction as I move
Do I not prove him wrong? And yet, it's true
    They will not change
There, on the stage of terror and of love.

The actors in that playhouse always sit
In fixed positions—father, mother, child
    With painted eyes.
How sad it is to be a little puppet!

Their heads are wooden. And you once pretended
To understand them! Shake them as you will,
    They cannot speak.
Do what you will, the comedy is ended.

Father, why did you work? Why did you weep,
Mother? Was the story so important?
    "*Listen!*" the wind
Said to the children, and they fell asleep.

On the Lawn at the Villa

On the lawn at the villa—
That's the way to start, eh, reader?
We know where we stand—somewhere expensive—
You and I *imperturbes*, as Walt would say,
Before the diversions of wealth, you and I *engagés*.

On the lawn at the villa
Sat a manufacturer of explosives,
His wife from Paris,
And a young man named Bruno,

And myself, being American,
Willing to talk to these malefactors,
The manufacturer of explosives, and so on,
But somehow superior. By that I mean democratic.
It's complicated, being an American,
Having the money and the bad conscience, both at the same time.
Perhaps, after all, this is not the right subject for a poem.

We were all sitting there paralyzed
In the hot Tuscan afternoon,
And the bodies of the machine-gun crew were draped over the balcony.
So we sat there all afternoon.

A Story about Chicken Soup

In my grandmother's house there was always chicken soup
And talk of the old country—mud and boards,
Poverty,
The snow falling down the necks of lovers.

Now and then, out of her savings
She sent them a dowry. Imagine
The rice-powdered faces!
And the smell of the bride, like chicken soup.

But the Germans killed them.
I know it's in bad taste to say it,
But it's true. The Germans killed them all.

* * *

In the ruins of Berchtesgaden
A child with yellow hair
Ran out of a doorway.

A German girl-child—
Cuckoo, all skin and bones—
Not even enough to make chicken soup.
She sat by the stream and smiled.

Then as we splashed in the sun
She laughed at us.
We had killed her mechanical brothers,
So we forgave her.

* * *

The sun is shining.
The shadows of the lovers have disappeared.
They are all eyes; they have some demand on me—
They want me to be more serious than I want to be.

They want me to stick in their mudhole
Where no one is elegant.

LOUIS SIMPSON   323

They want me to wear old clothes,
They want me to be poor, to sleep in a room with many others—

Not to walk in the painted sunshine
To a summer house,
But to live in the tragic world forever.

The Photographer

A bearded man seated on a camp-stool—
'The geologist. 1910.'

'Staying with friends'—a boy in a straw hat,
on a porch, surrounded with wisteria.

'Noontime'—a view of the Battery
with masts passing over the rooftops.

Then the old horse-cars on Broadway,
people standing around in the garment district.

A high view of Manhattan,
light-shelves with sweeps of shadow.

'Jumpers'—as they come plunging down
their hair bursts into fire.

Then there are photographs of a door-knob,
a chair, an unstrung tennis-racket.

'Still life. Yes, for a while.
It gives your ideas a connection

And a beautiful woman yawning
with the back of her hand, like this.'

Chocolates

Once some people were visiting Chekhov.
While they made remarks about his genius
the Master fidgeted. Finally
he said, "Do you like chocolates?"

They were astonished, and silent.
He repeated the question,
whereupon one lady plucked up her courage
and murmured shyly, "Yes."

"Tell me," he said, leaning forward,
light glinting from his spectacles,
"what kind? The light, sweet chocolate
or the dark, bitter kind?"

The conversation became general.
They spoke of cherry centers,
of almonds and Brazil nuts.
Losing their inhibitions
they interrupted one another.
For people may not know what they think
about politics in the Balkans,
or the vexed question of men and women,

but everyone has a definite opinion
about the flavor of shredded coconut.
Finally someone spoke of chocolates filled with liqueur,
and everyone, even the author of *Uncle Vanya*,
was at a loss for words.

As they were leaving he stood by the door
and took their hands.
     In the coach returning to Petersburg
they agreed that it had been a most
unusual conversation.

Why Do You Write about Russia?

When I was a child
my mother told stories about the country
she came from. Wolves were howling,
snow fell, the drunken Cossack
shouted in the snow.

Rats prowled the floor of the cellar
where the children slept.
Once, after an illness, she was sent
to Odessa, on the sea. There were battleships
painted white, and ladies and gentlemen
walking the esplanade . . . white naval uniforms
and parasols.

LOUIS SIMPSON   325

These stories were told
against a background of tropical night . . .
a sea breeze stirring the flowers
that open at dusk, smelling like perfume.
The voice that spoke of freezing cold
itself was warm and infinitely comforting.

So it is with poetry: whatever numbing horrors
it may speak of, the voice itself
tells of love and infinite wonder.

Later, when I came to New York,
I used to go to my grandmother's
in Brooklyn. The names of stations
return in their order like a charm:
Franklin, Nostrand, Kingston.

And members of the family gather:
the three sisters, the one brother,
one of the cousins from Washington,
and myself . . . a "student at Columbia."
But what am I really?

For when my grandmother says, "Eat!
People who work with their heads have to eat more" . . .
Work? Does it deserve a name
so full of seriousness and high purpose?
Gazing across Amsterdam Avenue
at the windows opposite, letting my mind
wander where it will, from the page
to Malaya, or some street in Paris . . .
Drifting smoke. The end will be as fatal
as an opium-eater's dream.

* * *

The view has changed—to evergreens,
a hedge, and my neighbor's roof.
This too is like a dream, the way we live
with our cars and power-mowers . . .
a life that shuns emotion
and the violence that goes with it,
the object being to live quietly
and bring up children to be happy.

Yes, but what are you going to tell them
of what lies ahead?

That the better life seems
the more it goes sour? The child no longer
a child, his happiness all of a sudden
behind him. And he in turn
expected to bring up his children
to be happy . . .

What then do I want?

A life in which there are depths
beyond happiness. As one of my friends,
Grigoryev, says, "Two things
constantly cry out in creation,
the sea and man's soul."

Reaching from where we are
to where we came from . . . *Thalassa!*
a view of the sea.

* * *

I sit listening to the rasp
of a power-saw, the puttering of a motorboat.
The whole meaningless life around me
affirming a positive attitude . . .

When a hat appears, a black felt hat,
gliding along the hedge . . .
then a long, black overcoat
that falls beneath the knee.

He produces a big, purple handkerchief,
brushes off a chair, and sits.

"It's hot," he says, "but I like to walk,
that way you get to see the world.
And so, what are you reading now?"
Chekhov, I tell him.

"Of course. But have you read Leskov?
There are sentences that will stay in your mind
a whole lifetime.
For instance, in the 'Lady Macbeth,'
when the woman says to her lover,
'You couldn't be nearly as desirous
as you say you are, for I heard you singing' . . .
he answers, 'What about gnats?
They sing all their lives, but it's not for joy.'"

So my imaginary friend tells stories
of the same far place the soul comes from.

When I think about Russia
it's not that area of the earth's surface
with Leningrad to the West and Siberia
to the East—I don't know anything
about the continental mass.

It's a sound, such as you hear
in a sea breaking along a shore.

My people came from Russia,
bringing with them nothing
but that sound.

Notes

On the Lawn at the Villa. Walt is Walt Whitman, the American poet, whom the fourth line paraphrases.

A Story about Chicken Soup. Berchtesgaden was where Hitler's retreat in the final days of World War II.

The Photographer. Jumpers—possibly parachutists, or the subjects of Richard Avedon, famous people who are shown jumping up in the air. The voice at the end seems to be the photographer's, reminding us, among other things, that all "still" photos of living subjects can be thought of as "still life."

Why Do You Write about Russia? *Thalassa* is the Greek word for the sea.

Louis Simpson

Books

The Arrivistes: Poems 1940–1949, 1949
Good News of Death and Other Poems, 1955
A Dream of Governors, 1959
Riverside Drive (novel), 1962
At the End of the Open Road, 1963
Selected Poems, 1965
An Introduction to Poetry (textbook), 1967
Adventures of the Letter I, 1971
North of Jamaica (autobiography), 1972
*Three on the Tower: The Lives and Works of Ezra Pound, T. S. Eliot and William Carlos
    Williams* (criticism), 1975
Searching for the Ox, 1976

A Revolution in Taste: Studies of Dylan Thomas, Allen Ginsberg, Sylvia Plath and Robert Lowell (criticism), 1978
A Company of Poets, 1981

Criticism

Ronald Moran, *Louis Simpson*, 1972; Lawrence R. Smith, "A Conversation with Louis Simpson," *Chicago Review* 27 (Summer 1975); George Lensing and Ronald Moran, *Four Poets of the Emotive Imagination: Robert Bly, James Wright, Louis Simpson, and William Stafford*, 1976

Alberta
Turner

(b. 1921)

L ike some other writers in this collection, Alberta Turner is very
much a teaching poet, with considerable editing and critical
work to her credit as well. Born in New York City, she graduated
from Hunter and Wellesley and received a Ph.D. from Ohio State Uni-
versity. She has been teaching at Cleveland State University since 1964,
where she also directs the Poetry Center and a lively Poetry Series. Her

interests range from Milton to contemporary poetics, and she has published essays, textbooks and poems for many years. With the publication of her first book of poems, *Need* (1971), she literally put her earlier ways with poems to rest. Having written extremely formal poems that no longer satisfied her, she began doing the exercises she assigned her students, participated in informal sessions with close poet-friends, and found her way to her own voice and her own material. She has since published two other collections, *Learning to Count* (1974)—from which we include the title poem—and *Lid and Spoon* (1977); these books have marked her as a highly original poet, of whom Adrienne Rich has said, "A poet of dark, forceful images, wrenched it seems from a life bristling with awareness. ... She takes materials of domestic life and sees them through the eye of nightmare. The milk bottle, the cracked egg..., the parts of the body, become Boschian. ... And the voice that is recalling all these things is measured, precise and unhysterical."

Rich goes on to stress that Turner's work must be read as a whole, and that is true because she frequently works from one fragment to the next; only when strung together (as the poems are in the books) do the fragments assume the shape of a necklace. As Turner herself has noted, "The greatest part of craftsmanship is recognizing what has happened after it has happened." First she follows the emotional thrust of the apparently inconspicuous details she selects. Then she teases them into larger wholes, where they take on surprising dimensions: from two or three coalesced images we look out on many complex, implied relationships. It is a poetry that is never rendered sterile by statements or "ideas."

Allowing that both poems included here are "assemblages"—like "Learning to Count," "Choosing a Death" is a long title poem of a book in progress—she says they were written in intervals, with no idea they would eventually become one poem, much less appear in their original sequence. What goes on inside each cell, or section, within the larger wholes, is something akin to how "Proverbs, Riddles, Spells" behave (title of a poem not presented here). The mode is close to what is called hermetic, a poetry that looks to heighten the lyrical quality of each word in such a way as to congeal it, or seal it in, with little emphasis on connections, which are left to the reader to make. The result is a delicate interplay between sound and silence, and the poems ultimately depend on her finding just the right word and the right cluster of words that will "explode" in this fashion. Aside from the obvious reason that working at this length allows her to say more than the tiny poems, or sections, might say by themselves, length also helps her test the sections one by one that can best agglutinate. Finally, she can keep working a major theme through several places, or clusters in the poem, at once.

Turner's poems often seem concerned with place—much of "Learning to Count" was written on bus trips, and is about what the poet can "name, one by one" (see the epigraph to the poem). She says she frequently writes while traveling, especially the islands of the world, which is her serious hobby. This love of islands may lead her to her forms, the sections in the poems functioning as stepping stones. But deeper down, as the two poems here illustrate (and many shorter works as well, e.g. "Pronoun Song: Trying to Get Used to a Death," "After You Died") there is a large concern with death, to which she returns again and again and finally perceives as the necessity we must come to terms with. There is nothing ghostly or maudlin about this concern. She has simply watched people die around her, and is dealing with the declarative, visible aspects of such loss. She adds, "These are uncomfortable poems to write—and to read." For a contrast, the reader might want to consult "Eight Small Comfort Poems" in *Learning to Count*.

SF

Learning to Count

"Count for: to be worth;
count in: to include;
count on: to depend;
count: to name, one by one."

1 CROSSHAIRS

Snake fence—peace sign—"Poodle Pups"
cords of bird baths and Virgins
hedge with two teeth missing

To the schoolbus, an armful of kittens

Meat
    (a dog's head?)

jet
pigeons
    wish I could like dying

*"Patient has been extremely well during
the past year, with no major problems
except for the brittle diabetes."*

Waiting, I smoke the cars ahead;
exhaling guns them;
one VW can't climb it
unless I cough.

*"Skin: in good condition.
Nose: no congestion.
Teeth: in repair."*

Angel tips on drifts
and trees turned stubble.

It was to have been
an egg with three yolks
or a python zucchini.

When milk freezes,
the bottle's supposed to leak.

*"Extremities: no edema.
Breasts: no abnormality.
Blood sugar: elevated."*

Under the bridge a small car,
woman driving;
she's shifting gears, headed south.
At low tide I call down.
"Turn your lights on."
But tide's in, and she's
forgotten.

*"EKG: normal
Chest X-ray: normal.
Smallpox vaccination ordered
(patient is going to Scotland
for two weeks)."*

Man in my crosshairs!
Remember to aim left
of him.

II FEMALE

The flowering tree she planted on the baby's
grave is no good.
Come spring, she'll hate it.

Thou shalt eat the tomato because
the grasshopper has made a hole in it.
Thou shalt press the sweaty collar back
on the dried horse.

He was born in November,
lived three months,
but he spends a lot of time with her in March:
"Not when I want him to, but
passing the rocking horse,
I know he needs to rock."

> *"Look for MARIGOLD SEEDS*
> *April 17 to April 22 on*
> *PEPPERIDGE FARM*
> *Cinnamon Raisin*
> *Bread. . . . Can be started*
> *indoors, but do best when*
> *not transplanted."*

"This one will be a girl:
    it will have brown hair and brown eyes,
    I shall not name it Carl.
    I hear its heartbeat everyday, on the machine."

> *The cat on your lap*
> *is the oldest living thing in the crib,*
> *the cat is female,*
> *this is the second swelling.*

III HE? YOU? LOVE POEM?

Frost and toast:

Telling you makes crystals start out on my coat
rain
run out of my mouth;
telling you is drawer slides and quart after quart
of milk.

If you deafen—moss over bone gongs—
and tray after tray of grenades
loads through wool,
how shall we count?

> *You tore out the wool.*

If you killed me, I'd have no joy of it.
Yet I keep asking and
the soup skins over and
the towel smells of you.

Would you like to lie down?
Can I bring you milk?

I'm dreaming that squirrel again: the legs
come off; the chick I stepped on by
mistake oozed pink.

No, I won't bring you a urinal.

Kill the chick.

Needles keep me alive.
I hate my body
and your body.
Tell me snow is unclean.

Snow is clean.

He may have no face;
if he walks, it's on crutches;
there's phlegm in his throat.

But pain is not
what he's about.
He's a sort of foot, scraping
along stone.
Don't look,
      don't talk about it.

Don't

IV NAME

Knew it was swimming and swam for it, running
and ran for it—
   sifted
      dusted a city
dusted a cantaloupe
        dusted a cat asleep
           a pigeon
  a beer can
    liked it

On any old man

      on any itchy baby
or sick pigeon

you could learn to count.
The old man has socks; you can tell
what color they were and what color they
will be. He has jaws; they
hinge open, they hinge shut. You know

they will do that again. He has
legs; every time he falls, he puts one
before him and never the same one
twice; he has claws—

I must love the woman on the bus who always
wants to feel my face
    and the fat driver who won't let her on
and the dog pissing my mailbox;
I must love the brown lumps on the back of my hand.

And when I find the baby rabbit dead in my fireplace,
I must scrape it out with the same hands
                      that fed it milk;

and I must   not   wash them.

        You shall walk out in rows of tall corn
        your crotch will itch,
        crickets will scrape you,
        you will drink milk and drink milk and drink milk.

        All the stars must be named.

In my dream I saw a foot,
longer than this room it was,
and the tops of the toes came to my knees.
It was white, blue white,
like the flesh of cucumbers, only finer,
like the flesh of radishes,
but finer than that,
and the veins that roped it
were dark blue and firm, thicker
than my arm and firm.

Where the foot rose and thickened
toward the ankle
a pulse breathed slowly
like a great milky lung, filling and emptying—

The toes were straight,
spaced wide apart and wrinkled like cheeks.
I touched one; it was warm
and dry and pushed back.
        Pus   cheese   pin
           rain
        milk
                    milkring
            raisins
        the hose jumps

                    squeeze it
        braid it   *not oil*
        never oil

                        stubble

              ox tongue

                     sand
            NAME

And in my dream I squatted down and pressed my face
between the great toe
and the next one.

Choosing a Death

1

It's I found the iron kettle
my choice to fill it
If it empties on my foot
if I cook a friend
my choice too

Nothing happens
the curtains straight   hollyhocks
waiting for frost
Blood moves so slow even reeds don't lean
So I need to make a gate   no knotholes
a waterfall on this side
and over the top twigs or a bulbous cloud
Or the maid's room in your house Weese
white iron bed   white spread
dry January flies
cracks between the boards (lemon)
stairs down to the kitchen (clove)
since your stroke   no sheets

Spit into the wind   and camphor balls
glass bells   salt flakes   Spit again
and every size glove   Cough
and jacks you can count with a red ball
Outside there's nothing to do
So I shut my eyes and wait
for snow hiss on teasel or
trickle down pine   I know
blood settles into sludge   You

felt your pulse   Mother
asked for breakfast   I
walk along a shelf   push
every bottle off

Superstitious? Of course
I raise my eyes to three soft candles
and I'm three
The street is cobble   the priest and saint
up ahead   chanting
I scuff in petals and coffee grounds
over my shoes   "Shame   bad"
You laugh and pull me back
But lying on my back   the warm wet
disgrace halfway to my waist
the blanket drawn up
I like that

The stalk that rain pushed down
turns up   but only at the tip
and come an east wind what about
pines bent only from the west
or the fat drop
in rain?

I'm afraid
I lean down and tie my shoe
But my sore throat is mine

And then outside a theater its picture
on tiptoe holding me straight up   my tutu
a stiff wing   laughing over its shoulder
at me in the rumble seat   curving
down from the trapeze to catch
my hands   pleading with me
from behind bars
Its face folds to the woman's
in the change booth
She is old and whimpers when I pull
the nipple from her gums
She grows small in my arms   I fold
the corner of the blanket over
her head

I wear a charm around my neck
The chin is almost worn away
I fold my thumb into my palm
lift it to my mouth

It plays cards in a tavern with three men
and mentions buried gold
It sits on a rock combing its hair
slips off and comes up under my boat
Through the planks I feel its playful butt
It floats by on a log
On the bank grass slants and trees lean
sun moves up or down   I have been and am
going to be   Do I really want
that rose explosion?
Back in the tavern one asks to be dummy
and leaves the room

In my fever I go looking for my death
It will have shape and weight
will come in a mason jar or hang
from a ring   If I pull and it snaps back
it may be mine   or if it bounces
higher than my hand   It won't
be a fistful of rubber crumbs

I walk into the shoe-repair shop
It's over thirty days but I have a ticket
Someone burrows in the back   I hear
the click of heels   the plop
of rubber soles   and his muffled
Will you please come and look

Or I look for a long horse   one of a row
tied to a rail   I walk slowly
behind them   One slaps its tail
and shifts weight   One twitches
off a fly   Hobson says "Take the first one
They're all the same"
He's lying

Or I find a fan   Ease right and the thin bones
slide apart   precise   overlapping   the veins of ribbon
taut   It's a wing folded   Folded how long?
How do I know the ribbon's young?
The ring in my hand is green
If I leave it folded it still looks strong

In the drawer all the underwear is dry
Blood and milk have been soaped
and squeezed   elastic relaxed

ALBERTA TURNER

the snags ironed and pulled through
Dark and camphor   I feel too good to move

Tell me   is this the way to—
                "How much rice in your pocket?
                Have you told birds?"
In the sky   clouds petal   and repetal
around a mouth

My brother was cut from that funnel womb
an arm at a time   To be I had to lift
the whole roof   but the roof's silted shut
and the way back will be an arm at a time

Are you my death?
                "I'm your earring"
Have you got it under your arm?
                "That's my kidney machine"
Phoenix   phoenix
who's got the phoenix?

3

Mueng Lin chose plum blossoms and river mist
one man with his one ox
and a wicker basket that might hold fish
Made a bet with himself   if the man were at least
seventy and if the sun had just set or the man
had just napped   he'd take whatever that man caught
and put in his basket

I slide in through a tube and walk around
Rails   a curving bed of Queen Anne's lace
Tracks I suppose
as if I were a crossing-keeper's lodge
the sunflowers and poppies growing in cinders
and edged with whitewashed stones   as if
the train would come

One of them will have warm flanks   a nibbling lip
a jingle of bells in the pasture   snort
when it comes toward me   nuzzle my pocket
I'll mount and trot in a soft thud of peat
and ammonia steam   dip under an apple tree
pull one off
One is loose just behind the rim of trees
I hold out sugar   trip over a vine
and pull myself down   When I sit up
I don't feel like riding

A horse less in the stall   the smell
of urine almost gone
Billy stamps in the next box
then walks out   holding his bit
bright with his own saliva   arching his neck

Did I say *death?*   I'm not sure it was
not even sure anyone rode out
now the manure's dried
                "Do you need a death?"
Yes Weese   I need one
                "Why?"
Suppose there were no traffic lights
and no exit signs and no speed limit
and no rest stops and—
                "You don't believe that"
But the caterpillars are woollier
and the acorns have thicker shells
                "They always do"
I *need* to pretend water   pretend feed
prop the door open a crack—
                "Stop this foolishness
                and run along"

But gravity's no pun
The mercury won't fall below the glass
And I'm used to lying still
while zero jumps up and down
And when I wasn't looking
you came Weese   And just before you left
your arms   my hands   your scratchy face—
                "What can you make?"

Woollier for one
ears so tall a whole herd
can winter under them
a horse that—

                "Choose then"

Notes

Learning to Count. The landscape, as in the first three lines, contains many literal
details from a bus trip. The italicized sections in Part 1 are from an actual
medical report. The child who died was a grandson of the author (named Carl).
Choosing a Death. The card game in Part 2 is an allusion to Chaucer's "Pardoner's

Tale." The "Rose Explosion" is from Dante's "Paradiso." Hobson's remark refers to "Hobson's Choice," which is in effect no choice at all. Hobson, who operated the livery stable at Cambridge University (where Milton studied and would come to ride horses), "forced" students to take the next horse in line, regardless of their preferences. The poem is largely a "dreaming-awake" that turns into a childhood landscape. "Weese" is the nickname the author-child used for her father.

Alberta Turner

Books

Need, 1971
Learning to Count, 1974
Lid and Spoon, 1977
Fifty Contemporary Poets: The Creative Process (textbook), 1977
Poets Teaching: The Creative Process (textbook), 1980
To Make a Poem (textbook), 1982
A Belfry of Knees (forthcoming)

Richard Wilbur

(b. 1921)

Rhoda Nathans

Richard Wilbur was recognized early as a poet of exceptional skill and consistency. In his first book, *The Beautiful Changes* (1947), he seemed more fully formed and in command of what he wanted than most young poets. In retrospect we can see that that book was full of influences not yet fully absorbed—Hopkins, Marianne Moore, John Crowe Ransom, Auden, Stevens—and that the poet was still feeling his way toward what would be his mature style; but it is also true that the level of technical skill was unusually high. In an era when formal values were especially prized, it was a dazzling debut.

"A Black November Turkey," from Wilbur's third collection, *Things of This World* (1956), reveals his poetic strengths and preferences very clearly. The subject is a barnyard scene, but one such as few of us have experienced, so transformed is it by what the poet has chosen to emphasize. Experience is here aesthetic, and reality is aesthetically seen. The chickens become an illustration of the wonderful phenomenon of light. The turkey is an opportunity for imaginative comparisons: his body its own cortege, then a cloud and a ship, his feathers ashes, his head a shepherd's crook and a saint's death mask. When Wilbur is through with him, the turkey is a natural wonder, part of a reality that is enigmatic as to meaning but unmistakable as to beauty, not least in its way of balancing the turkey's "timeless" look with the "clocking" (note the fragrant pun on "clucking") hens and roosters. It is partly that the world provides us with such brilliant contrasts—black and white, timeless and clocking, superb and vulgar—and partly, of course, that the artist finds or makes them, since we would scarcely have made all this from turkey and hens on our own.

The power of reality to assert its beauty can be as succinctly observed as it is in "Transit," "A Storm in April," and "Stop." It can be the product of a naturalist's close interest in the details of a plant's structure and foliage, as in "Thyme Flowering among Rocks." At the close of "Stop" the poet invokes Greek mythology to complete his comparison, bringing together the unlikely beauty of the baggage-truck with the distant legends of a dim and glowing underworld. "Thyme Flowering among Rocks" ends with a reference to Bashō, the great Japanese writer of haiku, and the spirit that finds the world "Truer than it seems" is certainly one that the American poet can be said to share with his Japanese counterpart.

More complex treatments of this view of the world as hard to fathom but easy to admire and love can be found in "Beasts" and "Walking to Sleep." The "tracking" of "Beasts"—how it gets from one image to another—is intriguing and mysterious. It is a kind of nocturne, a mapping of the night that moves from beasts to the man-beast threshold where the werewolf is giving himself up to the sharper senses that seem the very basis of the poem's own alert survey. The latter half of the poem shows us romantic idealists, "suitors of excellence," whose dreams seem at first to separate them sharply from the beast's world until we realize that their construings of "the painful / Beauty of heaven, the lucid moon / And the risen hunter" bring them and us back round to the animal world once more. It is hard to imagine a more civilized and witty celebration of the powerful connections we have to the animals, to "bestiality." "Walking to Sleep," another night-piece and the longest selection here, treats insomnia, dream, imagination, the unsounded depths of the self, and life itself (for which it seems a giant metaphor) with a mesmerizing and urbane penetration that grows cumulatively more engrossing as the poem unwinds.

Noting that some of these poems rhyme and that most of them employ meter in original and masterful ways does not really tell us as much about Wilbur the poet as we might think. More to the point, perhaps, is the impression that their detachment, completeness, and control make upon us. This poet does not write about his life and feelings in the way that so many do. His witty and impersonal manner runs through all his work, so that for the three decades covered by this anthology he has remained consistent in his commitments and artistic preferences, a choice that deserves understanding and respect. It has made him a stable point in a world where artistic and political currents have often swirled confusingly, and he has always had good lessons to teach young poets who have sent themselves to school among his poems, where the eye for detail and the ear for graceful music have never faltered.

Richard Wilbur taught for many years at Wesleyan University. An expert translator, he is famous for his versions of Molière's comedies. That stage experience may have led to his successful venture as a writer of song lyrics for the musical *Candide*. His program as a poet remains what he declared it to be in 1950, "an effort to articulate relationships not quite seen, to make or discover some pattern in the world" (*Mid-Century Poets*, ed. John Ciardi). This makes him an aesthete in the best sense, as Stevens was, and the uncertainty about whether the pattern is being discovered or imposed is one of the things that keeps his poems exciting.

DY

A Black November Turkey

to A.M. and A.M.

Nine white chickens come
With haunchy walk and heads
Jabbing among the chips, the chaff, the stones
And the cornhusk-shreds,

And bit by bit infringe
A pond of dusty light,
Spectral in shadow until they bobbingly one
    By one ignite.

Neither pale nor bright,
The turkey-cock parades
Through radiant squalors, darkly auspicious as
    The ace of spades,

Himself his own cortège
And puffed with the pomp of death,
Rehearsing over and over with strangled râle
    His latest breath.

The vast black body floats
Above the crossing knees
As a cloud over thrashed branches, a calm ship
    Over choppy seas,

Shuddering its fan and feathers
In fine soft clashes
With the cold sound that the wind makes, fondling
    Paper-ashes.

The pale-blue pony head
Set on its shepherd's-crook
Like a saint's death-mask, turns a vague, superb
    And timeless look

Upon these clocking hens
And the cocks that one by one,
Dawn after mortal dawn, with vulgar joy
    Acclaim the sun.

Beasts

Beasts in their major freedom
Slumber in peace tonight. The gull on his ledge
Dreams in the guts of himself the moon-plucked waves below,
    And the sunfish leans on a stone, slept
        By the lyric water,

In which the spotless feet
Of deer make dulcet splashes, and to which
The ripped mouse, safe in the owl's talon, cries
    Concordance. Here there is no such harm
        And no such darkness

As the selfsame moon observes
Where, warped in window-glass, it sponsors now
The werewolf's painful change. Turning his head away
On the sweaty bolster, he tries to remember
The mood of manhood,

But lies at last, as always,
Letting it happen, the fierce fur soft to his face,
Hearing with sharper ears the wind's exciting minors,
The leaves' panic, and the degradation
Of the heavy streams.

Meantime, at high windows
Far from thicket and pad-fall, suitors of excellence
Sigh and turn from their work to construe again the painful
Beauty of heaven, the lucid moon
And the risen hunter,

Making such dreams for men
As told will break their hearts as always, bringing
Monsters into the city, crows on the public statues,
Navies fed to the fish in the dark
Unbridled waters.

Stop

In grimy winter dusk
We slowed for a concrete platform;
The pillars passed more slowly;
A paper bag leapt up.

The train banged to a standstill.
Brake-steam rose and parted.
Three chipped-at blocks of ice
Sprawled on a baggage-truck.

Out in that glum, cold air
The broken ice lay glintless,
But the truck was painted blue
On side, wheels, and tongue,

A purple, glowering blue
Like the phosphorus of Lethe
Or Queen Persephone's gaze
In the numb fields of the dark.

RICHARD WILBUR

Thyme Flowering among Rocks

This, if Japanese,
Would represent grey boulders
Walloped by rough seas

So that, here or there,
The balked water tossed its froth
Straight into the air.

Here, where things are what
They are, it is thyme blooming,
Rocks, and nothing but—

Having, nonetheless,
Many small leaves implicit,
A green countlessness.

Crouching down, peering
Into perplexed recesses,
You find a clearing

Occupied by sun
Where, along prone, rachitic
Branches, one by one,

Pale stems arise, squared
In the manner of *Mentha*,
The oblong leaves paired.

One branch, in ending,
Lifts a little and begets
A straight-ascending

Spike, whorled with fine blue
Or purple trumpets, banked in
The leaf-axils. You

Are lost now in dense
Fact, fact which one might have thought
Hidden from the sense,

Blinking at detail
Peppery as this fragrance,
Lost to proper scale

As, in the motion
Of striped fins, a bathysphere
Forgets the ocean.

It makes the craned head
Spin. Unfathomed thyme! The world's
A dream, Basho said,

Not because that dream's
A falsehood, but because it's
Truer than it seems.

Walking to Sleep

As a queen sits down, knowing that a chair will be there,
Or a general raises his hand and is given the field-glasses,
Step off assuredly into the blank of your mind.
Something will come to you. Although at first
You nod through nothing like a fogbound prow,
Gravel will breed in the margins of your gaze,
Perhaps with tussocks or a dusty flower,
And, humped like dolphins playing in the bow-wave,
Hills will suggest themselves. All such suggestions
Are yours to take or leave, but hear this warning:
Let them not be too velvet green, the fields
Which the deft needle of your eye appoints,
Nor the old farm past which you make your way
Too shady-linteled, too instinct with home.
It is precisely from Potemkin barns
With their fresh-painted hex signs on the gables,
Their sparkling gloom within, their stanchion-rattle
And sweet breath of silage, that there comes
The trotting cat whose head is but a skull.
Try to remember this: what you project
Is what you will perceive; what you perceive
With any passion, be it love or terror,
May take on whims and powers of its own.
Therefore a numb and grudging circumspection
Will serve you best, unless you overdo it,
Watching your step too narrowly, refusing
To specify a world, shrinking your purview
To a tight vision of your inching shoes—
Which may, as soon you come to think, be crossing
An unseen gorge upon a rotten trestle.
What you must manage is to bring to mind
A landscape not worth looking at, some bleak
Champaign at dead November's end, its grass
As dry as lichen, and its lichens grey,

Such glumly simple country that a glance
Of flat indifference from time to time
Will stabilize it. Lifeless thus, and leafless,
The view should set at rest all thoughts of ambush.
Nevertheless, permit no roadside thickets
Which, as you pass, might shake with worse than wind;
Revoke all trees and other cover; blast
The upstart boulder which a flicking shape
Has stepped behind; above all, put a stop
To the known stranger up ahead, whose face
Half turns to mark you with a creased expression.
Here let me interject that steady trudging
Can make you drowsy, so that without transition,
As when an old film jumps in the projector,
You will be wading a dun hallway, rounding
A newel post, and starting up the stairs.
Should that occur, adjust to circumstances
And carry on, taking these few precautions:
Detach some portion of your thought to guard
The outside of the building; as you wind
From room to room, leave nothing at your back,
But slough all memories at every threshold;
Nor must you dream of opening any door
Until you have foreseen what lies beyond it.
Regardless of its seeming size, or what
May first impress you as its style or function,
The abrupt structure which involves you now
Will improvise like vapor. Groping down
The gritty cellar steps and past the fuse-box,
Brushing through sheeted lawn-chairs, you emerge
In some cathedral's pillared crypt, and thence,
Your brow alight with carbide, pick your way
To the main shaft through drifts and rubbly tunnels.
Promptly the hoist, ascending toward the pit-head,
Rolls downward past your gaze a dinted rock-face
Peppered with hacks and drill-holes, which acquire
Insensibly the look of hieroglyphics.
Whether to surface now within the vast
Stone tent where Cheops lay secure, or take
The proffered shed of corrugated iron
Which gives at once upon a vacant barracks,
Is up to you. Need I, at this point, tell you
What to avoid? Avoid the pleasant room
Where someone, smiling to herself, has placed
A bowl of yellow freesias. Do not let
The thought of her in yellow, lithe and sleek

As lemonwood, mislead you where the curtains,
Romping like spinnakers which taste the wind,
Bellying out and lifting till the sill
Has shipped a drench of sunlight, then subsiding,
Both warm and cool the love-bed. Your concern
Is not to be detained by dread, or by
Such dear acceptances as would entail it,
But to pursue an ever-dimming course
Of pure transition, treading as in water
Past crumbling tufa, down cloacal halls
Of boarded-up hotels, through attics full
Of glassy taxidermy, moping on
Like a drugged fire-inspector. What you hope for
Is that at some point of the pointless journey,
Indoors or out, and when you least expect it,
Right in the middle of your stride, like that,
So neatly that you never feel a thing,
The kind assassin Sleep will draw a bead
And blow your brains out.
                                        What, are you still awake?
Then you must risk another tack and footing.
Forget what I have said. Open your eyes
To the good blackness not of your room alone
But of the sky you trust is over it,
Whose stars, though foundering in the time to come,
Bequeath us constantly a jetsam beauty.
Now with your knuckles rub your eyelids, seeing
The phosphenes caper like St. Elmo's fire,
And let your head heel over on the pillow
Like a flung skiff on wild Gennesaret.
Let all things storm your thought with the moiled flocking
Of startled rookeries, or flak in air,
Or blossom-fall, and out of that come striding
In the strong dream by which you have been chosen.
Are you upon the roads again? If so,
Be led past honeyed meadows which might tempt
A wolf to graze, and groves which are not you
But answer to your suppler self, that nature
Able to bear the thrush's quirky glee
In stands of chuted light, yet praise as well,
All leaves aside, the barren bark of winter.
When, as you may, you find yourself approaching
A crossroads and its laden gallows tree,
Do not with hooded eyes allow the shadow
Of a man moored in air to bruise your forehead,
But lift your gaze and stare your brother down,

Though the swart crows have pecked his sockets hollow.
As for what turn your travels then will take,
I cannot guess. Long errantry perhaps
Will arm you to be gentle, or the claws
Of nightmare flap you pathless God knows where,
As the crow flies, to meet your dearest horror.
Still, if you are in luck, you may be granted,
As, inland, one can sometimes smell the sea,
A moment's perfect carelessness, in which
To stumble a few steps and sink to sleep
In the same clearing where, in the old story,
A holy man discovered Vishnu sleeping,
Wrapped in his maya, dreaming by a pool
On whose calm face all images whatever
Lay clear, unfathomed, taken as they came.

A Storm in April

for Ben

Some winters, taking leave,
Deal us a last, hard blow,
Salting the ground like Carthage
Before they will go.

But the bright, milling snow
Which throngs the air today—
It is a way of leaving
So as to stay.

The light flakes do not weigh
The willows down, but sift
Through the white catkins, loose
As petal-drift,

Or in an up-draft lift
And glitter at a height,
Dazzling as summer's leaf-stir
Chinked with light.

This storm, if I am right,
Will not be wholly over
Till green fields, here and there,
Turn white with clover,

And through chill air the puffs of milkweed hover.

Transit

A woman I have never seen before
Steps from the darkness of her town-house door
At just that crux of time when she is made
So beautiful that she or time must fade.

What use to claim that as she tugs her gloves
A phantom heraldry of all the loves
Blares from the lintel? That the staggered sun
Forgets, in his confusion, how to run?

Still, nothing changes as her perfect feet
Click down the walk that issues in the street,
Leaving the stations of her body there
As a whip maps the countries of the air.

Richard Wilbur

Books

The Beautiful Changes and Other Poems, 1947
Ceremony and Other Poems, 1950
A Bestiary (compilation), 1955
Molière, *The Misanthrope* (translation), 1955
Things of This World, 1956
Poems, 1943–1956, 1957
Candide: A Comic Operetta Based on Voltaire's Satire (lyrics by Wilbur, book by Hellman, score by Bernstein), 1957
Poe: Complete Poems (edition), 1959
Advice to a Prophet and Other Poems, 1961
Molière, *Tartuffe* (translation), 1963
The Poems of Richard Wilbur, 1963
Walking to Sleep, New Poems and Translations, 1969
Molière, *The School for Wives* (translation), 1972
Opposites, 1973
The Mind Reader, 1976
Responses: Prose Pieces, 1953–1976 (criticism), 1976
Molière, *The Learned Ladies* (translation), 1978
The Whale: Uncollected Translations, 1980

Interviews, Criticism

David Curry, "An Interview with Richard Wilbur," *Trinity Review* 17 (December 1962); Robert Frank and Stephen Mitchell, "Richard Wilbur: An Interview," *Amherst Library Magazine* 10 (Summer 1964); Edward Honig, "A Conversation with Richard Wilbur," *Modern Language Notes* 91 (October 1976); Peter Stitt, Ellesa High, Helen McCoy, "The Art of Poetry," *Paris Review* 19 (Winter 1977); Donald Hall, "The New Poetry: Notes on the Past Fifteen Years in America," in *New World Writing*, 1955; Ralph J. Mills, Jr., *Contemporary American Poetry*, 1965; Donald Hill, *Richard Wilbur*, 1967; John Field, *Richard Wilbur: A Bibliographical Checklist*, 1971

NINETEEN POETS BORN BETWEEN 1920 AND 1930

James
Wright

(1927–1980)

A broad vein of compassion and social concern runs through the poetry of James Wright. Growing up in Martin's Ferry, an industrial town on the Ohio River, in a working-class family and amid the considerable poverty of the Great Depression, he developed a sympathy for criminals, derelicts, minorities, and the uneducated poor that never left him. A note of sorrow, even of anguish, is never far away in his poems, though they can ring with celebration and reverberate with humor.

Educated at Kenyon College, where he studied with John Crowe Ransom, and at the University of Washington, where Theodore Roethke was his teacher and friend, James Wright began in the 1950s, like so many poets of his generation, writing poems of a formal cast. "Mutterings over the Crib of a Deaf Child," from his first collection, *The Green Wall* (1957), demonstrates this early manner at its most delicate and successful, in a poem that combines qualities of song with a dramatic exchange between two voices. "Saint Judas," the title poem of his second collection (1959), is technically impressive both as a sonnet and as a dramatic monologue. What makes it characteristically Wright's is the emphasis on suffering—even Judas cannot be free of compassion—along with the idea that altruism should involve no bargaining. Since he feels already "banished from heaven," Judas expects no reward for his kindness; he holds the man "for nothing" and presumably out of an empathy born of his own hopelessness.

After *Saint Judas*, Wright's style changed markedly. He had already moved to Minneapolis, and his friendship with another Minnesota poet, Robert Bly, as well as his interest in translation, brought the work of foreign poets to bear on his poetry in a dramatic way. Classical Chinese poetry, German expressionist poetry, especially Georg Trakl's, and Spanish surrealism, particularly as found in the work of Vallejo and Neruda—these influences enabled Bly and Wright to break sharply with their previous poems and forge a new style. The resulting poetry had a plainness, directness, and candor that made a considerable impact on American poetry during the 1960s. What is especially curious about this shift in Wright's case (Bly's too) is that it enabled the poet to write his most indelibly American poetry. Wright's earlier work had been mildly influenced by Robert Frost and Edward Arlington Robinson; but the new style, with its wild mixture of foreign influences, took Wright into his most impressive accounts of American settings and American experience. "Stages on a Journey Westward" is an obvious example of this, and "Twilights" is an even more interesting one: It behaves very much like a German expressionist or Spanish surrealist poem, but its maple leaves, shopping centers, steel mills, and barns make it indubitably American. The same observation can be made about "Outside Fargo, North Dakota," "Milkweed," "Two Hangovers," and "The Life." All these poems manage to capture scenes and feelings that are characteristic of American life but that had never gotten into our poetry before. They may be as mythic in cast as "The Life," which mentions Etruscans but is deeply American in its voice, movement, mood, and details—a poem that could come from no other culture. They may be as haunting and picturesque as "Outside Fargo, North Dakota," where middlewestern loneliness and the somber beauty of the Great Plains are caught in a breathtaking poem modeled after the Chinese lyric. And they may draw specifically on Wright's own experience growing up in Ohio, as the first part of "Two Hangovers" does. In their range and music, these poems of the 1960s had an effect on American poetry that is still to be fully assessed.

In the 1970s, living and teaching in New York City and traveling often to Europe, Wright began to produce poems that reflect a newfound fascination with the Mediterranean world, as the poems that conclude our selection tend to demonstrate. He could still treat American subjects effectively, as in "Snowfall: a Poem about Spring" and the bitter "Ohioan Pastoral"; but the poems "Mantova," "Apollo," "Against Surrealism," and "A Winter Daybreak above Vence" are much more typical of his last three volumes. Sometimes the poems of this phase make deliberate connections with the classical world. "Mantova" is built around a line by Catullus. "Apollo" finds "The only home where now, alone in the evening, / The god stays alive," meaning both the last light of the setting sun and the presence of divinity as they are reflected in the young fisherman's face. For all their classical leanings, however, these poems are mainly romantic lyrics, more celebratory and happy than the work of Wright's early and middle years. The last of them, and one of his last poems, "A Winter Daybreak above Vence," is an extraordinary account of a dawn that is comic, theatrical, dreamlike, mystical, and tender, all at the same time.

In 1980, shortly after he had completed his final collection of poems, *This Journey*, James Wright died in New York City.

DY

Mutterings over the Crib
of a Deaf Child

"How will he hear the bell at school
Arrange the broken afternoon,
And know to run across the cool
Grasses where the starlings cry,
Or understand the day is gone?"

Well, someone lifting curious brows
Will take the measure of the clock.
And he will see the birchen boughs
Outside sagging dark from the sky,
And the shade crawling upon the rock.

"And how will he know to rise at morning?
His mother has other sons to waken,
She has the stove she must build to burning
Before the coals of the nighttime die;
And he never stirs when he is shaken."

I take it the air affects the skin,
And you remember, when you were young,
Sometimes you could feel the dawn begin,
And the fire would call you, by and by,
Out of the bed and bring you along.

"Well, good enough. To serve his needs
All kinds of arrangements can be made.
But what will you do if his finger bleeds?
Or a bobwhite whistles invisibly
And flutes like an angel off in the shade?"

He will learn pain. And, as for the bird,
It is always darkening when that comes out.
I will putter as though I had not heard,
And lift him into my arms and sing
Whether he hears my song or not.

Saint Judas

When I went out to kill myself, I caught
A pack of hoodlums beating up a man.
Running to spare his suffering, I forgot
My name, my number, how my day began,
How soldiers milled around the garden stone
And sang amusing songs; how all that day
Their javelins measured crowds; how I alone
Bargained the proper coins, and slipped away.

Banished from heaven, I found this victim beaten,
Stripped, kneed, and left to cry. Dropping my rope
Aside, I ran, ignored the uniforms:
Then I remembered bread my flesh had eaten,
The kiss that ate my flesh. Flayed without hope,
I held the man for nothing in my arms.

Stages on a Journey Westward

1

I began in Ohio.
I still dream of home.
Near Mansfield, enormous dobbins enter dark barns in autumn,
Where they can be lazy, where they can munch little apples,
Or sleep long.
But by night now, in the bread lines my father
Prowls, I cannot find him: So far off,
1500 miles or so away, and yet
I can hardly sleep.
In a blue rag the old man limps to my bed,
Leading a blind horse
Of gentleness.
In 1932, grimy with machinery, he sang me
A lullaby of a goosegirl.
Outside the house, the slag heaps waited.

2

In western Minnesota, just now,
I slept again.
In my dream, I crouched over a fire.
The only human beings between me and the Pacific Ocean
Were old Indians, who wanted to kill me.
They squat and stare for hours into small fires
Far off in the mountains.
The blades of their hatchets are dirty with the grease
Of huge, silent buffaloes.

3

It is dawn.
I am shivering,
Even beneath a huge eiderdown.
I came in last night, drunk,
And left the oil stove cold.
I listen a long time, now, to the flurries.
Snow howls all around me, out of the abandoned prairies.
It sounds like the voices of bums and gamblers,
Rattling through the bare nineteenth-century whorehouses
In Nevada.

4

Defeated for re-election,
The half-educated sheriff of Mukilteo, Washington,

Has been drinking again.
He leads me up the cliff, tottering.
Both drunk, we stand among the graves.
Miners paused here on the way up to Alaska.
Angry, they spaded their broken women's bodies
Into ditches of crab grass.
I lie down between tombstones.
At the bottom of the cliff
America is over and done with.
America,
Plunged into the dark furrows
Of the sea again.

Twilights

The big stones of the cistern behind the barn
Are soaked in whitewash.
My grandmother's face is a small maple leaf
Pressed in a secret box.
Locusts are climbing down into the dark green crevices
Of my childhood. Latches click softly in the trees. Your hair is gray.

The arbors of the cities are withered.
Far off, the shopping centers empty and darken.

A red shadow of steel mills.

Two Hangovers

NUMBER ONE
I slouch in bed.
Beyond the streaked trees of my window,
All groves are bare.
Locusts and poplars change to unmarried women
Sorting slate from anthracite
Between railroad ties:
The yellow-bearded winter of the depression
Is still alive somewhere, an old man
Counting his collection of bottle caps
In a tarpaper shack under the cold trees
Of my grave.

I still feel half drunk,
And all those old women beyond my window
Are hunching toward the graveyard.

Drunk, mumbling Hungarian,
The sun staggers in,
And his big stupid face pitches
Into the stove.
For two hours I have been dreaming
Of green butterflies searching for diamonds
In coal seams;
And children chasing each other for a game
Through the hills of fresh graves.
But the sun has come home drunk from the sea,
And a sparrow outside
Sings of the Hanna Coal Co. and the dead moon.
The filaments of cold light bulbs tremble
In music like delicate birds.
Ah, turn it off.

NUMBER TWO: I TRY TO WAKEN AND GREET THE WORLD ONCE AGAIN
In a pine tree,
A few yards away from my window sill,
A brilliant blue jay is springing up and down, up and down,
On a branch.
I laugh, as I see him abandon himself
To entire delight, for he knows as well as I do
That the branch will not break.

Milkweed

While I stood here, in the open, lost in myself,
I must have looked a long time
Down the corn rows, beyond grass,
The small house,
White walls, animals lumbering toward the barn.
I look down now. It is all changed.
Whatever it was I lost, whatever I wept for
Was a wild, gentle thing, the small dark eyes
Loving me in secret.
It is here. At a touch of my hand,
The air fills with delicate creatures
From the other world.

JAMES WRIGHT

Outside Fargo, North Dakota

Along the sprawled body of the derailed
    Great Northern freight car,
I strike a match slowly and lift it slowly.
No wind.

Beyond town, three heavy white horses
Wade all the way to their shoulders
In a silo shadow.

Suddenly the freight car lurches.
The door slams back, a man with a flashlight
Calls me good evening.
I nod as I write good evening, lonely
And sick for home.

The Life

Murdered, I went, risen,
Where the murderers are,
That black ditch
Of river.

And if I come back to my only country
With a white rose on my shoulder,
What is that to you?
It is the grave
In blossom.

It is the trillium of darkness,
It is hell, it is the beginning of winter,
It is a ghost town of Etruscans who have no names
Any more.

It is the old loneliness.
It is.
And it is
The last time.

Mantova

optima dies prima fugit

The first thing I saw in the morning
Was a huge golden bee ploughing
His burly right shoulder into the belly
Of a sleek yellow pear
Low on a bough.
Before he could find that sudden black honey
That squirms around in there
Inside the seed, the tree could not bear any more.
The pear fell to the ground,
With the bee still half alive
Inside its body.
He would have died had I not knelt down
And sliced the pear gently
A little more open.
The bee shuddered, and returned.
Maybe I should have left him alone there
Drowning in his own delight.
The best days are the first
To flee.

Apollo

A young man, his face dark
With the sea's fire,
Quickens his needle bone through the webbing,
And passes away.
Out of my sight
And back again, as the moon
Braces its shoulders and disappears
And appears again, the young man's face
Begins to turn gray
In the evening light that cannot
Make up for loss.
It is morning and evening again, all over the water.
I know it is only moonlight that changes him, I know
It does not matter. The sea's fire
Is only the cold shadow of the moon's,

And the moon's
Fire itself only the cold
Shadow of the young
Fisherman's face:
The only home where now, alone in the evening,
The god stays alive.

Against Surrealism

There are some tiny obvious details in human life that survive the divine pur-
pose of boring fools to death. In France, all the way down south in Avallon, peo-
ple like to eat cake. The local bakers there spin up a little flour and chocolate
into the shape of a penguin. We came back again and again to a certain window
to admire a flock of them. But we never bought one.

We found ourselves wandering through Italy, homesick for penguins.

Then a terrible and savage fire of the dog-days roared all over the fourteenth
Arondissement: which is to say, it was August: and three chocolate penguins
appeared behind a window near Place Denfert-Rochereau. We were afraid the
Parisians would recognize them, so we bought them all and snuck them home
under cover.

We set them out on a small table above half the rooftops of Paris. I reached
out to brush a tiny obvious particle of dust from the tip of a beak. Suddenly the
dust dropped an inch and hovered there. Then it rose to the beak again.

It was a blue spider.

If I were a blue spider, I would certainly ride on a train all the way from
Avallon to Paris, and I would set up my house on the nose of a chocolate pen-
guin. It's just a matter of common sense.

Ohioan Pastoral

On the other side
Of Salt Creek, along the road, the barns topple
And snag among the orange-rinds,
Oil cans, cold balloons of lovers.
One barn there
Sags, sags and oozes
Down one side of the copperous gulley.

The limp whip of a sumac dangles
Gently against the body of a lost
Bathtub, while high in the flint-cracks
And the wild grimes trees, on the hill,
A buried gas-main
Long ago tore a black gutter into the mines.
And now it hisses among the green rings
On fingers in coffins.

Snowfall: a Poem about Spring

The field mouse follows its own shadow
Up out of the twelve inch fall
From a thin surface on one side of the path
Into a dark laurel some
Five feet away.

I take my little walk
Five feet beyond you and, all alone,
I follow the field mouse.
He and I track
The skeleton of an acorn, over
To the other side of the path.

He and I
Are gone a little,
But you
Somehow go over there at the other end of the snow tunnel, your throat

Bundled with laurel.

Ah, we breathe, we two,
We are not afraid of you, we will come out

And gather with you.

A Winter Daybreak above Vence

The night's drifts
Pile up below me and behind my back,
Slide down the hill, rise again, and build
Eerie little dunes on the roof of the house.

In the valley below me,
Miles between me and the town of Ste. Jeannet,
The road lamps glow.
They are so cold, they might as well be dark.
Trucks and cars
Cough and drone down there between the golden
Coffins of greenhouses, the startled squawk
Of a rooster claws heavily across
A grove, and drowns.
The gumming snarl of some grouchy dog sounds,
And a man bitterly shifts his broken gears,
True night still hands on,
Mist cluttered with a racket of its own.

Now on the mountain side,
A little way downhill among turning rocks,
A square takes form in the side of a dim wall.
I hear a bucket rattle or something, tinny,
No other stirring behind the dim face
Of the goatherd's house. I imagine
His goats are still sleeping, dreaming
Of the fresh roses
Beyond the walls of the greenhouse below them
And of lettuce leaves opening in Tunisia.

I turn, and somehow
Impossibly hovering in the air over everything,
The Mediterranean, nearer to the moon
Than this mountain is,
Shines. A voice clearly
Tells me to snap out of it. Galway
Mutters out of the house and up the stone stairs
To start the motor. The moon and the stars
Suddenly flicker out, and the whole mountain
Appears, pale as a shell.

Look, the sea has not fallen and broken
Our heads. How can I feel so warm
Here in the dead center of January? I can
Scarcely believe it, and yet I have to, this is
The only life I have. I get up from the stone.
My body mumbles something unseemly
And follows me. Now we are all sitting here strangely
On top of the sunlight.

NINETEEN POETS BORN BETWEEN 1920 AND 1930

James Wright

Books

The Green Wall, 1957
Saint Judas, 1959
Twenty Poems of Georg Trakl (translations, with Robert Bly), 1961
The Branch Will Not Break, 1963
The Rider on the White Horse: Selected Short Fiction of Theodor Storm (translations), 1964
Shall We Gather at the River, 1968
Poems by Hermann Hesse (translations), 1970
Collected Poems, 1971
Neruda and Vallejo: Selected Poems (translations, with Robert Bly and John Knoepfle), 1971
Wandering: Notes and Sketches by Hermann Hesse (translations, with Franz Wright), 1972
Two Citizens, 1973
To a Blossoming Pear Tree, 1977
This Journey, 1982

Interviews, Criticism

William Heyen and Jerome Mazzaro, "Something to be Said for the Light: A Conversation with James Wright," *Southern Humanities Review* 6 (1972); Interview, *Paris Review* 62 (1975); "Letters from Europe, Two Notes from Venice, Remarks on Two Poems, and Other Occasional Prose," in *American Poets in 1976*, ed. William Heyen, 1976; Michael Cuddihy, ed., *Ironwood: James Wright/A Special Issue*, vol. 5, no. 2, 1977; *see also* the Lensing and Moran book listed in the Robert Bly, Louis Simpson, and William Stafford entries.

Twelve Poets Born Between 1930 and 1940

PART FOUR

Marvin
Bell

(b. 1937)

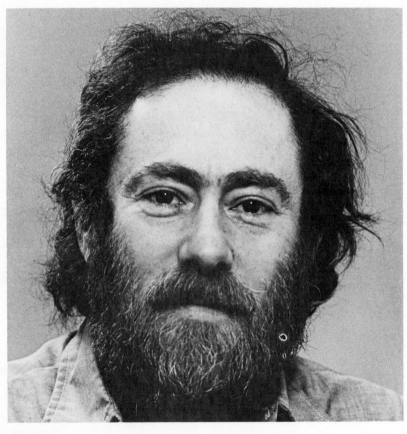

John Riley

M arvin Bell understands very well that, as Gertrude Stein re-
marked, "the contemporary thing is the thing you can't get
away from." Even if he writes about the past ("Fresh News

from the Past"), the emphasis is on updating, his eye and mind fixed on the present, which is fiercely, almost relentlessly, observed. Indeed, Bell's poetry is obsessed with observation, and he has defined the imagination as "a special way of seeing, not inventing."

He works with several basic techniques, chief among them a kind of silhouetting. By casting a dark image on a light background, or a light on a dark, he often seems to be taking two pictures simultaneously ("Two Pictures of a Leaf"; "Stars Which See, Stars Which Do Not See"), exploring reverse images, circling things, doubling back on them, in no hurry to strike the delicate balance between detachment and involvement that contemporary poetry honors. For example, he says of "Gemwood," which was originally called "How We Think Back," that it attempts "to follow mind and emotions backwards then forwards beyond the present."

In his early work, which attracted a good deal of attention for its musical properties and formal elegance, Bell admits he was too involved. The effect was sometimes one of straining. Though these early pieces had many redeeming qualities—notably his ability to laugh at himself—Bell has since discovered deeper feelings about the nature of human relationships. The result is more modest poems that explore the mind's random ways as it pokes around before taking the plunge into absorption. The selection from his most recent volume included here ("These Green-Going-to-Yellow," the title poem) is a good example of his maturing ability to follow the musing where it leads: "we look away, or look at the middles of things" seems startlingly true and plainly said.

Bell's way with syntax and diction is also a special contribution to what the contemporary poem can achieve. The first stanza of "Origin of Dreams," for instance, is one long sentence, a complex mix of voice and elaborate structure that incorporates surprising qualifications in such a smooth and quick manner that the listening ear accepts the large amount of information readily. In the middle of "The Mystery of Emily Dickinson" we are whirled physically and mentally around, ready for the final apparition: "This morning, not much after dawn, / in level country, not New England's, / through leftovers of summer rain I / went out rag-tag to the curb, only / a sleepy householder at his routine." Those "nots" bump us back, and words like "leftovers" and "rag-tag" dissemble; it is no wonder we are not ready for what we see next.

Bell's use of dialogue is another major technique that he takes full advantage of in pursuing his obsession: to outline all options and analyze them as if he were developing laws. If he is not addressing his father, or bringing a literary ancestor to life (Emily Dickinson), or engaging in a whole book of letter-poems with a friend (*Hunger for Stories: A Correspondence*, by William Stafford and Marvin Bell), he will conjure up something like a tree ("To an Adolescent Weeping Willow"—in his newest collection, but not included here) to have a long quiet talk with. Bell needs conversation desperately, with his father, his family, others, or himself if necessary. He has been called "a poet of the family," which is to say he cares deeply about people. It matters to him that we acknowledge how we feel about others, and his work is filled with "narrative, circumstance, and characters," which he himself suggests are what it takes to make myth.

The struggle to honor his father lies at the heart of Bell's work, from the earliest poems published in the 1960s through more recent poems printed here. It dominates "Obsessive" (from *The Escape into You*, 1971), "Origin of Dreams," and "Little Father Poem" (both from *Residue of Song*, 1974); is part of the issue in "Gemwood" (from *Stars Which See, Stars Which Do Not See*, 1977); and surfaces in many other poems as well. Like many poets of immigrant parents who survived terrible events, Bell has been paying and repaying the debt he feels is due his father. Returning as he does to the father stories, Bell seems resigned to accepting their legacy, as inevitable as it is paradoxical: "Father / forgave us when we did nothing wrong, / Father made us well when we were healthy." While admonishing us to keep our distance from our fathers, "Little Father Poem" admits that "Father in his grave / gives us everything we ever wanted." Bell is rightly content to leave matters at that, with the mystery of "who-knows-where" intact.

In addition to teaching at the Writer's Workshop at the University of Iowa, from which he also graduated, and writing vigorous essays on contemporary poetics, Marvin Bell has managed to publish eight volumes of poems since 1966, when *Things We Dreamt We Died For* appeared.

SF

Obsessive

It could be a clip, it could be a comb;
it could be your mother, coming home.
It could be a rooster; perhaps it's a comb;
it could be your father, coming home.

It could be a paper; it could be a pin.
It could be your childhood, sinking in.

The toys give off the nervousness of age.
It's useless pretending they aren't finished:
faces faded, unable to stand,
buttons lost down the drain during baths.
Those were the days we loved down there,
the soap disappearing as the water spoke,

saying, it could be a wheel, maybe a pipe;
it could be your father, taking his nap.
Legs propped straight, the head tilted back;
the end was near when he could keep track.
It could be the first one; it could be the second;
the father of a friend just sickened and sickened.

Origin of Dreams

Out from muted bee-sounds and musketry
(the hard works of our ears, dissembling),
under steeply-held birds (in that air
the mind draws of our laid breathing),
out from light dust and the retinal gray,
your face as in your forties appears
as if to be pictured, and will not go away.

I have shut up all my cameras, really,
Father, and thought I did not speak to you,
since you are dead. But you last;
are proved in the distance of a wrist.
Your face in dreams sends a crinkly static
and seems, in its mica- or leaf-like texture,
the nightworks of the viscera.

But feeling's not fancy, fancying you.
I don't forget you, or give stinks for thanks.
I think I think the bed's a balcony,
until we sleep. Then our good intentions
lower us to the dead, where we live.
I think that light's a sheet for the days,
which we lose. Then we go looking.

Little Father Poem

We must stay away from our fathers,
who have big ears. We must stay away
from our fathers, who are the snow.
We must avoid the touch of the leaves
who are our proud fathers. We must
watch out for father underfoot. Father
forgave us when we did nothing wrong,
Father made us well when we were healthy,
now Father wants to support us
when we weigh nothing, Father in his grave
gives us everything we ever wanted,
in a boat crossing who-knows-where,
mist flat over the water,
the sand smooth because soft.

The Mystery of Emily Dickinson

Sometimes the weather goes on for days
but you were different. You were divine.
While the others wrote more and longer,
you wrote much more and much shorter.
I held your white dress once: 12 buttons.
In the cupola, the wasps struck glass
as hard to escape as you hit your sound
again and again asking Welcome. No one.

Except for you, it were a trifle:
This morning, not much after dawn,
in level country, not New England's,
through leftovers of summer rain I
went out rag-tag to the curb, only
a sleepy householder at his routine
bending to trash, when a young girl
in a white dress your size passed,

so softly!, carrying her shoes. It must be
she surprised me—her barefoot quick-step
and the earliness of the hour, your dress—
or surely I'd have spoken of it sooner.
I should have called to her, but a neighbor
wore that look you see against happiness.
I won't say anything would have happened
unless there was time, and eternity's plenty.

Two Pictures of a Leaf

If I make up this leaf
in the shape of a fan, the day's cooler
and drier than any tree. But if
under a tree I place before me
this same leaf as on a plate,
dorsal side up and then its ribs
set down like the ribs of a fish—
then I know that fish are dead to us
from the trees, and the leaf
sprawls in the net of fall to be
boned and eaten while the wind gasps.
Ah then, the grounds are a formal ruin
whereon the lucky who lived
come to resemble so much that does not.

Stars Which See, Stars Which Do Not See

They sat by the water. The fine women
had large breasts, tightly checked.
At each point, at every moment,
they seemed happy by the water.
The women wore hats like umbrellas
or carried umbrellas shaped like hats.
The men wore no hats and the water,
which wore no hats, had that well-known
mirror finish which tempts sailors.
Although the men and women seemed at rest
they were looking toward the river
and some way out into it but not beyond.
The scene was one of hearts and flowers
though this may be unfair. Nevertheless,
it was probable that the Seine had hurt them,
that they were "taken back" by its beauty
to where a slight breeze broke the mirror
and then its promise, but never the water.

Fresh News from the Past

Many were happy.
It took a long time to make a wish.
Daffodils were trampled in play
and clover ripped up
by hands feeling for luck.
Ivy wouldn't stop.

There was a kind of weed made spinners
and a best grass reed
for making the hands a wind instrument.
No one who had seen Queen Anne's lace
knew it. There was suitable weather.
There was a road under the river.

Had we been to Paris? No,
but we had been to leg-of-lamb
and found it alive and moving.
Guns-and-butter had not yet become
rockets-and-pies. We were dumb
as ducks. We loved the word "propellor."

Gemwood

to Nathan and Jason, our sons

In the *shoppes*
they're showing "gemwood":
the buffed-up flakes of dye-fed pines—
bright concentrics or bull's-eyes,
wide-eyed on the rack of
this newest "joint effort
of man and nature." But then

those life-lines circling
each target chip of "gemwood"
look less like eyes, yours or mine,
when we have watched a while.
They are more like the whorls
at the tips of our fingers,
which no one can copy. Even on

the photocopy Jason made of
his upraised hands, palms down
to the machine, they do not appear.
His hands at five-years-old—
why did we want to copy them, and
why does the grey yet clear print
make me sad? That summer,

the Mad River followed us
through Vermont—a lusher state than
our own. A thunderous matinee
of late snows, and then the peak
at Camel's Hump was bleached.
As a yellow pear is to the sky—
that was our feeling. We had with us

a rat from the lab—no, a pet
we'd named, a pure friend who changed
our minds. When it rained near
the whole of the summer, in that
cabin Nathan made her a social creature.
She was all our diversion, and brave.
That's why, when she died

in the heat of our car
one accidental day we didn't intend,
it hurt her master first and most,
being his first loss like that,
and the rest of our family felt badly
even to tears, for a heart that small.
We buried her by the road

in the Adirondack Mountains,
and kept our way to Iowa.
Now it seems to me the heart
must enlarge to hold the losses
we have ahead of us. I hold to
a certain sadness the way others
search for joy, though I like joy.

Home, sunlight cleared the air
and all the green's of consequence. Still
when it ends, we won't remember
that it ended. If parents must receive
the sobbing, that is nothing
when put next to the last crucial fact
of who is doing the crying.

MARVIN BELL

These Green-Going-to-Yellow

This year,
I'm raising the emotional ante,
putting my face
in the leaves to be stepped on,
seeing myself among them, that is;
that is, likening
leaf-vein to artery, leaf to flesh,
the passage of a leaf in autumn
to the passage of autumn,
branch-tip and winter spaces
to possibilities, and possibility
to God. Even on East 61st Street
in the blowzy city of New York,
someone has planted a gingko
because it has leaves like fans like hands,
hand-leaves, and sex. Those lovely
Chinese hands on the sidewalks
so far from delicacy
or even, perhaps, another gender of gingko—
do we see them?
No one ever treated us so gently
as these green-going-to-yellow hands
fanned out where we walk.
No one ever fell down so quietly
and lay where we would look
when we were tired or embarrassed,
or so bowed down by humanity
that we had to watch out lest our shoes stumble,
and looked down not to look up
until something looked like parts of people
where we were walking. We have no
experience to make us see the gingko
or any other tree,
and in our admiration for whatever grows tall
and outlives us,
we look away, or look at the middles of things,
which would not be our way
if we truly thought we were gods.

Marvin Bell

Books

A Probable Volume of Dreams, 1969
The Escape into You, 1971
Residue of Song, 1974
Stars Which See, Stars Which Do Not See, 1977
These Green-Going-to-Yellow, 1981
Hunger for Stories: A Correspondence in Poetry (with William Stafford), 1982

Interview

Wayne Dodd and Stanley Plumly, "A Conversation with Marvin Bell," *Ohio Review* 17 (Spring–Summer 1976)

Russell
Edson

(b. 1935)

oming across the work of Russell Edson for the first time, the
reader is likely to wonder, are these poems or aren't they? Or,
whatever they are, how do they manage to be so simple and
mysterious at once? What forces are unleashed through them? One way
out of this befuddlement is to read the pieces aloud to others. People will
gradually begin to laugh, steadily, helplessly, realizing they are in the

grip of something both ferocious and serene, something that reminds them of games of logic or conundrums.

No discussion of Edson should go very far without recalling that he is a student of philosophy, with a love for argument about large questions. He feels that human intelligence is born out of a vast mindlessness and that therefore, like Kafka, we must look upon our situation as absurd. He builds his texts on this notion, calling them "islands of memory surrounded by nothing." Nor can one ignore the form he has been working with, passionately and relentlessly, for the past twenty years. From early collections that he designed and printed himself (he is an accomplished printmaker), to the later work issued by major publishers, Edson has, as he says, been singularly devoted to "feeding and caring for" the prose poem, a term that critics have settled on but one with which he himself is not entirely comfortable. In revealing and funny interviews, letters, and essays—especially the important "Portrait of the Writer as a Fat Man," from which most of the quotes used here are taken—he has had much to say about the fable form he has inherited, from Aesop on down to such other modern masters as George Ade and Thurber.

Central to his unique vision of the fable is his belief that the writer must "grow his own writing, his own meditation." Meditation is a useful term for what Edson is up to, but in a typically Edsonian gesture he immediately qualifies his remark to mean "the shape of a meditation, upon which surface pictures and speculations play." Underlying this is a preference for prose that is free from the self-consciousness of poetry, "a prose more compact than the storyteller's, removed from the formalities of literature." With no formal schooling to speak of, having learned to draw and printmake first and foremost (Edson's father was a well-known cartoonist), largely self-taught in language and literature, Edson has virtually isolated himself in his home in Connecticut with only occasional forays into the world of poetry readings and lecture circuits. This has provided him with a certain freedom to grow on his own, and he adds that he even desires to be free from himself, his own expectations of where his work might lead.

This isolation has led him to texts that depend entirely on their own geometries, proceeding as they do from their own givens to their own proofs, exploring inner life for itself, and not for "private expression or public anger," which Edson feels poetry has fallen prey to. He speaks with fervor of a shared responsibility for "imagining the universe," for mapping "the vague descriptions of the mind drifting through its own interior." His characters often maneuver their way through these pieces, from the old captain in "The Pilot" whose room has become his ship to the odd folk in "The Wheelbarrow," who steer their cows around. Edson keeps his language simple, his images direct, so that "the reader comes to recognitions long before consciousness of what has happened sets in." A key word is "intuition," and a key volume *The Intuitive Journey and Other Works* (1976), from which many of the texts presented here are taken. But even intuition is not enough, Edson feels, unless it is driven by the humor of "the deep, uncomfortable metaphor." Such humor will not only get us to laugh but will likely sink us in deep reservoirs of sadness. In "The Fall" the young man's parents conclude he is right, that is, they take him literally: "But his parents said look it is fall." It is too late to go back, once we accept the given; the man has told his parents he *is* a tree. The "situation" can only advance, inexorably, toward its logical conclusion. Edson's genius lies in tracking the emotional formations that have a compact psychological life of their own. The parents say things like "then go" and "do not grow" and "as your roots," which bespeak their admonishing power and control. The life has long left their son when he says, "I was fooling I am not a tree. . . ." Edson concentrates events that soon reach a peak on which all reconciliation is shattered. He is right to disclaim those formal means for developing pieces that other poets rely on (e.g., mood, tone and sound), settling instead for "the rough vision of discovery" we already feel upon reading the first line of a text by Edson.

Edson says he often works from first lines, the full meaning of which he's not sure of, but generally senses something "quaint and horrible at once about them" (from an essay on "Counting Sheep"). Second lines come "obbligato to the first, as attempts to repair the loss of scale" (that the sheep have suffered, in this instance), and further lines come as logical responses to the moves on the board. Moving in an opposite direction from the surrealists, who used irrational language to scorn rational thought, Edson keeps finding perfectly rational language to construct his irrational scenes. He can take on the nonsense of his stories because the language itself makes so much sense. Against much contemporary poetry that seems to insist on lack of content, Edson's style is to make something of nothing, to pull a whole little story out of an odd, dreamlike recollection of how something might have evolved: "I was combing some long hair coming out of a tree" ("In the Forest"); "A man had just married an automobile" ("The Automobile"); "A king had dropped his crown" ("Out of Whack"). Recently, he put this into Edson-like perspective, "We ask not necessarily to understand, in fact in most cases we'd rather not, we ask only to believe . . . Art makes us believe what we cannot understand."

SF

The Fall

There was a man who found two leaves and came indoors holding them out saying to his parents that he was a tree.

To which they said then go into the yard and do not grow in the living-room as your roots may ruin the carpet.

He said I was fooling I am not a tree and he dropped his leaves.

But his parents said look it is fall.

In the Forest

I was combing some long hair coming out of a tree...
I had noticed long hair coming out of a tree, and a comb on the ground by the roots of that same tree.
The hair and the comb seemed to belong together. Not so much that the hair needed combing, but the reassurance of the comb being drawn through it...
I stood in the gloom and silence that many forests have in the pages of fiction, combing the thick womanly hair, the mammal-warm hair; even as the evening slowly took the forest into night...

A Journey Through the Moonlight

In sleep when an old man's body is no longer aware of its boundaries, and lies flattened by gravity like a mere of wax in its bed... It drips down to the floor and moves there like a tear down a cheek... Under the back door into the silver meadow, like a pool of sperm, frosty under the moon, as if in his first nature, boneless and absurd.

The moon lifts him up into its white field, a cloud shaped like an old man, porous with stars.

He floats through high dark branches, a corpse tangled in a tree on a river.

The Wheelbarrow

Cows they had, many, like heavy clouds drifting in the meadow.
But they didn't have the wheelbarrow that they thought they had been promised. They had studied catalogs and prayed; but no wheel barrow.

RUSSELL EDSON

So at last they tied wheels to the front hooves of a cow and had a couple of stout gentlemen lift the hind legs and wheel the cow about the farm.

Although they admitted the cow made a very poor wheelbarrow, a make-do at best, still, they had done long enough without a wheelbarrow not to really need one, and could now relax in decorative values, for, as they said, time has long decayed utility from actual need.

The other cows look around at this new farm equipment; then turning they drift out like heavy clouds into the meadow.

The Pilot

Up in a dirty window in a dark room is a star which an old man can see. He looks at it. He can see it. It is the star of the room; an electrical freckle that has fallen out of his head and gotten stuck in the dirt on the window.

He thinks he can steer by that star. He thinks he can use the back of a chair as a ship's wheel to pilot this room through the night.

He says to himself, brave Captain, are you afraid?

Yes, I am afraid; I am not so brave.

Be brave, my Captain.

And all night the old man steers his room through the dark . . .

An Old Man's Son

There was an old man who had a kite for a son, which he would let up into the air attached to a string, when he had need to be alone.

. . . And, would watch this high bloom of himself, as something distant that will be close again . . .

The Wounded Breakfast

A huge shoe mounts up from the horizon, squealing and grinding forward on small wheels, even as a man sitting to breakfast on his veranda is suddenly engulfed in a great shadow almost the size of the night.

He looks up and sees a huge shoe ponderously mounting out of the earth. Up in the unlaced ankle-part an old woman stands at a helm behind the great tongue curled forward; the thick laces dragging like ships' rope on the ground as the huge thing squeals and grinds forward; children everywhere, they look from the shoelace holes, they crowd about the old woman, even as she pilots this huge shoe over the earth . . .

TWELVE POETS BORN BETWEEN 1930 AND 1940

Soon the huge shoe is descending the opposite horizon, a monstrous snail squealing and grinding into the earth . . .

The man turns to his breakfast again, but sees it's been wounded, the yolk of one of his eggs is bleeding . . .

The Automobile

A man had just married an automobile.

But I mean to say, said his father, that the automobile is not a person because it is something different.

For instance, compare it to your mother. Do you see how it is different from your mother? Somehow it seems wider, doesn't it? And besides, your mother wears her hair differently.

You ought to try to find something in the world that looks like mother.

I have mother, isn't that enough of a thing that looks like mother? Do I have to gather more mothers?

They are all old ladies who do not in the least excite any wish to procreate, said the son.

But you cannot procreate with an automobile, said father.

The son shows father an ignition key. See, here is a special penis which does with the automobile as the man with the woman; and the automobile gives birth to a place far from this place, dropping its puppy miles as it goes.

Does that make me a grandfather? said father.

That makes you where you are when I am far away, said the son.

Father and mother watch an automobile with a *just married* sign on it growing smaller in a road.

Out of Whack

A king had dropped his crown—Oh quite by accident, he screamed, for it likely foretells the fall of the king's pants, scattering his genital jewelry into the eyes of lusting peasants.

The crown was broken. His wife, the female king, cried, it's my crown which you broke.

Oh really? he screamed, I must have put it on by accident; I thought it was too small. Good thing it wasn't mine; yours is just a silly old girl's crown. Now you'll have to go down to the kitchen and clean pots.

RUSSELL EDSON   385

No no, I will wear the king's crown, which makes me the king, she screamed.

Oh no, that's only for the king to wear. The king wears the king's crown. Other than that is a perversion, you lesbian, he screamed.

You're the queer, wearing a lady's crown, you transvestite, screamed the queen.

But you see, I instinctively threw it off, because underneath my wayward delight is the true instinct, he screamed.

Too late, too late, because I am wearing the king's crown: and, in that we are married, and, in that the wearer of the king's crown is automatically the king, you are now *my* queen, who broke her crown like a typically silly woman, who doesn't quite realize the value of things, screamed the queen.

I will not play this naughty game, he screamed, and I will have you beheaded if you cannot come to terms with your disquiet.

I shall have *you* beheaded if you cannot come to terms with *your* disquiet, she screamed.

No no, I shall have you beheaded if you cannot come to terms with your disquiet, he screamed.

How dare you? It is I that has people beheaded when they cannot come to terms with their disquiet, she screamed.

I shall most certainly require that you be beheaded if you refuse to come to terms with your disquiet, he screamed.

Quiet, she screamed.
Silence, he screamed.

A page boy came and said, sirs, shall I bring your mouth-plugs now?
Of course, screamed the king and queen, are you blind, can't you see that our mouths have gone completely out of whack?

Counting Sheep

A scientist has a test tube full of sheep. He wonders if he should try to shrink a pasture for them.

They are like grains of rice.

He wonders if it is possible to shrink something out of existence.

He wonders if the sheep are aware of their tininess, if they have any sense of scale? Perhaps they just think the test tube is a glass barn . . .

He wonders what he should do with them; they certainly have less meat and wool than ordinary sheep. Has he reduced their commercial value?

He wonders if they could be used as a substitute for rice, a sort of woolly rice . . . ?

He wonders if he just shouldn't rub them into a red paste between his fingers?

He wonders if they're breeding, or if any of them have died.
He puts them under a microscope and falls asleep counting them . . .

The Death of an Angel

Being witless it said no prayer. Being pure it withered like a flower.

They could not tell its sex. It had neither anal nor genital opening.

The autopsy revealed no viscera, neither flesh nor bone. It was stuffed with pages from old Bibles and cotton.

When they opened the skull it played *Tales from the Vienna Woods*; instead of brain they found a vagina and a penis, testicles and an anus, packed in sexual hair.

Ah, that's better! cried one of the doctors.

The Long Picnic

An official document blows through a forest between the trees over the heads of the picnickers.
It is the end of summer, and there is only the snow to be looked forward to. The photosynthetic world is collapsing.
Those who have been picnicking all summer in the forest see that their food has gone bad. The blackberry jam is tar, the picnic baskets are full of bones wrapped in old newspapers.
A young man turns to his sweetheart. She's an old woman with white hair; her head bobs on her neck.
The picnickers try to catch the document as it flies over their heads. But the wind carries it away.
What is written on it is that *the summer is over* . . .

A Cottage in the Wood

He has built himself a cottage in a wood, near where the insect rubs its wings in song.
Yet, without measure, or proper sense of scale, he has made the cottage too small. He realizes this when only his hand will fit through the door. He tries the stairs to the second floor with his fingers, but his arm wedges in the entrance. He

wonders how he will cook his dinner. He might get his hands through the kitchen windows. But even so, he will not be able to cook enough on such a tiny stove.

He shall also lie unsheltered in the night, even though a bed with its covers turned down waits for him in the cottage.

He lies down and curls himself around the cottage, listening to the insect that rubs its wings in song.

Notes

A Journey Through the Moonlight. "Mere" (in the second line) has the archaic meaning of "lake" or "pond"—akin to Latin *mare*, sea.

Russell Edson

Books

The Very Thing That Happens, 1964
What a Man Can See, 1969
The Childhood of an Equestrian, 1973
The Clam Theater, 1973
The Reason Why The Closet-Man is Never Sad, 1974
The Falling Sickness: Four Plays, 1975
The Intuitive Journey and Other Works, 1976

Essays

"Portrait of the Writer as a Fat Man: Some Subjective Ideas or Notions on the Care & Feeding of Prose Poems," in *A Field Guide to Contemporary Poetry and Poetics*, ed. Friebert and Young, 1980

Michael Harper

(b. 1938)

M ichael Harper grew up in a home in Brooklyn where musi-
cians like Billie Holiday regularly came and went, bringing
their blues and jazz. When the Harper family moved to Los
Angeles in 1951, he started a dizzying collection of jobs and school

experiences that saw him trying everything from postal clerking to playing professional football under an assumed name. Along the way he managed to read voraciously and write a good deal, trying his hand at first on plays and fiction. He earned degrees from Los Angeles State and the University of Iowa, where he studied at the Writer's Workshop. In the 1960s he began publishing poems and journeyed to far-off places to deepen his understanding of the poetry and culture of other lands, the better to mirror "the wealth of human materials in my own life, its ethnic richness, complexity of language and stylization, the tension between stated moral idealism and brutal historical realities."

Working with landscapes rich in history and lore, he shapes his texts toward figurative moments marked by indelible images of personal pain and loss. To arrive at these images, he sometimes strains after the right turn of phrase, but there are no false notes on where he stands, who he is, what he has to say, and how he says it. While Harper writes as passionately as anyone of the threats to our civilization and our duty to struggle, to resist, his most affecting poems deal directly with family matters and center around the loss of a son (see especially "Nightmare Begins Responsibility" and "We Assume: On the Death of Our Son, Reuben Masai Harper"). This loss is a nightmare that Harper confronts again and again, in some kind of "ritualistic search for the presence and images of (all our?) children 'torn away,'" as the critic Robert Stepto sees it ("After Modernism, After Hibernation: Michael Harper, Robert Hayden, and Jay Wright"). "The Dance of the Elephants" is a poignant example of how Harper looks with bifocal vision at the horrors of holocaust the world would just as soon forget, and the ironic comfort our children find in the tiny possessions they take along for what may be the final journey. Our humanity persists, the poem suggests, in our taking with us whatever words and objects are most ours, even to the grave. Before Harper will tackle this powerful, even debilitating subject matter, he always starts by "finding a pattern for the poem at conception, a means of balancing form and content in formal rather than traditional lines" (from an essay on "Grandfather").

The ballad form suggested itself for "Grandfather," and of late Harper has been writing more and more ballads. Originally intended for preserving critical information orally, the ballad, or story-song, is dramatic and economical and thus attracts a poet like Harper, who has a lot of misinformation to correct—in the case of "Grandfather," the warped picture of a black family that D. W. Griffith's classic film *The Birth of a Nation* presented—and a lot of new information to pass on about such seemingly diverse matters as music, economics, railroads (above and underground, Harper is quick to note), history, race relations, hospital rooms, landfills, and rocking chairs. One of his strengths is his ability to bring much of this information together under one roof and send it spinning by like a carousel of human history. In his words, the struggle is "to portray clear images of heroic stances against adversity." A closer look reveals that Harper turns the ballad form inside out, fashioning of it a modern instrument that can carry today's tunes; his stories focus on several (not single) crucial episodes at once, begin frequently after (not before) the action that has resulted in catastrophe, and play back events in fractured fragments that match the complexity of the issues. But whatever the final forms of the poems, Harper makes sure he includes a persuasive amount of "circumstantial" detail, and does not fear intruding with subjective attitudes if he must. All this parallels the way contemporary black musicians play with traditional forms to discover dimensions hitherto unexplored. New forms emerge that are not tied to stock themes and standard rhetoric, with their rhythms loosened to accommodate human speech alongside poetic diction: "A woman who'd lost her first son / consoled us with an angel gone ahead / to pray for our family— / gone into that sky / seeking oxygen, / gone into autopsy, / a fine brown powdered sugar, / a disposable cremation."

While the titles of Harper's major collections underline the seriousness of his mission—*History Is Your Own Heartbeat* (1971), *Debridement* (1973), *Nightmare Begins Responsibility* (1975), and the new and selected poems, *Images of Kin* (1977)—many of the poems strike a beneficent chord, and there is a lighter side to his art that is just as affecting for the ways he can tune a tiny song to the sounds of others who have come before. "Br'er Sterling and the Rocker" is a witty, sly homage to black folktale, the sonnet form, and Harper's mentor and spiritual guide, Sterling Brown, all in one deft mix of the high and low talk that has always kept poetry vital. In his poems, his teaching, and his scholarship, Michael Harper works to keep us conscious of what is going on.

SF

The Dance of the Elephants

PART I

The trains ran through the eleven
nights it took to vacate the town;
relatives and lovers tacked in a row
on the button-board sidings,
wails of children tossed in a pile

wails of women tossed in a salad
to be eaten with soap and a rinse.
Those who took all they had to the borders,
those who took their bottles
three centuries old, those who
thought only of language, the written
word, are forgiven.
One daughter is riding on the train
above her mother, above her mother,
into the tunnel of the elephants.

Culture tells us most about its animals
singing our children asleep, or let them
slip into a room as smoothly as
refrigeration.

PART II

To be comforted by Swiss music
is a toy elephant in a box,
skimming the nickelplated air.
Beethoven's a passion dance
forgotten in a stamped coin—
it is magic—it is magic—

We dance the old beast round the fireplace,
coal engines fuming in a row,
elephant chimes in a toy rain—
human breath skimming the air.

We skim the air—
it is magic—the engines
smelling the chimes,
Beethoven chiming the magic—
we escape it on a train.

Sung in America,
the song some telescopic sight,
a nickelplated cream,
a small girl cuddles her elephant,
the song in the streets
leaping the train windows,
and what love as the elephant chimes.

Homage to the New World

Surrounded by scientists in a faculty
house, the trees wet with hot rain,
grass thickening under the trees,
welcomers come, ones and twos,
gifts of shoehorns, soap, combs,
half a subscription to the courier,
some news about changing
plates, the nearest market,
how to pick up the trash, a gallon
of milk twice a week, ok?

On the third day here,
a friend came in the night to announce
a phone call and a message,
and heard the shell go in
and the rifle cocking,
our next-door animal vet neighbor,
and cried out, "don't shoot",
and walked away to remember the phone
and the message, the crickets,
and the rifle cocking,
grass and hot rain.

I write in the night air
of the music of Coltrane,
the disc of his voice in this
contralto heart, my wife;
so what! Kind of Blue,
these fatherless whites
come to consciousness
with a history of the gun—
the New World, if misery had
a voice, would be a rifle cocking.

for Agnes & Ed Brandabur

Kin

When news came that your mother'd
smashed her hip, both feet caught
in rungs of the banquet table,
our wedding rebroken on the memory
of the long lake of silence
when the stones of her body
broke as an Irish fence of stones,
I saw your wet dugs drag
with the weight of our daughter
in the quick of her sleep
to another feeding;
then the shoulders dropped
their broken antenna branches
of fear at the knife
running the scars
which had borne into the colon
for the misspent enema,
the clubbed liver unclean
with the stones of the gall bladder,
and the broken arch of hip
lugging you to the lake,
the dough inner tube of lading
swollen with innerpatching.

I pick you up from the floor
of your ringing fears, the floor
where the photographs you have worked
into the cool sky of the gray you love,
and you are back at the compost pile
where the vegetables burn,
or swim in the storm of your childhood,
when your father egged you on with his
open machinery, the exhaust choking your sisters,
and your sisters choked still.

Now his voice stops you in accusation,
and the years pile up on themselves
in the eggs of your stretched sons,
one born on his birthday, both dead.
I pull you off into the sanctuary
of conciliation, of quiet tactics,
the uttered question, the referral,
which will quiet the condition you have seen
in your mother's shadow, the crutches
inching in the uncut grass,

and the worn body you will carry
as your own birthmark of his scream.

Grandfather

In 1915 my grandfather's
neighbors surrounded his house
near the dayline he ran
on the Hudson
in Catskill, NY
and thought they'd burn
his family out
in a movie they'd just seen
and be rid of his kind:
the death of a lone black
family is *the Birth*
of a Nation,
or so they thought.
His 5'4" waiter gait
quenched the white jacket smile
he'd brought back from watered
polish of my father
on the turning seats,
and he asked his neighbors
up on his thatched porch
for the first blossom of fire
that would burn him down.

They went away, his nation,
spittooning their torched necks
in the shadows of the riverboat
they'd seen, posse decomposing;
and I see him on Sutter
with white bag from your
restaurant, challenged by his first
grandson to a foot-race
he will win in white clothes.

I see him as he buys galoshes
for his railed yard near Mineo's
metal shop, where roses jump
as the el circles his house
towards Brooklyn, where his rain fell;
and I see cigar smoke in his eyes,

chocolate Madison Square Garden chews
he breaks on his set teeth,
stitched up after cancer,
the great white nation immovable
as his weight wilts
and he is on a porch
that won't hold my arms,
or the legs of the race run
forwards, or the film
played backwards on his grandson's eyes.

Nightmare Begins Responsibility

I place these numbed wrists to the pane
watching white uniforms whisk over
him in the tube-kept
prison
fear what they will do in experiment
watch my gloved stickshifting gasolined hands
breathe *boxcar-information-please* infirmary tubes
distrusting white-pink mending paperthin
silkened end hairs, distrusting tubes
shrunk in his *trunk-skincapped*
shaven head, in thighs
distrusting-white-hands-picking-baboon-light
on this son who will not make his second night
of this wardstrewn intensive airpocket
where his father's asthmatic
hymns of *night-train*, train done gone
his mother can only know that he has flown
up into essential calm unseen corridor
going boxscarred home, *mamaborn, sweetsonchild*
gonedowntown into *researchtestingwarehousebatteryacid*
mama-son-done-gone/me telling her 'nother
train tonight, no music, no breathstroked
heartbeat in my infinite distrust of them:

and of my distrusting self
white-doctor-who-breathed-for-him-all-night
say it for two sons gone,
say nightmare, say it loud
panebreaking heartmadness:
nightmare begins responsibility.

We Assume: On the Death of Our Son, Reuben Masai Harper

We assume
that in 28 hours,
lived in a collapsible isolette,
you learned to accept pure oxygen
as the natural sky;
the scant shallow breaths
that filled those hours
cannot, did not make you fly—
but dreams were there
like crooked palmprints on
the twin-thick windows of the nursery—
in the glands of your mother.

We assume
the sterile hands
drank chemicals in and out
from lungs opaque with mucus,
pumped your stomach,
eeked the bicarbonate in
crooked, green-winged veins,
out in a plastic mask;

A woman who'd lost her first son
consoled us with an angel gone ahead
to pray for our family—
gone into that sky
seeking oxygen,
gone into autopsy,
a fine brown powdered sugar,
a disposable cremation:

We assume
you did not know we loved you.

Landfill

Loads of trash and we light the match;
what can be in a cardboard box
can be in the bed of the pickup
and you jostle the containers onto the side road.

A match for this little road,
and a match for your son riding next to you firing,
and a match for the hole in the land filled with trees.
I will not mention concrete because theirs is the meshed
wire of concrete near the docks, and the concrete
of burned trees cut in cords of change-sawing,
and we will light a match to this too.

Work in anger for the final hour of adjustment
to the surveyors, and to the lawyers speaking of squatting,
and the land burning to no one.
This building of scrap metal, high as the storm that will
break it totally in the tornado dust,
and to the animals that have lived in the wheathay of their bedding
will beg for the cutting edge, or the ax,
or the electrified fencing that warms them in summer rain.

My son coughs on the tarred scrubble of cut trees,
and is cursed by the firelight, and beckoned to me to the pickup,
and washed of the soot of his sootskinned face,
and the dirt at the corners of my daughter's mouth will be trenchmouth;
and the worn moccasin of my woman will tear into the bulbed big toe,
and the blood will be black as the compost pile burning,
and the milk from her dugs will be the balm for the trenchmouth,
as she wipes her mouth from the smoke of the landfill filled with fire,
and these loads of trash will be the ashes for her to take:
and will be taken to the landfill, and filled, and filled.

Br'er Sterling and the Rocker

Any fool knows a Br'er in a rocker
is a boomerang incarnate; look at the blade
of the rocker, that wondrous crescent
rockin' in harness as poem.

To speak of poetry is the curled line straightened;
to speak of doubletalk, the tongue
gone pure, the stoic line a trestle
whistlin', a man a train comin' on:

Listen Br'er Sterling
steel-drivin' man, folk-said, folk-sayin',
that chair's a blues-harnessed star
turnin' on its earthy axis;

Miss Daisy, latch on that star's arc,
hold on sweet mama; Br'er Sterling's rocker glows.

Last Affair: Bessie's Blues Song

Disarticulated
arm torn out,
large veins cross
her shoulder intact,
her tourniquet
her blood in all-white big bands:

Can't you see
what love and heartache's done to me
I'm not the same as I used to be
this is my last affair

Mail truck or parked car
in the fast lane,
afloat at forty-three
on a Mississippi road,
Two-hundred-pound muscle on her ham bone,
'nother nigger dead 'fore noon:

Can't you see
what love and heartache's done to me
I'm not the same as I used to be
this is my last affair

Fifty-dollar record
cut the vein in her neck,
fool about her money
toll her black train wreck,
white press missed her fun'ral
in the same stacked deck:

Can't you see
what love and heartache's done to me
I'm not the same as I used to be
this is my last affair

Loved a little blackbird
heard she could sing,
Martha in her vineyard
pestle in her spring,
Bessie had a bad mouth
made my chimes ring:

Can't you see
what love and heartache's done to me
I'm not the same as I used to be
this is my last affair

MICHAEL HARPER

Notes

Grandfather. "Sutter" is a street name.

Br'er Sterling and the Rocker. The poem is a hymn to Harper's friend and mentor, Sterling Brown; "Miss Daisy" refers to Brown's wife.

Last Affair: Bessie's Blues Song. "Bessie" was the great blues singer Bessie Smith.

Michael Harper

Books

Dear John, Dear Coltrane, 1970
History Is Your Own Heartbeat, 1971
Song: I Want a Witness, 1972
Debridement, 1973
Nightmare Begins Responsibility, 1974
Images of Kin, 1977

Criticism, Interviews

Interviews with Black Writers, ed. J. O'Brien, 1973; Robert Stepto, "After Modernism, After Hibernation," in *Chant of Saints,* 1979; James Randall, "An Interview with Michael Harper," *Ploughshares 7,* no. 1 (1981)

Sylvia Plath

(1932–1963)

Rollie McKenna

The career of Sylvia Plath, a deeply unhappy and greatly gifted poet, was over before most people realized it had begun. Her major collection, *Ariel* (1965), appeared more than a year after she took her life in London. There are two other posthumous collections, *Crossing the Water* and *Winter Trees*. Only her first book of poems, *The Col-*

ossus (1960), appeared while she was still alive. To have a poet of brilliance come to notice in such circumstances was both disorienting and fascinating to most readers, and it is not surprising that a kind of cult has grown up around Sylvia Plath. She has been variously seen as a feminist martyr; a type of the romantic prodigy who burns out and dies young; and a psychotic whose poetry was a helpless, aberrant offshoot of her condition. While there is a grain of truth in each of these views, the actuality is more complex than any single label would suggest, though no less melancholy, and we may never fully understand how and why Sylvia Plath had to destroy herself.

What does seem clear from the poems is that she lived on a knife-edge, in the presence of a tremendous attraction to death and nothingness. This attraction informs her poems, giving them spiritual strength and adventurousness on the one hand, and psychological dislocation and occasional perversity on the other. To read Plath is to be first dazzled by her technical virtuosity and the flashing reach of her imagination; then, as the constant death wish, the romance of suicide, becomes clear, the reader is apt to react with dismay. Eventually, one adjusts to the intense negativity and tries to balance it with what is positive in the poems. The present selection aims to reflect the full range of her imaginative preoccupations without losing sight of the fact that her finest work is balanced between her fascination with death and her ability to observe and celebrate life. Her shrillest poems (e.g., "Daddy" and "Lady Lazarus") are not included here; their frequent appearance in anthologies has already tended to obscure her best accomplishment.

The first two poems of this selection, early pieces from *The Colossus*, show how her balance can operate. In "The Manor Garden" a mother addresses her unborn child, and the poem is marked by her consciousness that birth is also the onset of dying. Similarly, in "Watercolor of Grantchester Meadows," nature seems quaint and wholesome to the undergraduates boating in the springtime countryside, but the speaker is aware of the way that nature implies death and destruction too, and sees the students' black gowns as foreshadowing the night when "The owl shall stoop from his turret, the rat cry out."

These comparatively early poems also show Sylvia Plath's gifts for musical language and strong, resonant images, gifts she shared with her husband, Ted Hughes, the English poet, and her sometime teacher, Robert Lowell. The poems from *Ariel* (the rest of our selection, with the exception of "Winter Trees") suggest how distinctively she began to use those gifts in her last phase. "Sheep in Fog" is remarkable for the way it compresses the vision of "Watercolor" into something more powerful and mysterious, a tranquil landscape through which a dimension beyond life, both threatening and enticing, is thrillingly glimpsed. It is also an astonishing sequence, eccentric but absolutely precise in movement, a deftly sketched metaphor for existence—are we not all sheep in fog?—in which each detail rises inexorably but surprisingly from the last. Imagination, the image-making faculty, is the poet's special province, and the gift of thinking in images, sequences of astonishing links and leaps, is one that marks the greatest poetic talents. The sureness of "Sheep in Fog," a quality found again and again in *Ariel*, is perhaps Sylvia Plath's strongest hallmark as a poet. Sometimes, as in "The Couriers" and "Words," her track can be hard to follow, but we learn to trust her imagination as it moves among the things of this world, haunted and questing, for its sense of deep relations and illuminating connections. She sees the world with sharp clarity—the poppies in "Poppies in July" are flames, then mouths, then skirts, then wounds—and its color and vitality hurt her until she longs for transparency and nothingness. Agonizing, to have such a gift for observation and to receive so little solace from it!

Several of these poems, carrying on from "The Manor Garden," are about motherhood: "Morning Song," "The Night Dances," "Nick and the Candlestick." Again, their great originality with the subject can be seen to stem partly from the poet's consciousness of death in life. The mother's bemusement at the child's beauty and simplicity is colored by a sense of the coexistence and appeal of nothingness; birth, growth, and innocence are shadowed by their opposites. At the same time, that tension of opposites would mean nothing without its brilliant embodiment in poetic imagery: the watch, the museum, the cloud and puddle, the cow and cat and balloons of "Morning Song"; the cosmic trance of "The Night Dances," where lilies and snowflakes interact with comets and stars, all of them summoned to reflect a baby's random joy of movement; and the uncanny cave, both tomb and womb, that is so hauntingly and convincingly set forth in "Nick and the Candlestick."

Readers who are curious about Sylvia Plath's thirty-one years of life can learn more from her autobiographical novel, *The Bell Jar* (1963), and the fascinating collection of her letters; and her newly published Journals. But the best homage we can pay to her poetry is to recognize it as the accomplishment of a poet whose control and balance, however precarious, enabled her to produce poems of great beauty under tremendous pressure, like carbon turning to diamond. The existence of these poems is independent now of the life that produced them, and they can enter our own lives, becoming our strange and precious possessions, and troubling our complacency.

DY

Watercolor of Grantchester Meadows

There, spring lambs jam the sheepfold. In air
Stilled, silvered as water in a glass
Nothing is big or far.
The small shrew chitters from its wilderness
Of grassheads and is heard.
Each thumb-size bird
Flits nimble-winged in thickets, and of good color.

Cloudrack and owl-hollowed willows slanting over
The bland Granta double their white and green
World under the sheer water
And ride that flux at anchor, upside down.
The punter sinks his pole.
In Byron's pool
Cattails part where the tame cygnets steer.

It is a country on a nursery plate.
Spotted cows revolve their jaws and crop
Red clover or gnaw beetroot
Bellied on a nimbus of sun-glazed buttercup.
Hedging meadows of benign
Arcadian green
The blood-berried hawthorn hides its spines with white.

Droll, vegetarian, the water rat
Saws down a reed and swims from his limber grove,
While the students stroll or sit,
Hands laced, in a moony indolence of love—
Black-gowned, but unaware
How in such mild air
The owl shall stoop from his turret, the rat cry out.

The Manor Garden

The fountains are dry and the roses over.
Incense of death. Your day approaches.
The pears fatten like little buddhas.
A blue mist is dragging the lake.

You move through the era of fishes,
The smug centuries of the pig—
Head, toe and finger
Come clear of the shadow. History

Nourishes these broken flutings,
These crowns of acanthus,
And the crow settles her garments.
You inherit white heather, a bee's wing,

Two suicides, the family wolves,
Hours of blankness. Some hard stars
Already yellow the heavens.
The spider on its own string

Crosses the lake. The worms
Quit their usual habitations.
The small birds converge, converge
With their gifts to a difficult borning.

Morning Song

Love set you going like a fat gold watch.
The midwife slapped your footsoles, and your bald cry
Took its place among the elements.

Our voices echo, magnifying your arrival. New statue.
In a drafty museum, your nakedness
Shadows our safety. We stand round blankly as walls.

I'm no more your mother
Than the cloud that distils a mirror to reflect its own slow
Effacement at the wind's hand.

All night your moth-breath
Flickers among the flat pink roses. I wake to listen:
A far sea moves in my ear.

One cry, and I stumble from bed, cow-heavy and floral
In my Victorian nightgown.
Your mouth opens clean as a cat's. The window square

Whitens and swallows its dull stars. And now you try
Your handful of notes;
The clear vowels rise like balloons.

Poppies in July

Little poppies, little hell flames,
Do you do no harm?

SYLVIA PLATH

You flicker. I cannot touch you.
I put my hands among the flames. Nothing burns.

And it exhausts me to watch you
Flickering like that, wrinkly and clear red, like the skin of a mouth.

A mouth just bloodied.
Little bloody skirts!

There are fumes that I cannot touch.
Where are your opiates, your nauseous capsules?

If I could bleed, or sleep!—
If my mouth could marry a hurt like that!

Or your liquors seep to me, in this glass capsule,
Dulling and stilling.

But colourless. Colourless.

Ariel

Stasis in darkness.
Then the substanceless blue
Pour of tor and distances.

God's lioness,
How one we grow,
Pivot of heels and knees!—The furrow

Splits and passes, sister to
The brown arc
Of the neck I cannot catch,

Nigger-eye
Berries cast dark
Hooks—

Black sweet blood mouthfuls,
Shadows.
Something else

Hauls me through air—
Thighs, hair;
Flakes from my heels.

White
Godiva, I unpeel—
Dead hands, dead stringencies.

And now I
Foam to wheat, a glitter of seas.
The child's cry

Melts in the wall.
And I
Am the arrow,

The dew that flies
Suicidal, at one with the drive
Into the red

Eye, the cauldron of morning.

Poppies in October

Even the sun-clouds this morning cannot manage such skirts.
Nor the woman in the ambulance
Whose red heart blooms through her coat so astoundingly—

A gift, a love gift
Utterly unasked for
By a sky

Palely and flamily
Igniting its carbon monoxides, by eyes
Dulled to a halt under bowlers.

O my God, what am I
That these late mouths should cry open
In a forest of frost, in a dawn of cornflowers.

Nick and the Candlestick

I am a miner. The light burns blue.
Waxy stalactites
Drip and thicken, tears

The earthen womb
Exudes from its dead boredom.
Black bat airs

Wrap me, raggy shawls,
Cold homicides.
They weld to me like plums.

Old cave of calcium
Icicles, old echoer.
Even the newts are white,

Those holy Joes.
And the fish, the fish—
Christ! They are panes of ice,

A vice of knives,
A piranha
Religion, drinking

Its first communion out of my live toes.
The candle
Gulps and recovers its small altitude,

Its yellows hearten.
O love, how did you get here?
O embryo

Remembering, even in sleep,
Your crossed position.
The blood blooms clean

In you, ruby.
The pain
You wake to is not yours.

Love, love,
I have hung our cave with roses.
With soft rugs—

The last of Victoriana.
Let the stars
Plummet to their dark address,

Let the mercuric
Atoms that cripple drip
Into the terrible well,

You are the one
Solid the spaces lean on, envious.
You are the baby in the barn.

The Couriers

The word of a snail on the plate of a leaf?
It is not mine. Do not accept it.

Acetic acid in a sealed tin?
Do not accept it. It is not genuine.

A ring of gold with the sun in it?
Lies. Lies and a grief.

Frost on a leaf, the immaculate
Cauldron, talking and crackling

All to itself on the top of each
Of nine black Alps.

A disturbance in mirrors,
The sea shattering its grey one—

Love, love, my season.

The Night Dances

A smile fell in the grass.
Irretrievable!

And how will your night dances
Lose themselves. In mathematics?

Such pure leaps and spirals—
Surely they travel

The world forever, I shall not entirely
Sit emptied of beauties, the gift

Of your small breath, the drenched grass
Smell of your sleeps, lilies, lilies.

Their flesh bears no relation.
Cold folds of ego, the calla,

And the tiger, embellishing itself—
Spots, and a spread of hot petals.

The comets
Have such a space to cross,

Such coldness, forgetfulness.
So your gestures flake off—

Warm and human, then their pink light
Bleeding and peeling

Through the black amnesias of heaven.
Why am I given

SYLVIA PLATH

These lamps, these planets
Falling like blessings, like flakes

Six-sided, white
On my eyes, my lips, my hair

Touching and melting.
Nowhere.

Death & Co.

Two, of course there are two.
It seems perfectly natural now—
The one who never looks up, whose eyes are lidded
And balled, like Blake's,
Who exhibits

The birthmarks that are his trademark—
The scald scar of water,
The nude
Verdigris of the condor.
I am red meat. His beak

Claps sidewise: I am not his yet.
He tells me how badly I photograph.
He tells me how sweet
The babies look in their hospital
Icebox, a simple

Frill at the neck,
Then the flutings of their Ionian
Death-gowns,
Then two little feet.
He does not smile or smoke.

The other does that,
His hair long and plausive.
Bastard
Masturbating a glitter,
He wants to be loved.

I do not stir.
The frost makes a flower,

The dew makes a star,
The dead bell,
The dead bell.

Somebody's done for.

TWELVE POETS BORN BETWEEN 1930 AND 1940

Winter Trees

The wet dawn inks are doing their blue dissolve.
On their blotter of fog the trees
Seem a botanical drawing.
Memories growing, ring on ring,
A series of weddings.

Knowing neither abortions nor bitchery,
Truer than women,
They seed so effortlessly!
Tasting the winds, that are footless,
Waist-deep in history.

Full of wings, otherworldliness.
In this, they are Ledas.
O mother of leaves and sweetness
Who are these pietas?
The shadows of ringdoves chanting, but easing nothing.

Sheep in Fog

The hills step off into whiteness.
People or stars
Regard me sadly, I disappoint them.

The train leaves a line of breath.
O slow
Horse the colour of rust,

Hooves, dolorous bells—
All morning the
Morning has been blackening,

A flower left out.
My bones hold a stillness, the far
Fields melt my heart.

They threaten
To let me through to a heaven
Starless and fatherless, a dark water.

SYLVIA PLATH

411

Words

Axes
After whose stroke the wood rings,
And the echoes!
Echoes travelling
Off from the centre like horses.

The sap
Wells like tears, like the
Water striving
To re-establish its mirror
Over the rock

That drops and turns,
A white skull,
Eaten by weedy greens.
Years later I
Encounter them on the road—

Words dry and riderless,
The indefatigable hoof-taps.
While
From the bottom of the pool, fixed stars
Govern a life.

Notes

Watercolor of Grantchester Meadows. A favorite boating spot for Cambridge students (e.g., Lord Byron), who pole long flat boats called punts. A cygnet is a young swan.

Ariel. The title is the name of a favorite horse, and the poem is an account of a horseback ride at dawn; but the glance at the name of Prospero's familiar spirit, agent of his magic, in Shakespeare's *The Tempest*, is surely intentional.

Nick and the Candlestick. Nick: the second of Sylvia Plath's and Ted Hughes's two children.

The Night Dances. The poem is spoken by a mother who is watching her baby's random movements as it sleeps in its crib.

Death & Co. "Like Blake's": one of the personifications of Death resembles the death mask of the poet William Blake. The pair seem to be visiting the speaker in a hospital ward.

Sylvia Plath

Books

The Colossus, 1962
The Bell Jar (novel, written under the name of Victoria Lucas), 1963
Ariel, 1965
Crossing the Water, 1971
Winter Trees, 1972
Johnny Panic and The Bible of Dreams: Short Stories, Prose and Diary Excerpts, ed.
 Ted Hughes, 1979
The Collected Poems, ed. Ted Hughes, 1981
The Journals of Sylvia Plath, 1982

Letters, Criticism

Letters Home, ed. Aurelia Plath, 1975; Charles Newman, ed., *The Art of Sylvia Plath*, 1970; A. Alvarez, *The Savage God*, 1972; Eileen Aird, *Sylvia Plath: Her Life and Work*, 1973; Edward Butscher, *Sylvia Plath: Method and Madness*, 1976; David Holbrook, *Sylvia Plath: Poetry and Existence*, 1976; Judith Kroll, *Chapters in a Mythology: The Poetry of Sylvia Plath*, 1976; Gary Lane, ed., *Sylvia Plath: New Views on the Poetry*, 1979; Jon Rosenblatt, *Sylvia Plath: The Poetry of Initiation*, 1979

Stanley Plumly

(b. 1939)

Thomas Victor

What could an iron lung and a wildflower have in common? Nothing, you might say, until you begin to read Stanley Plumly. This poet hymns unlikely things, finding beauty and grace where they were overlooked so that a frightful contraption like an iron lung can become a miraculous vehicle for "out-of-the-body travel," the major metaphor as well as the title of Plumly's finest collection (1977). In the same way, wildflowers we may have scarcely noticed, like meadow-rue and peppergrass, are shown to have the same kind of unlikely and stirring beauty. Stirring, perhaps, *because* unlikely, rescued from a modest oblivion to enhance our sense of life.

One way that Plumly gets us to see his objects of praise in new ways is by strange and compelling associations. Thus, "Early Meadow-Rue" celebrates a flower, a certain light at dawn, a special sense of loneliness, and, once again, that image of the iron lung, "the girl looking into the mirror above her head, prone in paralysis." In "Out-of-the-Body Travel" the father's soulful violin playing and his careful slaughtering of a bull are seen as the same act, and as they mirror each other they also express the boy's ambivalence and shape the images of distance and closeness, harm and tenderness, that close the poem. "For Esther," dedicated to the poet's mother, shows a similar linking on a larger scale. It is about trains and railroads and a boy's fascination with them; but how, we wonder, does it also manage to be a poem about, and for, the boy's mother? The fact that mother and son share the memories might suffice as a reason for joining their uneasy love to images of railroads, but the connection goes much deeper. It touches on the mutual desire to be together and to be away from each other; the second possibility is represented both literally and metaphorically by the trains that pass through the little town where they live.

Writing about one's childhood and parents is never easy. The necessary perspective is hard to achieve, and the common temptation to make of childhood a lost paradise often lures us into nostalgia and sentimentality. Perhaps because his childhood was unhappy enough to resist idealization, and certainly because he writes with great honesty about all the divided feelings in his life and the lives of his family, Plumly achieves an elegiac tenderness about his past without falling into self-indulgence or self-pity. His poems are deeply personal and wonderfully impersonal at the same time. The past as he sees it is no less mixed in character and value than the present; the difference is that our having survived it gives us a calm perspective on it, a power over it—"Recovery is memory. / I never broke my arm"—and allows us to see its value, even in things as unlikely as iron lungs.

Not all these poems deal with memory and personal experience. They may tackle general subjects, as "Wildflower" does, or arise from a contemplation of art and the imagination, as "Another November" seems to. But "Wildflower" contains a memory ("the summer I picked everything"), and "Another November" makes the world of the picture as real as any remembered landscape. It's as if this poet were slowly furnishing a museum made up of the most cherished and sustaining objects he can find. Some come from "pain remembered" ("Out-of-the-Body Travel"); some from pain imagined (Plumly is not, after all, the speaker of "The Iron Lung"); but others center on minor and solitary pleasures, such as being alone, "poverty or purity of choice" in "Early Meadow-Rue," and the simple joy of naming and identifying expressed in "Wild-flower." Our selection closes with a long poem, "After Grief," in which the poet returns to the subject of the father in a lyric that ranges across life and death, past and present, waking and dreaming, with extraordinary authority and ease.

Stanley Plumly grew up in Ohio and Virginia and was educated at Wilmington College in Ohio, and Ohio University. He taught for a number of years at Ohio University, where he helped found the *Ohio Review*, and he has been a visiting writer at a number of other institutions, including Iowa, Princeton, Columbia and the University of Washington. At present, he teaches in the writing program at the University of Houston.

DY

Out-of-the-Body Travel

1

And then he would lift this finest
of furniture to his big left shoulder
and tuck it in and draw the bow
so carefully as to make the music

almost visible on the air. And play
and play until a whole roomful of the sad
relatives mourned. They knew this was
drawing of blood, threading and rethreading

the needle. They saw even in my father's
face how well he understood the pain
he put them to—his raw, red cheek
pressed against the cheek of the wood . . .

2

And in one stroke he brings the hammer
down, like mercy, so that the young bull's

legs suddenly fly out from under it . . .
While in the dream he is the good angel

in Chagall, the great ghost of his body
like light over the town. The violin
sustains him. It is pain remembered.
Either way, I know if I wake up cold,

and go out into the clear spring night,
still dark and precise with stars,
I will feel the wind coming down hard
like his hand, in fever, on my forehead.

Early Meadow-Rue

The fields in fog, the low, dull resonance of morning.

There never was an old country.
Only this privacy, the dream life of the deaf,
the girl looking into the mirror above her head,
prone in paralysis.

     And this one loneliness,
poverty or purity of choice, driving cold
in the general direction of the sun before dawn,
coffee in the truck, and bread, the cab light on,
and nobody, nobody else on the airstrip of the road,

going to work.

The Iron Lung

So this is the dust that passes through porcelain,
so this is the unwashed glass left over from supper,
so this is the air in the attic, in August,
and this the down on the breath of the sleeper . . .

If we could fold our arms, but we can't.
If we could cross our legs, but we can't.
If we could put the mind to rest . . .
But our fathers have set this task before us.

My face moons in the mirror, weightless,
without air, my head propped like a penny.
I'm dressed in a shoe, ready to walk out
of here. I'm wearing my father's body.

STANLEY PLUMLY

I remember my mother standing in the doorway
trying to tell me something. The day is thick
with the heat rising from the road. I am
too far away. She looks like my sister.

And I am dreaming of my mother in a doorway
telling my father to die or go away.
It is the front door, and my drunken father falls
to the porch on his knees like one of his children.

It is precisely at this moment I realize
I have polio and will never walk again.
And I am in the road on my knees, like my father,
but as if I were growing into the ground

I can neither move nor rise.
The neighborhood is gathering, and now
my father is lifting me into the ambulance
among the faces of my family. His face is

a blur or a bruise and he holds me
as if I had just been born. When I wake
I am breathing out of all proportion to myself.
My whole body is a lung; I am floating

above a doorway or a grave. And I know
I am in this breathing room as one
who understands how breath is passed
from father to son and passed back again.

At night, when my father comes to talk,
I tell him we have shared this body long enough.
He nods, like the speaker in a dream.
He knows that I know we're only talking.

Once there was a machine for breathing.
It would embrace the body and make a kind of love.
And when it was finished it would rise
like nothing at all above the earth

to drift through the daylight silence.
But at dark, in deep summer, if you thought you heard
something like your mother's voice calling you home,
you could lie down where you were and listen to the dead.

Peppergrass

Nothing you could know, or name, or say
in your sleep, nothing you'd remember,
poor-man's-pepper, wildflower, weed—
what the guidebook calls *the side*
of the road—as from the moon the earth
looks beautifully anonymous, this field
pennycress, this shepherd's purse, nothing
you could see: summer nights we'd look up
at the dark, the stars, and turn like toys . . .

Nothing you could hold on to
but the wet grass, cold as morning.

We were windmills where the wind came from,
nothing, nothing you could name,
blowing the lights out, one by one.

For Esther

1

From the back it looks like a porch,
portable, the filigree railing French.

And Truman, Bess and the girl each come out
waving, in short sleeves, because the heat
is worse than Washington.

The day is twelve hours old, Truman is talking.
You tell me to pay attention,
                         so I have my ball-
cap in my hands when he gets to the part that the sun

is suicidal, his dry voice barely audible above the train.

It makes a noise like steam.
He says, he says, he says.

His glasses silver in the sun. He says
there is never enough, and leans down to us.

2

Shultz and I put pennies on the track to make
the train jump. It jumps.

Afternoons you nap—one long pull of the body
through the heat.

                    I go down to the depot
against orders; it's practically abandoned
except for the guy who hangs out

the mail and looks for pennies. He's president
of this place, he says. We pepper his B & O
brick building with tar balls when he's gone.

You hate the heat and sleep and let
your full voice go when I get caught.

You can't stand my noise or silence.
And I can hear a train in each bent coin.

You're thirty. I still seem to burden that young body.

                         3

Light bar, dark bar, all the way down. The trick is
if a train comes there is room for only the river.

I look down between the crossties at the Great Miami.
Three miles back, near home,

Kessler has already climbed to his station.
The trick is waiting for the whistle.

                         I remember
your dream about bridges: how, as a child, they shook
you off, something the wind compelled.

You woke up holding on. And now this August morning

I don't know enough to be afraid or care.
I do my thinking here,

looking down at the long ladder on the water,
forty feet below.

                         4

The engine at idle, coasting in the yard, the call bell
back and forth, back and forth above the lull . . .

I hang on like the mail as the cars lock in
to one another, couple, and make a train.

The time I break my arm you swear
me to the ground—no more rivers,
no more side-car rides—

and stay up half
the night to rub my legs to sleep.

Sometimes you talk as if Roosevelt

were still alive. Recovery is memory.
I never broke my arm.

Back and forth. The names
of the states pass every day in front of us, single-file.

5

If a house were straw there'd be a wind,
if a house were wood there'd be a fire,

if a house were brick there'd be a track
and a train to tell the time.

I wish each passage
well—wind, fire, time, people on a train.
From here to there, three minutes, whistle-stop.

And the speech each night, the seconds clicking off.

The whole house shakes—or seems to. At intervals,
the ghost smoke fills

all the windows on the close-in side.
It's our weather. It's what we hear all night,
between Troy and anywhere, what you meant

to tell me, out of the body, out of the body travel.

Another November

In the blue eye of the medievalist there is a cart in the road.
There are brushfires and hedgerows and smoke and smoke
and the sun gold dollop going down.

The light has been falling all afternoon and the rain off and on.
There is a picture of a painting in a book in which the surface
of the paper, like the membrane of the canvas,

is nothing if not a light falling from another source.
The harvest is finished and figure, ground, trees lined up against
the sky all look like furniture—

STANLEY PLUMLY

even the man pushing the cart that looks like a chair,
even the people propped up in the fields, gleaning, or watching
the man, waving his passage on.

Part of a cloud has washed in to clarify or confound.
It is that time of the day between work and supper when the body
would lie down, like bread, or is so much of a piece

with the whole it is wood for a fire. Witness how
it is as difficult to paint rain as it is this light falling across
this page right now because there will always be

a plague of the luminous dead being wheeled to the edge of town.
The painting in the book is a landscape in a room, cart in the road,
someone's face at the window.

Wildflower

Some—the ones with fish names—grow so north
they last a month, six weeks at most.
Some others, named for the fields they look like,
last longer, smaller.

And these, in particular, whether trout- or corn-lily,
onion or bellwort, just cut
this morning and standing open in tapwater in the kitchen
will close with the sun.

It is June, wildflowers on the table.
They are fresh an hour ago, like sliced lemons,
with the whole day ahead of them.
They could be common mayflower lilies-of-the-valley,

day-lilies, or the clustering Canada, large, gold,
long-stemmed as pasture roses, belled out over the vase—
or maybe solomon's-seal, the petals
ranged in small toy pairs

or starry, tipped at the head like weeds.
They could be anonymous as weeds.
They are, in fact, the several names of the same thing,
lilies of the fields, butter-and-eggs.

toadflax almost, the way the whites and yellow juxtapose,
and have "the look of flowers that are looked at."
rooted as they are in water, glass, and air.
I remember the summer I picked everything

flower and wildflower, singled them out in jars
with a name attached. And when they had dried as stubborn
as paper I put them on pages and named them again.
They were all lilies, even the hyacinth,

even the great pale flower in the hand of the dead.
I picked it, kept it in the book for years
before I knew who she was,
her face lily-white, kissed and dry and cold.

After Grief

When you woke among them,
when you rose,
when you got up and they asked you
what you were—is it named?—
and you in your new clothes
and face and body lined dry with newspaper,

when you climbed out of the coffin
and began to walk,
alive (*like a rainbow* one of them said),
without a word, in this place of skull and femur,
stone and the sounds of water, when you walked up
to the one talking, his face a face
of the moon, and started to speak, he said

no need, I know who you are.

All this recorded in the first book, The Dream,
in the blessing of the death
of each day.

And tonight, bedded down,
the mind adrift, the body just a few feet
from the earth, it is written

there is the river,
go wash yourself.
And you asked

what is this place? And the one
without a face answered
look around you, this is where you are.

I remember how even near the end
you would go out to your garden
just before dark, in the blue air,
and brood over the failures
of corn or cabbage
or the crooked row
but meaning the day had once more
failed for you.

I watched you as any son watches his father,
like prophecy.

And in my mind I counted the thousand
things to say.

And tonight, again, it is written
that the one talking said
Father, forgive everything.
leave these clothes, this body.
lie down in the water.
be whole.

And having done so, you rose
among them, who are called The Bones,
without flesh or face.

All this recorded in the dream unending.

The first death was the death of the father.
And whosoever be reborn in sons
so shall they be also reborn.

In the Book of the Dead are names
the weight of the continents.
At each rising of the waters
shall the earth be washed.

This is the dream that holds the planet
in place.

And you, my anonymous father,
be with me when I wake.

Notes

For Esther. The first stanza recalls Harry Truman's whistlestop campaign in the summer and fall of 1948.

Wildflower. The quote "the look of flowers that are looked at" is from T. S. Eliot's *Four Quartets* ("Burnt Norton," I).

Stanley Plumly

Books

In the Outer Dark, 1970
Giraffe, 1974,
Out-of-the-Body Travel, 1977

Interviews, Essays

"The One Thing," in *American Poets in 1976*, ed. William Heyen, 1976; "The Path of Saying: An Interview with Stanley Plumly," *Poetry Miscellany* 9 (December 1979); "Interview with Stanley Plumly," *Ohio Review* 25 (Fall 1980)

Dennis Schmitz

(b. 1937)

D ennis Schmitz writes poems that let you know right away you have a challenge on your hands. The subject matter is often grotesque, the tone is dry and reticent, and the verse has a high specific density. In the absence of punctuation and capitalization the reader must make constant decisions about where one syntactical unit ends and another begins. Details crowd into the text in a dazzling and often bewildering succession. You take a deep breath before and after you read a Schmitz poem. In between, you call on quick wits and close attention.

Such efforts are well rewarded. The difficulties of these texts are not superficial features but muscle, sinew, and bone. Every element in a poem by Dennis Schmitz contributes to a well-constructed and compact whole. The reader doesn't have to supply order, just discover it. One acquaints oneself with these poems in the same way that one explores a well-made building, a process that can take time. In "A Letter to Ron Silliman on the Back of a Map of the Solar System," Greek myth and scientific fact are brought together in a fantastic combination that becomes a metaphor for our condition, or for the way we sometimes feel its weight and weirdness. Nothing in the poem, we realize upon pondering it closely, is incidental or casual. It is a thing to walk around and contemplate with astonishment, both as architecture and as music.

The pair of Chicago-based poems that follow, "Star & Garter Theater" and "Queen of Heaven Mausoleum," confirm the impression that Schmitz's poems are dense, complex structures to which we orient ourselves gradually and with growing delight. Both touch on the human need to create by constructing. The striptease and horror-movie world of the first is one where a monster is built ("my arm is sewn to your shoulder") and sex is a cumbersome assemblage ("now the fat ladies of the night // are lowered into the lace / stockings & strapped into their black / apparatus"). The poem's deft joinings become a superior reflection of the obsessive combinations of its subject. The construction worker who speaks in "Queen of Heaven Mausoleum" about the dreamlike work of finishing crypts is likewise a close cousin of the poet-maker who sketches his character's parodies of death and birth in a condensed, elegant style. Two later manifestations of the construction theme may be found in this selection: "Making a Door," in which a father and daughter work together on a dollhouse; and "Making Chicago," the most complex and explicit treatment of the human urge to build that Schmitz has yet undertaken.

The dry humor and deadpan manner of these poems keep them impersonal. Thus "Mile Hill," which is about Schmitz and his family, does not differ significantly in effect from "The Man Who Buys Hides," an extended dramatic monologue. So impressive is the amount of inward revelation in the latter poem, in fact, that it must be counted the more intimate of the two. It is as though the poles of what is personal and what is impersonal are reversed in Schmitz so that an excess of objectivity is what can take him into the subjective. His ability to move imaginatively into the lives and inner worlds of others is also illustrated by "A Picture of Okinawa." From a photograph and a few childhood memories of a distant war he is able to leap into the psyche of "the last Japanese soldier," who surrendered only thirty years later, having lived among the trees of the jungle. The poem is funny, touching, and grotesque; it makes us marvel at the poet's ability to combine imaginative sympathy with fierce powers of objectification.

Dennis Schmitz's vision, which is ultimately religious in character, is the greatest source of unity in his poetry. The human condition in an imperfect, fallen world is his chief preoccupation. He sees us as grounded or trapped in the physical world and in our bodies, yearning for some kind of transcendence. As "Mile Hill" puts it, "we are on our knees / everyday to find on the ground / what we'd lost to the sky." Knowing that the subject of any given Schmitz poem is apt to be the fallen world and the human search for transcendence, the reader will have an easier time with complex pieces like "Making Chicago" and "The Man Who Buys Hides." It is not that Schmitz writes the same poem over and over but that he brings, as all good artists do, a specific vision to bear on the world around him, a definite point of view. Locating the center of that vision or viewpoint is a logical step in coming to terms with the poet's work.

Dennis Schmitz grew up on a farm near Dubuque, Iowa. He was educated at Loras College and the University of Chicago, and lived and worked for a number of years in Chicago before moving to California, where since 1966 he has taught writing and literature at California State University at Sacramento. His collections of poems include *We Weep for Our Strangeness* (1969), *Double Exposures* (1971), *Goodwill, Inc.* (1976), and *String* (1980).

DY

A Letter to Ron Silliman on the Back
of a Map of the Solar System

I weigh 486 lbs on Jupiter
   I can't tell you why
I am crying why
        whole ridges of the memory
pull loose this immense gravity
keeps us down
under the slide I discarded first
   my old father who weighed more
here on my back a smaller hump somehow
my penis came out
   wrong or a strangely distended
heart girls touch for luck I threw
   down my weapons too what use
I said poor Aeneas is the afternoon
when distance turns our atmosphere
to frozen gas & shadows the gods give
        a discernible half-life
winks by the best
of our instruments the father
Jupiter ate the most promising
   of his children the Latin myths say

little that they were not grateful
to the sly Greeks a fallen
   city was given curiously foreign
buildings with supports constructed
   on heavenly principles Cassandra
for instance screamed & the water-clocks
ran faster in our color bands
   sodium insects & our smaller
life take on a radiance &
become explosive when it rains we know
it is a warning
   do not even cry the atmosphere
is unstable keep it under sawdust wet
with oil the moist armpits & loins
   are unstable for our use only
the subtle dust that drifts
   down when the last of the fallen memory
settles & Jupiter surrenders
a final disguise for our mothers
   were raped & we grow up half-gods in turn
to eat or forget our real origins

DENNIS SCHMITZ

Star & Garter Theater

for Roger Aplon

it is always night here
faces close but never heal
only the eyes develop

scabs when we sleep & head
by head the dream is drained
into the white pool

of the screen. we go on rehearsing
THE REVENGE OF FRANKENSTEIN:
my arm is sewn to your shoulder.
your father's awful hand
& an actual criminal brain

take root under the projector's
cold moon. I wanted to do
only good. I planted my mouth
& kisses grew all over skid row.
now the fat ladies of the night

are lowered into the lace
stockings & strapped into their black
apparatus. this body is grafted
to theirs. alone we are helpless,

but put together winos, whores
& ambivalent dead we walk the daytime
world charged with our beauty.

Queen of Heaven Mausoleum

white as coal-ash pressed
again in veins, fuel for the living
I lay all summer in the fourth

floor crypts chipping
the excess we poured in the footings
for the dead. the foreman kneels

to hand in the tools
his face framed by this inner
world square as an oven
in which my flesh warmed
death's inspired
ingredients. which was my hand
& which the dead hand wanting to pry
open the future, the concrete

forms a dead father reinforces
as he fills his son's
teetering flesh. after a moment
my eyes film, magnify
sparks dropping from the darkness
like snowflakes. I fall
back into the frozen position

of the dead or the foetus I once saw
in the clear icy jacket of a jar.
around my ankles something tightens
& pulls my legs straight
in this second more awkward birth
when the grinning foreman slaps
me from my faint, will I cry

to be buried or gratefully begin
to nurse at the world I thirsted for?

Making a Door

a weedy creek
peeled from cornfields,
the whole countryside
where I grew up
thaws from the front
windows of this dollhouse

we are making together.
my daughter kneels
to chalk night
on the back windows,
wanting for this one house
all that our family lived
her eight years—
even dreams reduced
to the neat minimum

DENNIS SCHMITZ

of her bedroom.
I ask to enter
the doll's world,
tell in altered size
what I dreamed

in my half of the house:
how I reached speech
through a series of dahs,
made my face a welt
on the five senses—
I go on distributing
myself over the assigned parts.
the house is almost done.

I hand her the saw.

Mile Hill

December: the trees chafing.
instead of a hole
at the horizon the focused light
of a welder's torch: the sun

& the iridescent this-world fuse.
6 days' drive, Calif to the cramped Iowa
farms. by the roadside we stretch
as I explain where my family

grew. below,
small preserved Dubuque bristles
in '90s plain-face
brick across the uneven hills,
circles where the river does

south to slough water.
Sara picks up
snow; molds it to her small hand,
tinges it with her pink

flesh: concomitant beauty
the bloodspot on the egg
we are on our knees
everyday to find on the ground
what we'd lost to the sky.

The Man Who Buys Hides

before I had a face
my mother supposed another horizon
aligned with that

wrong one contemporary hands fit
to relic Sioux.
maybe town behind the long
hills her brother's feedlot rode.
she was unmarried & wished

my face would never ripen
on the small stone memory left
of a necessary
lover. but I was born

white. & grew, bulky
& slow, never hearing my name
knotted in her tongue though
she must have sung

kneading father's pale
flesh, face to face drinking
distortion from each ripple
the other's body made.
or so I thought
when at night her lost
voice sounded the walls to the service
porch where at fourteen I dreamed
one pool dropping

to another hatchery trout threaded.
on the wall overhead
an exhausted
Jesus dried in milky shellac,

showing rain.

＊　＊　＊

summers I answered
her face surfacing in the bedroom
window to clean her eyes

or devotedly follow a crippled
hand through the word
"drink." my denim printed
blue sweat wherever I leaned
in her unquenchable

shadow. winters the ragged sky
my eyes folded as I slept
lost snow. the world formed under

our stamping feet & above it
breath drifted. with bare
hands uncle & I
shaped the cattle's frozen
noses, undid the ice their drool
tied through whatever
they ate. only the radio

spoke other names
when the lights were out
& eyes were adrift in their own

local winter.

*   *   *

forty years later never thinking
of Dakota I still go faceless
into sleep & dream myself

intaglio under the animal.
I never see the driver
of my truck as it weaves the dead
smells through eucalyptus rows
swerving for potholes

in the gravel till the bones
give & under the tarp
the burst organs suck & squeeze.
what is death?
at the tail end they put one drain
at the other end they put
the tongue back in, intractable
& too big—
what can the doctor say

who is tired of his own body?

*   *   *

the poplar leaves go on multiplying
basic July. July sun
is swollen in the basin

where I cool
my drunken face. once I loved
my smell as I loved the hoof tipped
with stink trailing from the stud

barn. I have become a talker
in bars who wanted
to be only a handspan of red
earth trembling with ants.
Dakota stays under the washed
face even if Calif
turns it dark. only man is dumb

whose tongue shapes before the fingers
know. did these dead
animals talk

with hooves or with tactile
fetlocks praise
the grass as they stepped

off the limits of their hunger,
touching with their mouths
last? as I load each distended

body the winch
squeals, the cable cuts new
boundaries across
a piebald hide. only the head
drags & the eyes roll

over, counter to the earth.

String

no one knows the way out of his mother
except as she leads him
the final knot is his head
which drags the nerves
along the spine like doublestitch
up the reverse
of the body & outside the soft fabric
currents which pucker
erogenous zones. no other joy

DENNIS SCHMITZ

but this string, this dorsal string
one end shit, the other end tongue.
who has not asked the way back?
who is not guilty of graceless longing,
& alone? watch that man who

puppet-dances through noon
traffic skinning light
off the chrome. though his hands
are broken his quarrel
goes on. his pants front soaked, shamed,

he sings for pedestrians.
his mouth will bunch with old stitches
but he will sing, "privacy is only

contraction, heavy
body, dangle of shriveled nuts . . ."

Making Chicago

*We cannot take a single step toward
heaven. It is not in our power to travel
in a vertical direction. If however we
look heavenward for a long time, God
comes and takes us up. He raises us
easily.*

SIMONE WEIL

let it end here where the blueprint
shows a doorway,
where it shows all of Chicago
reduced to a hundred prestressed floors,
fifty miles of conduit & ductwork

the nerve-impulse climbs to know God.
every floor we go up is one more down
for the flashy suicide, *for blessèd man who
by thought might lift himself*

to angel. how slowly we become only men!
I lift the torch away, push up the opaque
welder's lens to listen for the thud
& grind as they pour aggregate,

extrapolating the scarred forms resisting
all that weight & think
the years I gave away to reflexive anger,

to bad jobs, do not count
for the steps the suicide
divides & subdivides in order not to reach

the roof's edge. I count the family years
I didn't grow older with the stunted
locust trees in Columbus Park,
the ragweed an indifferent ground crew
couldn't kill, no matter the poison.
now I want to take up death more often

& taste it a little—
by this change I know I am not what I was:
the voice is the voice of Jacob
but the hands are the hands of Esau—
god & antigod mold what I say,

make me sweat inside the welding gloves,
make what I thought true turn heavy.
but there must be names
in its many names the concrete can't take.
what future race in the ruins
will trace out our shape from the bent

template of the soul,
find its orbit in the clouded atmosphere
of the alloy walls we used as a likeness

for the sky? the workmen stagger
under the weight of the window's nuptial
sheet—in its white reflected clouds
the sun leaves a virgin spot

of joy.

A Picture of Okinawa

out of adult hearing
the birds stammer this place
the animals intact
the remembered trees mismade
because a child painted them .

DENNIS SCHMITZ

from radio news & the interdicted
marsh back of Catfish Slough—
no Gl drab but the Rousseau greens
snakes shed in their turnings

from heaven-held aquas & cerulean.
when the last Japanese soldier
gave up thirty years late
crashed down in some islander's

backyard, the sniper webbings cradling
his navel to the bandoliers
& commando knife with the four
metal knuckle-rings, I still looked
for my soldier uncle in this picture

my aunt never sent
to show how I imagined the enemy
condemned to eat close to heaven
the lonely madness for another's flesh,
his greenish waste wrapped in leaves

& stabbed on treeforks,
one mottled arm reaching for birds,
leaf by leaf making himself
innocent of his weapons—
only thirty years to come down human.

Dennis Schmitz

Books

We Weep for our Strangeness, 1969
Double Exposures, 1971
Goodwill, Inc., 1976
String, 1980

Criticism

David Young, "Dennis Schmitz and Charles Simic," *FIELD* 24 (Spring 1981)

Charles
Simic

(b. 1938)

The poems of Charles Simic tend to be clear, compact, and mysteriously resonant. Some are quite short, others accumulate short sections as deliberate variations on a theme (e.g., "Bestiary for the Fingers of My Right Hand"). The reader senses the presence of distillation, as though large subjects had been reduced to pungent microcosms. We can conclude that Simic is a master of archetypes, but we need to remember that our sense of the archetypal is usually produced by a writer's careful manipulation of context. A loaf of bread can be just a loaf of bread in one poem, while it may summon powerful associations from history, myth, and the Bible in another. Simic's sense of the power of simple objects—tables, doors, brooms, stones—stems in part from his East European heritage (he spent the first ten years of his life in Yugoslavia) and in part from his careful study of folklore and myth while he was forming himself as a poet.

A glance at the first poem in our selection, "Butcher Shop," will serve to illustrate some of Simic's techniques. A place that most of us would pass without much thought is called back to our attention. A special time is invoked—"late at night"—and an atmosphere of suspense and drama is established by an ingenious comparison: "There is a single light in the store / Like the light in which the convict digs his tunnel." We are ready to look again at butcher shops, and as further figures of speech appear—the blood map on the apron, the church comparison in the third stanza—they lead us on into a sense of how fully the butcher shop can represent the dark side of our civilization, a place of destruction and nourishment that is as mysterious as any temple. The poet is not interested in judging the butcher or our habits of eating meat and slaughtering animals. Only a nonjudgmental attitude will take him as far as he wishes to go toward an encounter "Where I am fed, / Where deep in the night I hear a voice." Whose voice it is and what it says are left for the reader to decide; but the interlocking of life and death, creation and destruction that the poem envisions is one that most of us can respond to with a combination of terror and delight. It is part of the "gothic" side of our literature, akin to horror movies and monster myths, that cultivates this playing with our worst fears; and Simic is perfectly aware of his link with that side of the imagination. The poems crackle with a dark merriment about the whole human urge to the gothic and monstrous, and they bear titles like "Begotten of the Spleen" to make that allegiance clear.

"Butcher Shop" is set "late at night" and imagines "great continents" and "great rivers and oceans of blood." That expansion of horizon is also typical of Simic's cunning microcosms. In "Tapestry" we learn that the object (of which the poem seems a miniature replica), a tapestry out of Breughel or Bosch, "hangs from heaven to earth." "Psalm" discovers a woman who is a forest "standing at the beginning of time." The fork in "Fork" seems to have "crept / Right out of hell," while the brooms in the poem that follows invoke "Dawns a thousand years deep." Roads in Simic poems tend to be "long as sleep," and language is "as old as rain," while a stretch of tundra may be "on the scale of the universe." The poems reach out specifically to the vast areas of

space and time they attempt to represent in miniature, and their drama-
tic changes in scale keep our imaginations wide open, reminding us
constantly that we need to be in touch with the timeless and the unchang-
ing. It is with delight that we consent to recognize that brooms, for ex-
ample, give us ready links with the distant past and with realities beyond
the everyday. Such recognitions reopen our ties to the ancient world
of the peasant in which life and death, birth and growth, exist in a coher-
ent fabric. The modern world stands in danger of losing touch with this
sense of existence. Other poets have sought to rescue and prize it—one
thinks of Jarrell's fairy-tale poems—as have writers of fiction like Singer,
Garcia Marquez, and Calvino. Simic, among the poets of his generation,
is the authoritative imagination when it comes to the tradition that is
also manifested in nursery rhymes, proverbs, riddles, and spells—in
short, the world of magic.

A writer with such allegiances and of such mastery might not need
to develop or change, but Simic, careful to avoid artistic stagnation, has
experimented continually with new variations on the rich artistic possibil-
ities of his material. "Euclid Avenue," with its relative austerity of lan-
guage and tone, is one such departure. The final four poems of our selec-
tion—"Empire of Dreams," 'Begotten of the Spleen," "Classic Ballroom
Dances," and "Harsh Climate"—represent another. Drawn from
Simic's newest collection, *Classic Ballroom Dances* (1980), these poems
continue to reflect the "peasant" tradition of lively myth and folklore,
but they cross it with history and personal recollection: the "small, pro-
vincial city," the "floodlights / in the guard towers," the "dancefloor of
the Union Hall." These are not mythic or folkloric archetypes but direct
manifestations of twentieth-century history as it has made itself felt in
the world Simic grew up in (Eastern Europe during and after the Second
World War) and in the lives and imaginations of all of us. The "cross-
ventilating" of the mythic world by the historical and personal has pro-
tected Simic from simply repeating earlier successes and has opened his
poems up to new horizons.

Charles Simic came to the United States in 1949 and settled in Chi-
cago where he attended Oak Park High School and the University of
Chicago. After a stint in the army he completed his B.A. at New York Uni-
versity, where he also did graduate work. He has had jobs of all kinds,
but has for some years been a teacher, first in California and, since 1974,
at the University of New Hampshire. Besides his numerous books of poetry
(e.g., *Dismantling the Silence, Return to a Place Lit by a Glass of Milk, Charon's
Cosmology*), he has been an active translator of French, Russian, and
Yugoslav poetry, most notably the work of the Yugoslav poet Vasko
Popa in two collections: *The Little Box* (1970), and *Homage to the Lame
Wolf* (1979). The absence of self-indulgence in Simic's poetry, a reflection

of his urge to reach out to the lives and concerns of ordinary people, has helped win him a wide audience of enthusiastic readers.

DY

Butcher Shop

Sometimes walking late at night
I stop before a closed butcher shop.
There is a single light in the store
Like the light in which the convict digs his tunnel.

An apron hangs on the hook:
The blood on it smeared into a map
Of the great continents of blood,
The great rivers and oceans of blood.

There are knives that glitter like altars
In a dark church
Where they bring the cripple and the imbecile
To be healed.

There is a wooden slab where bones are broken.
Scraped clean:—a river dried to its bed
Where I am fed,
Where deep in the night I hear a voice.

Tapestry

It hangs from heaven to earth.
There are trees in it, cities, rivers,
small pigs and moons. In one corner
snow is falling over a charging cavalry,
in another women are planting rice.

You can also see:
a chicken carried off by a fox,
a naked couple on their wedding night,
a column of smoke,
an evil-eyed woman spitting into a pail of milk.

What is behind it?
—Space, plenty of empty space.

And who is talking now?
—A man asleep under a hat.

And when he wakes up?
—He'll go into the barbershop.
They'll shave his beard, nose, ears and hair
To look like everyone else.

Psalm

1

Old ones to the side.

If there's a tailor, let him sit
With his legs crossed.
My suit will arrive in a moment.

All priests into mouse-holes.
All merchants into pigs. We'll cut their throats later.

To the beggars a yawn,
We'll see how they'll climb into it.

To the one who thinks, to the one between yes and no,
A pound of onions to peel.

To the mad ones crowns, if they still want them.
To the soldier a manual to turn into a flea.

No one is to touch the children.
No one is to shovel out the dreamers.

2

I'm Joseph of the Joseph of the Joseph who rode on a donkey,
A wind-mill on the tongue humming with stars,
Columbus himself chained to a chair,
I'm anyone looking for a broom-closet.

3

You must understand that I write this at night
Their sleep surrounds me like an ocean.
Her name is Mary, the most mysterious of all.
She's a forest, standing at the beginning of time.
I'm someone lying within it. This light is our sperm.
The forest is old, older than sleep.
Older than this psalm I'm singing right to the end.

CHARLES SIMIC

Bestiary for the Fingers of My Right Hand

1

Thumb, loose tooth of a horse.
Rooster to his hens.
Horn of a devil. Fat worm
They have attached to my flesh
At the time of my birth.
It takes four to hold him down,
Bend him in half, until the bone
Begins to whimper.

Cut him off. He can take care
Of himself. Take root in the earth,
Or go hunting with wolves.

2

The second points the way.
True way. The path crosses the earth,
The moon and some stars.
Watch, he points further.
He points to himself.

3

The middle one has backache.
Stiff, still unaccustomed to this life;
An old man at birth. It's about something
That he had and lost,
That he looks for within my hand,
The way a dog looks
For fleas
With a sharp tooth.

4

The fourth is mystery.
Sometimes as my hand
Rests on the table
He jumps by himself
As though someone called his name.

After each bone, finger,
I come to him, troubled.

Something stirs in the fifth
Something perpetually at the point
Of birth. Weak and submissive,
His touch is gentle.
It weighs a tear.
It takes the mote out of the eye.

Fork

This strange thing must have crept
Right out of hell.
It resembles a bird's foot
Worn around the cannibal's neck.

As you hold it in your hand,
As you stab with it into a piece of meat,
It is possible to imagine the rest of the bird:
Its head which like your fist
Is large, bald, beakless and blind.

Brooms

for Tomaz, Susan and George

1

Only brooms
Know the devil
Still exists,

That the snow grows whiter
After a crow has flown over it,
That a dark dusty corner
Is the place of dreamers and children,

That a broom is also a tree
In the orchard of the poor,
That a hanging roach there
Is a mute dove.

CHARLES SIMIC

2

Brooms appear in dreambooks
As omens of approaching death.
This is their secret life.
In public, they act like flat-chested old maids
Preaching temperance.

They are sworn enemies of lyric poetry.
In prison they accompany the jailer,
Enter cells to hear confessions.
Their short-end comes down
When you least expect it.

Left alone behind a door
Of a condemned tenement,
They mutter to no one in particular,
Words like *virgin wind moon-eclipse*,
And that most sacred of all names:
Hieronymous Bosch.

3

In this and in no other manner
Was the first ancestral broom made:
Namely, they plucked all the arrows
From the bent back of Saint Sebastian.
They tied them with a rope
On which Judas hung himself.
Stuck in the stilt
On which Copernicus
Touched the morning star . . .

Then the broom was ready
To leave the monastery.
The dust welcomed it—
That great pornographer
Immediately wanted to
Look under its skirt.

4

The secret teaching of brooms
Excludes optimism, the consolation
Of laziness, the astonishing wonders
Of a glass of aged moonshine.

It says: the bones end up under the table.
Bread-crumbs have a mind of their own.
The milk is you-know-who's semen.
The mice have the last squeal.

As for the famous business
Of levitation, I suggest remembering:
There is only one God
And his prophet is Mohammed.

5

And then finally there's your grandmother
Sweeping the dust of the nineteenth century
Into the twentieth, and your grandfather plucking
A straw out of the broom to pick his teeth.

Long winter nights.
Dawns a thousand years deep.
Kitchen windows like heads
Bandaged for toothache.

The broom beyond them sweeping,
Tucking the lucent grains of dust
Into neat pyramids,
That have tombs in them,

Already sacked by robbers,
Once, long ago.

Ballad

What's that approaching like dusk like poverty
A little girl picking flowers in a forest
The migrant's fire of her long hair
Harm's way she comes and also the smile's round about way

In another life in another life
Aunt rain sewing orphan's buttons to each stone
Solitude's stitch
Let your horns out little stone

Screendoor screeching in the wind
Mother-hobble-gobble baking apples
Wooden spoons dancing ah the idyllic life of wooden spoons
I need a table to spread these memories on

Little girl fishing using me as bait
Me a gloomy woodcutter in the forest of words
I am going to say one thing and mean another
I'll tuck you in a matchbox like a hornet

CHARLES SIMIC

In another life in another life
Dandelion and red poppy grow in the back yard
Shoes in the rain bark at the milkman
Little girl alone playing blindman's buff

The words want to bring back more—
You are *it* she says laughing and is gone
Divination by one's own heartbeat
Draw near to what doesn't say yes or no

And she had nothing under her dress
Star like an eye the gamecocks have overlooked
Tune up your fingers and whistle
On a trail lined with elms she hides herself behind a tree

I tread the sod you walked on with kindness
Not even the wind blew to remind me of time
Approaches that which they insist on calling happiness
The nightbird says its name

On a tripod made of limbs hoist this vision
At eveningtime when they examine you in love
Glancing back on the road long as sleep
Little girl skipping the owl's hushed way.

Animal Acts

A bear who eats with a silver spoon.
Two apes adept at grave-digging.
Rats who do calculus.
A police dog who copulates with a woman,
Who takes undertaker's measurements.

A bedbug who suffers, who has doubts
About his existence. The miraculous
Laughing dove. A thousand-year-old turtle
Playing billiards. A chicken who
Cuts his own throat, who bleeds.

The trainer with his sugar-cubes,
With his chair and whip. The evenings
When they all huddle in a cage,
Smoking cheap cigars, lazily
Marking the cards in the new deck.

Euclid Avenue

All my dark thoughts
laid out
in a straight line.

An abstract street
on which an equally abstract intelligence
forever advances, doubting
the sound of its own footsteps.

✳ ✳ ✳

Interminable cortege.
Language
as old as rain.
Fortune-teller's spiel

from where it has its beginning,
its kennel and bone
the scent of a stick
I used to retrieve.

✳ ✳ ✳

A sort of darkness without the woods,
crow-light but without the crow,
Hotel Splendide
all locked up for the night.

And out there,
in sight of some ultimate bakery
the street-light
of my insomnia.

✳ ✳ ✳

A place
known as infinity
toward which that old self
advances.

The poor son of poor parents
who aspires to please
at such a late hour.

The magical coins
in his pocket
occupying all his thoughts.

CHARLES SIMIC   449

A place known
as infinity,
its screendoor screeching,
endlessly screeching.

Empire of Dreams

On the first page of my dreambook
It's always evening
In an occupied country.
Hour before the curfew.
A small provincial city.
The houses all dark.
The store-fronts gutted.

I am on a street corner
Where I shouldn't be.
Alone and coatless
I have gone out to look
For a black dog who answers to my whistle.
I have a kind of halloween mask
Which I am afraid to put on.

Begotten of the Spleen

The Virgin Mother walked barefoot
among the land mines.
She carried an old man in her arms.
The dove on her shoulder

barked at the moon.
The earth was an old people's home.
Judas was the night nurse.
He kept emptying bedpans into river Jordan.

The old man had two stumps for legs.
He was on a dog-chain. St. Peter pushed a cart
loaded with flying carpets.
They weren't flying carpets.

They were bloody diapers.
It was a cock-fighting neighborhood.
The Magi stood on street corners
cleaning their nails with German bayonets.

The old man gave Mary Magdalena
a mirror. She lit a candle,
and hid in the outhouse. When she got thirsty,
she licked the mist off the glass.

That leaves Joseph. Poor Joseph.
He only had a cockroach
to load his bundles on.
Even when the lights came on she wouldn't run
into her hole.

And the lights came on:
The floodlights
in the guard towers.

Classic Ballroom Dances

Grandmothers who wring the necks
Of chickens; old nuns
With names like Theresa, Marianne,
Who pull schoolboys by the ear;

The intricate steps of pickpockets
Working the crowd of the curious
At the scene of an accident; the slow shuffle
Of the evangelist with a sandwich-board;

The hesitation of the early morning customer
Peeking through the window-grille
Of a pawnshop; the weave of a little kid
Who is walking to school with eyes closed;

And the ancient lovers, cheek to cheek,
On the dancefloor of the Union Hall,
Where they also hold charity raffles
On rainy Monday nights of an eternal November.

Harsh Climate

The brain itself in its skull
Is very cold,
According to
Albertus Magnus.

CHARLES SIMIC   451

Something like a stretch of tundra
On the scale of the universe.
Galactic wind.
Lofty icebergs in the distance.

Polar night.
A large ocean liner caught in the ice.
A few lights still burning on the deck.
Silence and fierce cold.

Charles Simic

Books

What the Grass Says, 1967
Somewhere Among Us, A Stone Is Taking Notes, 1969
I. Lalic, *Fire Garden* (translations, with C. W. Truesdale), 1970
Vasko Popa, *The Little Box* (translations), 1970
Four Modern Yugoslav Poets (translations), 1970
White, 1970
Dismantling the Silence, 1971
Return to a Place Lit by a Glass of Milk, 1974
Another Republic (anthology, ed. with Mark Strand), 1976
Charon's Cosmology, 1977
Vasko Popa, *Homage to the Lame Wolf* (translations), 1979
Classic Ballroom Dances, 1980

Criticism, Interviews

Interview, *Ohio Review* 14, no. 2 (Winter 1973); David Walker, "O What Solitude," and James Carpenter "Charles Simic's *White*," Ironwood 7/8 (1976); Manassas Review 1, no. 2 (Winter 1978) issue devoted to Simic, with interview, six articles, and bibliography

Gary
Snyder

(b. 1930)

T he poems of Gary Snyder have large and long perspectives.
They bring together different cultures (e.g., "Hitch Haiku") and
survey vast tracts of history and geography (e.g., "Mother

Earth: Her Whales"). A poet's values, as Snyder has noted, go back to the Neolithic: "the fertility of the soil, the magic of animals, the power-vision in solitude, the terrifying initiation and rebirth, the love and ecstasy of the dance, the common work of the tribe." When Snyder can make the past and the present jump together, as he does, for example, in "Above Pate Valley," there is a sense of enlightenment, of opening vistas, that is exhilarating. The speaker's sense of community expands to include those long-ago makers of arrowheads who were drawn to the same mountain meadow. A comparable lift comes from the sudden uniting of man and nature in "Water," where the comic encounters with rattlesnake and trout (the magic of animals) carry the reader, along with the speaker, into a kind of *satori*, awakening, the Zen term for sudden spiritual understanding that also brings a oneness with the universe.

"Above Pate Valley" and "Water" are from Gary Snyder's first collection, *Riprap* (1959), which reflects his experiences as a logger, firewatcher, and mountaineer in the western states—California and Oregon—where he grew up. It also reflects his interest in Chinese poetry, which he studied and translated in those years (especially Han Shan, *Cold Mountain Poems*, published in a joint edition with *Riprap* in 1965). A work experience and a literary interest coming together: that is typical of Gary Snyder's poetry. He brings the attention of an anthropologist, a student of human culture and languages, to bear on his subjects; but he also draws directly, again and again, on his own active life, his own experience of "the work and play of the tribe." "Oil" is firsthand reportage by someone who has worked long hours on tankers, the same sailor who, in "Hitch Haiku," realizes that scrap brass dumped from the ship when it is crossing the Mindinao Deep will be "falling six miles." This same character picks peppers and cabbages in "Nature Green Shit" and reads Blake during a Japanese typhoon. He has traveled widely, worked a lot with his hands, read voraciously, and pondered deeply. Involved in a casual game of hopscotch on the beach, he does not try to suppress his knowledge that the game is an ancient divining ritual, a way of foretelling one's life and fate. The work and play of the tribe can come to the same thing, and children's games are one more meaningful way of learning and knowing. Enlightenment can come from standing on the deck of an oil tanker or noticing some arrowhead chippings in a mountain meadow or reading a long-dead English poet in an Oriental cowshed. We learn not to despise the means by which the world makes itself known to us.

Studying Zen in Japan might have tempted Gary Snyder to withdraw from the world, but he is too much a naturalist and activist, with a deep concern for our good and bad ways with the planet. Seeing what was happening to Japan made him decide to return to the nation the

TWELVE POETS BORN BETWEEN 1930 AND 1940

Japanese were emulating. If pollution, environmental problems, and misuse of technology were to be confronted directly, it made the most sense to come home to the heart of the problem. He settled back in California in the late 1960s and has been active ever since in the conservation movement, not simply protesting the misuse of resources and pointing out our civilization's errors but trying to help educate Americans to new styles of living and thinking, new ways of valuing themselves and the world around them. He continues, it might be noted, in the native tradition of Emerson and Thoreau. The awareness he wants to share—of ecosystems, cycles, primitive wisdom about holistic ways of seeing the world—is not always easy to put into poems, and Synder is willing to risk the didactic in the interest of making his poetry of a piece with the rest of his life and beliefs. Recent poems, represented here by "Song of the Taste" and "Mother Earth: Her Whales," are explicit about the nature of his commitments.

It is difficult to represent Gary Snyder's work with a selection of poems because some of his best efforts have gone into the writing of two long poems. *Myths and Texts* (1960), from which anthologists sometimes excerpt portions, is much better read in its entirety. An even more ambitious conception, *Mountains and Rivers Without End*, based on the form of a Chinese scroll unrolling horizontally, has had many of its projected forty sections appear in print but has yet to see full completion. The reader is urged to investigate these longer texts and to sample Snyder's essays, as represented by collections like *The Real Work* (1980). In his energy and resourcefulness, Gary Snyder is properly a particular inspiration to young people. They share his concerns and his ideals, and can respond readily to the openness and directness of his poems.

DY

Above Pate Valley

We finished clearing the last
Section of trail by noon,
High on the ridge-side
Two thousand feet above the creek—
Reached the pass, went on
Beyond the white pine groves,
Granite shoulders, to a small
Green meadow watered by the snow,
Edged with Aspen—sun

Straight high and blazing
But the air was cool.
Ate a cold fried trout in the
Trembling shadows.   I spied
A glitter, and found a flake
Black volcanic glass—obsidian—
By a flower. Hands and knees
Pushing the Bear grass, thousands
Of arrowhead leavings over a
Hundred yards. Not one good
Head, just razor flakes
On a hill snowed all but summer,
A land of fat summer deer,
They came to camp. On their
Own trails. I followed my own
Trail here. Picked up the cold-drill,
Pick, singlejack, and sack
Of dynamite.
Ten thousand years.

Water

Pressure of sun on the rockslide
Whirled me in dizzy hop-and-step descent,
Pool of pebbles buzzed in a Juniper shadow,
Tiny tongue of a this-year rattlesnake flicked,
I leaped, laughing for little boulder-color coil—
Pounded by heat raced down the slabs to the creek
Deep tumbling under arching walls and stuck
Whole head and shoulders in the water:
Stretched full on cobble—ears roaring
Eyes open aching from the cold and faced a trout.

Hitch Haiku

They didn't hire him
        so he ate his lunch alone:
the noon whistle

* * *

Cats shut down
           deer thread through
men all eating lunch

* * *

Frying hotcakes in a dripping shelter
         Fu Manchu
Queets Indian Reservation in the rain

* * *

A truck went by
           three hours ago:
Smoke Creek desert

* * *

Jackrabbit eyes all night
  breakfast in Elko.

* * *

Old kanji hid by dirt
on skidroad Jap town walls
          down the hill
to the Wobbly hall

                  Seattle

* * *

Spray drips from the cargo-booms
a fresh-chipped winch
         spotted with red lead
young fir—
         soaking in summer rain

* * *

Over the Mindanao Deep

Scrap brass
         dumpt off the fantail
falling six miles

GARY SNYDER

* * *

*[The following two were written on classical
themes while travelling through Sappho, Washington.
The first is by Thomas L. Hoodlatch.]*

Moonlight on the burned-out temple—
       wooden horse shit.

Sunday dinner in Ithaca—
       the twang of a bowstring

* * *

After weeks of watching the roof leak
      I fixed it tonight
by moving a single board

* * *

*A freezing morning in October in the high
Sierra crossing Five Lakes Basin to the
Kaweahs with Bob Greensfelder and Claude Dalenburg*

Stray white mare
       neck rope dangling
forty miles from farms.

* * *

Back from the Kaweahs

Sundown, Timber Gap
      —sat down—
         dark firs.
  dirty;   cold;
too tired to talk

* * *

Cherry blossoms at Hood river
      rusty sand near Tucson
mudflats of Willapa Bay

Pronghorn country

Steering into the sun
          glittering jewel-road
shattered obsidian

* * *

The mountain walks over the water!
Rain down from the mountain!
          high bleat of a
crow elk
          over blackberries

* * *

A great freight truck
          lit like a town
through the dark stony desert

* * *

Drinking hot saké
                    toasting fish on coals
     the motorcycle
out   parked in the rain.

* * *

Switchback

turn, turn,
and again,   hard-
scrabble
steep travel a-
head.

Oil

soft rainsqualls on the swells
south of the Bonins, late at night. Light
from the empty mess-hall
throws back bulky shadows
of winch and fairlead
over the slanting fantail where I stand.

but for men on watch in the engine room,
the man at the wheel, the lookout in the bow,
the crew sleeps. in cots on deck
or narrow iron bunks down drumming
passageways below.

the ship burns with a furnace heart
steam veins and copper nerves
quivers and slightly twists and always goes—
easy roll of the hull and deep
vibration of the turbine underfoot.

bearing what all these
crazed, hooked nations need:
steel plates and
long injections of pure oil.

Nature   Green Shit

The brittle hollow stalks of sunflower
    heads broke over full of dusty seed
    peeld, it tastes good, small

Why should dirt be dirty when you clean up.
    stop to like the dead or dying plants,
    twisted witherd grass

Picking the last peppers
Soft and wrinkld; bright green, cool

    what a lump of red flesh *I* am!

Violet dawn sky—no more Arcturus—
    beside the sugi nursery where we
    pulld down vines
    house lights constellations
    still   on the hill.

TWELVE POETS BORN BETWEEN 1930 AND 1940

Heavy frosted cabbage.
   (all night porch bulb—)
   paper boy squealing bike brakes

   hey that's my cat!
Coming home.

Hop, Skip, and Jump

for Jim and Annie Hatch

   the curvd lines toe-drawn, round cornerd squares
bulge out doubles from its single pillar line, like,
Venus of the Stone Age.
she takes stone,
with a white quartz band for her lagger.
                              she
   takes a brown-staind salt-sticky cigarette
                              butt.
he takes a mussel shell. he takes a clamshell. she takes
a stick.
he is tiny, with a flying run & leap—
shaggy blond—misses all the laggers,
            tumbles from one foot.
            they are dousing
a girl in a bikini down the beach
            first with cold seawater
                then with wine.
double-leg   single-leg   stork stalk turn
on the end-square—   hop, fork, hop, scoop the lagger,
   we have all trippt and fallen.
      surf rough and full of kelp,
   all the ages—
draw a line on another stretch of sand—
                        and—
                  everybody try
to do the hop, skip, and jump.

4.X.1964 Muir Beach

It

*[Reading Blake in a cowshed during a typhoon on an island in the
East China Sea]*

Cloud—cloud—cloud—hurls
     up and on over;
Bison herds stamp-
eding   on Shantung

Fists of rain
     flail half down the length of the floor
Bamboo hills
     bend and regain;
          fields follow the laws of waves.

     puppy scuds in wet
     squats on the slat bed
        —on the edge of a spiral
centered five hundred miles southwest.

Reading in English:
     the way the words join
     the weights, the warps

     I know   what it means.

     my language is home.

          mind-fronts meeting
          bite back at each other,
          whirl up a Mother Tongue.

     one hundred knot gusts dump palms
     over somebody's morning cream—
Cowshed skull
its windows open

     swallows and strains
     gulfs of wild-slung
          quivering ocean air.
          breathe it;
          taste it;   how it

Feeds the brain.

Song of the Taste

Eating the living germs of grasses
Eating the ova of large birds

    the fleshy sweetness packed
    around the sperm of swaying trees

The muscles of the flanks and thighs of
         soft-voiced cows
    the bounce in the lamb's leap
    the swish in the ox's tail

Eating roots grown swoll
      inside the soil

Drawing on life of living
   clustered points of light spun
      out of space
hidden in the grape.

Eating each other's seed
      eating
  ah, each other.

Kissing the lover in the mouth of bread:
    lip to lip.

Mother Earth: Her Whales

An owl winks in the shadows
A lizard lifts on tiptoe, breathing hard
Young male sparrow stretches up his neck,
      big head, watching—

The grasses are working in the sun. Turn it green.
Turn it sweet. That we may eat.
Grow our meat.

Brazil says "sovereign use of Natural Resources"
Thirty thousand kinds of unknown plants.
The living actual people of the jungle
    sold and tortured—
And a robot in a suit who peddles a delusion called "Brazil"
    can speak for *them?*

GARY SNYDER

463

The whales turn and glisten, plunge
     and sound and rise again,
Hanging over subtly darkening deeps
Flowing like breathing planets
     in the sparkling whorls of
          living light—

And Japan quibbles for words on
     what kinds of whales they can kill?
A once-great Buddhist nation
     dribbles methyl mercury
     like gonorrhea
          in the sea.

Père David's Deer, the Elaphure,
Lived in the tule marshes of the Yellow River
Two thousand years ago—and lost its home to rice—
The forests of Lo-yang were logged and all the silt &
Sand flowed down, and gone, by 1200 AD—

Wild Geese hatched out in Siberia
          head south over basins of the Yang, the Huang,
          what we call "China"
On flyways they have used a million years.
Ah China, where are the tigers, the wild boars,
          the monkeys,
               like the snows of yesteryear
Gone in a mist, a flash, and the dry hard ground
Is parking space for fifty thousand trucks.
IS man most precious of all things?
—then let us love him, and his brothers, all those
Fading living beings—

North America, Turtle Island, taken by invaders
          who wage war around the world.
May ants, may abalone, otters, wolves and elk
Rise! and pull away their giving
          from the robot nations.

Solidarity. The People.
Standing Tree People!
Flying Bird People!
Swimming Sea People!
Four-legged, two-legged, people!

How can the head-heavy power-hungry politic scientist
Government   two-world   Capitalist-Imperialist
Third-world   Communist   paper-shuffling male
          non-farmer   jet-set   bureaucrats
Speak for the green of the leaf? Speak for the soil?

(Ah Margaret Mead . . . do you sometimes dream of Samoa?)

The robots argue how to parcel out our Mother Earth
To last a little longer
        like vultures flapping
Belching, gurgling,
          near a dying Doe.

"In yonder field a slain knight lies—
We'll fly to him and eat his eyes
      with a down
  derry derry derry down down."

      An Owl winks in the shadow
      A lizard lifts on tiptoe
          breathing hard
      The whales turn and glisten
          plunge and
      Sound, and rise again
      Flowing like breathing planets

      In the sparkling whorls

      Of living light.

Stockholm: Summer Solstice 40072

Gary Snyder

Books

Riprap, 1959
Myths and Texts, 1960, 1978
Riprap and Cold Mountain Poems, 1965
Six Sections from Mountains and Rivers Without End, 1965, 1970
Three Worlds, Three Realms, Six Roads, 1966
The Back Country, 1968
Earth House Hold, 1969
Regarding Wave, 1970
Turtle Island, 1974
The Old Ways, 1977

Interviews, Criticism

The Real Work: Interviews and Talks, 1964–1979, 1980; Kenneth Rexroth, *American Poetry in the Twentieth Century*, 1971; Bob Steuding, *Gary Snyder*, 1976

Mark Strand

(b. 1934)

Jack Driscoll

Mark Strand, one of the best-known poets of his generation, writes poems that explore silence, absence, and nullity. In this he somewhat resembles W. S. Merwin, but Strand's world is more painterly and his gothic sense more·playful. His land-scapes are mysterious without necessarily being austere. They remind us of silent movies, old photographs, and the work of atmospheric painters of loneliness like Edward Hopper: "When somebody spoke, there was no answer. / Clouds came down / And buried the buildings along the water, / And the water was silent. / The gulls stared" ("Elegy for My Father," 1). In one sense, this is a perfectly natural scene with fog and a calm sea, but the insistence on solitude is unmistakable. Strand's initial efforts to become a painter were not wasted. Just as the landscapes tend to be deserted and mysterious, so the people in these poems tend to move about like ghosts or robots: "They mourn for you. / They lead you back into the empty house. / They carry the chairs and tables inside. / They sit you down and teach you to breathe. / And your breath burns" ("Elegy for My Father," 5). There is contact here, but it does not break the essential sense of isolation. The sleepwalking people belong to the hushed and dreamlike landscapes, and both project an existential bleakness that is fascinating and troubling.

The style that makes such projections so powerful is based on a rhetoric of simple forms. Short, declarative sentences abound. Repetition is frequent. Questions and answers sound like a primer or a language-learning manual; in "Elegy for My Father," that heightens the strangeness of the interview of a dead father by a living son. Everywhere in Strand's poetry language tends to slow down and grow rigid, eschewing its lusher and suppler ways. The result reminds us of ritualized language as we know it from the Bible and other primitive texts in which chant and psalm, proverb and catalogue, express an obsessive and supernatural version of reality.

The primitive rhythms and wooden constructions are of course very self-conscious; we are meant to share in the artist's deliberate sense of exploring extremes. "The Prediction" is partly a poem about itself, its own validation, and whether its self-contained quality is a strength or a weakness is left for the reader to decide. Sophisticated readers will surely appreciate the poem's rueful acknowledgement of the limits of its magic: It can "predict," but only within its own frame. The "Elegy for My Father," centerpiece of our selection from Strand, is a poem that seems as intent on an exploration of the esthetics of grief as on the expression of grief itself. In a way, it makes the emotion more powerful by muting and muffling it. It also seems able to acknowledge that our emotions are seldom unmixed. In approaching a work of art called an elegy, for example, we are in search of aesthetic pleasure as much as pain or grief. Since art is artful, why not acknowledge that (the analogy of John Ashbery's work is useful here) and let the reader share the poet's sense of the task before him? As a son, Strand grieves profoundly for his father. As an artist, he is fascinated with the way a stylized treatment, a rhetoric of chant and repetition, may help re-create the experience and emotion of grief. Both son and artist are before us in the "Elegy," and the result is one of the most distinctive poems of the 1970s. Call it, if you like, the first great postmodern elegy.

One of the sections of the "Elegy" concerns the fate of the father's shadow, and that use of the shadow, the archetype of the dark and unknown part of the self, serves to remind us how much Strand shares an interest in magic with contemporaries like Simic, Merwin, and Willard. "The Prediction," after all, deals with a vivid experience of premonition. The conversation in the second section of the "Elegy" is like part of a seance or a strange recasting of the ghost scene in *Hamlet*. Other moments in that poem remind us of rituals of exorcism. "Where Are the Waters of Childhood?" guides us on a dream journey to life's beginnings. "Shooting Whales" is based on childhood memory, but the sense of animal magic and of an encounter with the dark forces beyond life is its most pervasive effect. While these ventures into the extraordinary and the supernatural are tinged with self-consciousness and a hint of self-mockery, it remains Strand's special knack that he can produce effects of having released secret forces or penetrated to the heart of certain mysteries, so that his poems carry both authority and fascination.

Born in Canada (Prince Edward Island), Mark Strand grew up in various parts of Canada and the United States, attended Antioch College and, for a time, the Yale Art School. He has taught widely, at schools like Iowa, Yale, Brandeis, and Columbia. He lived for a number of years in New York City before his recent move to Utah, where he is writer-in-residence at the University of Utah in Salt Lake City. The publication of his *Selected Poems* in 1980 clarified the nature and extent of his achievement as a poet, and his recent experiments with fiction suggest a new direction for his very special artistry.

DY

Keeping Things Whole

In a field
I am the absence
of field.
This is
always the case.
Wherever I am
I am what is missing.

When I walk
I part the air
and always
the air moves in
to fill the spaces
where my body's been.

We all have reasons
for moving.
I move
to keep things whole.

The Prediction

That night the moon drifted over the pond,
turning the water to milk, and under
the boughs of the trees, the blue trees,
a young woman walked, and for an instant

the future came to her:
rain falling on her husband's grave, rain falling
on the lawns of her children, her own mouth
filling with cold air, strangers moving into her house.

a man in her room writing a poem, the moon drifting into it,
a woman strolling under its trees, thinking of death,
thinking of him thinking of her, and the wind rising
and taking the moon and leaving the paper dark.

Elegy for My Father
(*Robert Strand 1908–68*)

1 THE EMPTY BODY

The hands were yours, the arms were yours,
But you were not there.
The eyes were yours, but they were closed and would not open.
The distant sun was there.
The moon poised on the hill's white shoulder was there.
The wind on Bedford Basin was there.

MARK STRAND

The pale green light of winter was there.
Your mouth was there,
But you were not there.
When somebody spoke, there was no answer.
Clouds came down
And buried the buildings along the water,
And the water was silent.
The gulls stared.
The years, the hours, that would not find you
Turned in the wrists of others.
There was no pain. It had gone.
There were no secrets. There was nothing to say.
The shade scattered its ashes.
The body was yours, but you were not there.
The air shivered against its skin.
The dark leaned into its eyes.
But you were not there.

2 ANSWERS

Why did you travel?
Because the house was cold.
Why did you travel?
Because it is what I have always done between sunset and sunrise.
What did you wear?
I wore a blue suit, a white shirt, yellow tie, and yellow socks.
What did you wear?
I wore nothing. A scarf of pain kept me warm.
Who did you sleep with?
I slept with a different woman each night.
Who did you sleep with?
I slept alone. I have always slept alone.
Why did you lie to me?
I always thought I told the truth.
Why did you lie to me?
Because the truth lies like nothing else and I love the truth.
Why are you going?
Because nothing means much to me anymore.
Why are you going?
I don't know. I have never known.
How long shall I wait for you?
Do not wait for me. I am tired and I want to lie down.
Are you tired and do you want to lie down?
Yes, I am tired and I want to lie down.

3 YOUR DYING

Nothing could stop you.
Not the best day. Not the quiet. Not the ocean rocking.
You went on with your dying.
Not the trees
Under which you walked, not the trees that shaded you.
Not the doctor
Who warned you, the white-haired young doctor who saved you once.

You went on with your dying.
Nothing could stop you. Not your son. Not your daughter
Who fed you and made you into a child again.
Not your son who thought you would live forever.
Not the wind that shook your lapels.
Not the stillness that offered itself to your motion.
Not your shoes that grew heavier.
Not your eyes that refused to look ahead.
Nothing could stop you.
You sat in your room and stared at the city
And went on with your dying.
You went to work and let the cold enter your clothes.
You let blood seep into your socks.
Your face turned white.
Your voice cracked in two.
You leaned on your cane.
But nothing could stop you.
Not your friends who gave you advice.
Not your son. Not your daughter who watched you grow small.
Not fatigue that lived in your sighs.
Not your lungs that would fill with water.
Not your sleeves that carried the pain of your arms.
Nothing could stop you.
You went on with your dying.
When you played with children you went on with your dying.
When you sat down to eat,
When you woke up at night, wet with tears, your body sobbing,
You went on with your dying.
Nothing could stop you.
Not the past.
Not the future with its good weather.
Not the view from your window, the view of the graveyard.
Not the city. Not the terrible city with its wooden buildings.
Not defeat. Not success.

MARK STRAND

471

You did nothing but go on with your dying.
You put your watch to your ear.
You felt yourself slipping.
You lay on the bed.
You folded your arms over your chest and you dreamed of the world without
    you.
Of the space under the trees.
Of the space in your room,
Of the spaces that would now be empty of you,
And you went on with your dying.

Nothing could stop you.
Not your breathing. Not your life.
Not the life you wanted.
Not the life you had.
Nothing could stop you.

4 YOUR SHADOW

You have your shadow.
The places where you were have given it back.
The hallways and bare lawns of the orphanage have given it back.
The Newsboys Home has given it back.
The streets of New York have given it back and so have the streets of Montreal.
The rooms in Belém where lizards would snap at mosquitos have given it back.
The dark streets of Manaus and the damp streets of Rio have given it back.
Mexico City where you wanted to leave it has given it back.
And Halifax where the harbor would wash its hands of you has given it back.
You have your shadow.
When you traveled the white wake of your going sent your shadow below, but
    when you arrived it was there to greet you. You had your shadow.
The doorways you entered lifted your shadow from you and when you went out,
    gave it back. You had your shadow.
Even when you forgot your shadow, you found it again; it had been with you.
Once in the country the shade of a tree covered your shadow and you were not
    known.
Once in the country you thought your shadow had been cast by somebody else.
    Your shadow said nothing.
Your clothes carried your shadow inside; when you took them off, it spread like
    the dark of your past.
And your words that float like leaves in an air that is lost, in a place no one
    knows, gave you back your shadow.
Your friends gave you back your shadow.
Your enemies gave you back your shadow. They said it was heavy and would
    cover your grave.
When you died your shadow slept at the mouth of the furnace and ate ashes for
    bread.

It rejoiced among ruins.
It watched while others slept.
It shone like crystal among the tombs.
It composed itself like air.
It wanted to be like snow on water.
It wanted to be nothing, but that was not possible.
It came to my house.
It sat on my shoulders.
Your shadow is yours. I told it so. I said it was yours.
I have carried it with me too long. I give it back.

5 MOURNING

They mourn for you.
When you rise at midnight,
And the dew glitters on the stone of your cheeks,
They mourn for you.
They lead you back into the empty house.
They carry the chairs and tables inside.
They sit you down and teach you to breathe.
And your breath burns,
It burns the pine box and the ashes fall like sunlight.
They give you a book and tell you to read.
They listen and their eyes fill with tears.
The women stroke your fingers.
They comb the yellow back into your hair.
They shave the frost from your beard.
They knead your thighs.
They dress you in fine clothes.
They rub your hands to keep them warm.
They feed you. They offer you money.
They get on their knees and beg you not to die.
When you rise at midnight they mourn for you.
They close their eyes and whisper your name over and over.
But they cannot drag the buried light from your veins.
They cannot reach your dreams.
Old man, there is no way.
Rise and keep rising, it does no good.
They mourn for you the way they can.

6 THE NEW YEAR

It is winter and the new year.
Nobody knows you.
Away from the stars, from the rain of light,
You lie under the weather of stones.
There is no thread to lead you back.

Your friends doze in the dark
Of pleasure and cannot remember.
Nobody knows you. You are the neighbor of nothing.
You do not see the rain falling and the man walking away,
The soiled wind blowing its ashes across the city.
You do not see the sun dragging the moon like an echo.
You do not see the bruised heart go up in flames,
The skulls of the innocent turn into smoke.
You do not see the scars of plenty, the eyes without light.
It is over. It is winter and the new year.
The meek are hauling their skins into heaven.
The hopeless are suffering the cold with those who have nothing to hide.
It is over and nobody knows you.
There is starlight drifting on the black water.
There are stones in the sea no one has seen.
There is a shore and people are waiting.
And nothing comes back.
Because it is over.
Because there is silence instead of a name.
Because it is winter and the new year.

Where Are the Waters of Childhood?

See where the windows are boarded up,
where the gray siding shines in the sun and salt air
and the asphalt shingles on the roof have peeled or fallen off,
where tiers of oxeye daisies float on a sea of grass?
That's the place to begin.

Enter the kingdom of rot,
smell the damp plaster, step over the shattered glass,
the pockets of dust, the rags, the soiled remains of a mattress,
look at the rusted stove and sink, at the rectangular stain
on the wall where Winslow Homer's *Gulf Stream* hung.

Go to the room where your father and mother
would let themselves go in the drift and pitch of love,
and hear, if you can, the creak of their bed,
then go to the place where you hid.

Go to your room, to all the rooms whose cold, damp air you breathed,
to all the unwanted places where summer, fall, winter, spring,
seem the same unwanted season, where the trees you knew have died
and other trees have risen. Visit that other place
you barely recall, that other house half hidden.

See the two dogs burst into sight. When you leave,
they will cease, snuffed out in the glare of an earlier light.
Visit the neighbors down the block; he waters his lawn,
she sits on her porch, but not for long.
When you look again they are gone.

Keep going back, back to the field, flat and sealed in mist.
On the other side, a man and a woman are waiting;
they have come back, your mother before she was gray,
your father before he was white.

Now look at the North West Arm, how it glows a deep cerulean blue.
See the light on the grass, the one leaf burning, the cloud
that flares. You're almost there, in a moment your parents
will disappear, leaving you under the light of a vanished star,
under the dark of a star newly born. Now is the time.

Now you invent the boat of your flesh and set it upon the waters
and drift in the gradual swell, in the laboring salt.
Now you look down. The waters of childhood are there.

Shooting Whales

for Judith and Leon Major

When the shoals of plankton
swarmed into St. Margaret's Bay,
turning the beaches pink,
we saw from our place on the hill
the sperm whales feeding,
fouling the nets
in their play,
and breaching clean
so the humps of their backs
rose over the wide sea meadows.

Day after day
we waited inside
for the rotting plankton to disappear.
The smell stilled even the wind,
and the oxen looked stunned,
pulling hay on the slope
of our hill.
But the plankton kept coming in
and the whales would not go.

That's when the shooting began.
The fishermen got in their boats
and went after the whales,
and my father and uncle
and we children went, too.
The froth of our wake sank fast
in the wind-shaken water.

The whales surfaced close by.
Their foreheads were huge,
the doors of their faces were closed.
Before sounding, they lifted
their flukes into the air
and brought them down hard.
They beat the sea into foam,
and the path that they made
shone after them.

Though I did not see their eyes,
I imagined they were
like the eyes of mourning,
glazed with rheum,
watching us, sweeping along
under the darkening sheets of salt.

When we cut our engine and waited
for the whales to surface again,
the sun was setting,
turning the rock-strewn barrens a gaudy salmon.
A cold wind flailed at our skin.
When finally the sun went down
and it seemed like the whales had gone.
my uncle, no longer afraid,
shot aimlessly into the sky.

Three miles out
in the rolling dark
under the moon's astonished eyes,
our engine would not start
and we headed home in the dinghy.
And my father, hunched over the oars,
brought us in. I watched him,
rapt in his effort, rowing against the tide,
his blond hair glistening with salt.
I saw the slick spillage of moonlight
being blown over his shoulders,
and the sea and spindrift
suddenly silver.

He did not speak the entire way.

At midnight
when I went to bed,
I imagined the whales
moving beneath me,
sliding over the weed-covered hills of the deep;
they knew where I was;
they were luring me
downward and downward
into the murmurous
waters of sleep.

Mark Strand

Books

Reasons for Moving, 1968
The Contemporary American Poets: American Poetry Since 1940 (anthology, ed.), 1969
Darker, 1970
The Poetry of Mexico (anthology, ed.), 1970
The Story of Our Lives, 1973
The Owl's Insomnia: Selected Poems of Rafael Alberti (translations), 1973
Souvenir of the Ancient World: Carlos Drummond de Andrade (translations), 1976
Another Republic: 17 European & South American Writers (ed. with Charles Simic), 1976
The Late Hour, 1978
The Monument (prose), 1978
Selected Poems, 1980

Interviews, Criticism

"A Conversation with Mark Strand," *Ohio Review* 13 (Winter 1972); Richard Howard, *Alone with America: Essays on the Art of Poetry in the United States Since 1950*, 1969; Harold Bloom, "Dark and Radiant Peripheries: Mark Strand and A. R. Ammons," *Southern Review*, new series 8 (Winter 1972); Mark Strand, "The Need to Change or the Anxiety of Self-Influence," FIELD 16 (Spring 1977); *Strand: A Profile* (Profile Editions, Grilled Flowers Press; with an interview, critical essays, poems and prose by Mark Strand and a select bibliography), 1980

Jean
Valentine

(b. 1934)

In his essay "Word Against Object," George Steiner discusses what he calls "the tactic of silence" that has come about in modern poetry, he feels, because of a discrepancy between "individual perception and the frozen generalities of speech." Writers fall silent at terrible moments in history, when language has been so corrupted by despotic, demonic forces as to defy attempts to cleanse it. "Rather silence than a betrayal of felt meanings," Steiner concludes, citing Wittgenstein's remark that what one does *not* write at such times is the important part of a writer's contribution. More than any other poet in this anthology, perhaps, Jean Valentine seeks refuge in a language of silence, or extreme privacy, choosing as she does to provide so little exposition or context for her poems that some readers complain of inscrutability. Words like "spare, brilliant," but also "baffling, mysterious" are used to characterize her style, which admittedly depends on eerie juxtapositions, floating images, dizzying leaps, and enigmatic structures that leave the lazy reader behind. If one word can be helpful, perhaps Hayden Carruth's adjective "notational" best gets at Valentine's strategies for dealing with the intimate spheres of dream and reality that have merged in our nightmarish world. By noting things, by relying on an abbreviated system, a kind of shorthand, she is able to track things as fast as they happen, from words countered by other words to objects that displace other objects.

If we relax our need for instant understanding and participate with Valentine as she locates her poems visually before us, we have a better chance of following her poetic process. It is a process that insists on the inherent, tenuous quality of things and requires her to sort her way among the contradictions of what we say and mean to say, what we see and mean to see. This struggle with intention and implication is ultimately provocative because as she merely sketches but never fully colors in her landscapes, the reader must provide additional images to help develop the picture. Glimpses of things seen, snatches of conversation overheard, are filtered through scrims that soften their outlines as they alter our perspectives. In effect, the poems permit one last look at a past that can only be imagined now, in part because it was so horrible, in part because there are few survivors. We encounter these ghostly figures in luminous, ominous landscapes reminiscent of Bergman films: "He pointed at the window, the trees, or the snow, / or our silver auditorium" ("The Forgiveness Dream: Man from the Warsaw Ghetto"). These are kin who "are here. / Were here." Because the poet never tells us what to feel or think, we sometimes grow frightened, but this is a poetry that frees the mind and reassures us that we are capable of spiritual powers with which to face our visions. We must only keep looking, listening, and speaking, however fitfully, to ourselves, or our lost selves, to our friends, family and lovers, and on back to our beginnings, for "our lives have been a minute, a feather, our sex was chaff" ("The Field").

Jean Valentine's first collection, *Dream Barker*, won the Yale Series of Younger Poets Award in 1965. Of all its poems, "The Second Dream" most closely resembles what has continued to absorb her: some sort of destructive force approaches, from an unlikely place—"the planes were out / And coming, from a friendly country." The briefest time remains, what can one do? Nothing, perhaps, save use that brief moment to locate our spiritual center, acknowledge our love for those around us, and thus preserve whatever humanity is left in the world. In poem after poem, we see life from its most fragile to its most resolute, in one sweeping motion. Under such stress, "every molecule of every object here will swell / with life" ("The Knife"). Above all, the threat must not be met on its own ground. Survivors will forgive us, if we can't forgive ourselves, for doing "nothing" but turning inward, living with our grief: "I said to him in English, 'I've lived the whole time / here, in peace. A private life.' 'In shame,' / I said." The old man understands, "... he nodded, / and wrote in my notebook—'Let it be good'" ("The Forgiveness Dream...").

Pilgrims, Valentine's second book, appeared in 1969. Almost all the poems, especially the remarkable title poem with its quiet, deliberate circling over accepted destiny, reach such compact, final form that one can understand why she waited nearly a decade to publish her next book, *Ordinary Things* (1977). Valentine found a way out of the finality *Pilgrims* had achieved by sacrificing some of her previous range and going deeper in one direction. *Ordinary Things* is a treatise on developing contemplative powers to deal with what has been called the "aesthetic surfaces" in our lives. Straining to regard things as simple as a coffee cup, or "a child's handprint in a clay plate," Valentine argues for a contemplation that in its intensity will train us for the spiritual problems we face in troubled times. In *The Messenger* (1979), her most recent collection, the stakes are higher still. With an archaeologist's care she digs up "The Field," and comes across the last room: "Incised on stone, bronze, silver, / eyes, belly, mouth, circle on circle." The room in which love is made, children are born, is also the tomb. Prefigured in the early poems, called "an opened ground" in "Pilgrims," and "a northern still life" in "December 21st," this place, this room of Valentine's own, with its look down at our beginnings, and its glance up to what we still face is finally where "you must be still. Touch nothing. / Here, in this room. To look at nothing, to listen to nothing. / A long time" ("The Messenger"). This long title poem is a history of one family's struggle to undo its fears and remain together no matter what the future nature of "the message." Jean Valentine likes to quote from a letter Sarah Orne Jewett wrote to Willa Cather: "You must find a quiet place. You must find your own quiet center of life and write from that." It is the only hope.

Jean Valentine was born and raised in Chicago. While studying at Radcliffe, she worked closely with the poet and playwright William Alfred. Having taught at a variety of places such as Barnard, Swarthmore, Yale and Hunter, she has been teaching writing at Sarah

Lawrence College since 1974. She also serves on the staff of the 92nd Street YM-YWHA in New York City, where she makes her home.

SF

The Second Dream

We all heard the alarm. The planes were out
And coming, from a friendly country. You, I thought,
Would know what to do. But you said,
'There is nothing to do. Last time
The bodies were like charred trees.'

We had so many minutes. The leaves
Over the street left the light silver as dimes.
The children hung around in slow motion, loud,
Liquid as butterflies, with nothing to do.

Orpheus and Eurydice

What we spent, we had.
What we had, we have.
What we lost, we leave.
—*Epitaph for his wife and himself,*
by the DUKE OF DEVON, *12th century*

i

You. You running across the field.

A hissing second, not a word,
and there it was, our underworld:
behind your face another, and another,
and I

away.

—And you alive: staring,
almost smiling;

hearing them come down, tearing
air from air.

'This dark is everywhere'
we said, and called it light,
coming to ourselves.
                    Fear
has at me, dearest. Even this night
drags down. The moon's gone. Someone
shakes an old black camera-cloth
in front of our eyes.
Yours glint like a snowman's eyes.
We just look on, at each other.

What we had, we have. They circle down.
You draw them down like flies.
You laugh, we run
over a red field, turning at the end to blue air,—
you turning, turning again! the river
tossing a shoe up, a handful of hair.

Pilgrims

Standing there they began to grow skins
dappled as trees, alone in the flare
of their own selves: the fire
died down in the open ground

and they made a place for themselves.
It wasn't much good,
they'd fall, and freeze,

some of them said
Well, it was all they could,

some said it was beautiful, some days,
the way the little ones took to the water,
and some lay smoking, smoking,

and some burned up for good,
and some waited,
lasting, staring
over each other's merciful shoulders,
listening:
            only high in a sudden January thaw
or safe a second in some unsmiling eyes
they'd known always

whispering
Why are we in this life.

After Elegies

Almost two years now I've been sleeping,
a hand on a table that was in a kitchen.

Five or six times you have come by
the window; as if I'd been on a bus

sleeping through the Northwest, waking up,
seeing old villages pass in your face,

sleeping.
               A doctor and his wife, a doctor too, are in the kitchen
area, wide awake. We notice things
differently: a child's handprint in a clay plate, a geranium,
    aluminum
balconies rail to rail, the car horns of a wedding,

blurs of children in white. *LIFE* shots
of other children.   Fire to paper; black

faces, judge faces, Asian faces; flat
earth   your face   fern   coal

The Knife

Thought: Zero.   Fell at his feet   wanted to eat him right up

           would have   but
           even better
           he talked to me.

           Did I ask you to?
           Were those words a blood-sucking too?

Thought: Now I will have a body again
           move differently, easier   back to the plan
           a little house   a woman and a man

           crossed against yours my soul will show
           glow through my breastbone
           back down into the kitchen
           yours

Thought: Here   I will save you
         others have failed, even died, but I
         my darling will save   you save me
           devour me away
         up

Woke up:
Thought: I can cry but I can't wake up
         today again   don't answer the door
         then did   couldn't look at you   talk

         couldn't place the bed in the room, or where the room was
         when I closed my eyes

Thought: This is the same old knife   my knife
         I know it as well as I know my own mouth
         it will be lying there on the desk if

         I open my eyes I will know the room very well
         there will be the little thrown-out globe of blood we left
         and every molecule of every object here will swell
         with life. And someone will be at the door.

The Forgiveness Dream:
Man from the Warsaw Ghetto

He looked about six or seven, only much too thin.
It seemed right he would be there, but everything,
every lineation, was slow. . . . He was speaking in Polish,
I couldn't answer him.
He pointed at the window, the trees, or the snow,
or our silver auditorium.

I said to him in English, "I've lived the whole time
here, in peace. A private life."   "In shame,"
I said. He nodded. He was old now, kind,
my age, or my mother's age: he nodded,
and wrote in my notebook—"Let it be good."

He frowned, and stopped,
as if he'd forgotten something,
and wrote again,
"Let it."

I walk, and stop, and walk—
touch the birchbark   shining, powdery, cold:
taste the snow, hot on my tongue—
pure cold, licked from the salt of my hand;
This quiet, these still unvisitable stars
move with choices.
Our kin are here.
Were here.

The Field

Chemicals in peat bogs keep
bodies so nearly perfectly, that
men cutting peat, who have
come across them, have sup-
posed these people, dead for as
long as 2000 years, were just
recently drowned or murdered.

A sculpture in a bare white gallery:
Pike jaws arch, in a shining transparent space
without locality: levels of peat, sand, air.
Bones. Teeth.
Fine, thin white jaws: the willingness to do harm—Odysseus
leaving—

At forty we have always been parents; we hold each other's sex
in a new tenderness . . . As we were; hardly breathing
over the pulse in the infant's lucent temple—

Our breath comes shorter,
our lives have been a minute, a feather, our sex is chaff . . .

Sleep: the room
breaks up into blue and red
film, long muscles crossing bones, raw pelvis pulled
to birth: Incised on stone, bronze, silver,
eyes, belly, mouth, circle on circle—

Look, by morning noises, in this city island flickering with blue flame,
These photographs.
The Tollund man. The Windeby girl. The goddess
Nerthus.

In the middle of a light wood   of tall forked trees stripped white
at the edge of a bog, in Denmark,
we walk   slowly out to the field   walk slowly by
the hacked-out cots of silk
bog children.

The Messenger
I / The Father

In the strange house
in the strange town
going barefoot past the parents' empty room
I hear the horses   the fire   the wheel   bone wings
your voice.

I make my corners:
this table
this letter
this walk.

2

The night you died
by the time I got there to the Peter Bent Brigham Hospital
the guard said, It's no use your going up.
That was the first time you spoke to me dead—
from the high corner of the lobby.

The next night a friend said, Well these deaths
bring our own deaths, close.

I stand on all fours, my fur
is warm; warm organs, the male and the female.
The earth is light and warm around us.
We lick our cracked old worries
like blood away from our faces, our haunches, we
nudge each other, all our white fur, goodbye, goodbye . . .

saying again there is a last
even of last times

I wake up with one hand holding hard to the other hand.
My head rests on oilcloth. A quiet voice laughs, and says again,

—You were going to go without me?
That was always your story.

But now, this is your voice
younger than mine; leaning over—say goodbye—
the fake gold Navy officer's sword
the square real gun.

4

Every night the freight train crossed the grown-over road
at the foot of the Neilsens' field, trailing its rusty
whistle. The fire, the wheel; fireflies.
The wall of stars. Real horses. I could go
anywhere. I could go to where you are.
I lie under the bank, my face on the wall of wet grass.
I can't go anywhere, No such thing my dear.

My mother has flour on her hands,
on her cheekbone. My father smiles his one smile
gray and white on the wall. She pushes
her hair back from her eyes. His eyes
settle. On us.

II / The Messenger

You are the messenger
my half-brother, I have seen you before,
you have visited me before.
in the hallways of a school, a hospital,
in a narrow hotel room once,
once on a dirt road in August.

I lean on the oak grain of this desk,
the grain of your body, your hair,
your long back. This plum
is darker than your mouth
I drink its salty sweetness   its leaf-smell
from your tongue. Sleep;
your dark head at my breasts
                                        Turns
to a boy's head, you are Allan   my brother
Johnny DeSoto, nine
Philip   my brother
David

JEAN VALENTINE   487

Your hand is my father's sure, square hand,
it is not too late, digging down through the sand
to show me the water

You turn, say something in your sleep

You are my sister   I hold you warm in my hand   her breast
You trace my breasts

3

My eyes were clenched, they are opening . . .
everything, nothing . . .
We aren't afraid.
The earth drips through us

Now I want to live forever
Now I could scatter my body easily
if it was any use

now that the earth
has rained through us
green   white
green green grass.

You say you came to say if I live without you
I'll live. That's always been your story.

III / The Hill

The dogwood blossoms stand in still, horizontal planes
at the window. In mist. Small gray figures
climb away up the green hill. Carrying precision tools wrapped in oilcloth.
Some push their bicycles.—Wait, I'm coming, no this time I mean it

now I could scatter my body
if it was any use

saying again
if you do not teach me I shall not learn

—First, you see, you must be still. Touch nothing.
Here, in this room. To look at nothing, to listen to nothing.
A long time. First, you see, you must open your clenched hands.
You must carry your mother and your father at your breasts.

Silences: A Dream of Governments

From your eyes I thought
you could almost say
what it was you were thinking
And so could I   We could almost move
But that voice, speaking out our names—
And the way our hands
held there in the yellow air   And the way the sun
shone right through us
Done with us

        Then
the plain astonishment—the air
broken open: just ourselves
sitting, talking; like always;
the kitchen window
propped open by the same
blue-gray dictionary.
August. Rain. A Tuesday.

Then, absence. The open room
suspended   The long street
gone off   quiet, dark.
The ocean floor. Slow
shapes glide by

Then, day
keeps beginning again: the same
stubborn pulse against our throats:
Listening for a human voice
our names

December 21st

How will I think of you
"God-with-us"
a name: a word

and trees paths stars this earth
how will I think of them

and the dead I love   and all absent friends
here-with-me

and table: hand: white coffee mug:
a northern still life:

and you
without a body

quietness

and the infant's red-brown mouth   a star
at the star of the girl's nipple . . .

Notes

Orpheus and Eurydice. Orpheus was given a lyre he learned to play so well that rivers stopped flowing and savage beasts grew tame. He married Eurydice, who died from a serpent's bite. Diconsolate, Orpheus visited the infernal regions to recover her, and Pluto consented to return Eurydice if Orpheus agreed not to look back while leaving. Orpheus forgot his promise, and as he turned to look at Eurydice, she vanished.

The Forgiveness Dream: Man from the Warsaw Ghetto. On April 19, 1943, the Jews in the Warsaw Ghetto (Poland) rose against the Germans, and after a few weeks of fierce fighting, the whole area was razed and the Jews annihilated.

The Messenger. The italicized lines in Part 3 are from Samuel Beckett's poem "Cascando" (from *Poems in English*). The poem draws from William Blake's notions of the angel Gabriel.

December 21st. The words in quotations, "God-with-us," are a literal translation of "Emmanuel" and the next phrase, "a name: a word" recalls Jesus Christ. The "girl" offering her nipple to the infant is Mary.

Jean Valentine

Books

Dream Barker, 1965
Pilgrims, 1969
Ordinary Things, 1977
The Messenger, 1979

Criticism

Philip Booth, "Jean Valentine's *The Messenger*," *American Poetry Review*, January–February 1980

Nancy Willard

(b. 1936)

To use Roethke's phrase, "we hark back to the condition of the child" in the poems of Nancy Willard. It is a condition that encourages beliefs in many things, from angels to talking hens and vegetable saints, made real by Willard's sharp eye for detail; her witty, crafty ways of making things talk; and natural speech rhythms (which some critics have called psalmic) that present startling and strange elements in matter-of-fact tones. In addition, she has an uncanny feeling for the "magic" in ordinary things, turning them over and over till they take on a living presence—an egg will never be the same after "How the Hen Sold Her Eggs to the Stingy Priest"—or scooping out their essences, as she does with the pumpkin in "Saint Pumpkin." Children turn up frequently and easily in these pieces, because, like Willard, they love things for themselves and are more interested in how they look and work and fit together than in our presuppositions or notions of them. An early poem, "Picture Puzzles," darkly celebrates a family's joint enterprise of assembling Fra Angelico's *Nativity*, or "how the shapes of our healing lie / dumb in our hand."

Willard's critical study, *Testimony of the Invisible Man* (1970), a collection of essays on Ponge, Rilke, Williams, and Neruda, examines how these modern masters place objects (in all their myriad forms) at the center of their poetic worlds. One is reminded of what the German poet Günter Eich added to this dialogue: "Real language is a falling together of the word and the object. Our task is to translate from the language that is around us but not 'given.' . . . I must admit . . . I am still not beyond the 'thing-word' or noun . . . like a child who says 'tree,' 'moon,' 'mountain' and thus orients himself" (from "Some Remarks on Literature and Reality"). Nancy Willard has written many books for and about children, all of which center on similar definitions, naming things that have been badly named or that must still be named. As one of her characters reports, "Naming things we already know wouldn't change a thing." Similarly, many of the poems have to do with seeing things for the first time. There is "the first strawberry" of "Original Strawberry." Insects we thought we knew, seen through the microscope of Willard's encyclopedic imagination, become something "that does not belong to the habits / of our globe" ("The Insects"). And moons and pumpkins need to be seen without the "false face" we give them, "a light of our own making" ("Saint Pumpkin").

While Willard mentions in an essay that many of her poems start from common or domestic experiences, "working in the kitchen, picking up toys, bringing a bottle to a child at night," they quickly turn to large matters of faith and belief, which they explore in oracular ways. In both the poems and prose, her characters search for "faith and greater faith" as they "lie down in white pastures" ("Angels in Winter") or move among the signs and symbols of the complicated laws of life. Her story "The Hucklebone of a Saint," begins, "In my father's house, moral ambiguity was not allowed." If the child drops her knife, her father commands her to pick it up, while her mother adds, "A man is coming."

TWELVE POETS BORN BETWEEN 1930 AND 1940

And if she were to drop a spoon, "A child is coming." As the mother in this story demonstrates that "faith takes root in the insignificant," it is frequently a mother figure in the poems who helps a child make sense of the "innocent" power of animals and objects encountered on the journey from birth to death. Mother and child develop, with delicate wordplay in parablelike exchanges, their imaginary powers as they heighten their sense of self in a world in which nothing human survives (see especially, "Questions My Son Asked Me, Answers I Never Gave Him"). Willard's most recent poems move toward even more complex, involved relationships with other spirits in the world, exploring the nature of deities we must make room for in our minds or perish. From Great Danes to mangy cats to "No-kings," Willard's odd assortment of characters seems destined to roam some sort of purgatory until finding the right language to describe things.

Nancy Willard was born in Michigan and received a Ph.D. from the University of Michigan. She has lived in Oslo and Paris, and now makes her home in Poughkeepsie, New York, where she teaches at Vassar College. In addition to more than a dozen children's books, she has published several collections of stories and poems. *Skin of Grace* won the Devins Memorial Award for poetry in 1967.

SF

The Insects

They pass like a warning of snow,
    the dragonfly, mother of millions,
the scarab, the shepherd spider,
    the bee. Our boundaries break
on their jeweled eyes,
    blind as reflectors.
The black beetle
    under the microscope wears the
blue of Chartres. The armored
    mantis, a tank in clover,
folds its wings like a flawless
    inlay of wood, over and over.

"There is something about insects
            that does not belong to the habits
of our globe," said Maeterlinck,
            touching the slick
upholstery of the spider,
            the watchspring and cunning
tongue of the butterfly, blown out
            like a paper bugle. Their humming
warns us of sickness, their silence
            of honey and frost. Asleep
in clapboards and rafters,
            their bodies keep

the cost of our apples and wool,
            A hand smashes their wings,
tearing the veined
            landscape of winter trees.
In the slow oozing of our days
            who can avoid remembering

their silken tents on the air,
            the spiders wearing their eggs
like pearls, born on muscles
            of silk, the pulse of a rose, baiting
the fly that lives for three hours,
            lives only for mating?

Under a burning glass, the creature
            we understand disappears. The dragonfly
is a hawk, the roach
            cocks his enormous legs at your acre,
eyes like turrets piercing
            eons of chitin and shale. Drummers
under the earth, the cicadas
            have waited for seventeen summers
to break their shell,
            shape of your oldest fear
of a first world
            of monsters. We are not here.

Original Strawberry

The first strawberry:
plain as a teething ring.
And God blessed the strawberry
and eying the future made it
three leaved for the Trinity
and red for His son's blood.

The strawberry was tasty but sad.
Lord, why make me so low?
And God decreed that the meek
should inherit the earth.

But has a strawberry ears?

On the seventh day it seceded
from creation like a grieving nun.
On the eighth, stars pocked its body
(my sky at sunset, said the strawberry)
and a green sun grew on its north pole.
(My vernal equinox, said the strawberry.)

Pick a strawberry as if you were paying court.
From which constellation shall you sail
to the mandala
that only a knife can find?

Angels in Winter

Mercy is whiter than laundry,
great baskets of it, packed like snowmen.
In the cellar I fold and sort and watch
through a squint in the dirty window
the plain bright snow.

Unlike the earth, snow is neuter.
Unlike the moon, it stays.
It falls, not from grace but a silence
which nourishes crystals.
My son catches them on his tongue.

Whatever I try to hold perishes.
My son and I lie down in white pastures
and flap like the last survivors
of a species that couldn't adapt to the air.
Jumping free, we look back at

angels, blurred fossils of majesty and justice
from the time when a ladder of angels
joined the house of the snow
to the houses of those whom it covered
with a dangerous blanket or a healing sleep.

As I lift my body from the angel's,
I remember the mad preacher of Indiana
who chose for the site of his kingdom
the footprint of an angel and named the place
New Harmony. Nothing of it survives.

The angels do not look backward
to see how their passing changes the earth,
the way I do, watching the snow,
and the waffles our boots print on its unleavened face,
and the nervous alphabet of the pheasant's feet,

and the five-petaled footprint of the cat;
and the shape of snowshoes, white and expensive as tennis,
and the deep ribbons tied and untied by the sleds.
I remember the millions who left the earth;
it holds no trace of them

as it holds of us, tracking through snow,
so tame and defenseless
even the air could kill us.

How the Hen Sold Her Eggs
to the Stingy Priest

An egg is a grand thing for a journey.

It will make you a small meal on the road
and a shape most serviceable to the hand

for darning socks, and for barter
a purse of gold opens doors anywhere.

If I wished for a world better than this one
I would keep, in an egg till it was wanted,

the gold earth floating on a clear sea.
If I wished for an angel, that would be my way,

the wings in gold waiting to wake,
the feet in gold waiting to walk,

and the heart that no one believed in
beating and beating the gold alive.

Questions My Son Asked Me,
Answers I Never Gave Him

1. Do gorillas have birthdays?
    Yes. Like the rainbow they happen,
    like the air they are not observed.

2. Do butterflies make a noise?
    The wire in the butterfly's tongue
    hums gold.
    Some men hear butterflies
    even in winter.

3. Are they part of our family?
    They forgot us, who forgot how to fly.

4. Who tied my navel? Did God tie it?
    God made the thread: O man, live forever!
    Man made the knot: enough is enough.

5. If I drop my tooth in the telephone
    will it go through the wires and bite someone's ear?
    I have seen earlobes pierced by a tooth of steel.
    It loves what lasts.
    It does not love flesh.
    It leaves a ring of gold in the wound.

6. If I stand on my head
    will the sleep in my eye roll up into my head?
    Does the dream know its own father?
    Can bread go back to the field of its birth?

7. Can I eat a star?
    Yes, with the mouth of time
    that enjoys everything.

8. Could we xerox the moon?
    This is the first commandment:
    I am the moon, thy moon.
    Thou shalt have no other moons before thee.

9. Who invented water?
    The hands of the air, that wanted to wash each other.

10. What happens at the end of numbers?
     I see three men running toward a field.
     At the edge of the tall grass, they turn into light.

11. Do the years ever run out?
     God said, I will break time's heart.
     Time ran down like an old phonograph.
     It lay flat as a carpet.
     At rest on its threads I am learning to fly.

Lightness Remembered

Nor do these heads sing,
though our breath pushes
a blizzard of glass grapes
through the female wand,

a ring of red plastic,
the better
to blow bubbles with.
Through a bowl of soap soup

the melts of moonlight,
the seduction of sherbet,
my son draws the wand,
and now in the ring shines

a lens
on which he blows
as if he would clean it,
the better to see

the wind with.
O breath, lovely
shaper that makes
a silken windsock,

a nervous tunnel,
a sack soft enough
to hold the unborn,
a glass egg that breaks free

and floats like a planet
over the rose bush,
casting
its rainbow-lipped

shadow on leaves,
on stones—
O, wet nose of a spirit,
cold cheek of

the apples of the air,
though he waves the wand,
though he fans you awake,
though you rise again,

there's no saving you.

Night Light

The moon is not green cheese.
It is china and stands in this room.
It has a ten-watt bulb and a motto:
made in Japan.

Whey-faced, doll-faced,
it's closed as a tooth
and cold as the dead are cold
till I touch the switch.

Then the moon performs
its one trick:
it turns into a banana.
It warms to its subjects,

it draws us into its light,
just as I knew it would
when I gave ten dollars
to the pale clerk

in the store that sold
everything.
She asked, did I have a car?
She shrouded the moon in tissue

and laid it to rest in a box.
The box did not say *moon*.
It said *This side up*.
I tucked the moon into my basket

and bicycled into the world.
By the light of the sun
I could not see the
moon under my sack of apples,

NANCY WILLARD

moon under slab of salmon,
moon under clean laundry,
under milk its sister
and bread its brother,

moon under meat.
Now supper is eaten.
Now laundry is folded away.
I shake out the old comforters.

My nine cats find their places
and go on dreaming where they left off.
My son snuggles under the heap.
His father loses his way in a book.

It is time to turn on the moon.
It is time to live by a different light.

Saint Pumpkin

Somebody's in there.
Somebody's sealed himself up
in this round room,
this hassock upholstered in rind,
this padded cell.
He believes if nothing unbinds him
he'll live forever.

Like our first room
it is dark and crowded.
Hunger knows no tongue
to tell it.
Water is glad there.
In this room with two navels
somebody wants to be born again.

So I unlock the pumpkin.
I carve out the lid
from which the stem raises
a dry handle on a damp world.
Lifting, I pull away
wet webs, vines on which hang
the flat tears of the pumpkin,

like fingernails or the currency
of bats. How the seeds shine,
as if water had put out
hundreds of lanterns.
Hundreds of eyes in the windless wood
gaze peacefully past me,
hacking the thickets,

and now a white dew beads the blade.
Has the saint surrendered
himself to his beard?
Has his beard taken root in his cell?
 Saint Pumpkin, pray for me,
 because when I looked for you, I found nothing,
 because unsealed and unkempt, your tomb rots,
 because I gave you a false face
 and a light of my own making.

No-Kings and the Calling of Spirits

*The first stringent rule in Ireland was that no one with a physical blemish could
rule as king. The historic King Cormac was forced to abdicate when he lost an
eye...*
    CELTIC MYSTERIES: THE ANCIENT RELIGION

My cat can look at a king
but can never be
king of his own kind,
this hero of the highway,
spinner
and winner
under the dark wheels.

A real loser:
one eye's stitched over
a dark hole.
One tooth icicles out.
His jaw mended badly.
"On our right we have
Doctor Jekyll,

on our left, Mr. Hyde,"
says my small brother
who can never be
king of the mountain.
"With his right he'll hear
radios, birds.
With his left, silence,"

says the doctor,
tracing horizons
on a graph designed
to unravel improvement.
I think of losses
greater than his:
lives, limbs, a mind fallen

asleep. I think of the reasons
for giving up
yourself
or a part of yourself,
your eye for an eye,
your arm to an enemy,
your liver and lights

to disease.
I think of wisdom,
its peddlers
and prices.
I think of Odin
who traded his eye for it
and how only then

did the other eye show him
spirits,
their beauty grazing
the mountains,
their shadows skimming his heart.
At a dark hole my one-eyed cat
worships the invisible mouse.

Little brother,
gifted with silence,
watch over us hunters,
watch over our hands,
our holding on
and our letting go
and our letting go

Notes

The Insects. Chartres, a city in Northern France, is famous for its cathedral. Maeterlinck (1862–1949) was a Belgian essayist, dramatist and poet. A burning glass is a lens for focusing the sun's rays.

Original Strawberry. A *mandala* is a Hindu or Buddhist symbol of the universe: a circle enclosing a square with a deity on each side.

How the Hen Sold Her Eggs to the Stingy Priest. The hen is speaking.

Lightness Remembered. The mother and son are blowing bubbles together. The "female wand" (a play on words) is the "red plastic ring" one soaks in the mixture of soap and water and blows through to produce bubbles.

Nancy Willard

Books

Skin of Grace, 1967
The Lively Anatomy of God (stories), 1968
A New Herball, 1968
Testimony of the Invisible Man: William Carlos Williams, Francis Ponge, Rainer Maria Rilke, Pablo Neruda (criticism), 1970
19 Masks for the Naked Poet, 1971
Childhood of the Magician (prose), 1973
Carpenter of the Sun, 1974
William Blake's Inn for Innocent and Experienced Travelers, 1981

Criticism

Judith Baughman, "Nancy Willard," in *Dictionary of Literary Biography*, 1980

Charles Wright

(b. 1935)

T he poems of Charles Wright are filled with expressive language. Dense in detail, brimming with vitality, they strike us both as powerful representations of their subjects and as compelling verbal worlds in their own right. Certain stylistic features stand out right away. This poet loves proper names, for their weight and particularity—"It's hard freight / From Ducktown to Copper Hill, from Six / To Piled High"—and compound nouns for their way of fusing objects and movements, nouns and verbs, striking off small metaphors—"Spindrift and windfall; woodrot"—even as they enter the poem. Charles Wright is not afraid to use repetition and exaggeration, perhaps because he is a southerner, perhaps because his urge to write poetry was born while he was serving in the army and stationed in Italy, a country where the love of spoken language and high-flown expressiveness is both ancient and unabashed.

The music and energy of Wright's poems are always fitted to his subjects. The lush abundance of Dog Creek (near Hiwassee, North Carolina) is carefully re-created by the texture and emphasis of the verse in "Dog Creek Mainline," by the itemizing and elaborating and by the figures of speech—turtles' heads as tomahawks, pike as knives in a drawer, the trees "in their jade death-suits." We feel that language and reality are being drawn closer together than is ordinarily possible. The poem begins to emerge as an exercise in memory, in which the obsessive ways of the imagination are matched to a landscape that reflects them. In "Nightdream," on the other hand, the poet creates a different movement and atmosphere in order to convince us that we have entered the floating and continually metamorphosing world of nightmare. The diction is more elusive and more surprising: "The chambers you've reached, the stones touched, / All stall and worm to a dot." We sense the rightness of those last two verbs even before we've understood them, and that enables us to give the poem and poet our trust. Both "Dog Creek Mainline" and "Nightdreams," from Wright's 1973 volume, *Hard Freight*, end with parenthetical stanzas, as though the knowledge they moved toward, a kind of anatomy in one case and an ambiguous celebration in the other, almost had to be whispered.

Hard Freight is the first volume of a carefully planned trilogy, and the two poems that follow in our selection, "Delta Traveller" and "Virgo Descending," are from the second volume, *Bloodlines* (1975). "Delta Traveller" is an elegy for the poet's mother, and it takes the form of a series of variations on the theme of loss and grief. Again, the extraordinary details and musical effects are faithful to the subject. Some of the nine-line stanzas are one long sentence, but the moving tale of the empty dress is full of its own inevitable stops and starts: "The dress gets up, windbone and windskin, / To open the window. It is not there. / It goes to the door. It is not there. / The dress goes back and sits down. The dress gets up. ..." The pair of compound nouns here show how much compression Wright gets from his deft use of such words. They are the shortest possible way of saying what is and isn't inside the dress, but they force the language into the foreground so that we sense the pressure of emotion, contorting its own expression. To read this poem aloud is to experience its cumulative force and superb control. The same can be said for "Virgo Descending," which might be called a family elegy for the way in which it imagines death as a gradual re-creation of the family home. Here, as in "Delta Traveller," there is an extraordinary mixture of dreaming and waking, real and surreal, cast in the form of a narrative that draws us forward powerfully, mixing humor and suspense, toward its thrilling, unparaphrasable ending.

The series of shorter poems that follow in this selection—"Snow," "Self-Portrait in 2035," "Invisible Landscape," "Stone Canyon Nocturne," "Spider Crystal Ascension," and "Sitting at Night on the Front Porch"—are from the third volume of the trilogy, *China Trace* (1978). The poems in this volume are relatively short, twelve lines or less, and if they take some of their inspiration from the journal-like meditations on landscape of Chinese poetry, their distinctiveness comes from their metaphysical subject—they are poems about belief, a spiritual quest—and the fact that they ask even more from language than Wright's previous poems, pushing expression to the limits of possibility. "Spider Crystal Ascension," a poem about looking at the night sky, particularly the Milky Way, illustrates this tendency. Its very title, as the poet has explained, consists of "three separate words that are supposed to give you the idea of what's coming in the whole poem." It represents an effort to "compress the language and the thought to such a point that they stop being small and start to enlarge." The short poems of *China Trace* do tend to expand enormously upon consideration, so that they repay careful study and rereading.

The final group of poems in our selection—"Mount Caribou at Night," "Dog Yoga," "Dog Day Vespers," "Dead Color," and "Hawaii Dantesca"—comes from Charles Wright's new collection, *The Southern Cross* (1981). These new poems combine characteristics from all three volumes of the trilogy, and their vigor and range suggest that this poet's love affair with language continues unabated. After a boyhood and education in Tennessee and North Carolina, some years in Italy first through the army and later through Fulbright fellowships, Charles Wright studied at the Iowa Writer's Workshop. For some years now, he has lived on the Pacific coast of Southern California, teaching in the Writing Program at the University of California at Irvine.

DY

Dog Creek Mainline

Dog Creek: cat track and bird splay,
Spindrift and windfall; woodrot;
Odor of muscadine, the blue creep
Of kingsnake and copperhead;
Nightweed; frog spit and floating heart,
Backwash and snag pool: Dog Creek

Starts in the leaf reach and shoal run of the blood;
Starts in the falling light just back
Of the fingertips; starts
Forever in the black throat
You ask redemption of, in wants
You waken to, the odd door:

Its sky, old empty valise,
Stands open, departure in mind; its three streets,
Y-shaped and brown,
Go up the hills like a fever;
Its houses link and deploy
—This ointment, false flesh in another color.

✳   ✳   ✳

Five cutouts, five silhouettes
Against the American twilight; the year
Is 1941; remembered names
—Rosendale, Perry and Smith—
Rise like dust in the deaf air;
The tops spin, the poison swells in the arm:

The trees in their jade death-suits,
The birds with their opal feet,
Shimmer and weave on the shoreline;
The moths, like forget-me-nots, blow
Up from the earth, their wet teeth
Breaking the dark, the raw grain;

The lake in its cradle hums
The old songs: out of its ooze, their heads
Like tomahawks, the turtles ascend
And settle back, leaving their chill breath
In blisters along the bank;
Locked in their wide drawer, the pike lie still as knives.

Hard freight. It's hard freight
From Ducktown to Copper Hill, from Six
To Piled High: Dog Creek is on this line,
Indigent spur; cross-tie by cross-tie it takes
You back, the red wind
Caught at your neck like a prize:

(The heart is a hieroglyph;
The fingers, like praying mantises, poise
Over what they have once loved;
The ear, cold cave, is an absence,
Tapping its own thin wires;
The eye turns in on itself.

The tongue is a white water.
In its slick ceremonies the light
Gathers, and is refracted, and moves
Outward, over the lips,
Over the dry skin of the world.
The tongue is a white water).

Nightdream

Each day is an iceberg,
Dragging its chill paunch underfoot;
Each night is a tree to hang from.
The wooden knife, the mud rope
You scratch your initials on—
Panoply, panoply.

Up and up from his green grave, your father
Wheels in the wind, split scrap of smoke;
Under him stretch, in one file, Bob's Valley, Bald Knob,
The infinite rectitude
Of all that is past: Ouachita,
Ocoee, the slow slide of the Arkansas.

Listen, the old roads are taking flight;
Like bits of string, they, too,
Rise in the pendulous sky,
Whispering, whispering:
Echo has turned a deaf ear,
The wayside is full of leaves.

Your mother floats from her bed
In slow-motion, her loose gown like a fog
Approaching, offering
Meat; across the room, a hand
Again and again
Rises and falls back, clenching, unclenching.

The chambers you've reached, the stones touched,
All stall and worm to a dot;
Sirens drain through the night; lights
Flick and release; the fields, the wet stumps,
Shed their hair and retire;
The bedroom becomes a rose:

(In Kingsport, beneath the trees,
A Captain is singing Dixie; sons
Dance in their gold suits, clapping their hands;
And mothers and fathers, each
In a soft hat, fill
With dust-dolls their long boxes).

Delta Traveller

—MWW, 1910–1964

Born in the quarter-night, brash
Tongue on the tongueless ward, the moon down,
The lake rising on schedule and Dr Hurt
Already across the water, and headed home—
And so I came sailing out, first child,
A stream with no bed to lie in,
A root with no branch to leaf,
The black balloon of promise tied to your wrist,
One inch of pain and an inch of light.

*　*　*

No wonder the children stand by those moist graves.
And produce is spread on the cobbled streets,
And portraits are carried out, and horns play.
And women, in single file, untangle
Corn from the storage bins, and soft cheese.
I shield my eyes against the sunlight,
Holding, in one hand, a death's-head,
Spun sugar and marzipan. I call it Love,
And shield my eyes against the sunlight.

I lie down with you, I rise up with you.
If a grain turns in my eye,
I know it is you, entering, leaving,
Your name like a lozenge upon my tongue.
You drift through the antilife,
Scrim and snow-scud, fluff stem, hair
And tendril. You bloom in your own throat,
Frost flame in the frost dust,
One scratch on the slipstream, a closed mouth.

* * *

High-necked and high-collared, slumped and creased,
A dress sits in a chair. Your dress,
Or your mother's dress, a dress
On a wooden chair, in a cold room, a room
With no windows and no doors, full of the east wind.
The dress gets up, windbone and windskin,
To open the window. It is not there.
It goes to the door. It is not there.
The dress goes back and sits down. The dress gets up . . .

* * *

Three teeth and a thumbnail, white, white; four
Fingers that cradle a black chin;
Outline of eye-hole and nose-hole. This skull
And its one hand float up from the tar
And lime pit of dreams, night after slick night,
To lodge in the fork of the gum tree,
Its three teeth in the leaflight,
Its thumbnail in flash and foil,
Its mouth-hole a nothing I need to know.

* * *

Cat's-eye and cloud, you survive.
The porcelain corridors
That glide forever beneath your feet,
The armed lawn chair you sit in,
Your bones like paint, your skin the wrong color—
All this you survive, and hold on,
A way of remembering, a pulse
That comes and goes in the night,
Match flare and wink, that comes and goes in the night.

If the wafer of light offends me,
If the split tongue in the snake's mouth offends me,
I am not listening. They make the sound,
Which is the same sound, of the ant hill,
The hollow trunk, the fruit of the tree.
It is the Echo, the one transmitter of things:
Transcendent and inescapable,
It is the cloud, the mosquito's buzz,
The trickle of water across the leaf's vein.

* * *

And so with the dead, the rock dead and the dust:
Worm and worm-fill, pearl, milk-eye
And light in the earth, the dead are brought
Back to us, piece by piece—
Under the sponged log, inside the stump,
They shine with their secret lives, and grow
Big with their messages, wings
Beginning to stir, paths fixed and hearts clocked,
Rising and falling back and rising.

Virgo Descending

Through the viridian (and black of the burnt match),
Through ox-blood and ochre, the ham-colored clay,
Through plate after plate, down
Where the worm and the mole will not go,
Through ore-seam and fire-seam,
My grandmother, senile and 89, crimpbacked, stands
Like a door ajar on her soft bed,
The open beams and bare studs of the hall
Pink as an infant's skin in the floating dark;
Shavings and curls swing down like snowflakes across her face.

My aunt and I walk past. As always, my father
Is planning rooms, dragging his lame leg,
Stroke-straightened and foreign, behind him,
An aberrant 2-by-4 he can't fit snug.
I lay my head on my aunt's shoulder, feeling
At home, and walk on.

CHARLES WRIGHT

Through arches and door jambs, the spidery wires
And coiled cables, the blueprint takes shape:
My mother's room to the left, the door closed;
My father's room to the left, the door closed—

Ahead, my brother's room, unfinished;
Behind, my sister's room, also unfinished.
Buttresses, winches, block-and-tackle: the scale of everything
Is enormous. We keep on walking. And pass
My aunt's room, almost complete, the curtains up,
The lamp and the medicine arranged
In their proper places, in arm's reach of where the bed will go . . .
The next one is mine, now more than half done,
Cloyed by the scent of jasmine,
White-gummed and anxious, their mouths sucking the air dry.

Home is what you lie in, or hang above, the house
Your father made, or keeps on making,
The dirt you moisten, the sap you push up and nourish . . .
I enter the living room, it, too, unfinished, its far wall
Not there, opening on to a radiance
I can't begin to imagine, a light
My father walks from, approaching me,
Dragging his right leg, rolling his plans into a perfect curl.
That light, he mutters, that damned light.
We can't keep it out. It keeps on filling your room.

Snow

If we, as we are, are dust, and dust, as it will, rises,
Then we will rise, and recongregate
In the wind, in the cloud, and be their issue,

Things in a fall in a world of fall, and slip
Through the spiked branches and snapped joints of the evergreens,
White ants, white ants and the little ribs.

Self-Portrait in 2035

The root becomes him, the road ruts
That are sift and grain in the powderlight
Recast him, sink bone in him,
Blanket and creep up, fine, fine:

Worm-waste and pillow tick; hair
Prickly and dust-dangled, his arms and black shoes
Unlinked and laceless, his face false
In the wood-rot, and past pause . . .

Darkness, erase these lines, forget these words.
Spider recite his one sin.

Invisible Landscape

This is the way it must have been in the first dusk:
Smokeclouds sculling into their slips in the Claw Mountains,
Bats jerked through the plumlight by strings of white sound;
The wind clicks through its turnstiles
Over the high country, the hush of a steady pulse . . .

I bring to this landscape a bare hand, these knuckles
Slick as a cake of soap,
The black snag of a tamarack,
The oddments and brown jewelry of early September evenings
In wet weather, a Colt-colored sky . . .

God is the sleight-of-hand in the fireweed, the lost
Moment that stopped to grieve and moved on . . .

Stone Canyon Nocturne

Ancient of Days, old friend, no one believes you'll come back.
No one believes in his own life anymore.

The moon, like a dead heart, cold and unstartable, hangs by a thread
At the earth's edge,
Unfaithful at last, splotching the ferns and the pink shrubs.

In the other world, children undo the knots in their tally strings.
They sing songs, and their fingers blear.

And here, where the swan hums in his socket, where bloodroot
And belladonna insist on our comforting,
Where the fox in the canyon wall empties our hands, ecstatic for more,

Like a bead of clear oil the Healer revolves through the night wind,
Part eye, part tear, unwilling to recognize us.

CHARLES WRIGHT   513

Spider Crystal Ascension

The spider, juiced crystal and Milky Way, drifts on his web through the night
    sky
And looks down, waiting for us to ascend . . .

At dawn he is still there, invisible, short of breath, mending his net.

All morning we look for the white face to rise from the lake like a tiny star.
And when it does, we lie back in our watery hair and rock.

Sitting at Night on the Front Porch

I'm here, on the dark porch, restyled in my mother's chair.
10:45 and no moon.
Below the house, car lights
Swing down, on the canyon floor, to the sea.

In this they resemble us,
Dropping like match flames through the great void
Under our feet.
In this they resemble her, burning and disappearing.

Everyone's gone
And I'm here, sizing the dark, saving my mother's seat.

Mount Caribou at Night

Just north of the Yaak River, one man sits bolt up-right,
A little bonnet of dirt and bunch grass above his head:
Northwestern Montana is hard relief,
And harder still the lying down and the rising up . . .

I speak to the others there, lodged in their stone wedges, the blocks
And slashes that vein the ground, and tell them that Walter Smoot,
Starched and at ease in his bony duds
Under the tamaracks, still holds the nightfall between his knees.

Work stars, drop by inveterate drop, begin
Cassiopeia's sails and electric paste
Across the sky. And down
Toward the cadmium waters that carry them back to the dawn,

They squeeze out Andromeda and the Whale,
Everything on the move, everything flowing and folding back
And starting again,
Star-slick, the flaking and crusting duff at my feet,

Smoot and Runyan and August Binder
Still in the black pulse of the earth, cloud-gouache
Over the tree-line, Mount Caribou
Massive and on the rise and taking it in. And taking it back

To the future we occupied, and will wake to again, ourselves
And our children's children snug in our monk's robes,
Pushing the cauly hoods back, ready to walk out
Into the same night and the meadow grass, in step and on time . . .

Dog Yoga

A spring day in the weeds.
A thread of spittle across the sky, and a thread of ash.
Mournful cadences from the clouds.

Through the drives and the cypress beds,
                              25 years of sad news.

Mother of Thrushes, Our Lady of Crows,
Brief as a handkerchief,
                              25 years of sad news.

Later, stars and sea winds in and out of the open window.

Later, and lonesome among the sleepers,
                              the day's thunder in hidden places,
One lissome cheek a notch in the noontide's leash,

A ghostly rain of sunlight among the ferns.

Year in, year out, the same loom from the dark.
Year in, year out, the same sound in the wind.

Near dawn, the void in the heart,
The last coat of lacquer along the leaves,
                              the quench in the west.

Dog Day Vespers

Sun like an orange mousse through the trees,
A snowfall of trumpet bells on the oleander;

                                    mantis paws
Craning out of the new wisteria; fruit smears in the west . . .
DeStael knifes a sail on the bay;
A mother's summons hangs like a towel on the dusk's hook . . .

Everything drips and spins
In the pepper trees, the pastel glide of the evening
Slowing to mother-of-pearl and the night sky.
Venus breaks clear in the third heaven.
Quickly the world is capped, and the seal turned.

I drag my chair to the deck's edge and the blue ferns.
I'm writing you now by flashlight,
The same news and the same story I've told you often before.
As the stag-stars begin to shine,
A wing brushes my left hand,
                       but it's not my wing.

Dead Color

I lie for a long time on my left side and my right side
And eat nothing,
                  but no voice comes on the wind
And no voice drops from the cloud.
Between the grey spiders and the orange spiders,
                         no voice comes on the wind . . .

Later, I sit for a long time by the waters of Har,
And no face appears on the face of the deep.

Meanwhile, the heavens assemble their dark map.
The traffic begins to thin.
Aphids munch on the sweet meat of the lemon trees.
The lawn sprinklers rise and fall . . .

And here's a line of brown ants cleaning a possum's skull.
And here's another, come from the opposite side.

Over my head, star-pieces dip in their yellow scarves toward their
                                    black desire.
Windows, rapturous windows!

Hawaii Dantesca

White-sided flowers are thrusting up on the hillside,
$$\text{blank love letters from the dead.}$$
It's autumn, and nobody seems to mind.

Or the broken shadows of those missing for hundreds of years
Moving over the sugar cane
$$\text{like storks, which nobody marks or mends.}$$

This is the story line.

And the viridescent shirtwaists of light the trees wear.
And the sutra-circles of cattle egrets wheeling out past the rain showers.
And the spiked marimbas of dawn rattling their amulets...

Soon it will be time for the long walk under the earth toward the sea.

And time to retrieve the yellow sunsuit and little shoes
$$\text{they took my picture in}$$
In Knoxville, in 1938.

Time to gather the fire in its quartz bowl.

I hope the one with the white wings will come.
I hope the island of reeds is as far away as I think it is.

When I get there, I hope they forgive me if the knot I tie is the
$$\text{wrong knot.}$$

Notes

Dead Color. Wright's own note quotes from A. Vollard: "When I saw Degas again, he happened to have a box of pastels in his hand, and was spreading them out on a board in front of the window. Seeing me watching him: 'I take all the color out of them that I can, by putting them in the sun.'
    'But what do you use, then, to get colors of such brightness?'
    'Dead color, Monsieur.'"

Hawaii Dantesca. The Dante reference is to the reed of humility in the first book of the *Purgatorio.*

Charles Wright

Books

The Grave of the Right Hand, 1970
Hard Freight, 1973

Bloodlines, 1975
China Trace, 1977
Eugenio Montale, The Storm and Other Poems (translations), 1978
The Southern Cross, 1981

Interviews, Criticism

"Charles Wright at Oberlin," in *A Field Guide to Contemporary Poetry and Poetics*, ed. Friebert and Young, 1980; Helen Vendler, *Part·of Nature, Part of Us: Modern American Poets*, 1980; *Wright: A Profile* (Profile Editions, Grilled Flowers Press; with an interview, an essay, new poems by Charles Wright, and a select bibliography), 1979; Sherod Santos, "An Interview with Charles Wright," in *Quarterly West*, No. 12, 1981

Six Poets Born After 1940

PART FIVE

Norman
Dubie

(b. 1945)

I n his first major collection, the *Alehouse Sonnets* (1971), Norman Dubie conducted highly inventive, spirited conversations with the nineteenth-century British essayist William Hazlitt, in which both men's lives seemed to merge. Dubie had hit on a method that, in one form or another, has served him ever since, up to and through such recent books as *The City of the Olesha Fruit* (1979). Eschewing his own personality and voice more than any other contemporary poet, Dubie slips into a dazzling variety of historical figures: Queen Elizabeth I, Coleridge, Beethoven, Ibsen, Kafka, and the World War II saboteur-singer, Marie Triste, among others! He has taught himself to speak in character for all of them. Working with what might be called historical narratives, or dramatic fictions—some poems within this larger frame are purely dramatic monologues—Dubie goes about collecting and making up "facts" for the past and present as he takes up, in Marvin Bell's apt phrase, "the difficulties of personal histories, intimate and cultural, told or insinuated." The results are unlikely histories, which we enter as if through a seance, from an unlikely historian. One is reminded of similar efforts in contemporary fiction, where novelists like E. L. Doctorow and D. M. Thomas weave living and dead, real and fictional, personalities into vibrant tapestries. While it would be foolish to claim that Dubie's poetic constructions can be approached as historical documents, they make us feel, like the best recorded history, the dynamic interplay among their unlikely protagonists. Dubie achieves this by carefully linking events, which are bathed in suggestive details that illuminate, or illustrate, rather than merely characterize, those moments in history that he takes to be formative. Without this linkage of events, history, or human activity, would amount to a series of random happenings.

Dubie mentions starting to write once by staring at his wall, on which hung "a narrow photograph of Dresden in a snowstorm, my only window." That is a useful way to think about his poems as well. All taught history is circumvented, and we are left with one slit into the past through these picture-poems, or, as he called an entire book of them, *The Illustrations* (1975). By staring at them, one enters a double consciousness in which the mass of history is blacked out so we can concentrate on a particular series of events that are projected before us. As we share in these images, and these images alone (see "The Ganges"), a new sense of history is born. As if to stress the importance of having but one window, or vantage point, Dubie moves his characters to where they can look out on a narrow scene and thus intensify their vision. In "The Fox Who Watched for the Midnight Sun," Henrik Ibsen "looks out / Into the March storm for an illustration," a sign of what to follow in his bafflement. Obsessed by these windows on the world, Dubie calls his latest book *The Window in the Field* (1981).

Both for Dubie and for his characters, caught in the frozen frames of their histories, events are clarified when seen through literal, or figurative, windows. In "Coleridge Crossing the Plain of Jars: 1833," Coleridge can no longer walk his English fields without coming upon Keats's funeral in Italy, and simultaneously upon the Vietnamese-French battle fought at the Plain of Jars in the 1950s, both but a brief historical leap away from a Biblical Armageddon, said to have occurred on the Plain of Jars. Once we step "under the bitter waterfall" time warp sets in, and we are no longer innocent. The "funeral ghats" in "The Ganges" afford the same sort of passageway as Dubie's "narrow photograph" or the walk under the waterfall: They are a birth-chute through which we enter the next level and the next and the next—"It will be dark with a mist / Where the stairs jump into the water" ("The Ganges"). Upon his return, Coleridge's wife can only manage, "I thought / The elements had swallowed you / Just as you passed the last sycamore?" ("Coleridge Crossing the Plain of Jars: 1833"). In "February: The Boy Breughel," something happens out past the trees as well, as "a boy in a red shirt who woke / A moment ago / Watches from the window" to see the fox eat his kill. It is something to do with lost innocence, with paying witness, something tiny at first that prefigures, or "inaugurates," as Dubie says of another poem, "something as huge as our Second World War."

Dubie can also cast his visions on a much larger scale if the story merits amplification. In an essay on his methods of composition, he speaks of having a basic instinct "toward the sentence." From sentences, he works toward stanzas that are built like paragraphs. The long poem that concludes our selection, "The Composer's Winter Dream," rings out like a hymn, as Dubie fashions an heroic account of Beethoven's bout with deafness and death. It is as close as a contemporary poet can come to the novelist's way with the forces that drove Beethoven mad. At an almost cacophonous pitch, Dubie's "score" follows Beethoven as he stumbles and shuffles and eats his way through the great halls of Vienna, at the mercy of drunken physicians. The curtain comes down on a history about to break loose from its cage—"The same March storm that swept through Vienna just an hour before / Has turned in its tracks like the black, caged panther / On exhibit in the Esterhazys' candlelit ballroom." We can see into the Götterdämmerung of a Richard Wagner and beyond to the coming storm of the 1930s.

Norman Dubie was born in Vermont and grew up in the Northeast. He has degrees from Goddard College and the Writer's Workshop at the University of Iowa, and currently teaches at Arizona State University in Tempe. He counts his experiences working in hospitals as having most shaped his understanding of others' lives.

SF

February: The Boy Breughel

The birches stand in their beggar's row:
Each poor tree
Has had its wrists nearly
Torn from the clear sleeves of bone,
These icy trees
Are hanging by their thumbs
Under a sun
That will begin to heal them soon,
Each will climb out
Of its own blue, oval mouth;
The river groans,
Two birds call out from the woods

And a fox crosses through snow
Down a hill; then, he runs,
He has overcome something white
Beside a white bush, he shakes
It twice, and as he turns
For the woods, the blood on the snow

Looks like the red fox,
At a distance, running down the hill:
A white rabbit in his mouth killed
By the fox in snow
Is killed over and over as just
Two colors, now, on a winter hill:

Two colors! Red and white. A barber's bowl!
Two colors like the peppers
In the windows
Of the town below the hill. Smoke comes
From the chimneys. Everything is still.

Ice in the river begins to move,
And a boy in a red shirt who woke
A moment ago
Watches from his window
The street where an ox
Who's broken out of his hut
Stands in the fresh snow
Staring cross-eyed at the boy
Who smiles and looks out
Across the roof to the hill;
And the sun is reaching down
Into the woods

NORMAN DUBIE   525

Where the smoky red fox still
Eats his kill. Two colors.
Just two colors!
A sunrise. The snow.

The Ganges

I'm sorry but we can't go to the immersions tonight
For the poor will not get down from the wheel, and
The musicians and the lorry won't budge
Without the money. We don't have it. But, we could

Walk to the cremations. It will be dark with a mist
Where the stairs jump into the water. These are
The funeral ghats. The corpses are brought in drapes
And that one will be dipped in the river and then
She will be anointed with clarified butter. To the
Left of us four men waist deep in the river sift
Through mud and ashes for gold rings.
With a straw torch
The dead mother's son starts the fire;
With a bone cudgel
He smashes her skull to release the images shared
By her with these

Postcards I am now passing to you:
Of the family pond entirely filled with limes,
White pigs rooting in coconut husks, and her six
Children watering their charges, the black lulled elephants.

Elizabeth's War with the Christmas Bear: 1601

For Paul Zimmer

The bears are kept by hundreds within fences, are fed cracked
Eggs; the weakest are
Slaughtered and fed to the others after being scented
With the blood of deer brought to the pastures by Elizabeth's
Men—the blood spills from deep pails with bottoms of slate.

The balding Queen had bear-gardens in London and in the country.
The bear is baited: the nostrils
Are blown full with pepper, the Irish wolf dogs
Are starved, then, emptied, made crazy with fermented barley;

And the bear's hind leg is chained to a stake, the bear
Is blinded and whipped, kneeling in his own blood and slaver, he is
Almost instantly worried by the dogs. At the very moment that
Elizabeth took Essex's head, a giant brown bear
Stood in the gardens with dogs hanging from his fur . . .
He took away the sun, took
A wolfhound in his mouth and tossed it into
The white lap of Elizabeth I—arrows and staves rained

On his chest, and standing, he, then, stood even taller, seeing
Into the Queen's private boxes—he grinned into her battered eggshell face.
Another volley of arrows and poles, and opening his mouth he showered
Blood all over Elizabeth and her Privy Council.

The very next evening, a cool evening, the Queen demanded
13 bears and the justice of 113 dogs: She slept
All that Sunday night and much of the next morning.
Some said she was guilty of *this* and *that*.
The Protestant Queen gave the defeated bear
A grave in a Catholic cemetery. The marker said:
Peter, a Solstice Bear, a gift of the Tsarevitch to Elizabeth.

After a long winter she had the grave opened. The bear's skeleton
Was cleared with lye, she placed it at her bedside.
Put a candle inside behind the sockets of the eyes, and, then
She spoke to it:

You were a Christmas bear—behind your eyes
I see the walls of a snow cave where you are a cub still smelling
Of your mother's blood which has dried in your hair; you have
Troubled a Queen who was afraid when seated in *shade* which, standing,
You had created! A Queen who often wakes with a dream of you at night—
Now, you'll stand by my bed in your long white bones; alone, you
Will frighten away at night all visions of bear, and all day
You will be in this cold room—your constant grin,
You'll stand in the long, white prodigy of your bones, and you are,
Every inch of you, a terrible vision, not bear, but virgin!

The Fox Who Watched for the Midnight Sun

Across the snowy pastures of the estate
Open snares drift like pawprints under rain, everywhere
There is the conjured rabbit being dragged
Up into blowing snow: it struggles
Upside down by a leg, its belly
Is the slaked white of cottages along the North Sea.

Inside the parlor Ibsen writes of a summer garden, of a
Butterfly sunken inside the blossoming tulip.
He describes the snapdragon with its little sconce of dew.
He moves from the desk to a window. Remembers his studies
In medicine, picturing the sticky
Overlapping eyelids of drowned children. On the corner
Of the sofa wrapped in Empress-silks there's a box
Of fresh chocolates. He mimics the deceptively distant,
Chittering birdsong within the cat's throat.
How it attracts finches to her open window.
He turns toward the fire, now thinking of late sessions in Storting.
Ibsen had written earlier of an emotional girl
With sunburnt shoulders,

Her surprise when the heavy dipper came up
From the well with frogs' eggs bobbing in her water.
He smiles.

Crosses the room like the fox walking away
From the woodpile.
He picks up his lamp and takes it
To the soft chair beneath the window. Brandy is poured.
Weary, he closes his eyes and dreams
Of his mother at a loom, how she would dip, dressing
The warp with a handful of coarse wool.

Henrik reaches for tobacco—tomorrow, he'll write
Of summer some more, he'll begin with a fragrance . . .
Now, though, he wonders about the long
Devotion of his muscles to his bones. He's worried by
The wind which hurries the pages in this drafty room.
He looks out
Into the March storm for an illustration: under a tree
A large frozen hare swings at the end of a snare-string.
The fox sits beneath it, his upturned head swinging with it,
The jaws are locked in concentration,

As if the dead hare were soon to awaken!

Coleridge Crossing the Plain of Jars: 1833

For Sherod Santos

The gypsies carry sacks of walnuts out of the groves.
A dog
Whimpers below the cemetery, near to the peat field.

With regard to color primarily, but also
Scent and form,
The browsing deer under the sycamores
Have the very properties of a peach
Spoiled on the branch by a blanketing frost . . .

The deer, in Asia,
Rise out of fog as though it were a pond.

I walk. And over the wind, I hear the crushing
Of talc for the shaping of a death mask. Why is it?

Young Keats is lost!

Joseph Severn's hurried sketch of the rouged corpse
Was like that deep violet thumbprint, this morning,
In the soft breast of the goose
Hung in a draughty printshop of my publishers!

Sarah watched from her window above the philodendron
While I crossed against the West Wind
Through the drifting snow. She lost sight of me
For a moment. She guessed I was again wrestling
The angel.
I did die there, briefly, in the blizzard
As I had once with my mother as a boy—
The first of April, nude except for our canvas shoes,
We stepped
Under the bitter waterfall fed with a run-off of snow.

My brain empties

As it will when I've stood under the compass
Of a great low chandelier, weighted
In the purity
Of vertical tiers of burning citron candles.

The gypsies' bonfire climbs the stone face
Of the nunnery . . .
A Christmas pie, already sampled by the children,

Sits on the cleared table.

NORMAN DUBIE

I stepped into the parlor, and Sarah said, "I thought
The elements had swallowed you
Just as you passed the last sycamore?"

She smiled in her chair, from half-dark,
And sewed—
I knew the chipped fire of pond ice
Was in her eyes like a widow's soul.

The Composer's Winter Dream

Vivid and heavy, he strolls through dark brick kitchens
Within the great house of Esterhazy:
A deaf servant's candle
Is tipped toward bakers who are quarreling about
The green kindling! The wassail is
Being made by pouring beer and sherry from dusty bottles

Over thirty baked apples in a large bowl: into
The wassail, young girls empty their aprons of
Cinnamon, ground mace and allspice berries. A cook adds
Egg whites and brandy. The giant, glass snifters
On a silver tray are taken from the kitchens by two maids.
The anxious pianist eats just the edges of a fig

Stuffed with Devonshire cream. In the sinks the gall bladders
Of geese are soaking in cold salted water.
Walking in the storm, this evening, he passed
Children in rags, singing carols; they were roped together
In the drifting snow outside the palace gate.
He knew he would remember those boys' faces . . .

There's a procession into the kitchens: larger boys, each
With a heavy shoe of coal. The pianist sits and looks
Hard at a long black sausage. He will not eat

Before playing the new sonata. Beside him
The table sags with hams, kidney pies and two shoulders
Of lamb. *A hand rings a bell in the parlour!*

No longer able to hide, he walks
Straight into the large room that blinds him with light.
He sits before the piano still thinking of hulled berries . . .
The simple sonata which

He is playing has little
To do with what he's feeling: something larger
Where a viola builds, in air, an infinite staircase.
An oboe joins the viola, they struggle
For a more florid harmony.
But the silent violins now emerge,

And like the big wing of a bird, smother everything
In a darkness from which only a single horn escapes—
Successively but in strict imitation of the viola
That feels effaced by the composer's dream . . .
But he is not dreaming,
The composer is finishing two performances simultaneously!

He is back in the dark kitchens, sulking and counting
His few florins—they have paid him
With a snuff-box that was pressed
With two diamonds, in Holland!
This century discovers quinine.
And the sketchbooks of a mad, sad musician

Who threw a lantern at his landlord who was standing beside
A critic. He screamed: *here, take a snuff-box, I've filled
It with the dander of dragons!* He apologizes
The next morning, instructing the landlord to take
This *stuff* (Da Ist Der Wisch) to a publisher,
And sell it! *You'll have your velvet garters, Pig!*

The composer is deaf, loud and feverish . . . he went
To the countryside in a wet sedan-chair.
He said to himself: for the piper, seventy ducats! He'd curse
While running his fingers through his tousled hair, he made
The poor viola climb the stairs.
He desired loquats, loquats with small pears!

Ludwig, there are Spring-bears under the pepper trees!
The picnic by the stone house . . . the minnows
Could have been sunlight striking fissures
In the stream; Ludwig, where your feet are
In the cold stream
Everything is horizontal like the land and living.

The stream sang, "In the beginning was the word
And without the word
Was not anything made that was made . . .
But let us believe in the word, Ludwig,
For it is like the sea grasses
Off which the giant snails eat, at twilight!" But then

The dream turns to autumn; the tinctures he
Swallows are doing nothing for him, and he shows
The physicians his spoon which has dissolved
In the mixtures the chemist has given him!
After the sonata was heard; the standing for applause
Over, he walked out where it was snowing.

It had been dark early that evening. It's here that the
Dream becomes shocking: he sees a doctor
In white sleeves
Who is sawing at the temporal bones of his ears. There is
A bag of dampened plaster for the death mask. And
Though he *is* dead, a pool of urine runs to the

Middle of the sickroom. A brass urinal is on the floor, it is
The shape of his ears rusting on gauze. The doctors
Drink stale wassail. They frown over the dead Beethoven. Outside,
The same March storm that swept through Vienna just an hour before
Has turned in its tracks like the black, caged panther
On exhibit in the Esterhazys' candlelit ballroom. The storm crosses
Over Vienna once more: lightning strikes the Opera House, its eaves
And awnings filled with hailstones,
Flames leaping to the adjacent stables! Someone had known,
As thunder dropped flower-boxes off window sills,
            Someone *must* have known
That, at this moment, the violins would emerge
            in a struggle with the loud, combatant horns . . .

Notes

February: The Boy Breughel. Pieter Breughel (1525?–1569), the Flemish painter.

The Ganges. Ganges is a river flowing from the Himalayas in Northern India to the Bay of Bengal. It is sacred to the Hindus. A *ghat* is a passage or stairway descending to a river.

Elizabeth's War with the Christmas Bear: 1601. The Earl of Essex was a British soldier and a favorite of Queen Elizabeth I. Tsarevitch refers to the eldest son of the Emperor (Tsar) of Russia.

Coleridge Crossing the Plain of Jars: 1833. The Plain of Jars refers to the landscape where the Biblical Armageddon will occur. It is also the place where one of the last major battles of the French Indochina War was fought in 1954. Joseph Severn (1793–1879) was an English artist who accompanied his friend, John Keats (1795–1821), to Italy and attended him at his death there. Sarah was Coleridge's (1772–1834) wife. The date sets the poem one year before his death, and the author may in the title have also been alluding to Coleridge's bouts of drinking and drugging as he entered a world of hallucinations he would only be freed from in death.

SIX POETS BORN AFTER 1940

The Composer's Winter Dream. "The great house of Esterhazy" refers to the noble Magyar family prominent in Hungarian history. They were the largest landowners in Hungary and with their wealth staunch supporters of the Habsburg dynasty, as well as great patrons of art, music, and science.

Norman Dubie

Books

Alehouse Sonnets, 1971
In the Dead of the Night, 1975
The Illustrations, 1977
The City of the Olesha Fruit, 1979
The Everlastings, 1980
The Window in the Field, 1981

Interviews

American Poetry Review 7, no. 4 (July/August 1978)

Laura Jensen

(b. 1948)

L aura Jensen writes a good deal about fear and distress, but her
poems are also filled with surges of pleasure and delight. The
voice that speaks of these emotional extremes is calm, and the
poems have a lyrical lilt so that an interesting discrepancy sometimes
arises between subject matter and tone. In addition, that quiet voice
keeps turning unexpected corners; readers face new and sudden pros-

pects without knowing how they got there. Altogether, the challenge of a Laura Jensen poem is not undertaken lightly, though the rewards for plucky readers are considerable.

Sometimes the speaker of a Jensen poem is in the presence of another person, and this "implied listener," whose position is more or less the same as the reader's, may find the relationship disquieting. In "The Red Dog," for instance, the speaker is moved to announce that the dog's lively vigor, his utter happiness on the beach, is a sign of his death, indeed that "this is the best time for it." The insistence, as though "you" was reluctant to accept this idea, suggests that the relation between speaker and listener constitutes the poem's real drama. Even more mysterious is the relation in "Tapwater," where the speaker knows more about what has happened to the "you" of the poem than is ever disclosed to the reader. We can piece a story together and put ourselves in the position of the "you" being addressed, but the mystery that envelops the speaker—and the title—will never be fully solved.

More often, however, the poetic voice in a Jensen poem is alone, reflecting. It may be remembering the pleasures of childhood, as in "The Ajax Samples" and "The Kite," or re-exploring childhood dislocation, as in "The Age." It may move into considerations of the domestic, as in "Household," which grows fascinated with needles, or "House Is an Enigma," which maps a convincing psychological terrain. Other poems touch on night fears: in "Winter Evening Poem" the "believer" the speaker has created grows more real and more ominous as the poem moves forward, and in "The Candles Draw Well After All" a journey through fear ends with a dismissal: "Reel up the little masquerade. / The summer will not be dreadful."

A closer look at one of Jensen's finest poems, "As the Window Darkens," should clarify some of her methods. In the series of clauses that open the poem, "as" can mean both "while" and "in the same way that." This elaborate sentence, evoking dusk, turns out to be a reflexive statement about the poem. The reader-poem relationship is now equated with that of the protagonist, gazing out a darkening window that gradually becomes a mirror. The mirror tells us we aren't beautiful, and we remember how we have learned to live with our clumsiness. In the confusion of inner and outer that the window-mirror creates, the past seems manageable and friendly. But isn't that because we want it that way? "What the world likes," the poetic speaker says reflectively, "is a bootstrap and locket," comfortable tokens that stand for "work and sentiment ebbing with the light." But the poem goes on to give us another kind of token, the huge and unfathomable ocean that is "a dark vase / of flowers before a dark window" and "a dish of water carried by a woman, / where the worry of our lives lies down." The images translate it into a token, but it also remains the world beyond our ken, acting as it did when it was first made, and going on "forever." The deft and quiet progression of this poem, its beautiful comparisons, its steady tone and surprising reach, all show how expertly this unusual poet puts her poetic worlds together.

While some stress on the fears and difficulties in Jensen's poems is necessary to a good account of her work, it would be a serious oversight to neglect the elements of joy and celebration in her poetry, evident throughout this selection and epitomized by two poems: "The Cloud Parade," a wild and exuberant response to its subject; and "Kite," a tender, wry and praising poem that calls forth Jensen's dual talents of close observation and imaginative comparison.

Laura Jensen is a native of the Pacific Northwest, and except for a brief period of study at the Iowa Writer's Workshop, that is where she has always lived and worked. At present, she is living in Tacoma.

DY

The Red Dog

You know that he is going to die
as soon as I tell you
he is standing beside me
his hair in spikes and dripping
from his body. He turns his head.
Canadian geese
all of them floating along the shore.
The red dog is swimming for them
only his head shows now
they flap into a curve and move
farther along the bay.
You know that he is going to die
this is the time for it
this is the best time for it
while there is a way to vanish
while the geese are moving off
to be their hard sounds
as their bodies leave the water.

The Ajax Samples

They gave us the mysterious deep warehouse
filled with lavender and telephone books.
We emptied it.
I gave the last box to a beach house
on Brown's Point.
It was like running down into a stadium
crowds cheered in the blackberries on both sides
there was a wide blue field
with a sailboat anchored
the house with its shingles and screen door.

They gave us Alan Gentili.
He was our inspector.
Alan Gentili how beautiful your eyes are
your thin brown legs in your khaki shorts.

They released the pigeons over Melrose Street.
The pigeons turned together in the afternoon
again and again
and their shadow was a blessing.

It was like a sign to us.
It was like starting our lives in another way.
Saint Nicholas, the tooth fairy
they have nothing on us now.
We are so glorious that halos shine around us.
Jewels glint on Alan Gentili's panel truck.

We are the magi traveling by moonlight.
We are Michael Anthony
giving million dollar checks to strangers.
We are the holy sunlit wanderers
and we leave gifts behind.

An Age

There is a growth that hurts the child
one was, the child who still knew
the ocean rock from a distance,
flocked like cloth, white like sugar,
a flower out of focus in the waves,

the waves, the thousands of horizons
seen again and again as blue Japan—
something that changes the freighters
twined with lights and evergreen
in the port of Seattle.

I remember being nowhere in the early light,
halfway over ocean to a northbound freighter
and walking back to my sister
where our white wood caught fire
in the white sand.

Tapwater

You live where the sounds of trucks
come through the open window,
packers bringing carcasses at night.
All this time on the side of the market
hang, like eclipses, six round lamps.

But once you went into song, went
into dance, when the rock of night
was lifted, before you thought of all
the things a rock could do to you,
on its own.

Out on the beach the mussels caught
at it, what you overturned;
the crabs scattered, running
with one glance
at some horrible maturity.

You pray to the bird in your hands
that you will never wake again
to the dilemma, or wake without
breath, or without the familiar town,
or without the others.

Household

Grudges mend and wear and turn in winter
but they turn again, astounded
if the wish has not been made,
not the stars considered,
nor time kept useful in absence.

These are the needles.
They are not thrown down
when they are stubborn.

But a fingertip is sleeping in a thimble.
There is a haystack of needles
leaving every farm with the country daughter,
needles spending their lives now
forgotten from raincoats in a rush,
shaking from cuffs and emptying from shoes.

It is not easy to sew with an ignorant needle.

Once building a needle, once building a weed
was a young time, once, that leaves itself be
a wheedling eye, a thread of light
between pins and the reputable grasses,
their brass teaching eyes to believe.

If there were no trouble, borrowing,
the troubles would be in the rivers
and the rivers would be rivers
that the troubled find.

The lake is rising like an argyle sock
on a darning egg grown wings.
And even with everything there would be
the fear, the warning, and the needles

looking down at my knees from my mind.
The needles close up in their packets
as they are remembered, what the feminine
should have kept in their lives,
so many eyes and only one authority of paper.

The Cloud Parade

In deference to the cloud parade,
the horse has shed its winter red,
stamped its last horseshoe out of the shed,
has moved away, leaving no forwarding
address. The heavens turn furniture,
attics and beds, men with moustaches
heels over heads; they cover the sun
to a gloomy shade,
in deference to the cloud parade.

LAURA JENSEN

Scarves! Echoes! Pavillions!
The meat grain in bacon, the star-stun
in roast, the bone down the well, the moon
down the wane, the smoke from the fireplace,
beautifully made,
in deference to the cloud parade.

Winter Evening Poem

I remember how I came here
unraveling.
The words find a believer
and skate idly
on the frozen pond of his surface.

The ocean is given to night—
night, blue as mussel shell.
The lamp post in its quiet habit
spills light onto nothing below it.
There are no stars. We are all safe
in something better than ourselves.

The winter reached a tide
and the night was hidden
behind each winter tree
looking shy and biting its lips.
Wearing a heavy coat,
the believer holds fast.

He is night's hope,
within it a hundred false springs
that are the scent of moist
brilliantine,
the sight of a limber muscle,
the light of the moon
that was last sighted
barking down the door.

A twig snaps.
Though we kneel to no stick
and fall to no knee
wouldn't you run
from what seems like a crack in the land
from a place that will not mend for you?

House Is an Enigma

House is an enigma. It directs what is near
and what is far away. Under the north wind,
under the hill, the broad bay is dark blue-cold.
The cold does not matter. The whitecaps are heavy
and heavily wrapped, under the wind
in a pauper whiteness, deceptive brides
one by one drowned and pulled under.

The gull was born to a task—sorting
the park and the houses from his eye, from the air;
there is no secret. Some whitecaps
reach the rocks. They thought rocks were safety.
They pound for the railroad; they reach no railroad,
no hill, no high peace on land.

But no, do not run, though you have
no instinct and small reason to be proud.
The ashes are cold and the image
is image no longer.

House alleys are rutted and glorified
by wild grasses, wild plants, California Poppies.
Afternoons, mornings, behind cement-blocked
walls, the walls fluted for light and pattern
cling the vines. Garage doors are heavy wooden burdens.
The young trees, the sweet peas, the Hubbard Squashes
are no burden. The rest is fence. Garbage cans.
Cats. Dogs. The great memory of the torn-away
raspberry jumble. And the cynical gravel.

I have been a poet for a time
before I hear a pot at home setting down
without finality. The spoon taps the sides
and the television glows and speaks out
in a language it says has been shattered,
and a light goes on in me; somewhere, inside.

But no, do not run, though you have
no instinct and small reason to be proud.
The ashes are cold and the image
is image no longer.

The Candles Draw Well After All

The candles draw well after all.
By night they might have been
flickering.
Tallow; wax and tallow;
the story is a circle and a band.
The unseen circles of air
make a silent story. So tells
the ring and the rowboat round the isle,
the zero and the handles of scissors.
So tells the circle swinging from the cord,
the noose of the windowshade.

The sun is passing
from the Atlantic to your day.
The sun has passed the eddies of rain
and is coming fast as a runner.
It is coming from a bath of rain
to its absence.

Sister braid, the skull
is not along today. Elemental word!
She is never ready for morning.
Reel up the little masquerade.
The summer will not be dreadful.

As the Window Darkens

As the window darkens, as the light yearns
over the couch, as the plants drift like swans,
this is a silent poem. It will not flower
in water like a party favor, nor
will it bleed like the universe. It will
be the knot of wood that looks like a rabbit.
A knot of wood tense and growing stiffer.

The window darkens to mirror. It chimes
the reflection and what it should have been.
Have the trees and antennas seen this
blot for years, pumping like a gauge?
No wonder the birds flew away, crying out.

SIX POETS BORN AFTER 1940

It is not true that the beautiful
are always false and the ugly philosophical.
But the clumsy stand as surely as the deft
at dark windows, knowing they have been deceived.
This is unbearable because we know
we see a door closing and we wait to see
that door close in our dreams, shutting us out.

How many years can come as gently as lamplight
out of the wind, each year with its own place
and the circle it made around a friend?
What the world likes is a bootstrap and locket,
work and sentiment ebbing with the light.

The ocean is a sigh at night, a dark vase
of flowers before a dark window, salt water,
someone pouring it from an abalone shell
when it first was made. It goes on forever,
a fountain, a fortuneteller in the palm of sand.
The ocean is a dish of water carried by a woman,
where the worry of our lives lies down.

Kite

Dime store. The goldfish swam in the murky
back. I was a child there, where the helmeted
diver bubbled, where, in an enameled
white basin below, the turtles struggled.
They were a moist delight.
And, as I realize,
shaped as a child draws any animal:
round body, legs and head extending.

Kites are separate from toys, for they are
Seasonal. Toys are in the inner aisles
that follow age so faithfully a child
might guess what the next step might be.
Of skeins of baby yarn, of bibs and rattles
sings the hardwood floor—of mother. Then
of pencils, parties, powder, bobby pins, barrettes.
Suddenly, at the counter, a life has passed—
a history, an age, a generation.

But the kites, like the pleated paper bells,
are Seasonal. Making conversation,
the young father tells, "We're not looking
for some expensive kites now," As his son
and little daughters skip around grandly.

For months it was
Wouldn't your mother like a handkerchief
or perhaps a teapot for Christmas?
in the window display,
but now it is kites and flowers.

Not kites in trees or kites like heroines
in wires, but the kite that was a speck,
the opposite of fishing: to want nothing
caught in anything but the pretty sky,
to reel the color back down again
beside you, a celebrity who tells
what it is like in the altitude.

Laura Jensen

Books

Anxiety and Ashes, 1976
Bad Boats, 1977
Memory, 1981

Larry
Levis

(b. 1946)

Randall Tosh

L arry Levis grew up on a farm near Fresno, California, with a rev-
erence for nature and human labor. He is fond of saying, "the
romance of poetry needs to be soiled by the human." In an essay,
"Some Notes on the Gazer Within," he writes of the need to rediscover

those landscapes where someone has actually lived and left a mark, places where "some delicate linkage is preserved between past and present"—the deserted streets of a small town, the closed warehouse, the steel mill. His first book, which won the U.S. Award of the International Poetry Forum, was called *Wrecking Crew*; a recent poem is titled "To a Wall of Flame in a Steel Mill, Syracuse, New York, 1969." Given the sterility of so much modern landscape, Levis worries about "the eye's starvation" and subscribes to the poetic tradition, redefined by modern masters like Rilke and Montale, that the more we forget our personalities and let our subjects find us, the more we will have to say after "a necessary immersion into voicelessness, the prophet's apprenticeship." If we write with no real subject in mind, it will lead to our superimposing values instead of discovering anything fresh about the world. This has led Levis, in an interesting extension, to cast his poems as "fables with no values." He turns things over and over to let their own meanings evolve, and the emphasis is on precision about things, rather than predisposed feelings.

Inside his "fables," on a line-by-line basis, Levis explores the conflict between the ways we experience things and the ways we think about our experiences. In rhythms that recite more than speak, that behave like arias in which elaborate melodies for a single voice work their way around a single repeated theme, Levis's poetry makes a case against prescribed meaning; repeated errors of mind, repeated lapses, are carefully tracked to suggest that nothing can be trusted. Going round and round feelings that are more complex than we imagine, Levis finds that more has gone wrong than we suppose. He takes these powers of observation farthest in "Linnets," in which he becomes a listener to those of our fears and worries that, as he notes, "assume a life more powerful than their sources."

We are representing Levis's work chiefly by "Linnets," a long poem from his second book, *The Afterlife* (the Lamont Poetry Selection for 1976). Not only does it rank as one of the most moving, sustained elegies of our time, it is a compendium of Levis's ways with his poems. Reminiscent of Coleridge's "The Rime of the Ancient Mariner" in its subject, and of Mark Strand's elegy for his father in its structure, "Linnets" begins plainly, almost bluntly, with the facts of an incident from the poet's childhood. Levis chose the subject because he thought it was the least likely subject for a poem, and he was interested in exploring the mood "of having nothing to say." By the final line of the first section, however, he has given himself up to the story and become aware of the possibilities in his subject: "He drove on the roads with a little hole in the air behind him." Now the poet relaxes and lets the connections come as they will; Section 2 is "a fable of some kind of wild justice" meted out to his brother; and then he simply leaps from "bird to bestiary" in sections 3 to

5. Finally, writer, reader, and the brothers are whirled about so that we cannot be sure any longer who did the shooting or if there was a gun at all. What we do come to realize is that Levis has followed the poem, with appropriate gravity and a relieving sense of humor, to the secret places of our ghosts and guilts. Stanley Plumly has written of Levis's ability to "surrender completely to what he sees and suffers," which not only makes him vulnerable but renders what he says genuine. At the end of "Linnets," we ache with the tiredness of having survived some kind of long illness, ready for the backfiring car that drives off to put an end to all future sound.

The other poems we include are from Levis's latest book, *The Doll-maker's Ghost* (1981), a winner of the National Poetry Series competition. While several poems pay homage to foreign poets he has come to revere, and reflect his ongoing interest in the poetry of other cultures, Levis is particularly drawn to a poet like Zbigniew Herbert, who believes that "the world without imagination is a lie—such a world tries to assure its inhabitants that there's no death, passion, vision." In his poem for Herbert, Levis celebrates a story that Herbert has entrusted to him, and one he can only reach with his imagination because he has no real knowledge of where it happened or how. Levis must simply listen a long time to what he has been told, until he hears "the black blood rushing over / The stone of my skull, and believe it is music." The empathy and compassion may not suffice, however: "But some things are not possible on this earth" ("For Zbigniew Herbert, Summer, 1971, Los Angeles"). As in "Linnets," what can happen, if we keep after that "delicate linkage between past and present," is a mystical exchange: The dead will watch over the poems that we make about them "until they are finished." Levis understands that he does not have to do it all, find the subject, the form, the "way out." The wordlessness beyond these poems points to a place where "... everything is muted and / Real. The way laughter is real / When it ends, suddenly, between two strangers, / And you step quickly past them, into the night" ("The Ownership of the Night").

Larry Levis studied with Philip Levine in Fresno, earned a master's degree at Syracuse University, and has a Ph.D. from the University of Iowa, where he has taught in the Writer's Workshop. He is currently teaching at the University of Missouri in Columbia, where he helps edit the *Missouri Review*.

SF

Linnets

1

One morning with a 12-gauge my brother shot what he said was a linnet. He did this at close range where it sang on a flowering almond branch. Anyone could have done the same and shrugged it off, but my brother joked about it for days, describing how nothing remained of it, how he watched for feathers and counted only two gold ones which he slipped behind his ear. He grew uneasy and careless; nothing remained. He wore loud ties and two tone shoes. He sold shoes, he sold soap. Nothing remained. He drove on the roads with a little hole in the air behind him.

2

But in the high court of linnets he does not get off so easily. He is judged and sentenced to pull me on a rough cart through town. He is further punished since each feather of the dead bird falls around *me*, not him, and each falls as a separate linnet, and each feather lost from one of these becomes a linnet. While he is condemned to feel nothing ever settle on his shoulders, which are hunched over and still, linnets gather around me. In their singing, they cleanse my ears of all language but that of linnets. My gaze takes on the terrible gaze of song birds. And I find that I too am condemned, and must stitch together, out of glue, loose feathers, droppings, weeds and garbage I find along the street, the original linnet, or, if I fail, be condemned to be pulled in a cart by my brother forever. We are tired of each other, tired of being brothers like this. The backside of his head, close cropped, is what I notice when I look up from work. To fashion the eyes, the gaze, the tongue and trance of a linnet is impossible. The eyelids are impossibly delicate and thin. I am dragged through the striped zoo of the town. One day I throw down the first stillborn linnet, then another, then more. Then one of them begins singing.

3

As my brother walks through an intersection the noise from hundreds of thin wings, linnet wings, becomes his silence. He shouts in his loud clothes all day. God grows balder.

4

Whales dry up on beaches by themselves.
The large bones in their heads, their silence,
Is a way of turning inward.

Elephants die in exile.
Their tusks begin curling, begin growing
into their skulls.

My father once stopped a stray dog
With a 12-gauge, a blast in the spine.
But you see them on the roads, trotting through rain.

Cattle are slaughtered routinely.
But pigs are intelligent and vicious to the end.
Their squeals burn circles.

Mice are running over the freezing snow.
Wolverines will destroy kitchens for pleasure.
Wolverines are so terrible you must give in.

The waist of a weasel is also lovely. It slips away.

The skies under the turtle's shell are birdless.

* * *

These shadows become carp rising slowly. The black
Trees are green again. The creeks are full
And the wooden bridge trembles.

The suicides slip beneath you, shining.
You think if you watched them long enough
You would become fluent in their ten foreign tongues

Of light and drummed fingers and inbreedings.

5

Snakes swallow birds, mice, anything warm.
Beaten to death with a length of pipe,
A snake will move for hours afterward, digesting.

In fact their death takes too long.
In their stillness it may be they outlast death.
They are like stones the moment after

A wind passes over.
The tough skin around a snake's eyes
Is ignorant and eternal.

They are made into belts and wallets.
Their delicate meat can be eaten.
But you can't be sure.

In the morning another snake lies curled
On the branch just over your head.

LARRY LEVIS

* * *

Under the saint's heel in the painting,
A gopher snake sleeps.
The saint's eyes are syphilitic with vision.

He looks the Lord in the face.
He is like the bridge the laborers shrug at
As they wade across the water at night.

* * *

When LaBonna Stivers brought a 4 foot bullsnake to High Mass, she stroked its
lifted throat; she smiled: "Snakes don't have no minds."

6

You can't be sure. Your whole family
May be wiped out by cholera. As the plums
Blossom, you may hang yourself.

Or you may love a woman whose low laugh
Makes her belly shake softly.
She wants you to stay, and you should have.

* * *

Or like your brother, you may go
Into the almond orchard to kill
Whatever moves. You may want to go

Against the little psalms and clear gazings
Of birds, against yourself, a 12-gauge
Crooked negligently over your shoulder.

You're tired of summer.
You want to stop all the singing.
And everything is singing.

At close range you blow a linnet
Into nothing at all, into the silence
Of stumps, where everyone sits and whittles.

* * *

Your brother grows into a stranger.
He walks into town in the rain.
Two gold feathers behind his ear.

He is too indifferent to wave.
He buys all the rain ahead of him,
And sells all the silence behind him.

7. LINNET TAXIDERMY

I thought when finished
it would break into flight, its beak
a Chinese trumpet over the deepest lakes.
But with each feather it grows colder to the touch.
I attach the wings which wait for the glacier
to slide under them. The viewpoint of ice
is birdless. I close my eyes,
I give up.

* * *

I meet my brother in Los Angeles.
I offer him rain
but he clears his throat.
He offers me
the freeway and the sullen huts;
the ring fingers stiffening;
the bitten words.

There are no birds he remembers.
He does not remember owning a gun.
He remembers nothing of the past.

He is whistling "Kansas City"
on Hollywood Boulevard, a bird
with half its skull eaten away
in the shoebox tucked under his arm.

* * *

When the matinee ends, the lights come on
and we blink slowly
and walk out. It is the hour
when the bald usher
falls in love.

* * *

When we are the night and the rain,
the leper on his crutch will spit once,
and go on singing.

LARRY LEVIS

8. MATINEE

Your family stands over your bed
like Auks of estrangement.
You ask them to look you in the eye,
in the flaming aviary.
But they float over in dirigibles:

in one of them
a girl is undressing; in another
you are waking your father.

Your wife lies hurt on the roadside
and you must find her.
You drive slowly, looking.

They lift higher and higher
over the snow on the Great Plains.
Goodbye, tender blimps.

9. 1973

At the end of winter
the hogs are eating abandoned cars.
We must choose between Jesus and seconal
as we walk under the big, casual spiders whitening
in ice, in tree tops. These great elms rooted in hell
hum so calmly.

My brother marching through Prussia
wears a chrome tie and sings.
Girls smoothing their dresses
become mothers. Trees grow more deeply
into the still farms.

The war ends.
A widow cradles her husband's
acetylene torch,
the flame turns blue,
a sparrow flies out of the bare elm
and it begins again.

I'm no one's father.
I whittle a linnet out of wood until
the bus goes completely dark around me.
The farms in their white patients' smocks join hands.
Only the blind can smell water,
the streams moving a little,
freezing and thawing.

In Illinois one bridge is made entirely
of dead linnets. When the river sings under them,
their ruffled feathers turn large and black.

10. AT THE HIGH MEADOW

In March the arthritic horses
stand in the same place
all day.
A piebald mare flicks her ears back.

Ants have already taken over
the eyes of the house finch
on the sill.

So you think someone
is coming,
someone already passing the burned mill,
someone with news of a city
built on snow.

But over the bare table
in the morning
a glass of water goes blind
from staring upward.

For you
it's not so easy.
You begin the long witnessing:
Table. Glass of water. Lone crow
circling.

You witness the rain for weeks
and there are only the two of you.
You divide yourself in two and witness yourself,
and it makes no difference.

* * *

You think of God dying of anthrax
in a little shed, of a matinee
in which three people sit
with their hands folded and a fourth
coughs. You come down the mountain.

LARRY LEVIS   553

11

Until one day in a diner in Oakland
you begin dying.
It is peace time.
You have no brother.
You never had a brother.
In the matinees no one sat next to you.
This brother for whom
you have been repairing linnets all your life,
unthankful stuffed little corpses,
hoping they'd perch behind glass in museums that have
been levelled, this brother
who slept under the fig tree
turning its dark glove inside out at noon, is no one;
the strong back you rode while
the quail sang perfect triangles, was no one's.
Your shy father extinct in a single footprint,
your mother a stone growing a cuticle.
It is being suggested that you were never born, that
it never happened in linnet feathers
clinging to the storm fence along the freeway;
in the Sierra Nevadas,
in the long azure of your wife's glance,
in the roads and the standing water,
in the trembling of a spider web gone suddenly still,
it never happened.

12

This is a good page.
It is blank,
and getting blanker.
My mother and father
are falling asleep over it.
My brother is finishing a cigarette;
he looks at the blank moon.
My sisters walk gravely in circles.
My wife sees through it, through blankness.
My friends stop laughing, they listen
to the wind in a room in Fresno, to the wind
of this page, which is theirs,
which is blank.

They are all tired of reading,
they want to go home,
they won't be waving goodbye.

When they are gone,
the page will be crumpled,
thrown into the street.
Around it, sparrows will be feeding
on bits of garbage.
The linnet will be singing.
A man will awaken on his death bed,
not yet cured.

I will not have written these words,
I will be that silence slipping around the bend
in the river, where it curves out of sight among weeds,
the silence in which a car backfires and drives away,
and the father of that silence.

For Zbigniew Herbert, Summer, 1971, Los Angeles

No matter how hard I listen, the wind speaks
One syllable, which has no comfort in it—
Only a rasping of air through the dead elm.

✳ ✳ ✳

Once a poet told me of his friend who was torn apart
By two pigs in a field in Poland. The man
Was a prisoner of the Nazis, and they watched,
He said, with interest and a drunken approval.
If terror is a state of complete understanding,

Then there was probably a point at which the man
Went mad, and felt nothing, though certainly
He understood everything that was there: after all,
He could see blood splash beneath him on the stubble,
He could hear singing float toward him from the barracks.

✳ ✳ ✳

And though I don't know much about madness,
I know it lives in the thin body like a harp
Behind the rib cage. It makes it painful to move.
And when you kneel in madness your knees are glass,
And so you must stand up again with great care.

Maybe this wind was what he heard in 1941.
Maybe I have raised a dead man into this air
And now I will have to bury him inside my body,
And breathe him in, and do nothing but listen—
Until I hear the black blood rushing over
The stone of my skull, and believe it is music.

But some things are not possible on the earth.
And that is why people make poems about the dead.
And the dead watch over them, until they are finished:
Until their hands feel like glass on the page,
And snow collects in the blind eyes of statues.

The Ownership of the Night

1

After five years,
I'm in the kitchen of my parents' house
Again, hearing the aging refrigerator
Go on with its music,
And watching an insect die on the table
By turning in circles.
My face reflected in the window at night
Is paler, duller, even in summer.
And each year
I dislike sleeping a little more,
And all the hours spent
Inside something as black
As my own skull . . .
I watch
This fruit moth flutter.
Now it's stopped.

2

Once,
Celebrating a good year for Muscatel,
My parents got away to Pismo Beach,
Shuttered and cold in the off season.
When I stare out at its surf at night,
It could be a girl in a black and white slip,
It could be nothing.

But I no longer believe this is where
America ends. I know
It continues as oil, or sorrow, or a tiny
Island with palm trees lining
The sun-baked, crumbling
Asphalt of its air strip.
A large snake sleeps in the middle of it,
And it is not necessary to think of war,
Or the isolation of any father
Alone on a raft in the Pacific
At night, or how deep the water can get
Beneath him . . .
Not when I can think of the look of distance
That must have spread
Over my parents' faces as they
Conceived me here,
And each fell back, alone,
As the waves glinted, and fell back.

3

This evening my thoughts
Build one white bridge after another
Into the twilight, and now the tiny couple
In the distance,
In the picture I have of them there,
This woman pregnant after a war,
And this man who whistles with a dog at his heels,
And who thinks all this is his country,
Cross over them without
Looking back, without waving.
Already, in the orchards behind them,
The solitary hives are things;
They have the dignity of things,
A gray, precise look,
While the new wasps swarm sullenly out of them,
And the trees hold up cold blossoms,
And, in the distance, the sky
Does not mind the one bird in it,
Which by now is only a frail brush stroke
On a canvas in which everything is muted and
Real. The way laughter is real
When it ends, suddenly, between two strangers,
And you step quickly past them, into the night.

LARRY LEVIS

557

Larry Levis

Books

Wrecking Crew, 1972
The Afterlife, 1977
The Dollmaker's Ghost, 1981

Essays

"Some Notes on the Gazer Within," in *A Field Guide to Contemporary Poetry & Poetics*, ed. Friebert & Young, 1980; "The Nature and Use of Place in Contemporary Poetry," *FIELD* 26 (Spring 1982)

Thomas Lux

(b. 1946)

Michael Lauchlin

Among other things, Thomas Lux writes about the imagination, stressing both its pleasures and its limits. "Man Asleep in the Desert," for instance, proposes a figurative situation in which reality is a desert and imagination the series of dreams granted to the sleeper. There's no question but that the dreams give interest and meaning to the sleeper's existence, but there's also no question about the fact that the desert is the true reality: Sleep is a window that has "Nothing on the other side." Even when we are awake, Lux seems to suggest, we are "asleep in the desert" of reality, trying to nourish ourselves with fictions and mirages. This poet would seem to be continuing the imagination-reality dialectic that was the central theme of Wallace Stevens's poetry.

As an image, the desert sleeper has elements of deliberate cliché about him, a source in the pop world of comics, movies, and overfamiliar reproduction of famous works of art (e.g., Rousseau's "Sleeping Gypsy"). It's important to recognize why Lux casts his existential propositions in such popular forms. It gives an edge of self-mockery to his poetry, and it complicates the dialectic mentioned above: The meaning of imagination is different when it includes the silly and debased images that fill our lives. In one of the sections of "Flying Noises" the lovers in their rowboat drift past an older-style poet: "On the opposite shore Mallarmé's / feeding some swans." Unlike Mallarmé, who could exalt the imagination as an alternative to life, Lux sees the poet as unable to draw away from life; instead of purifying the dialectic of the tribe and enshrining the artistic imagination, the poet is a poor clown like everybody else, soiled by the necessary entanglements of dreaming and waking, subject to pratfalls and ludicrous occupations: "Force-feeding swans—let me tell / you—was hard" ("Farmers").

Lux's wit is the element that gives his poems buoyancy and promise, a kind of implied counterweight to their pessimistic sense of human isolation and ignorance. The wit is verbal—"all the solunar tables / set with silver linen!"—but it is situational too: Elements of parody lace through all Lux's poems. He borrows from melodrama in writing about destruction ("Barn Fire"), and from science fiction in writing about isolation ("Solo Native"). The pastoral's traditional celebration of country life comes in for various kinds of teasing in "Farmers," "There Were Some Summers" and two sections of "Flying Noises," but the ribbing is not a dismissal; it's more like an acknowledgment of our dependence on nature as a source of wisdom and comfort, a dependence the poet shares. "The Graveyard by the Sea" echoes the situation of countless poems, not least Valéry's famous "Le Cimetière marin," but here too the speaker is a foolish figure, stumbling around before dawn in a bad state and then down on his hands and knees trying to figure out the purpose of the mirror fragments embedded in the grave crosses. He is at one with a frightened and foolish humanity, laughing at our fears but participating in them too.

Getting adjusted to the complex tone of Lux's poetry in shorter

pieces will prepare the reader for one of his longer sequences, repre-
sented here by "Flying Noises." This kind of poem, journal-like and
loose as to subject, allows Lux to extend and deepen his poetic world by
a technique that resembles the fugue: Sections start but never fully stop
(no periods), and when they break off abruptly they go on reverberating
while new sections replace them. The resulting series of anecdotes, lists,
meditations, parodies, and constantly shifting rhythms and moods creates
a single poem that is rich and echoing both as to structure and subject.
As an exploration of love and solitude it might be thought of simply as a
larger and fuller catalogue of the dreams of that man asleep in the desert,
though the sleep, in this case, is tinged with self-consciousness and mor-
dant wit. Lux is an expert whistler in the dark, like the "solo native"
who sees that "the stars are pinholes, / slits in the hangman's mask," but
who nevertheless, "after a few chiliads," begins to produce "an awkward
first audible / called language."

Tom Lux grew up in the Boston area and was educated at Emerson
College. His collections include *Memory's Handgrenade* (1972), *The Glass-
blower's Breath* (1976), and *Sunday* (1979). He has taught at a number of
schools, including Oberlin and the University of Houston, but for some
years now has been part of the writing staff of Sarah Lawrence College.

DY

Man Asleep in the Desert

He's the man—we all recognize
him—he's the man
in the desert who sees a mirage

of a frozen lake whose skaters glide
across its cold thirstless face.
On the warmer side of a dune

he reclines and pulls the palest sheet
up to his chin and sleeps, fitfully,
as only he deserves.

He dreams: Love as a tool,
love as a bribe.
He dreams: X, X, X, X, and he interprets these

as the particular zones of passion
he does not remember.
The moonlight, like a blue welt

THOMAS LUX

of indignation, doesn't disturb him.
In his sleep he nods toward
the curved leaf of calm

and his pulse slows its vital imaginings. . . .
There is only one flaw in the window
of his sleep: Nothing on the other side.

Graveyard by the Sea

I wonder if they sleep better here
so close to the elemental pentameter
of the sea which comes in incessantly?
Just a few square acres of sand
studded mainly with thick posts
as if the coffins beneath were boats
tied fast to prevent further drift.
I half stumble around one pre-dawn,
just a dog following the footprints
of another dog with me, and stop

before one particular grave: a cross
inlaid with large splinters of mirror.
Whoever lies here is distinguished,
certainly, but I wonder—why mirrors?
For signaling? Who? No, they're embedded
in the stone and so can't be flicked
to reflect the sun or moonlight.
Is the sleeper here unusually vain
and the glass set for those times of dark
ascensions—to smooth the death gown,

to apply a little lipstick to the white
worms of the lips? No again. I think
they're for me and the ones who come,
like me, at this hour, in this half-light.
The ones who come half-drunk, half-wild,
and wholly in fear—so we may gaze
into the ghosts of our own faces,
and be touched by this chill of all
chills,—and then go home, alive,
to sleep the sleep of the awake.

Barn Fire

It starts, somehow, in the hot damp
and soon the lit bales
throb in the hayloft. The tails

of mice quake in the dust,
the bins of grain, the mangers stuffed
with clover, the barrels of oats
shivering individually in their pale

husks—animate and inanimate: they know
with the first whiff in the dark.
And we knew, or should have: that day
the calendar refused its nail

on the wall and the crab apples hurling
themselves to the ground . . . Only moments
and the flames like a blue fist curl

all around the black. There is some
small blaring from the calves and the cows'
nostrils flare only once
more, or twice, above the dead dry

metal troughs. . . . No more fat tongues worrying
the salt licks, no more heady smells
of deep green from silos rising now

like huge twin chimneys above all this.
With the lofts full there is no stopping
nor even getting close: it will rage

until dawn and beyond,—and the horses,
because they know they are safe there,
the horses run back into the barn.

Farmers

Force-feeding swans—let me tell
you—was hard. And up
every morning 4:30 counting

the lambs out to pasture,
each one tapped on the forehead with a stick
to be sure it's there.

THOMAS LUX   563

Uncle Reaper half the time so drunk
he'd pull his milkstool
under the horse: more work

explaining the difference. Gramma
and Cousin Shroud putting up
8000 jars of beets, Auntie Bones

rapping her wooden spoon
against my ear: "More bushels, bumbler!"

I'll tell you—I understand
how come the dancing bear tore off his skirt

and headed back to the Yukon,
how come all of a sudden jewels in avalanche
down the spine of my sleep. . . .

But still, still when it rains
I remember all of us: farmers, simple sweat mongers
of the dirt whose turnips depend on it,

I remember how we called it down, how down
we desired it to fall: the rain.

Solo Native

Suppose you're a solo native here
on one planet rolling, the lily
of the pad and valley.

You're alone and you know
a few things: the stars are pinholes,
slits in the hangman's mask.
And the crabs walk sideways
as they were taught by the waves.

You're the one thing upright
on hind legs, an imaginer,
an interested transient.
Look—all the solunar tables
set with silver linen!

This is where you'll live, exactly
here in a hut on the green and gray belly
of the veldt. You'll be

a metaphor, a meatpacker,
a tree dropping or gaining
its credentials. You'll be

a dancer with two feet dancing
in the dirt-colored dirt. All this,
and after a few chiliads,

from your throat a noise,
an awkward first audible
called language.

Flying Noises

* * *

The horses out of their brains bored all
winter gnawing on stalls
Outside the snow several fetlocks deep
Pounding our noses
against the ice everywhere
you could say
we had our souls in backwards
we were dumb from trudging away from noon
we were lame like the bread that lies on the table
One child's dream sledding down a slagheap
every day going at it with the cold

* * *

So he deposits the moth in a matchbox
and flails with a flashlight
into the forest a mile or two fox-
like crosses a few gullies streams
stopping finally before a final ravine
where he slides open removes the moth
lays down the light on the perfect
theater of moss
as backdrop a few slim branches
and on that greenly illumined stage it dances
to an audience of darkness plus one

THOMAS LUX

He was absolved prematurely they forgot
what he might do from the point
of absolution to the next point what's it called
So he filled in he could do anything
He disregarded the live hearts
of live humans he did misconduct before
his mother and father he coveted
his neighbor's wife and speedboat
he propped open a baby's eyes with matches
He did it like a good thief
having already been absolved

* * *

The mattress always acts as a boat
He's aware of that that's why he hopes
to bob in the wakes there
He never takes a path nonchalantly solo
knowing that's of course where
beasts do their dreaming also
Joining nothing he joins the other peasants
waving pitchforks not getting
dung for our wheat we've had it
up to our haircuts thinking we're salved
until we're mistaken is obvious

* * *

Approximately dawn some people exercise Take X
He goes out to a dirt road
with a club and bashes small stones
like in a ballgame Sending
a shot deep into the east slows down dawn
The first peeps of light In India
they have a word for it it's a child's name
you can't make a close paraphrase
The very beginning light
when roof and bush and animal
become apart from air

* * *

As if hands undoing our clothes from the inside
we fumble around in a rowboat
One oar floats downriver What a day
On the opposite shore Mallarmé's
feeding some swans How will we row
Which port our oars arriving
days ahead of us With you
voyaging you also voyaging
There's the lovely sword of moon
There's the cricket warming up his cello
There's the various positions in which we exult

* * *

Once gone like gloss in a flashflood
Once an animal loving another of another species
Once one joyful crumb of the fully individual
Once a convict dreaming of mowing a hayfield
Once an avenue upon a bench sits one moment of present
Once under deep enough to ring the literal sleep-bells
Once the dead changing shirts in their small booths
Once farmers merely bored by drought
Once all the birds invented as toys
Once the heart-angles the trillion u-turns of blood
Once the flying noise

* * *

Slow tarantula slow blink by blink
the afternoon unspools a wind primping
the fir tree's common hair
A blue calf bleats in the far pasture
Reduced by bucholia
it always hauls him back
gaping like a lump of gold shocked
in the sludge-sifter's hand
One water mocassin rolls over a few times
A hill hunches somewhat
while memorizing the earth's sore fictions

THOMAS LUX

His mouth connecting lines the puzzle
from nape to the slope beneath
her ankles the dunes He takes
pleasure there and giving it it's simply the hearts
simply the lungs simply two
to swerve beneath the fell cleavers of day to day
Their nerves on overdrive together
two odd ones warbling around an oasis
alert to the blue thuds in the wrist
And that other pulse the pulse of top lip
to bottom lip and bottom lip to top

* * *

Loving the incunabula the beginnings
like one obsessed by desert
loving its freeze at night
because it reminds him more of water
than the heat of afternoon Lined
up and loaded like something on wheels
small wafers of anger off his bureau
spinning A window is open
On the table there is sky
And behind the curtain one marvelous belly
or else the wind is bringing the usual

There Were Some Summers

There were some summers
like this: The blue barn steaming,
some cow-birds dozing with their heads
on each other's shoulders, the electric fences
humming low in the mid-August heat . . .
So calm the slow sweat existing
in half-fictive memory: a boy
wandering from house, to hayloft, to coop,
past a dump where a saddle rots
on a sawhorse, through the still forest
of a cornfield, to a pasture talking to himself
or the bored, baleful Holsteins nodding
beneath the round shade of catalpa, the boy
walking his trail towards the brook

in a deep but mediocre gully,
through skunk cabbage and pop-weed,
down sandbanks (a descending
quarter-acre Sahara), the boy wandering,
thinking nothing, thinking:
Sweatbox, sweatbox, the boy
moving towards a minnow whose slight beard
tells the subtleties of the current, holding there,
in water cold enough to break your ankles.

Thomas Lux

Books

Memory's Handgrenade, 1972
The Glassblower's Breath, 1976
Sunday, 1979

Sandra
McPherson

(b. 1943)

William Stafford

To take a common subject—slicing meat, a children's story, a coconut—or an uncommon subject—a mummy, a collapsar, a morning glory pool—and do more with it, take it further than we could have foreseen, is the specialty of Sandra McPherson. The thoughtfulness of her poems is striking; they are the products of a complex mind as well as a vivid imagination. A poem like "Collapsars," with its dialectical structure—cold fact versus emotional involvement, cosmic events counterpointing neighborhood disaster—demonstrates that. So does the complex design and emotional configuration of "Gnawing the Breast," where the little zoo (we're not told precisely where we are until stanza four) affords a consideration of life stretching all the way from birth to death. The cool detachment the speaker brings to watching the prairie dogs, a naturalist's unsentimental observation, is trained on the children as well: "Pretty things, when will you have earned // your beauty sleep? And when have eaten enough love to live on love / though you throw so much away?" This poem ends with a snatch of mystic speculation that gives it a fuller tone and ampler meaning. The little hill, a new grave, is climbed in imagination, with the discovery that it provides cooler and fresher air and that "the hill might even move a little, feeling the kick of a child."

The engagement-detachment polarity that provides the structure of "Collapsars" and the drama of "Gnawing the Breast" is fascinating to trace through Sandra McPherson's work. In "Games," for example, which involves a mother and daughter, we get not the warmth we might expect but a coolness in the mother toward the child's innocent cruelty—"She forgets it easily, / Who never speaks of losing"—that is almost scornful. Contrarily, when alienation might seem the most natural state of affairs, as in the imaginary possession of a mummy, we get closeness and sympathy: "My room-temperature friend and I / I with my hands like peaches // And my friend all / Shortbread and roots." The poem about the natural historians—dioramicist, skinner, taxidermist, stringer, egg-gatherer, even janitor—who collaborate to create the natural history museum ("The Museum of the Second Creation") is, similarly, more involved and passionate than we might expect.

These reversals of expectation about how close or distant the speaker is going to be have the rhetorical advantage of keeping us off balance, pleasantly surprised; but they go deeper as well, to reveal an essential soundness and sanity in the poet. She knows how to redress imbalances and correct one-sided impressions, and she brings a clear-eyed fairness to her account of things. "Resigning from a Job in a Defense Industry" might easily have become a condemnation both of the industry and its workers; instead it finds magic in the technical vocabulary and sympathy for the awkward creative urges expressed in the company art show. "A Coconut for Katerina," about a friend's miscarriage, has good reason to lose itself in anger or sorrow, but it finds hope and wonder instead by taking the coconut, "This baby's head, this dog's head, this dangerous acorn," as a microcosm, a world in which life can begin again, a token of human resiliency and imaginative strength.

Perhaps the need to strike balance and assert sanity stems from the strong influence of Sylvia Plath on McPherson's early poems, as if she had to define the ways in which she was different from an obsessed and self-destructive model. Perhaps it is just a leading characteristic of her personality. Whatever its origin, it makes her a poet whom readers can trust and return to. Whether she is mainly exercising her great powers of observation and association, as she does with the colors and details of "Michael," or undertaking a complex meditation like "Collapsars," Sandra McPherson shows herself a poet who is never content with easy judgments or haphazard effects. Before reading "Peter Rabbit," try imagining what you might have to say about that familiar story; then compare the imagery, diction, and tonal complexity of McPherson's treatment. You'll soon recognize that you are in the presence of an extraordinary poet.

Born in San Jose, California, where she grew up and went to San Jose State College, Sandra McPherson continued her education at the University of Washington and worked for a short time as a technical writer for Honeywell. With the exception of two stints of teaching at Iowa, she has for many years made her home in Portland, Oregon. She has published three book-length collections of poetry: *Elegies for the Hot Season* (1970), *Radiation* (1973) and *The Year of Our Birth* (1978).

DY

Resigning from a Job
in a Defense Industry

The names of things—sparks!
I ran on them like a component:
henries, microhenries, blue
beavers, wee wee ductors:
biographer of small lives,
of a plug and his girl named Jack,
of Utopian colonies which worked—
steel, germanium, brass, aluminum,
replaceables.
        Outside, afloat, my words
swung an arm charting the woman
who was the river bottom.

We tried, beyond work, at work,
to keep what we loved. Near
Christmas I remember the office
women trimming their desperately
glittering holy day trees. And,
just as I left, the company
talent show, the oils and sentiment
thick on still lifes and seacoasts,
the brush strokes tortured as a child's
first script. Someone
had studied driftwood; another man,
the spray of a wave, the mania
of waters above torpedoes.

Butchery

They're like the valentines from old schoolmates—
We were going to love each other forever.
Now I turn the beasts in the fields under my hands
And slice
Against the grain.
The table settles,
On meats, its earth.
A raw piece: fat skims it like the froth on beer.
I hammer it.
Something for the family, O our
Solicitous eunuch.
I like to think of the green fields where steers revolve
Beneath such a blue thumb,
Their hoarse announcements seeming never to express despair
Or more specific sadness
Than that the sky is darkening.
I can feel their necks breathe
And see their sides slapping like heavy suitcases.
Belly within belly now
We lie down to sleep,
Dull with each other.
I have washed the cutting board,
I have dried the fine knife that it will not rust,
I have scrubbed knowing the smell will stay on my hands
A few more hours, like perfume or gloves.

SANDRA MCPHERSON

Collapsars

The problem with
black holes is

She would see
if I had a problem.
She read my birth
and I grew cold.
The chart held a "dark time"
for a "near" woman
in the snow stars of Christmas.
No, I said,
tragedies like that—

there is no way
to see them
or hear them.

As one hears
even in sleep
a man shouting Fire!
in the street.

They are stars
that have collapsed,
suffered what

even hard winter
doesn't bring:
snow fallen between houses
like a body
between bed and door.
Inhaling then choking

is called an implosion.

Without realizing
what happens,
you reach intensity . . .

The matter
in such stars
has been squashed together

like a victim
of a fire
carried down in a bag,
half size,
but then again and again,
fire after fire,

> *into forms*
> *unknown on earth,*

because our knowledge
has made us rare
and cold. How
can I look at it,

> *matter so dense*
> *its gravitational field*
> *prevents any kind*
> *of radiation*
> *from escaping.*

I have kept my body heat
in heavy sweaters
and weatherstripping,
while earth's night grows colder
and what was burned
freezes.
          From that body
could a soul be escaping?

> *You couldn't see one*
> *if it was right*
> *next to you;*

Miss Nugent was like that.
She must have walked
right by our house
twice a day. I never
saw her, never saw
her take the steps
one by one up to her apartment
after work and switch
on the light.

> *if you shone*
> *a light on it*

today, in the noon
after the fire broke out
like the sun's own rooster
rising from her window,
way too early
in the dark holiday morning,
licking up story after story,

> *the light would*
> *simply disappear*

SANDRA MCPHERSON   575

like a Christmas present
we missed
and sifted the ashes for,
thrown away with its wrapping,

into the black hole.

And what spark doesn't
desire all? And what
kind of star
visited a woman that night,
thirty-five,
of a secretary's passions,
ninety-eight point six?

Wanting a Mummy

I've always wanted one,
A connection,

Leaning against the bureau, an in
To atrocious kingships,

To stone passages,
Those nights carrying the planets of the dead.

I'd like being able to ask it,
How do you like the rain?

Are you 3000 years old or still 25?
And to hear it replying,

Voluble with symbols
And medallions.

There we would debate, faced off
Across the room,

My room-temperature friend and I,
I with my hands like peaches

And my friend all
Shortbread and roots.

Peter Rabbit

Mushrooms grew near the tree
Nearly black with foliage.
Each footfall was a special touch.
Mother Rabbit wore a carrot-
Colored jacket and a broad purple skirt,
She was beyond hopping.
Over her paw a basket; her forearm, umbrella.
No no no! we're waiting for her to demand.
She looks that way though kind.

Father father's in the pie.
It was an accident.
It was a stupid way to die.
Peter knows how to be very naughty.
There is a shimmer
About the lettuce, French beans,
Radishes, and parsley—
Of evil or of humanity.
Peter is a thief.

Peter my hero I am a thief.
Peter I am a child.

Peter was most dreadfully frightened
And shed big tears.
Mr. McGregor was upon him
With his size huge shoe.
Of course we are going to win.

Lippity-lippity we wander
With puzzled Peter
But I don't want the story to be over.
They will make us wash the green
From our hands and our knees.

Gnawing the Breast

of a fallen sparrow, the prairie dog first softens
it with his teeth then frees and finishes the piece,
        his head high.
    The she-dog eats stems of grass.
Meat-eater tries to make love to grass-eater.
But no, she'd rather lie almost flat as water,
    contracting and rolling while she sleeps.

SANDRA MCPHERSON

Young girls keep running up and asking me if she
    is dying.
She sleeps, smaller and darker of the two.
They attribute despair inside her to her shade and size.
    She might also be old-fashioned,
    a baby could kill her.
And then, inclusive kids, they nose about what I am

doing; why I am doing it; what I do when I'm not
    doing this;
till one squeals that she hates what I do because
    it puts her to sleep.
When they run off kicking, the prairie dog wakes
and otters through the grass: while I think,
    Pretty things, when will you have earned

your beauty sleep? And when have eaten enough love
    to live on love
though you throw so much away? Well, it's just a tiny
guilty zoo. The keeper wishes he could feed
    the animals more blossoms.
I ask him, "Where did you get that hill that wasn't
    there before?"

    "A new grave," he says.
Maybe it was Aesop, diving, doing research as a
universal bird and ending up in the mouth of this dog.
    The hill will give it a viewpoint.
I think if I could climb that hill,
the air would be cooler, fresher, as it always used to be
    on ones I didn't know the source of.

And the hill might even move a little, feeling the kick
    of a child.

Morning Glory Pool

1

The boy who fell into the Morning Glory Pool met earth's fire and its water all at
once. Neither could quench the other. The boy, the water flowing, the fire, the
flower, and rising from them the steam or smoke. To think there are people who
sit down at a desk spread with wires and feathers to make *artificial flowers*. What
hallucination of evil are they adding to this world which already cradles its
capacity? What destruction is each of their creations a model of. . . .

Synthesis as a principle is dangerous. Sometimes we "collect ourselves" and make a good impression. Then we find that those whom we have impressed are in as many pieces as we. We lock the door. Motherhood is another synthesis. I am the devouring Morning Glory Pool and my child has made my name a symbol of death. My door cannot be locked. It must flow and scald.

Michael

The archangel's silver panties glint as he flies. Hooting softly, his trumpet dangles from a cord too weak to hang himself with. Lilac wings like crocuses in winter. Weather of lullabyes and impregnations. The sky handwritten.

Michael, I thought of you when I saw a mink in terror swim into the suffused lacustrine evening. And now again—though celestiality maroons you—as a heron opens rising from a snag.

A Coconut for Katerina

Inside the coconut is Katerina's baby. The coconut's hair, like Katerina's
    brown hair.
Like an auctioneer Katerina holds the coconut, Katerina in her dark furcoat
covering winter's baby, feet in the snow. Katerina's baby is the milk
and will not be drinking it.

Ropes hanging down from the trees—are they well ropes? Ropes on a moss
wall. Not to ring bells but used for climbing up and down
or pulling, I mean bringing. Anchor ropes on which succulent ropy sea-
    plants grow.

And floating like a bucket of oak or like a light wooden dory, the coconut bobs,
creaking slowly, like a piling or a telephone pole with wet wires
downed by a thunderstorm over its face.

This baby's head, this dog's head, this dangerous acorn is the grocer
of a sky-borne grocery store where the white-aproned grocer or doctor
        imprints it
with three shady fingerprints, three flat abysses the ropes will not cross.

SANDRA MCPHERSON

What of it? There is enough business for tightrope walkers in this jungle.
The colonizers make a clearing
for a three-cornered complex of gas-stations, lit with a milky spotlight
at night.

And here we dedicate this coconut to Katerina. We put our hand
on the round stomach of Katerina. We put our five short ropes of fingers on
the lost
baby of Katerina and haul it in to the light of day and wash it with sand.

Coconut, you reverse of the eye, the brown iris in white, the white center
in brown sees so differently. The exposed fibrous iris,
the sphere on which memory or recognizing must have latitude and longi-
tude
to be moored

or preserved in the big sky, the sea's tug of war. The tugging of water
held in and not clear. Lappings and gurglings of living hollows half filled,
half with room
for more empty and hopeful boats and their sails.

Games

I play pool. I aim toward the faces
    Across the room. My daughter
Takes these quarters for the pinball
    She plays with a dying

Butterfly on her left hand. It
    Will not leave, it is tired,
And all its strength is in its legs.
    I set it on my arm

Then give it back. I'll take her hand
    That way when dying, stick
Out my tongue, like its curled black one,
    Green crutch of a Kentucky

Wonder Bean, and *Look*, she cries,
    Its body fell away.
It's all wings and head. Short life
    Has culled mistaken

Parts and dropped the mite-sized heart and
    Killed the steering place.
Or else she did this, quickened its
    Death among the games

           SIX POETS BORN AFTER 1940

And flunked it too soon. And even so
　　The golden-mica'd wings
Are best. She forgets it easily,
　　Who never speaks of losing.

The Museum of the Second Creation

The dioramacist does not know
How the Creator shows emotion.
So he flings the passenger pigeon across the sunset
As a guess. And the pigeons look joyous.
In fact, he says, I could call it a sunrise,
No one will ever know.

If there is a whole
Table of feet, and one
Of skulls, and a rugful of antlers, a bench of pelts,
A skinner has loved to give samples to touch,
A collector has strewn away the danger
By pooling big and little teeth.

And the taxidermist must be happy each time
He's given a weasel to stuff, maybe that's
His favorite animal, and best if it's a Least
Weasel, once full of night courage, at the neck
Of a cat or the heel
Of a cow.

Who fills museums
Loves to recreate little horses.
I have seen them in most big cities, little horses
In a rodeo through swamps, little horses
That could companion us
Like dogs.

Joining the fruit-bat's bones,
The stringer loves to reveal its outgrown fingers,
Strokes of fossil longer than our own. Flying on a wire
At dusk, its mouseflesh gone, its tarp wings rotted,
Big starlight hands.
The visitor says: Lost love, your body is so

Recreated in me
That I can look in the glass
Polished round the animal we loved the most
And see how nearly real you are.

SANDRA MCPHERSON   581

What reincarnation is there? What can I learn
From the egg-gatherer

Sitting on his license to clean a new lilac shell,
Turning its most ecstatic face upward?
What can I glean from the late-late janitor
Sweeping up moths that fall
Through seal ribs strung near the light?
Their wings are now his—

Their sparkle's on his broomstraws.

Sandra McPherson

Books

Elegies for the Hot Season, 1970
Radiation, 1973
The Year of Our Birth, 1978

David
St. John
(b. 1949)

In the poems of David St. John, "there's only one story, but it's told many times" ("Portrait, 1949") to expose the painful and frightening, but also the joyous, aspects of experience in order that the process of healing can begin. The poems focus primarily on love and friendship, with their corollaries of jealousy and desire. He tells them

583

slowly, in deliberate, muted tones, but is not afraid to resort to pulsing rhythms that evoke Eliot and Yeats at times. St. John works with exquisite pastels—lavender boats, orange and yellow smoke, lemon derbies, and reddened walls—that soften his landscapes so we can bear the harsh events. These stories need time to unfold. They are studded with qualifying detail, questions of who said what, memories that pile up and must be sorted out. Frequently, the people in the poems seek solace in sleep, using their dreams to try to order their lives. However, "When you are asleep, dreaming of another country, / This is the country" ("Dolls"): One longs for elsewhere, but has perhaps been in the right place all the while. In spite of feeling dislocated, confronting paradoxes they cannot resolve, no one gives up in these poems—"those who give up finally give up too much" ("Four O'Clock in Summer: Hope"). In honest fights, in meditative asides, the characters salvage something from their sometimes wicked, sometimes loving encounters with each other. We admire them as we watch, in Anthony Hecht's phrase, "the grime and sadness turn to melody and grace." Grace follows, because St. John does not foreshorten the "grime and sadness." The poems, the people in them, take the long way around, as here, in "Slow Dance," they sail back into the past and move out again toward the future:

> ... We know lovers who quarrel
> At a party stay in the cool trajectory
> Of the other's glance,
> Spinning through the pockets of conversation, sliding in & out
> Of the little gaps between us all until they brush or stand at last
> Back to back, & the one hooks
> An ankle around the other's foot. Even the woman
> Undressing to music on a stage & the man going home the longest
> Way after a night of drinking remember
> The brave lyric of a heel-&-toe.

This distance we must travel to flesh out the full story of our lives is emphasized in poem after poem. "The Boathouse" puts it this way: "Homer had it right. A man sails / The long way home." Anything less would not do justice to what people have been through together.

Things are not what they seem in these poems, but they reveal themselves in private moments if we are as patient as the poet with his material: "the young / Acolyte ... / ... twirling his gold & white satin / Skirts so that everyone can see his woolen socks & rough shoes" ("Slow Dance"). Catching sight of the primitive footwear under the acolyte's sacred robes, we are struck with the full meaning of revelation: "an act of grace & disgust." Staged comically here—as other incidents are tragically staged—the moment celebrates the secular in the liturgical and thus avoids a false romanticism. In a spirit of art for life's sake, "Slow Dance" keeps going from image to Fellini-like image and makes it possible for us to accept the rhythms of the human dance, from the kicking of Anna Karenina's heels to the "nervous goose-step" of puppet-soldiers to today's dance between parents and children who are beginning to learn the right steps. The mood invokes Eliot's "lifting heavy feet in clumsy shoes, / Earth feet, loam feet, lifted in country mirth / Mirth of those long since under earth / . . . Keeping time / Keeping the rhythm in their dancing" ("East Coker": *Four Quartets*) as the poem takes its place in a long tradition that continues to find new forms.

Two somber but delicate family poems, "Hush" and "Iris," would seem to be in sharp contrast to St. John's large concerns for what has been happening in the world, whether seen through his story of a young soldier killed in the Second World War ("Six/Nine/Forty-Four," not presented here) or a latter-day biblical man standing alone on dangerous ground ("The Shore," "Elegy"). In effect, as they "let go a whole cadenza of beliefs," "Hush" and "Iris" are of the same cloth we have been looking at in the other texts: loss and absence. In "Hush," father and son are far apart and getting farther: "Sometimes, you ask / About the world; sometimes, I answer back." Only a nightmare can console the father, "as sleep returns sleep / To a landscape ravaged / & familiar. The dark watermark of your absence, a hush." As in "Dolls," the doll the father makes of his son is a deformed gesture. In "Iris," mesmerized by the double image of train and flower (over which the eye's iris passes), there is only the long good-bye to savor, detail by pitifully beautiful detail. For grandmother and grandson are dead; "you remain" to respect the intimacy of their private grief, but your (our) memory is fading fast.

David St. John grew up in California and like Larry Levis studied with Philip Levine in Fresno. He did graduate work at the Writer's Workshop at the University of Iowa and currently teaches in the Writing Seminars at Johns Hopkins University.

SF

Iris

Vivian St. John (1891–1974)

There is a train inside this iris:

You think I'm crazy, & like to say boyish
& outrageous things. No, there is
A train inside this iris.

It's a child's finger bearded in black banners.
A single window like a child's nail,

A darkened porthole lit by the white, angular face

Of an old woman, or perhaps the boy beside her in the stuffy,
Hot compartment. Her hair is silver, & sweeps

Back off her forehead, onto her cold & bruised shoulders.

The prairies fail along Chicago. Past the five
Lakes. Into the black woods of her New York; & as I bend

Close above the iris, I see the train

Drive deep into the damp heart of its stem, & the gravel
Of the garden path

Cracks under my feet as I walk this long corridor

Of elms, arched
Like the ceiling of a French railway pier where a boy

With pale curls holding

A fresh iris is waving goodbye to a grandmother, gazing
A long time

Into the flower, as if he were looking some great

Distance, or down an empty garden path & he believes a man
Is walking toward him, working

Dull shears in one hand; & now believe me: The train

Is gone. The old woman is dead, & the boy. The iris curls,
On its stalk, in the shade

Of those elms: Where something like the icy & bitter fragrance

In the wake of a woman who's just swept past you on her way
Home

& you remain.

Hush

For My Son

The way a tired Chippewa woman
Who's lost a child gathers up black feathers,
Black quills & leaves
That she wraps & swaddles in a little bale, a shag
Cocoon she carries with her & speaks to always
As if it were the child,
Until she knows the soul has grown fat & clever,
That the child can find its own way at last;
Well, I go everywhere
Picking the dust out of the dust, scraping the breezes
Up off the floor, & gather them into a doll

SIX POETS BORN AFTER 1940

Of you, to touch at the nape of the neck, to slip
Under my shirt like a rag—the way
Another man's wallet rides above his heart. As you
Cry out, as if calling to a father you conjure
In the paling light, the voice rises, instead, in me.
Nothing stops it, the crying. Not the clove of moon,
Not the woman raking my back with her words. Our letters
Close. Sometimes, you ask
About the world; sometimes, I answer back. Nights
Return you to me for a while, as sleep returns sleep
To a landscape ravaged
& familiar. The dark watermark of your absence, a hush.

Slow Dance

It's like the riddle Tolstoy
Put to his son, pacing off the long fields
Deepening in ice. Or the little song
Of Anna's heels, knocking
Through the cold ballroom. It's the relief
A rain enters in a diary, left open under the sky.
The night releases
Its stars, & the birds the new morning. It is an act of grace
& disgust. A gesture of light:
The lamp turned low in the window, the harvest
Fire across the far warp of the land. The somber
Cadence of boots returns. A village
Pocked with soldiers, the dishes rattling in the cupboard
As an old serving woman carries a huge, silver spoon
Into the room & as she polishes she holds it just
So in the light, & the fat
Of her jowls
Goes taut in the reflection. It's what shapes
The sag of those cheeks, & has
Nothing to do with death though it is as simple, & insistent.
Like a coat too tight at the shoulders, or a bedroom
Weary of its single guest. At last, a body
Is spent by sleep: A dream stealing the arms, the legs.
A lover who has left you
Walking constantly away, beyond that stand
Of bare, autumnal trees: Vague, & loose. Yet, it's only
The dirt that consoles the root. You must begin
Again to move, towards the icy sill. A small
Girl behind a hedge of snow
Working a stick puppet so furiously the passers-by bump
Into one another, watching the stiff arms

Fling out to either side, & the nervous goose-step, the dances
Going on, & on
Though the girl is growing cold in her thin coat & silver
Leotard. She lays her cheek to the frozen bank
& lets the puppet sprawl upon her,
Across her face, & a single man is left twirling very
Slowly, until the street
Is empty of everything but snow. The snow
Falling, & the puppet. *That girl.* You close the window,
& for the night's affair slip on the gloves
Sewn of the delicate
Hides of mice. They are like the redemption
Of a drastic weather: Your boat
Put out too soon to sea,
Come back. Like the last testimony, & trace of desire. Or,
How your blouse considers your breasts,
How your lips preface your tongue, & how a man
Assigns a silence to his words. We know lovers who quarrel
At a party stay in the cool trajectory
Of the other's glance,
Spinning through pockets of conversation, sliding in & out
Of the little gaps between us all until they brush or stand at last
Back to back, & the one hooks
An ankle around the other's foot. Even the woman
Undressing to music on a stage & the man going home the longest
Way after a night of drinking remember
The brave lyric of a heel-&-toe. As we remember the young
Acolyte tipping
The flame to the farthest candle & turning
To the congregation, twirling his gold & white satin
Skirts so that everyone can see his woolen socks & rough shoes
Thick as the hunter's boots that disappear & rise
Again in the tall rice
Of the marsh. The dogs, the heavy musk of duck. How the leaves
Introduce us to the tree. How the tree signals
The season, & we begin
Once more to move: Place to place. Hand
To smoother & more lovely hand. A slow dance. To get along.
You toss your corsage onto the waters turning
Under the fountain, & walk back
To the haze of men & women, the lazy amber & pink lanterns
Where you will wait for nothing more than the slight gesture
Of a hand, asking
For this slow dance, & another thick & breathless night.
Yet, you want none of it. Only, to return
To the countryside. The fields & long grasses:
The scent of your son's hair, & his face
Against your side,
As the cattle knock against the walls of the barn

Like the awkward dancers in this room
You must leave, knowing the leaving as the casual
& careful betrayal of what comes
Too easily, but not without its cost, like an old white
Wine out of its bottle, or the pages
Sliding from a worn hymnal. At home, you walk
With your son under your arm, asking of his day, & how
It went, & he begins the story
How he balanced on the sheer hem of a rock, to pick that shock
Of aster nodding in the vase, in the hall. You pull him closer,
& turn your back to any other life. You want
Only the peace of walking in the first light of morning,
As the petals of ice bunch one
Upon another at the lip of the iron pump & soon a whole blossom
Hangs above the trough, a crowd of children teasing it
With sticks until the pale neck snaps, & flakes spray everyone,
& everyone simply dances away.

Dolls

They are so like
Us, frozen in a bald passion
Or absent
Gaze, like the cows whose lashes
Sag beneath their frail sacks of ice.
Your eyes are white with fever, a long
Sickness. When you are asleep,
Dreaming of another country, the wheat's
Pale surface sliding
In the wind, you are walking in every breath
Away from me. I gave you a stone doll,
Its face a dry apple, wizened, yet untroubled.
It taught us the arrogance of silence,
How stone and God reward us, how dolls give us
Nothing. Look at your cane,
Look how even the touch that wears it away
Draws up a shine, as the handle
Gives to the hand. As a girl, you boiled
Your dolls, to keep them clean, presentable;
You'd stir them in enormous pots,
As the arms and legs bent to those incredible
Postures you preferred, not that ordinary, human
Pose. How would you like me?—
Leaning back, reading aloud from a delirious
Book. Or sprawled across your bed,
As if I'd been tossed off a high building
Into the street,
A lesson from a young government to its people.
When you are asleep, walking the fields of another
Country, a series of shadows slowly falling

DAVID ST. JOHN

Away, marking a way,
The sky leaning like a curious girl above a new
Sister, your face a doll's deliberate
Ache of white, you walk along that grove of madness,
Where your mother waits. Hungry, very still.
When you are asleep, dreaming of another country,
This is the country.

The Shore

So the tide forgets, as morning
Grows too far delivered, as the bowls
Of rock and wood run dry.
What is left seems pearled and lit,
As those cases
Of the museum stood lit
With milk jade, rows of opaque vases
Streaked with orange and yellow smoke.
You found a lavender boat, a single
Figure poling upstream, baskets
Of pale fish wedged between his legs.
Today, the debris of winter
Stands stacked against the walls,
The coils of kelp lie scattered
Across the floor. The oil fire
Smokes. You turn down the lantern
Hung on its nail. Outside,
The boats aligned like sentinels.
Here beside the blue depot, walking
The pier, you can see the way
The shore
Approximates the dream, how distances
Repeat their deaths
Above these tables and panes of water—
As climbing the hills above
The harbor, up to the lupine drifting
Among the lichen-masked pines,
The night is pocked with lamps lit
On every boat off shore,
Galleries of floating stars. Below,
On its narrow tracks shelved
Into the cliff's face,
The train begins its slide down
To the warehouses by the harbor. Loaded
With diesel, coal, paychecks, whiskey,
Bedsheets, slabs of ice—for the fish,
For the men. You lean on my arm,
As once

I watched you lean at the window;
The bookstalls below stretched a mile
To the quay, the afternoon crowd
Picking over the novels and histories.
You walked out as you walked out last
Night, onto the stone porch. Dusk
Reddened the walls, the winds sliced
Off the reefs. The vines of the gourds
Shook on their lattice. You talked
About that night you stood
Behind the black pane of the French
Window, watching my father read some long
Passage
Of a famous voyager's book. You hated
That voice filling the room,
Its light. So tonight we make a soft
Parenthesis upon the sand's black bed.
In that dream we share, there is
One shore, where we look out upon nothing
And the sea our whole lives;
Until turning from those waves, we find
One shore, where we look out upon nothing
And the earth our whole lives.
Where what is left between shore and sky
Is traced in the vague wake of
(The stars, the sandpipers whistling)
What we forgive. *If you wake soon, wake me.*

Elegy

> *If there is any dwelling place*
> *for the spirits of the just;*
> *if, as the wise believe, noble souls*
> *do not perish with the body,*
> *rest thou in peace . . .*
> TACITUS

Who keeps the owl's breath? Whose eyes desire?
Why do the stars rhyme? Where does
The flush cargo sail? Why does the daybook close?

So sleep and do not sleep.

The opaque stroke lost across the mirror,
The clamp turned.
The polished nails begin the curl into your palms.
The opal hammock of rain falls out of its cloud.

I name you, *Gloat-of-*
The-stalks, drowse-my-embers, old-lily-bum.
No matter how well a man sucks praise in the end

He sucks earth. Go ahead, step
Out into that promised, rasp gratitude of night.

Seeds and nerves. *Seeds*

And nerves. I'll be waiting for you, in some
Obscure and clarifying light;
I will say, Look, there is a ghost ice on the land.

If the page of marble bleeds in the yellow grass,
If the moon-charts glow useless and cold,
If the grains of the lamp outlast you, as they must—
As the tide of black gloss, the marls, and nectar rise

I will understand.

Here are my gifts: *smudges of bud,*
A blame of lime. Everything you remember crowds
Away. Stubble memory,
The wallpaper peeling its leaves. Fog. Fog
In the attic; this pod of black milk. Anymore,

Only a road like August approaches.

Sometimes the drawers of the earth close;
Sometimes our stories keep on and on. So listen—

Leave no address. Fold your clothes into a little
Island. Kiss the hinges goodbye. Sand the fire. Bitch
About *time.* Hymn away this reliquary fever.

How the sun stands crossing itself in the cut glass.

How the jonquils and bare orchards fill each morning
In mist. The branches in the distance stiffen,
Again. The city of stars pales.
In my fires the cinders rise like black angels;
The trunks of the olives twist once towards the world.

Once. I will walk out into the day.

David St. John

Books

Hush, 1976
The Shore, 1980